05

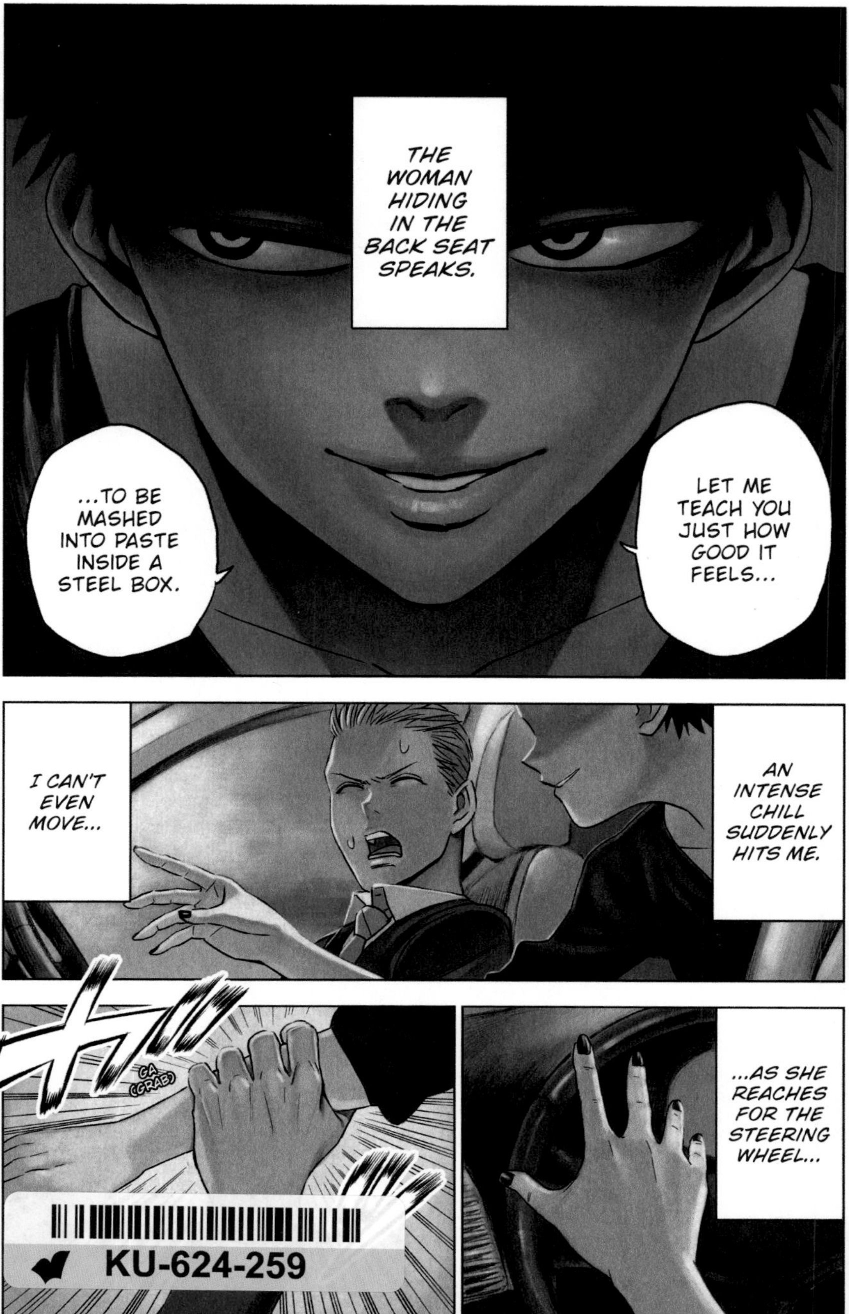
THE WOMAN HIDING IN THE BACK SEAT SPEAKS.
LET ME TEACH YOU JUST HOW GOOD IT FEELS...
...TO BE MASHED INTO PASTE INSIDE A STEEL BOX.
AN INTENSE CHILL SUDDENLY HITS ME.
I CAN'T EVEN MOVE...
...AS SHE REACHES FOR THE STEERING WHEEL...
GA (GRAB)

ID:INVADED

#BRAKE-BROKEN

#05 BRINK OF DEATH

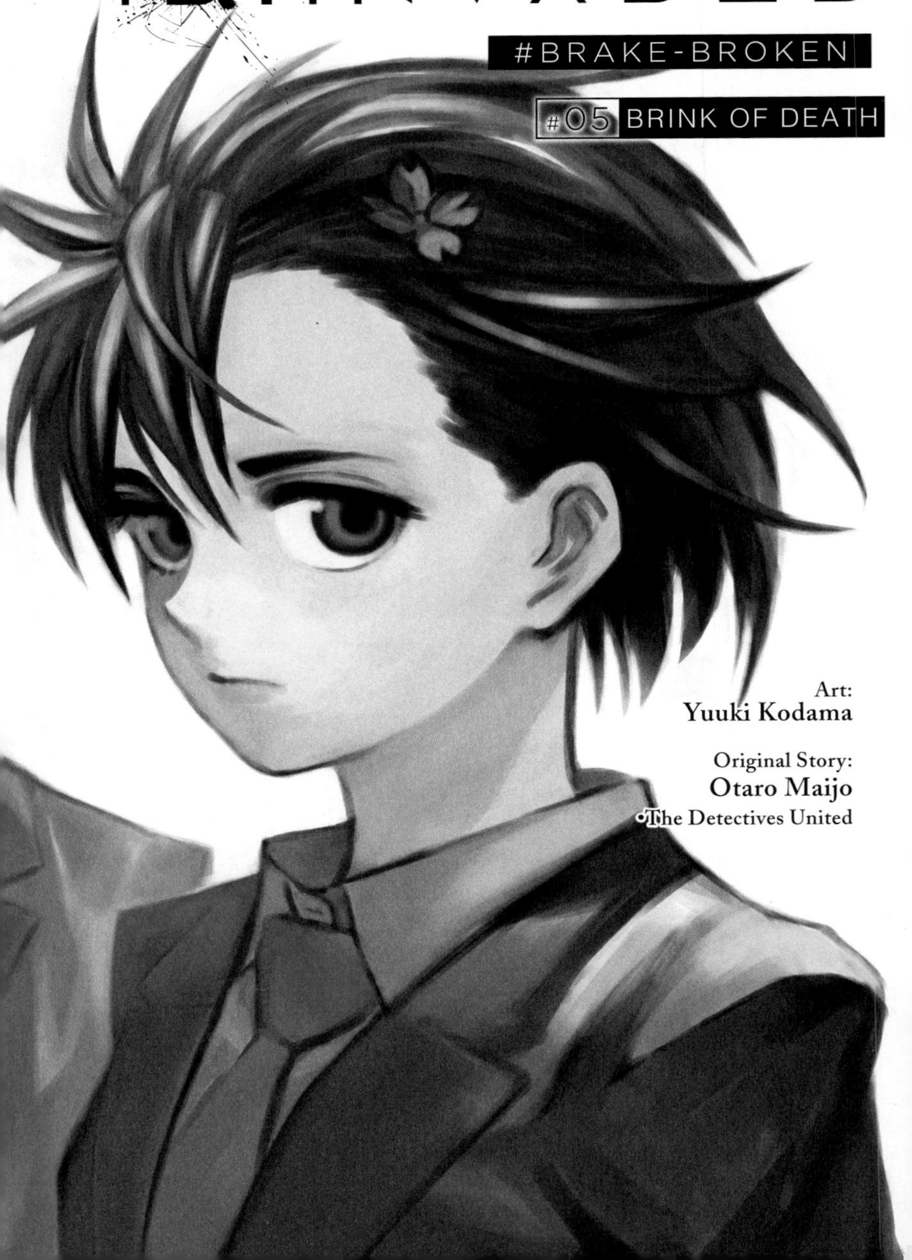

Art:
Yuuki Kodama

Original Story:
Otaro Maijo
•The Detectives United

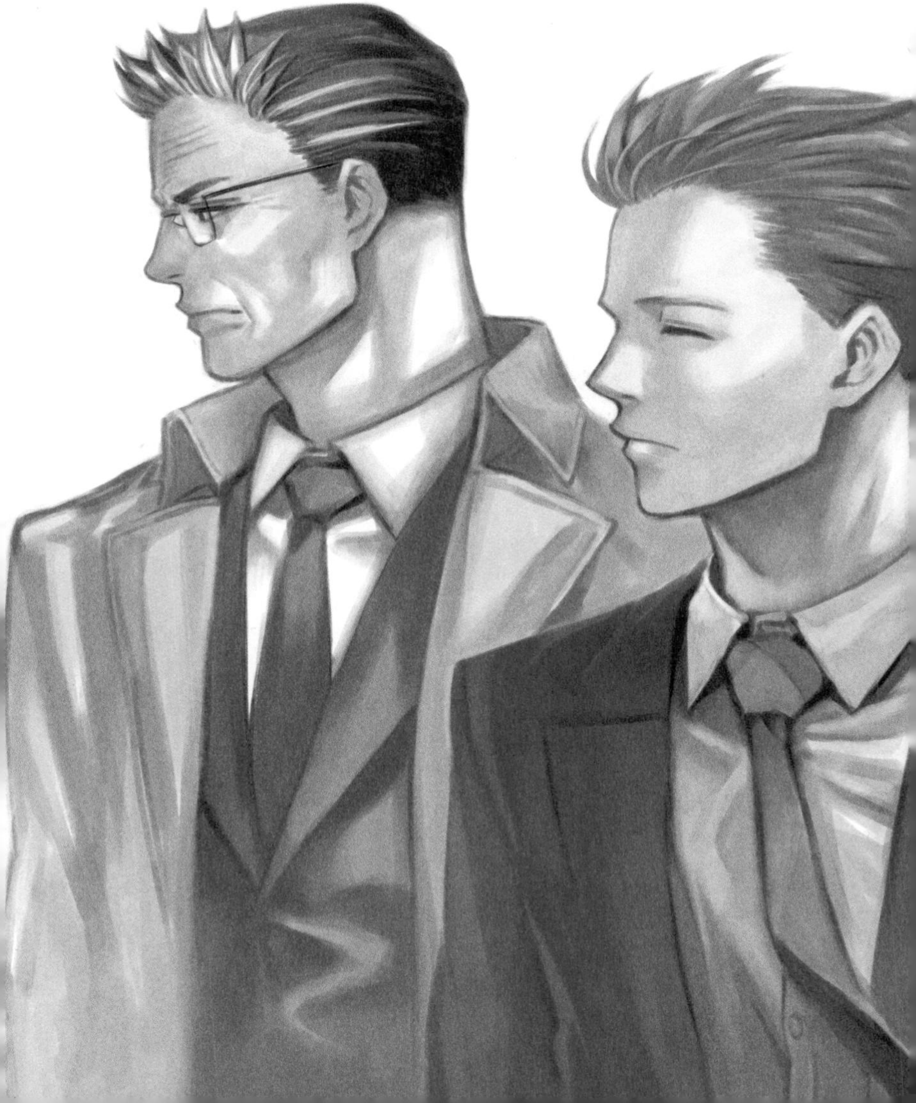

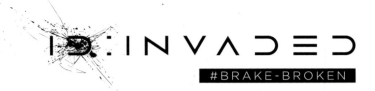

ID:INVADED

#BRAKE-BROKEN

Contents

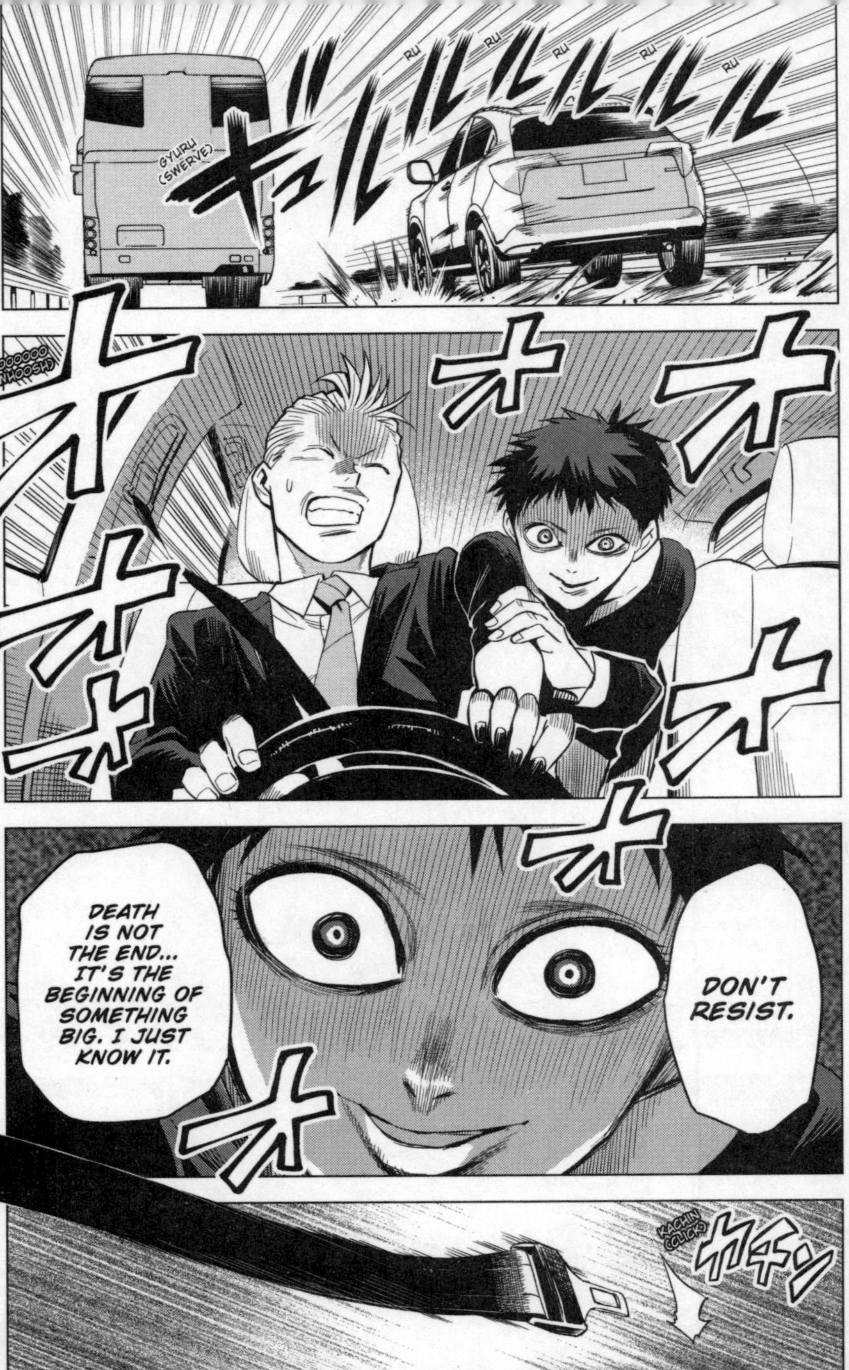
RU RU RU RU RU
GYURU (SWERVE)
OOOOOOO (WHOOSH)
DON'T RESIST.
DEATH IS NOT THE END... IT'S THE BEGINNING OF SOMETHING BIG. I JUST KNOW IT.
KACHIN (CLICK)

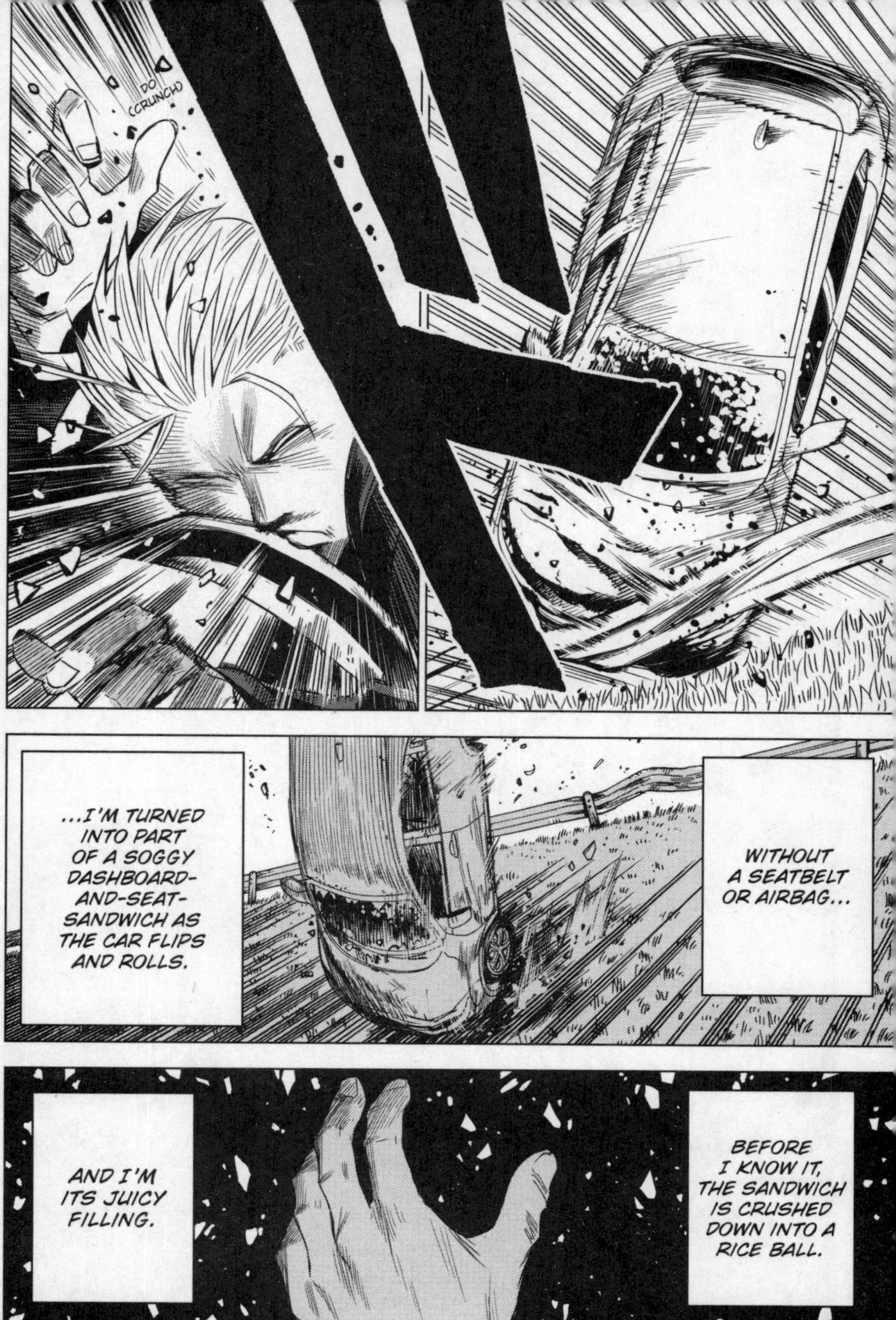
DO (CRUNCH)
WITHOUT A SEATBELT OR AIRBAG...
...I'M TURNED INTO PART OF A SOGGY DASHBOARD-AND-SEAT-SANDWICH AS THE CAR FLIPS AND ROLLS.
BEFORE I KNOW IT, THE SANDWICH IS CRUSHED DOWN INTO A RICE BALL.
AND I'M ITS JUICY FILLING.

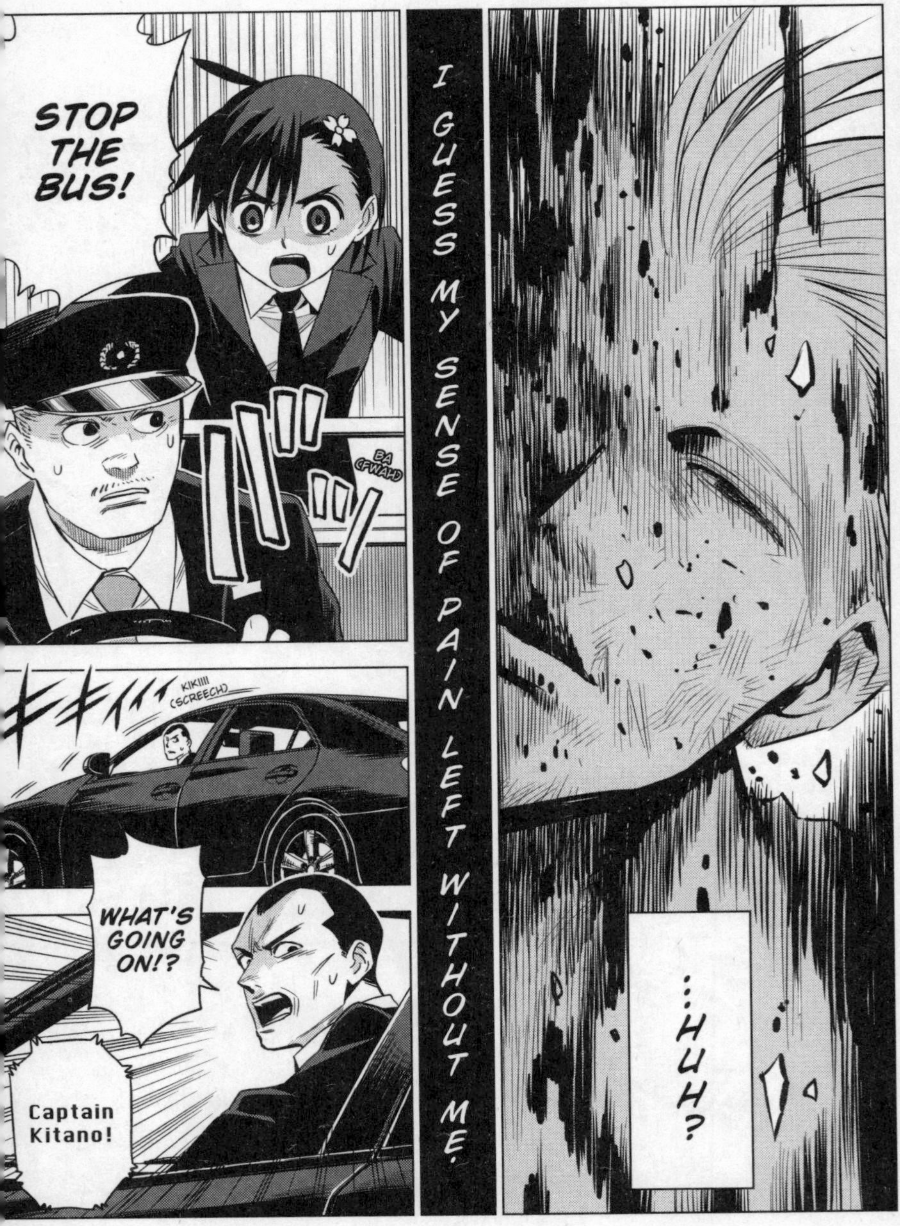
...HUH?
I GUESS MY SENSE OF PAIN LEFT WITHOUT ME.
STOP THE BUS!
BA (FWAH)
KIKIIII (SCREECH)
WHAT'S GOING ON!?
Captain Kitano!

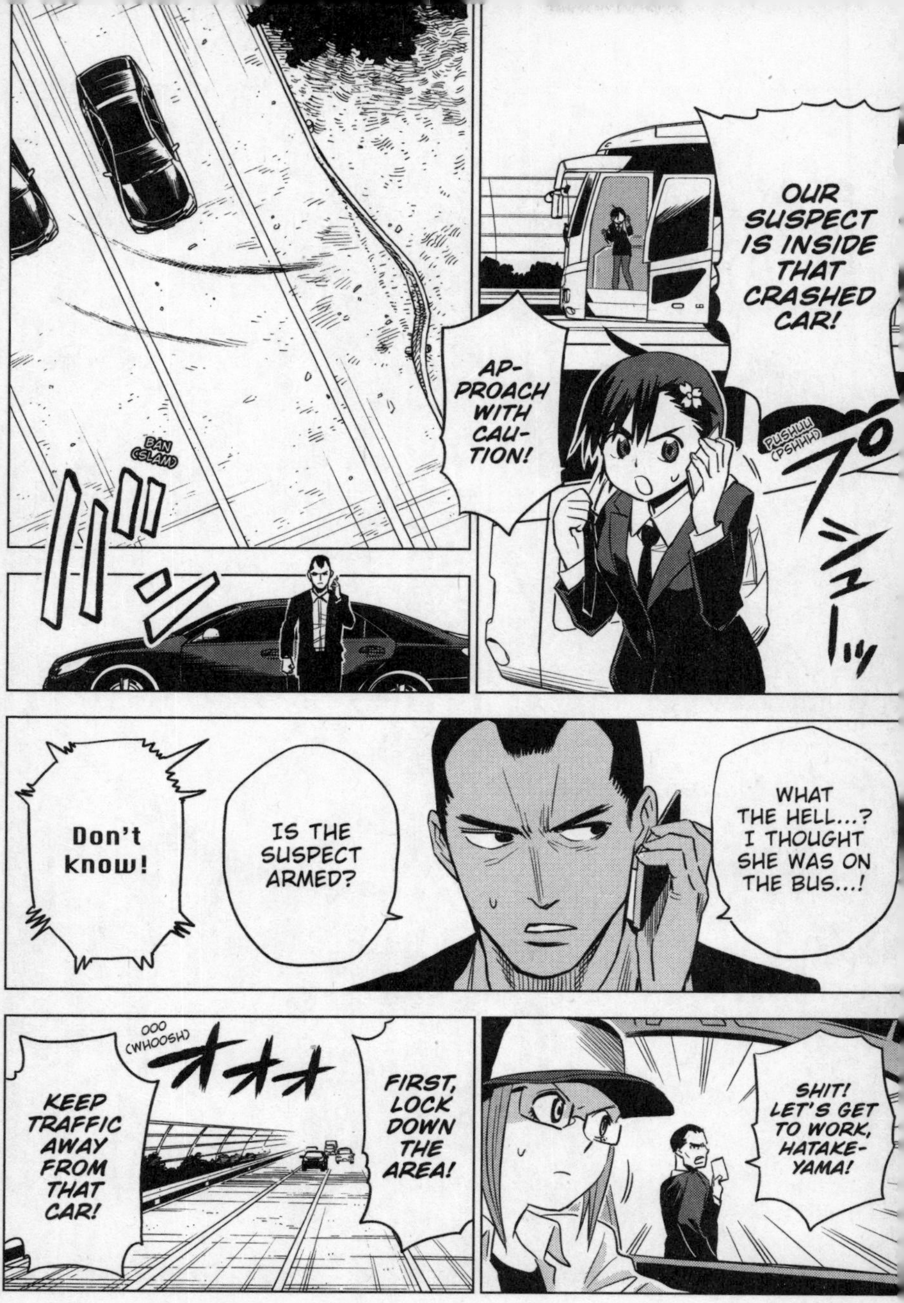
OUR SUSPECT IS INSIDE THAT CRASHED CAR!
AP-PROACH WITH CAU-TION!
PUSHUU (PSHHH)
BAN (SLAM)
WHAT THE HELL...? I THOUGHT SHE WAS ON THE BUS...!
IS THE SUSPECT ARMED?
Don't know!
SHIT! LET'S GET TO WORK, HATAKE-YAMA!
FIRST, LOCK DOWN THE AREA!
OOO (WHOOSH)
KEEP TRAFFIC AWAY FROM THAT CAR!

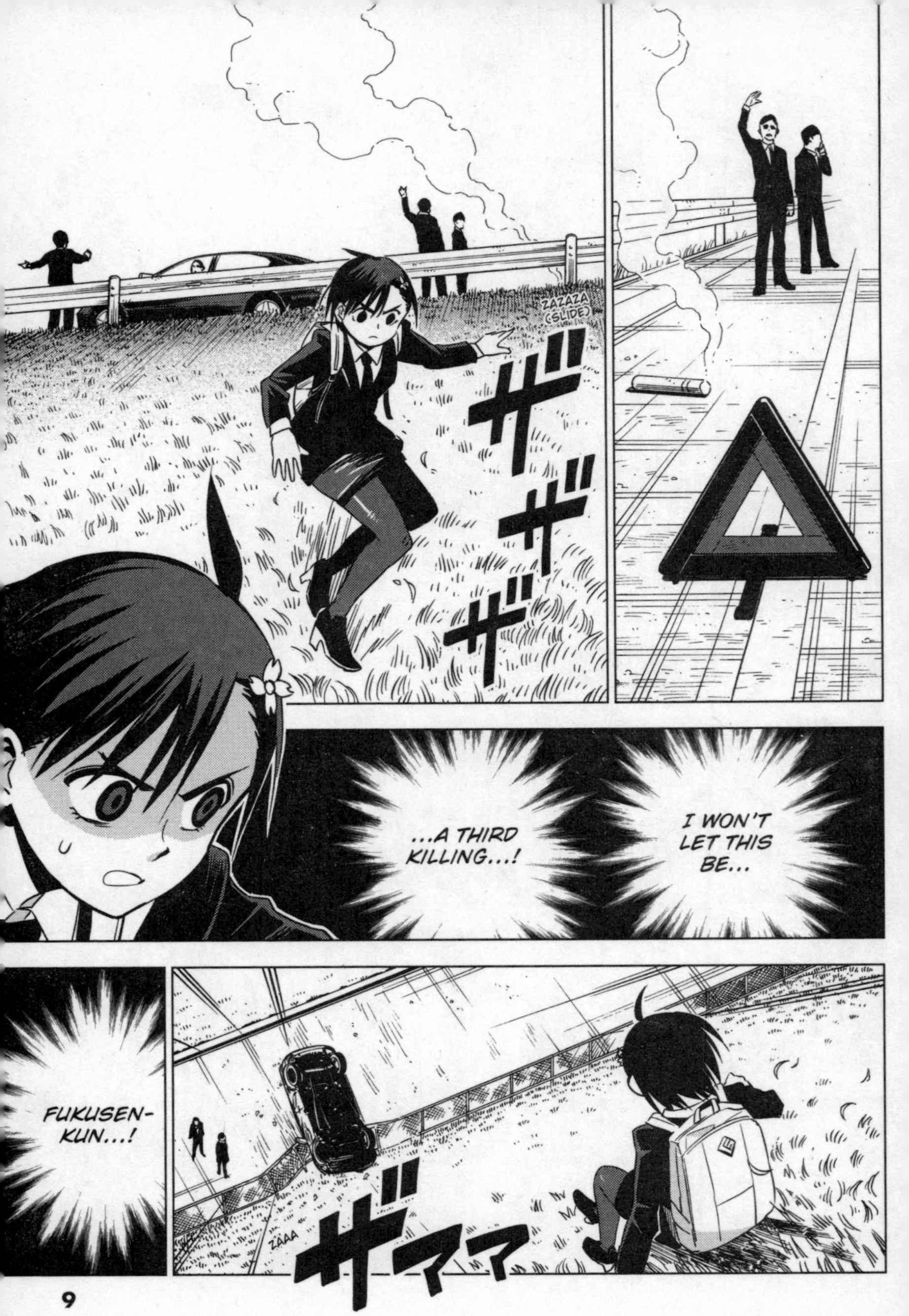
ZAZAZA (SLIDE)
ザザザザ
I WON'T LET THIS BE...
...A THIRD KILLING...!
ザァア
ZAAA
FUKUSEN-KUN...!

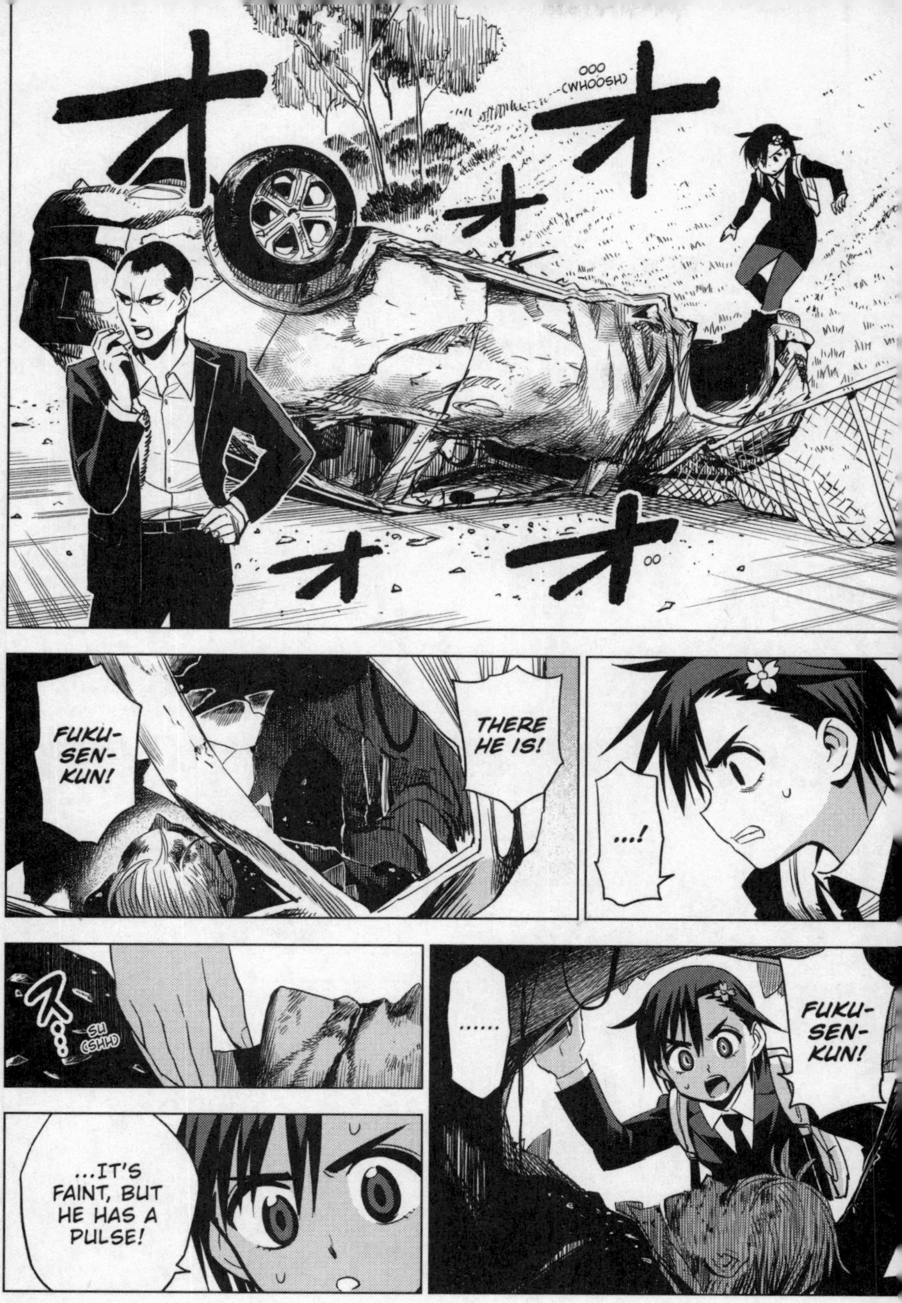
OOO
(WHOOSH)
...!
THERE HE IS!
FUKU-SEN-KUN!
FUKU-SEN-KUN!
......
SU
(SHH)
...IT'S FAINT, BUT HE HAS A PULSE!

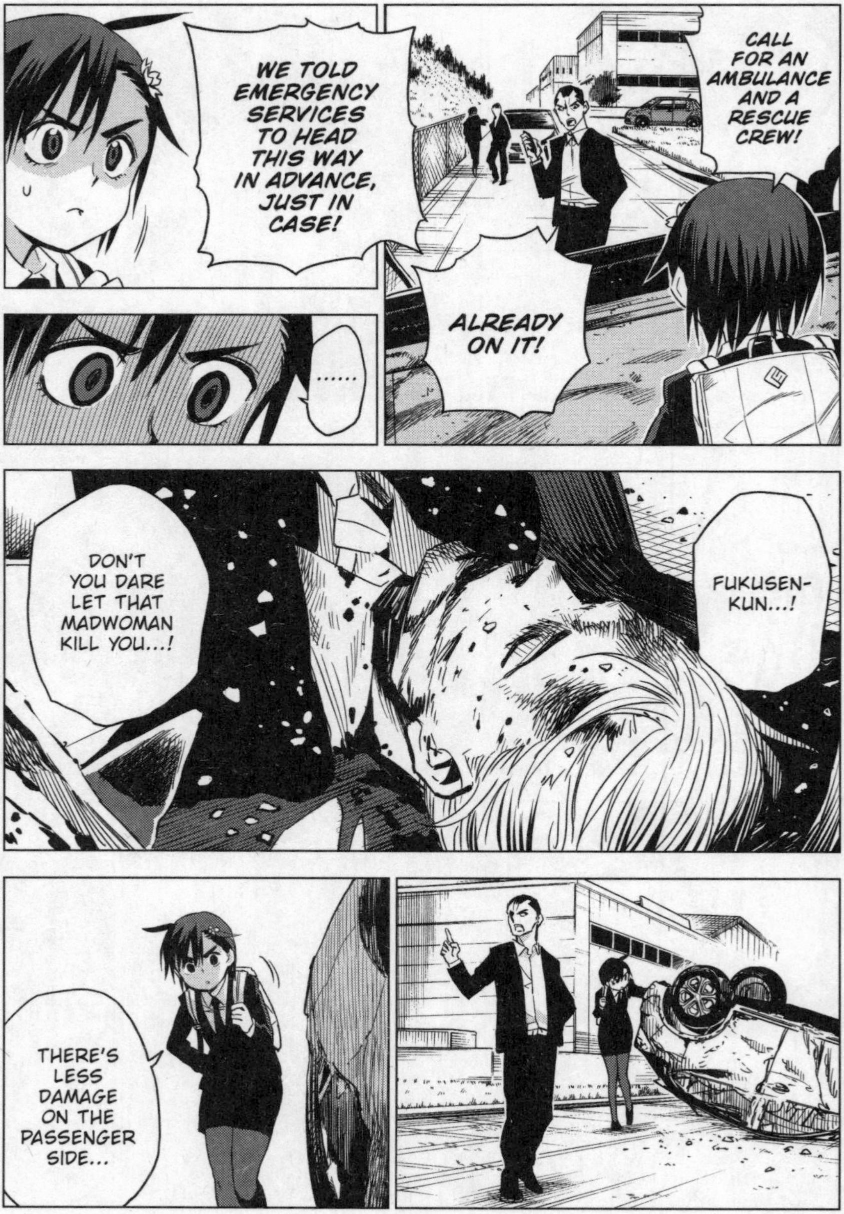
CALL FOR AN AMBULANCE AND A RESCUE CREW!
ALREADY ON IT!
WE TOLD EMERGENCY SERVICES TO HEAD THIS WAY IN ADVANCE, JUST IN CASE!
......
FUKUSEN-KUN...!
DON'T YOU DARE LET THAT MADWOMAN KILL YOU...!
THERE'S LESS DAMAGE ON THE PASSENGER SIDE...

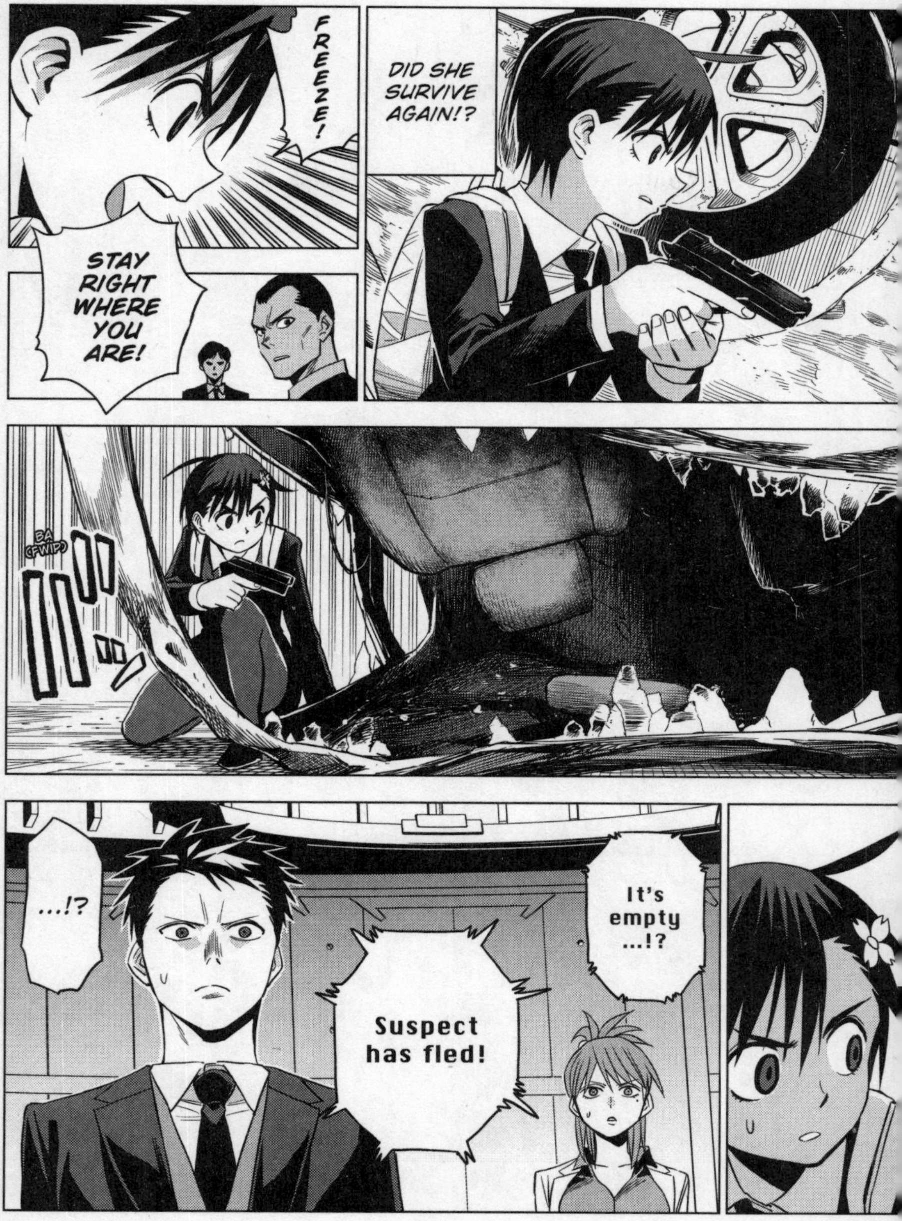
DID SHE SURVIVE AGAIN!?
FREEZE!
STAY RIGHT WHERE YOU ARE!
BA (FWIP)
It's empty ...!?
...!?
Suspect has fled!

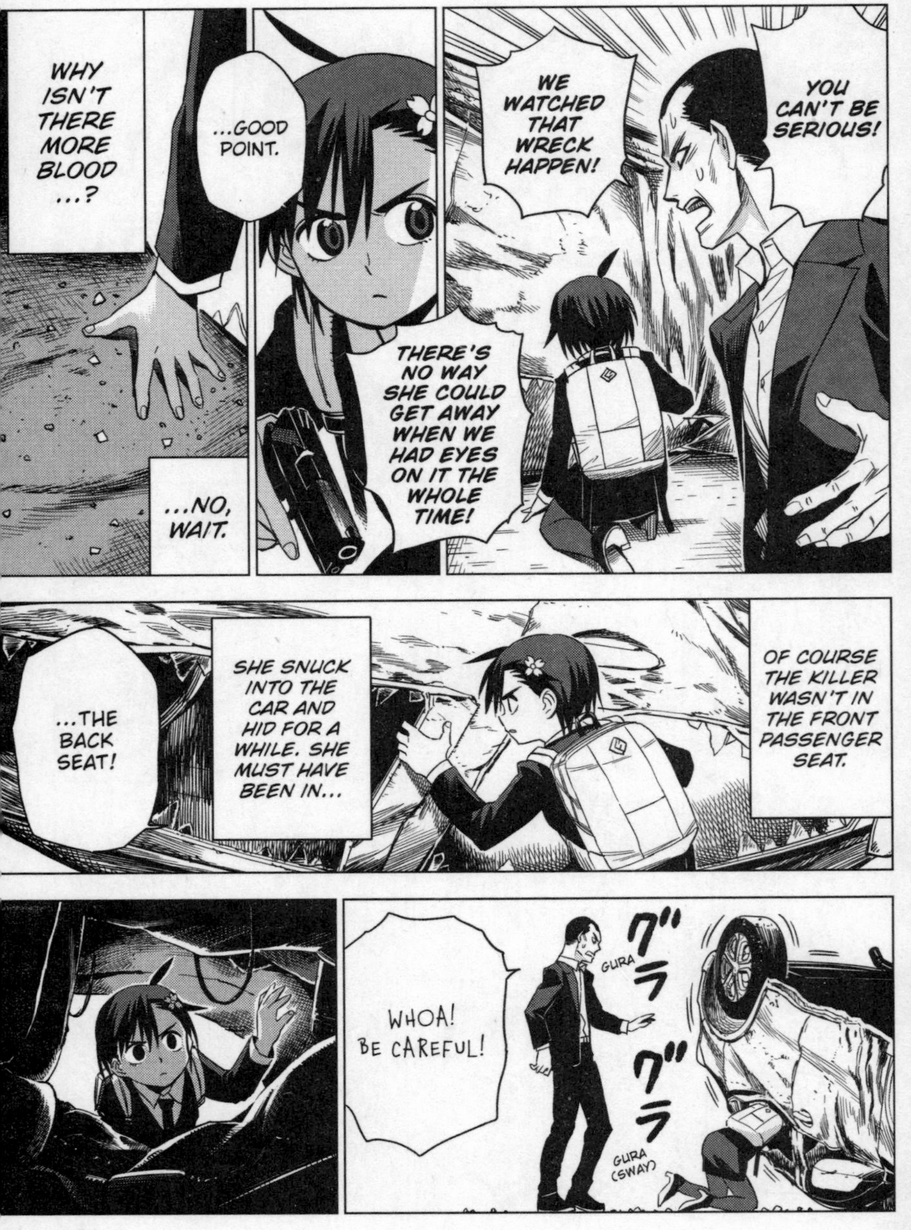
YOU CAN'T BE SERIOUS!
WE WATCHED THAT WRECK HAPPEN!
THERE'S NO WAY SHE COULD GET AWAY WHEN WE HAD EYES ON IT THE WHOLE TIME!
...GOOD POINT.
WHY ISN'T THERE MORE BLOOD ...?
...NO, WAIT.
OF COURSE THE KILLER WASN'T IN THE FRONT PASSENGER SEAT.
SHE SNUCK INTO THE CAR AND HID FOR A WHILE. SHE MUST HAVE BEEN IN...
...THE BACK SEAT!
グラ
GURA
グラ
GURA (SWAY)
WHOA! BE CAREFUL!

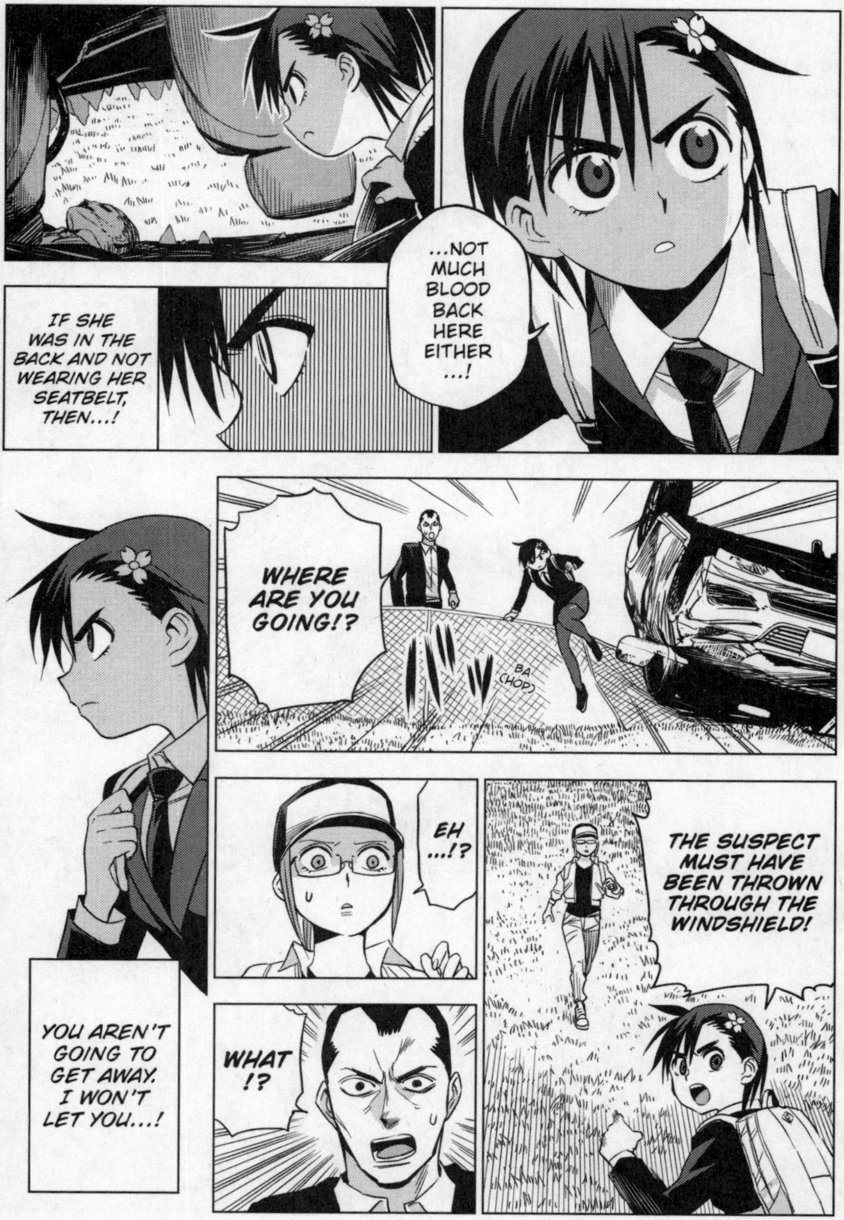
...NOT MUCH BLOOD BACK HERE EITHER ...!
IF SHE WAS IN THE BACK AND NOT WEARING HER SEATBELT, THEN...!
WHERE ARE YOU GOING!?
BA (HOP)
THE SUSPECT MUST HAVE BEEN THROWN THROUGH THE WINDSHIELD!
EH ...!?
WHAT !?
YOU AREN'T GOING TO GET AWAY. I WON'T LET YOU...!

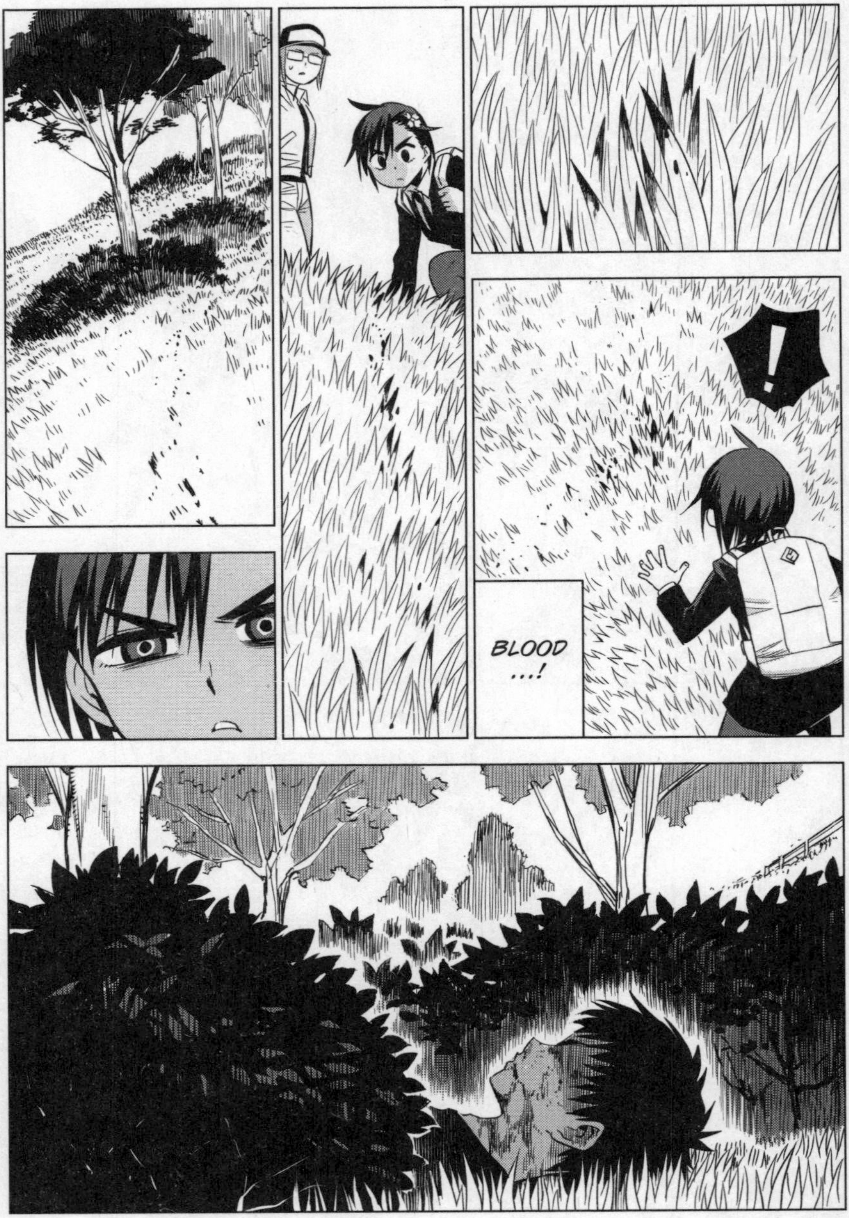
!
BLOOD ...!

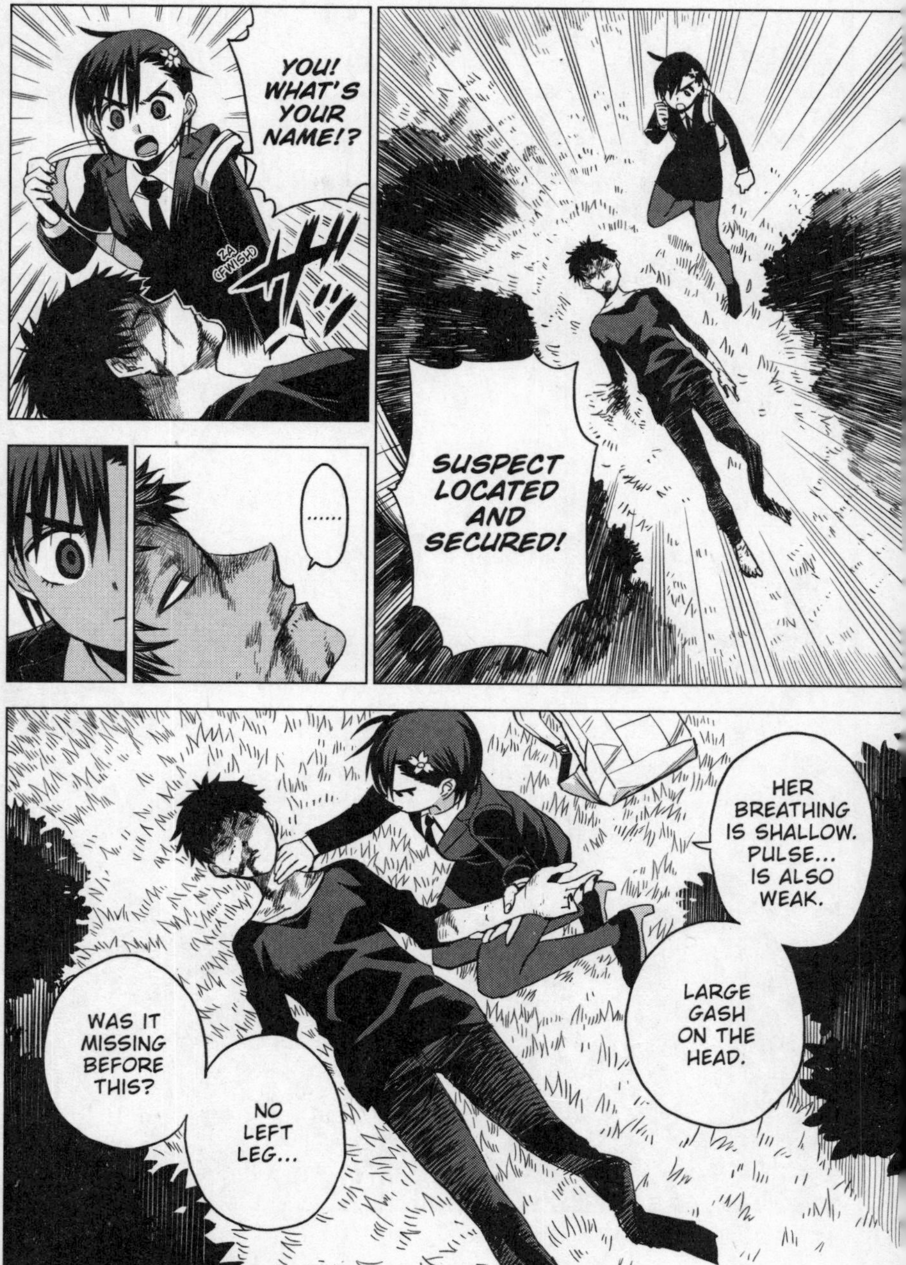
SUSPECT LOCATED AND SECURED!
YOU! WHAT'S YOUR NAME!?
ZA (FWISH)
......
HER BREATHING IS SHALLOW. PULSE... IS ALSO WEAK.
LARGE GASH ON THE HEAD.
NO LEFT LEG...
WAS IT MISSING BEFORE THIS?

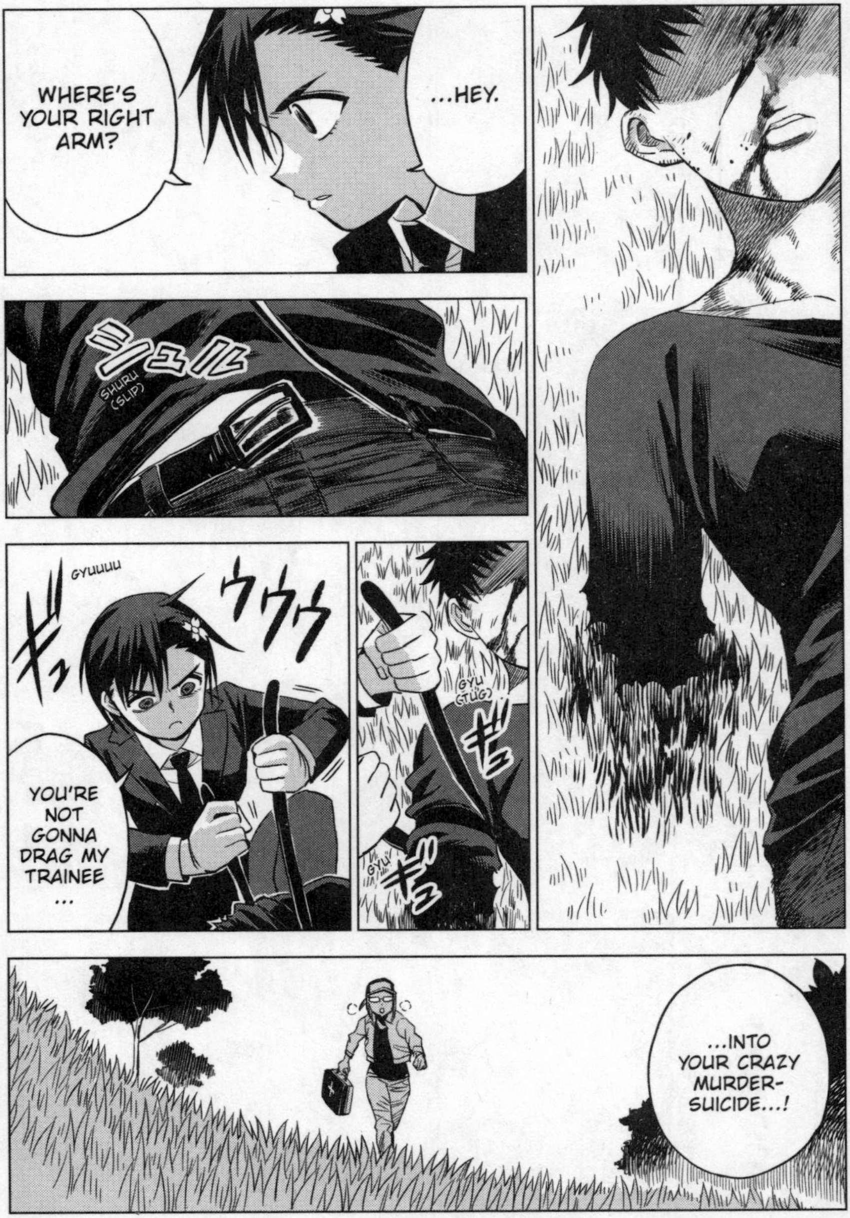
...HEY.
WHERE'S YOUR RIGHT ARM?
シュル
SHURU (SLIP)
GYU (TUG)
ギュ
GYU
ギュ
ギュウウウ
GYUUUU
YOU'RE NOT GONNA DRAG MY TRAINEE ...
...INTO YOUR CRAZY MURDER-SUICIDE...!

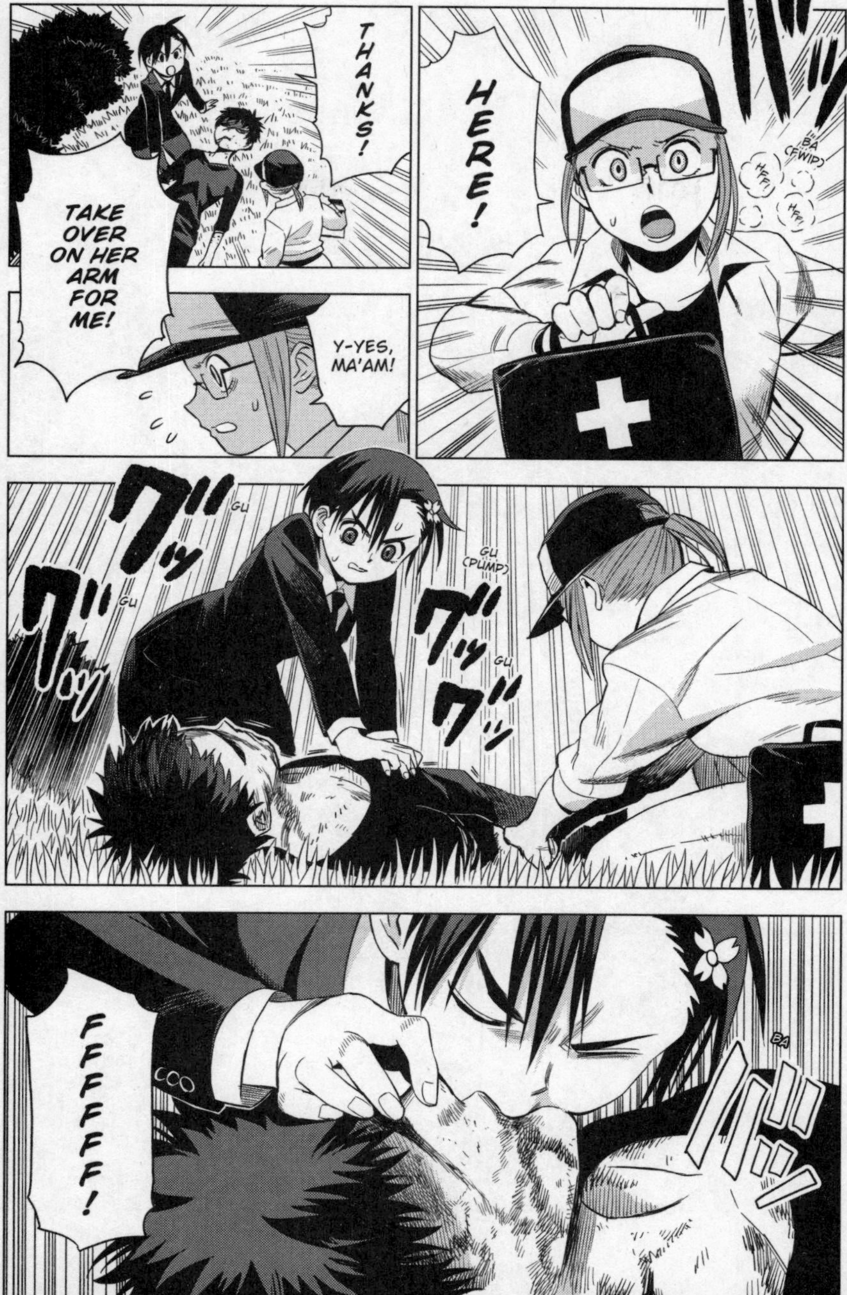
HERE!
BA (FWIP)
HFF!
HFF!
THANKS!
TAKE OVER ON HER ARM FOR ME!
Y-YES, MA'AM!
GU
GU (PUMP)
GU
GU
BA
FFFFFF!

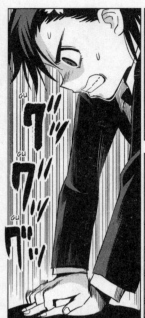

GU
GU
GU

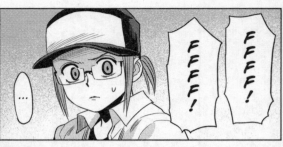

...

FFFF!

FFFF!

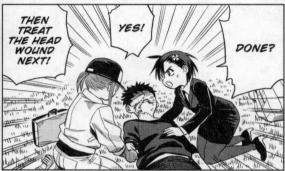

THEN TREAT THE HEAD WOUND NEXT!

YES!

DONE?

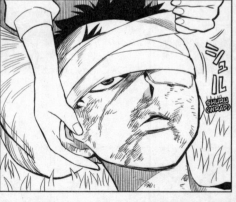

SHURU
(WRAP)

OKAY! MOVE!

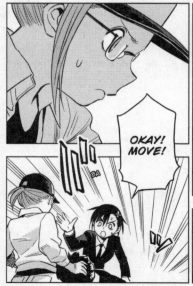

BA

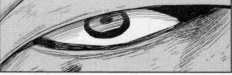

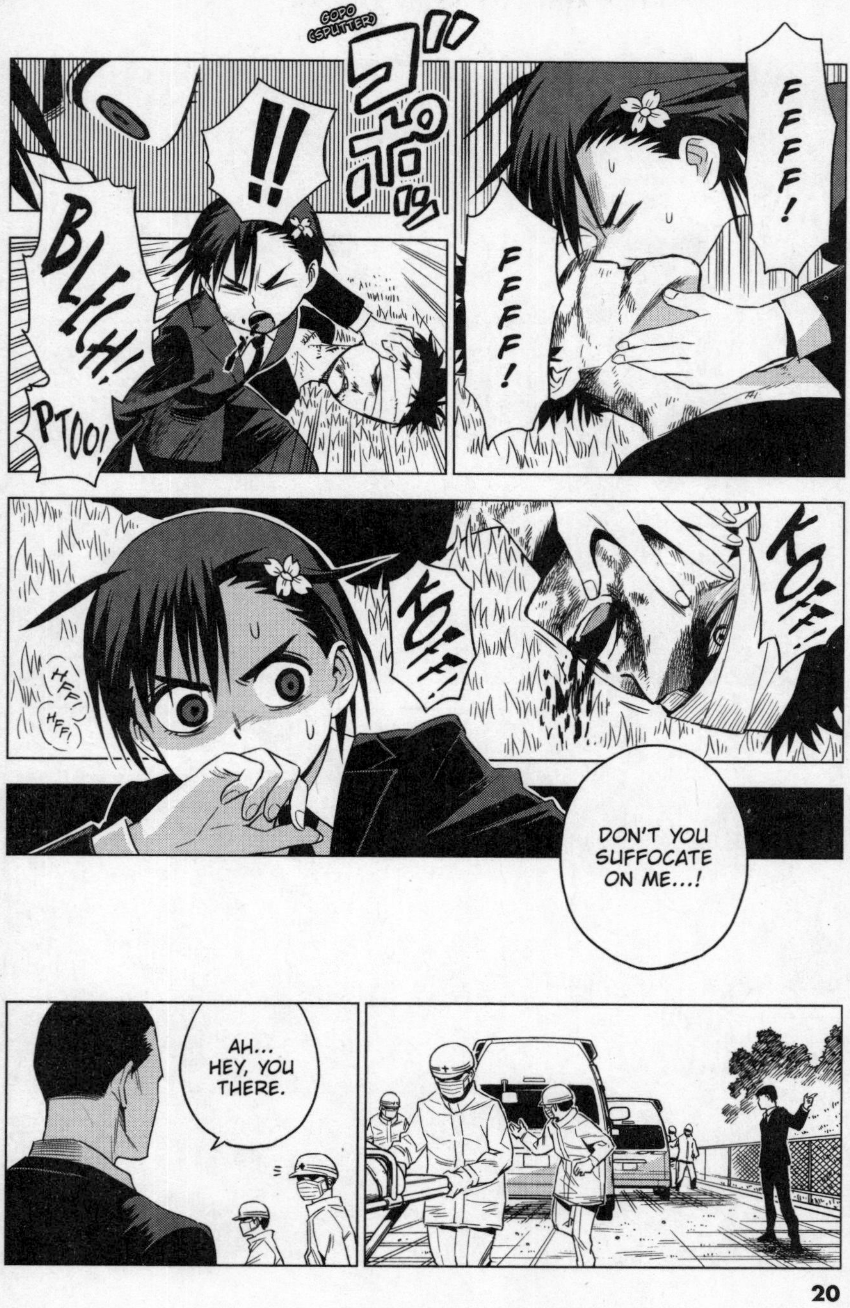
FFFFF!
FFFFF!
!!
GOPO (SPLUTTER)
BLECH!
PTOO!
KOFF!
KOFF!
HFF! HFF!
DON'T YOU SUFFOCATE ON ME...!
AH... HEY, YOU THERE.

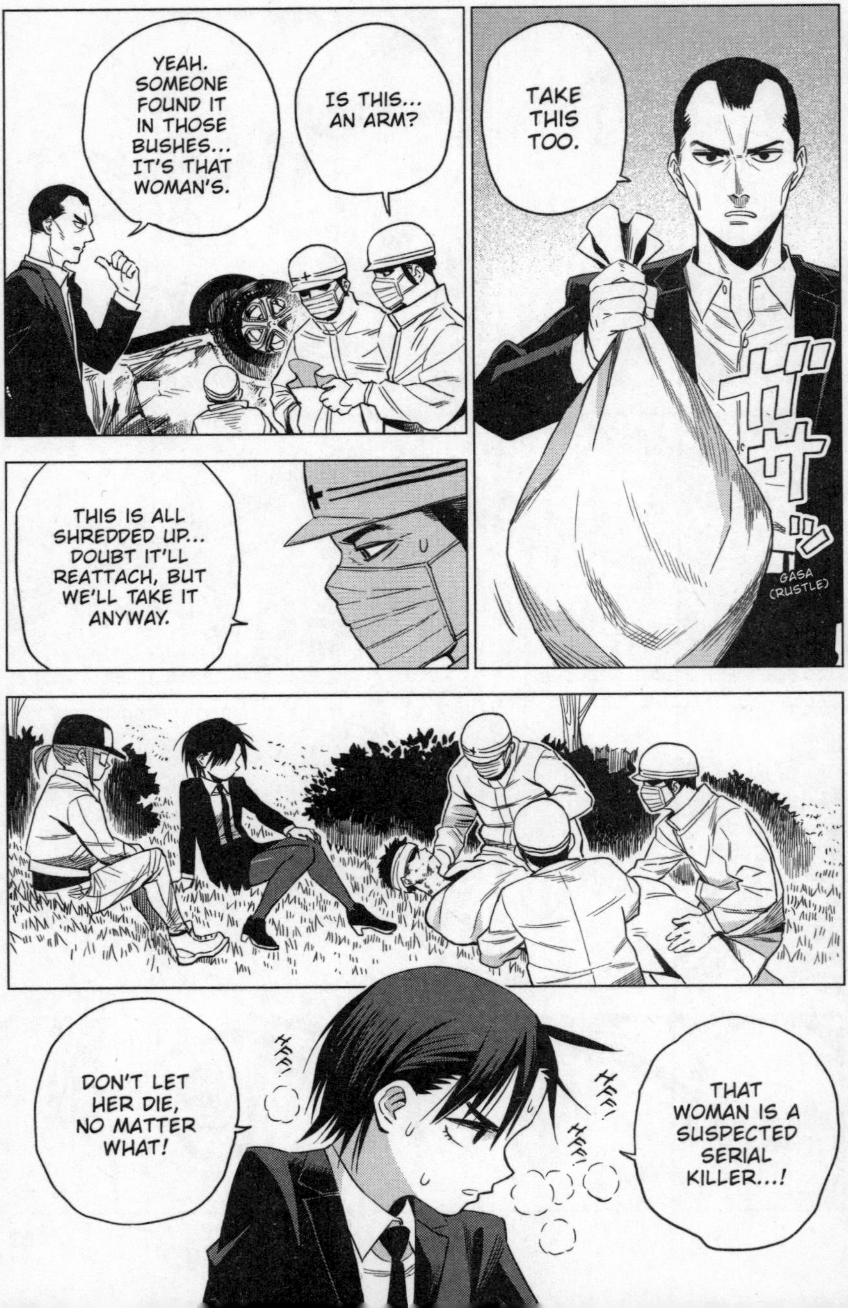
TAKE THIS TOO.
GASA (RUSTLE)
IS THIS... AN ARM?
YEAH. SOMEONE FOUND IT IN THOSE BUSHES... IT'S THAT WOMAN'S.
THIS IS ALL SHREDDED UP... DOUBT IT'LL REATTACH, BUT WE'LL TAKE IT ANYWAY.
THAT WOMAN IS A SUSPECTED SERIAL KILLER...!
DON'T LET HER DIE, NO MATTER WHAT!

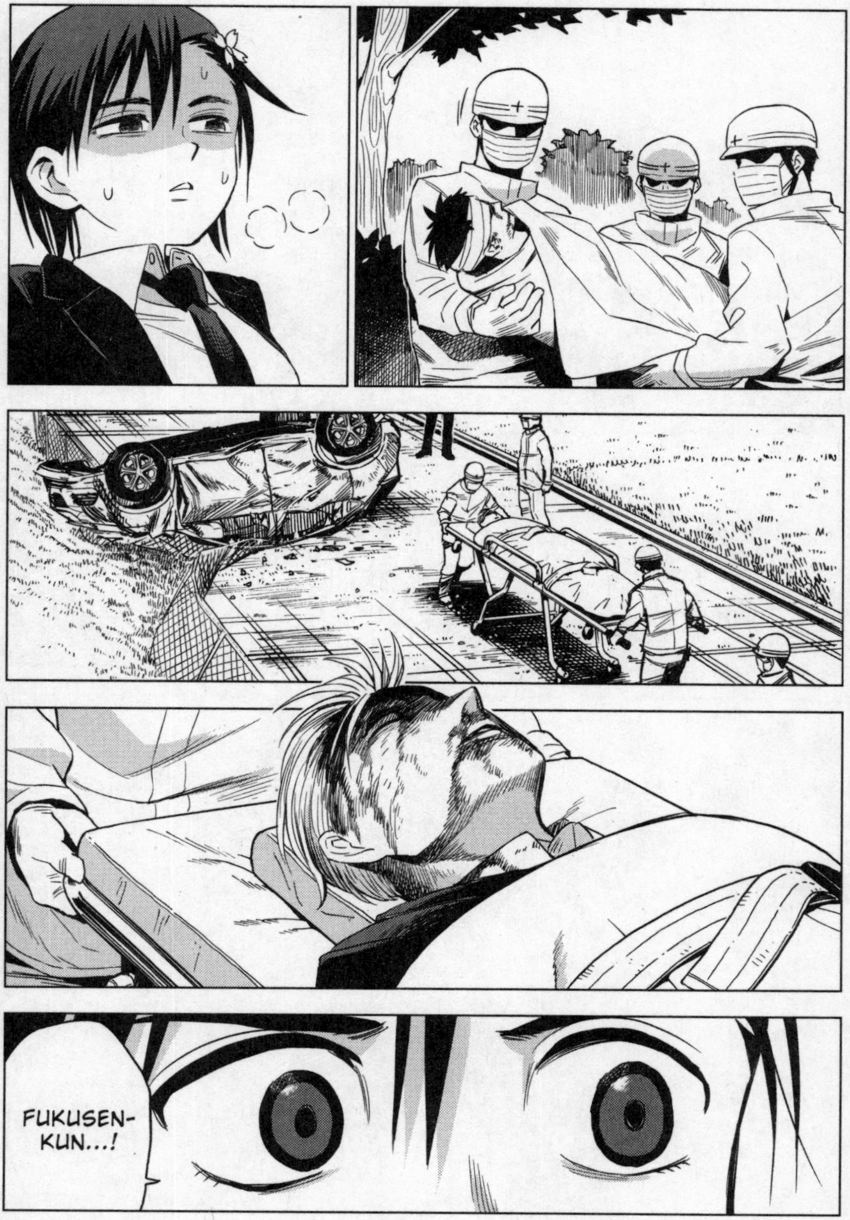
FUKUSEN-KUN...!

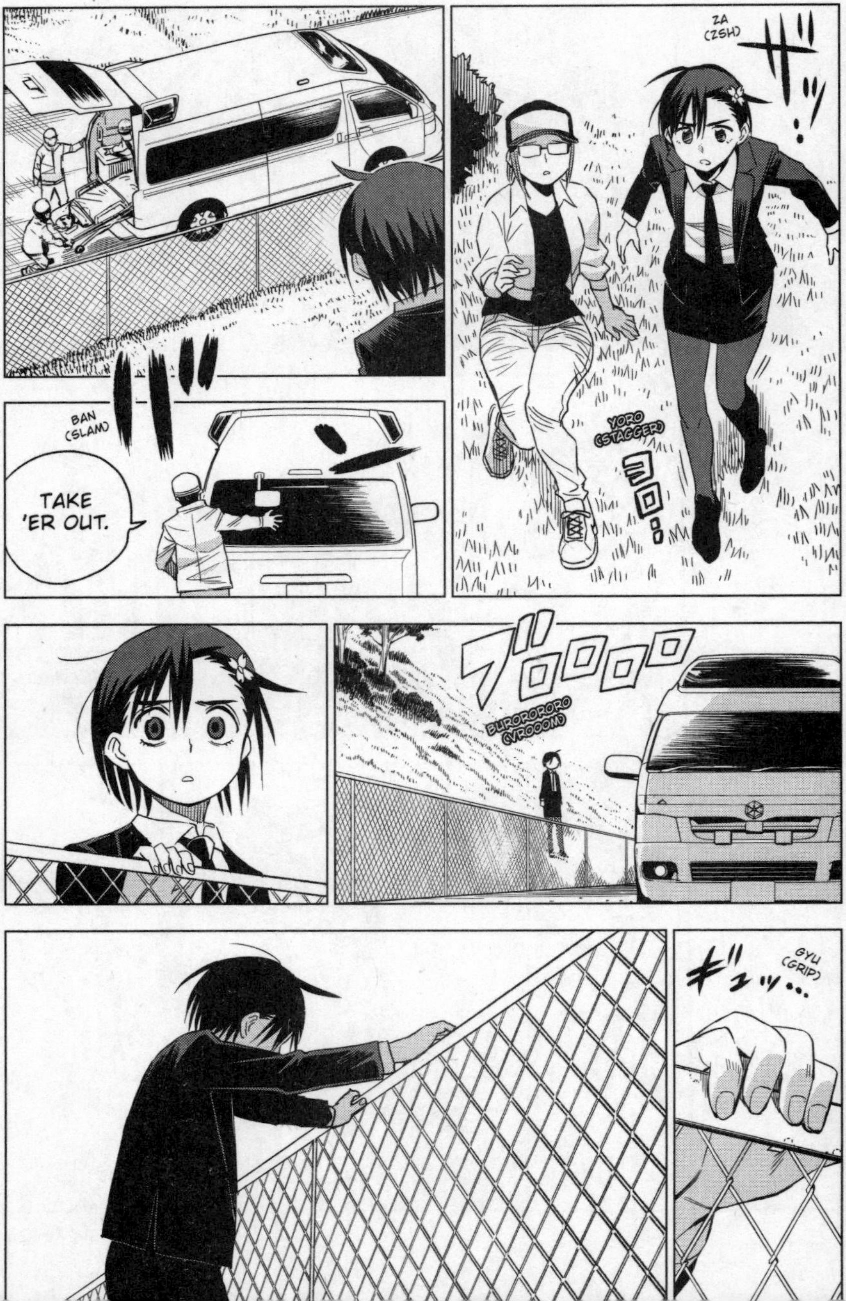
ZA (ZSH)
ザッ!
YORO (STAGGER)
ヨロ..
BAN (SLAM)
TAKE 'ER OUT.
ブロロロロ
BUROROROROR (VROOOM)
GYU (GRIP)
ギュッ...

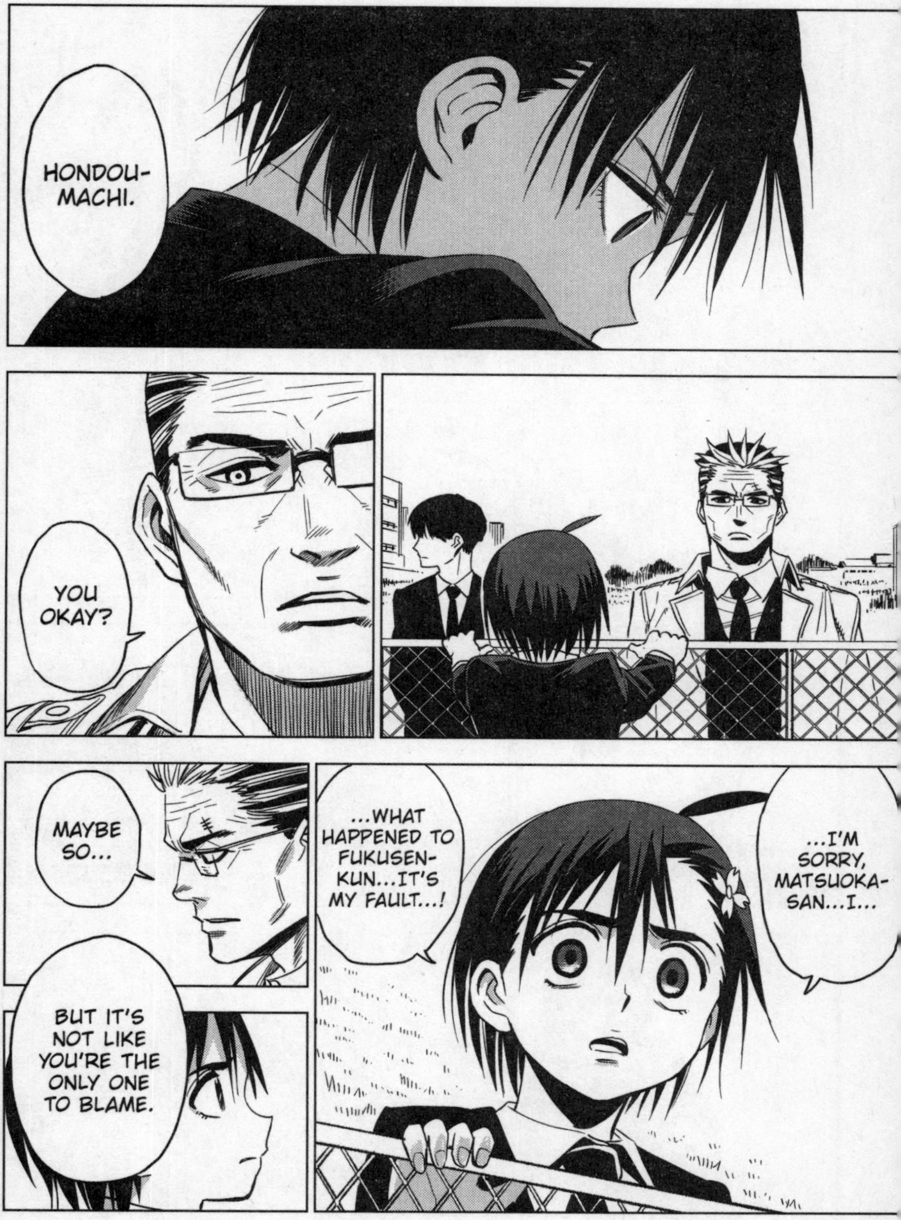
HONDOU-MACHI.
YOU OKAY?
...I'M SORRY, MATSUOKA-SAN...I...
...WHAT HAPPENED TO FUKUSEN-KUN...IT'S MY FAULT...!
MAYBE SO...
BUT IT'S NOT LIKE YOU'RE THE ONLY ONE TO BLAME.

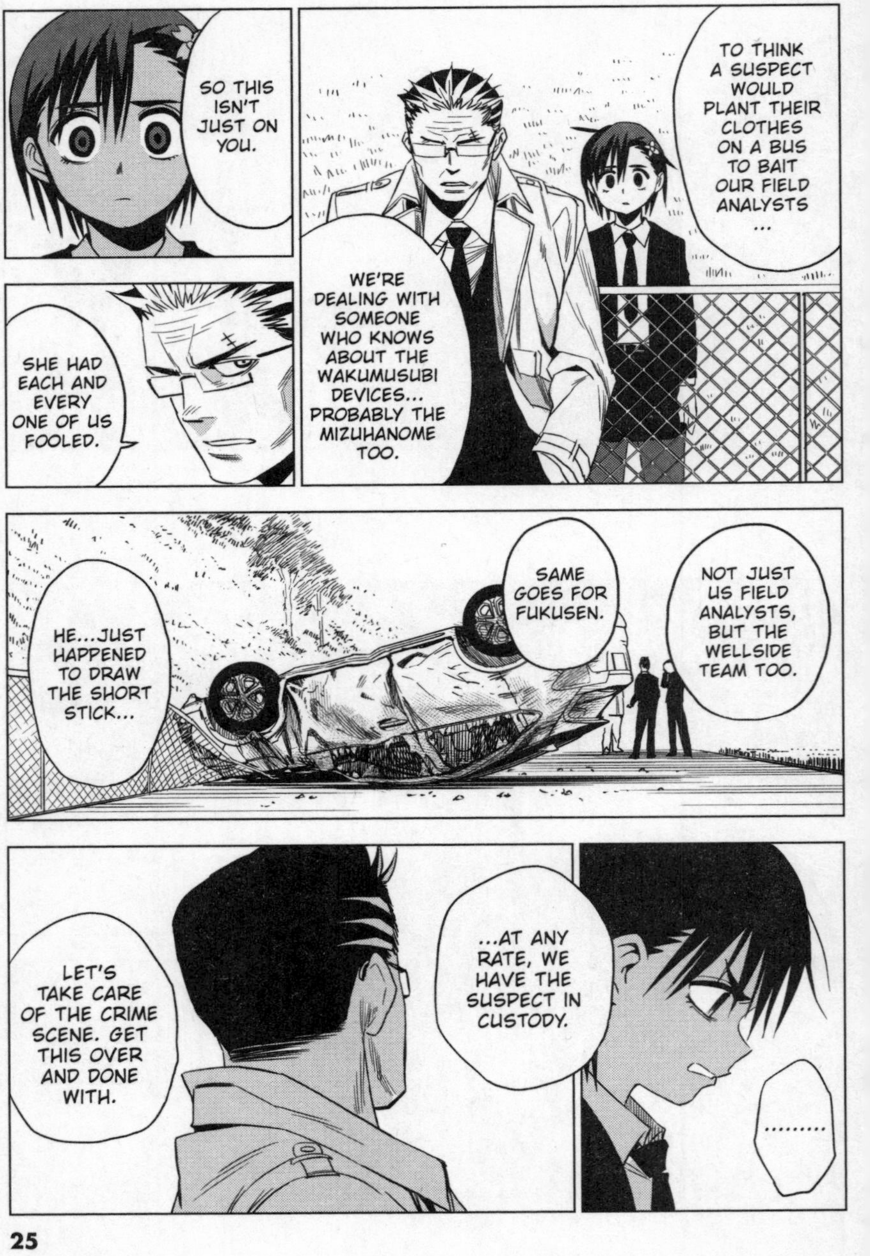
TO THINK A SUSPECT WOULD PLANT THEIR CLOTHES ON A BUS TO BAIT OUR FIELD ANALYSTS ...
WE'RE DEALING WITH SOMEONE WHO KNOWS ABOUT THE WAKUMUSUBI DEVICES... PROBABLY THE MIZUHANOME TOO.
SO THIS ISN'T JUST ON YOU.
SHE HAD EACH AND EVERY ONE OF US FOOLED.
NOT JUST US FIELD ANALYSTS, BUT THE WELLSIDE TEAM TOO.
SAME GOES FOR FUKUSEN.
HE...JUST HAPPENED TO DRAW THE SHORT STICK...
....
...AT ANY RATE, WE HAVE THE SUSPECT IN CUSTODY.
LET'S TAKE CARE OF THE CRIME SCENE. GET THIS OVER AND DONE WITH.

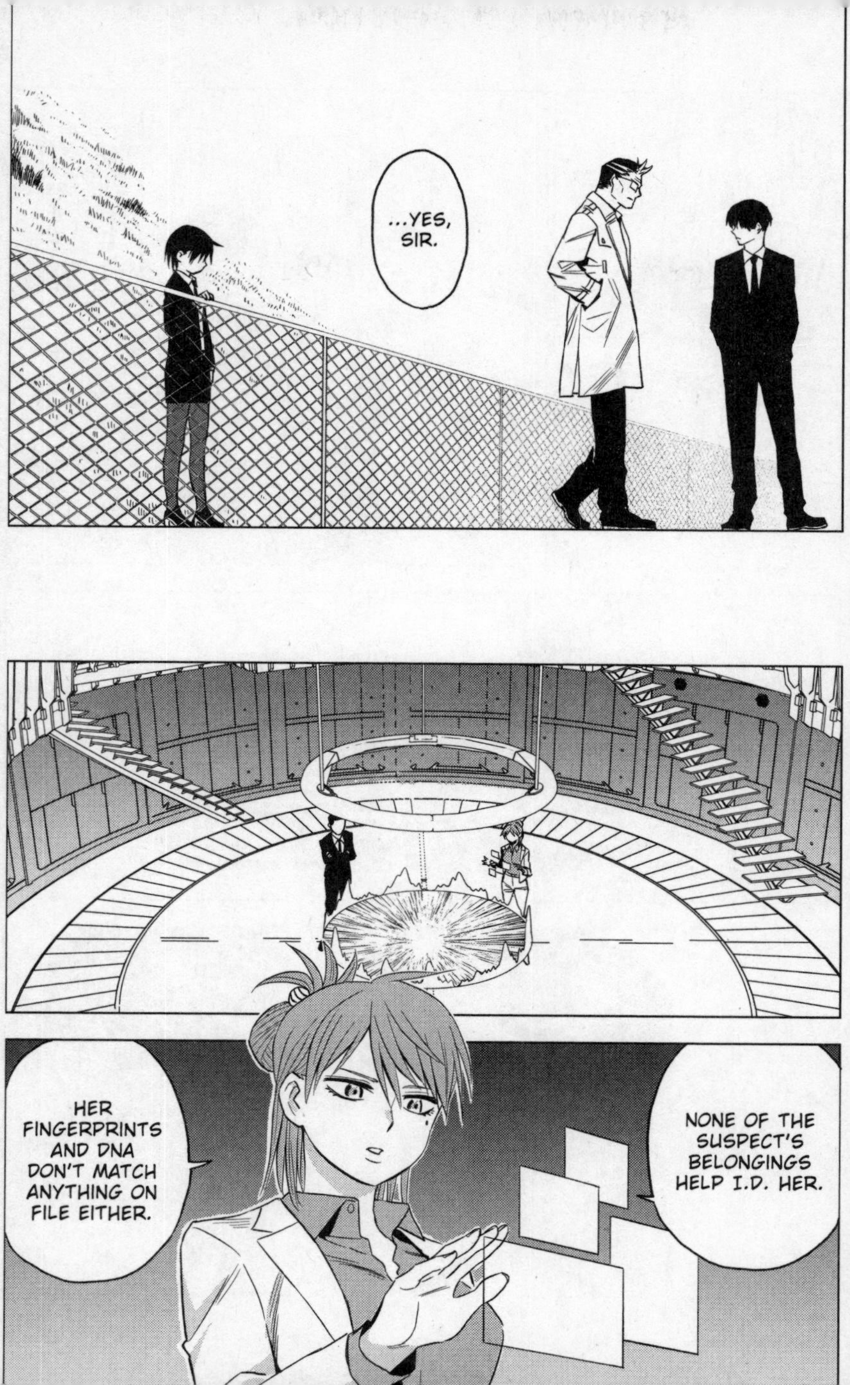
...YES, SIR.
NONE OF THE SUSPECT'S BELONGINGS HELP I.D. HER.
HER FINGERPRINTS AND DNA DON'T MATCH ANYTHING ON FILE EITHER.

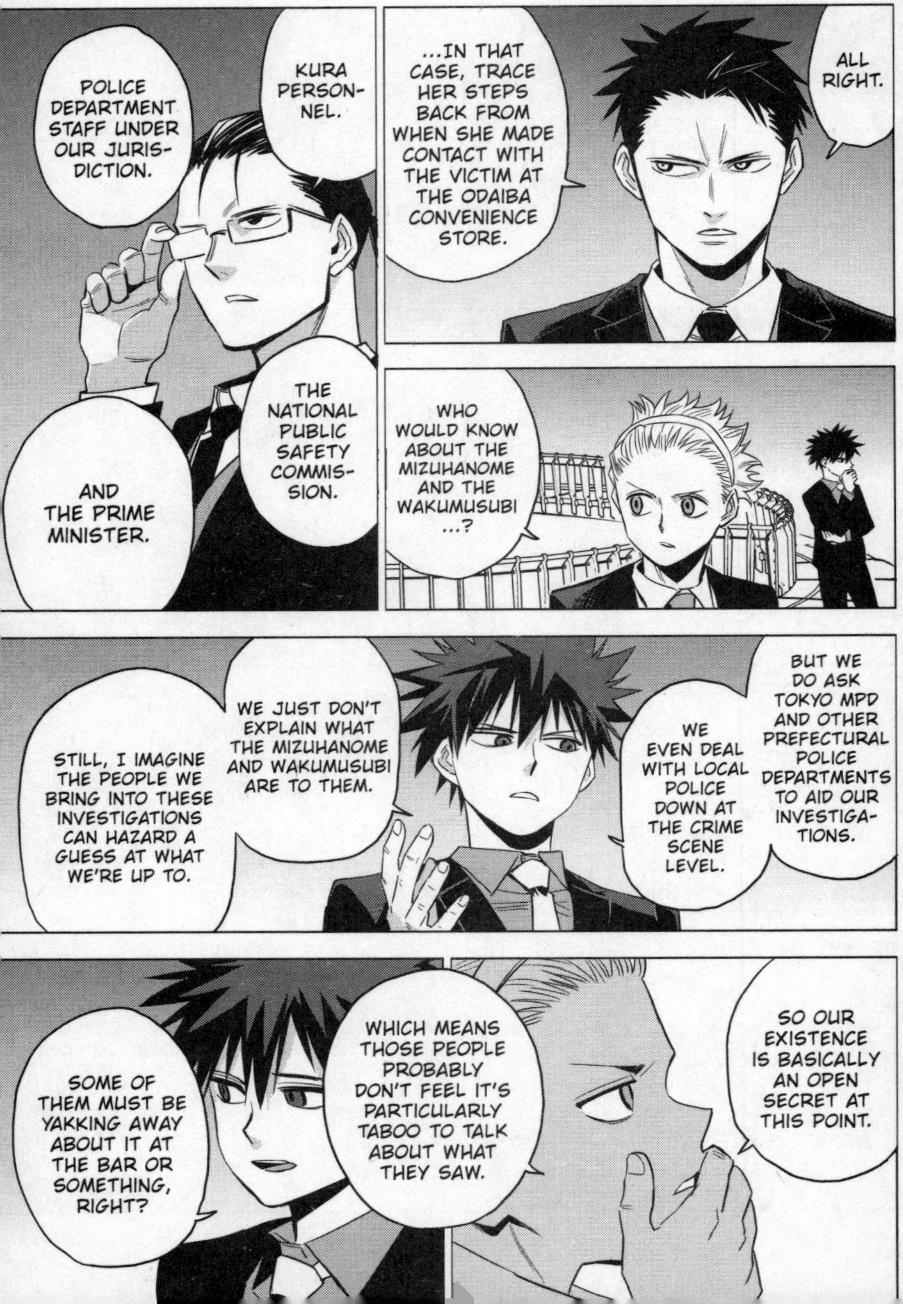
ALL RIGHT.
...IN THAT CASE, TRACE HER STEPS BACK FROM WHEN SHE MADE CONTACT WITH THE VICTIM AT THE ODAIBA CONVENIENCE STORE.
WHO WOULD KNOW ABOUT THE MIZUHANOME AND THE WAKUMUSUBI ...?
KURA PERSONNEL.
POLICE DEPARTMENT STAFF UNDER OUR JURISDICTION.
THE NATIONAL PUBLIC SAFETY COMMISSION.
AND THE PRIME MINISTER.
BUT WE DO ASK TOKYO MPD AND OTHER PREFECTURAL POLICE DEPARTMENTS TO AID OUR INVESTIGATIONS.
WE EVEN DEAL WITH LOCAL POLICE DOWN AT THE CRIME SCENE LEVEL.
WE JUST DON'T EXPLAIN WHAT THE MIZUHANOME AND WAKUMUSUBI ARE TO THEM.
STILL, I IMAGINE THE PEOPLE WE BRING INTO THESE INVESTIGATIONS CAN HAZARD A GUESS AT WHAT WE'RE UP TO.
SO OUR EXISTENCE IS BASICALLY AN OPEN SECRET AT THIS POINT.
WHICH MEANS THOSE PEOPLE PROBABLY DON'T FEEL IT'S PARTICULARLY TABOO TO TALK ABOUT WHAT THEY SAW.
SOME OF THEM MUST BE YAKKING AWAY ABOUT IT AT THE BAR OR SOMETHING, RIGHT?

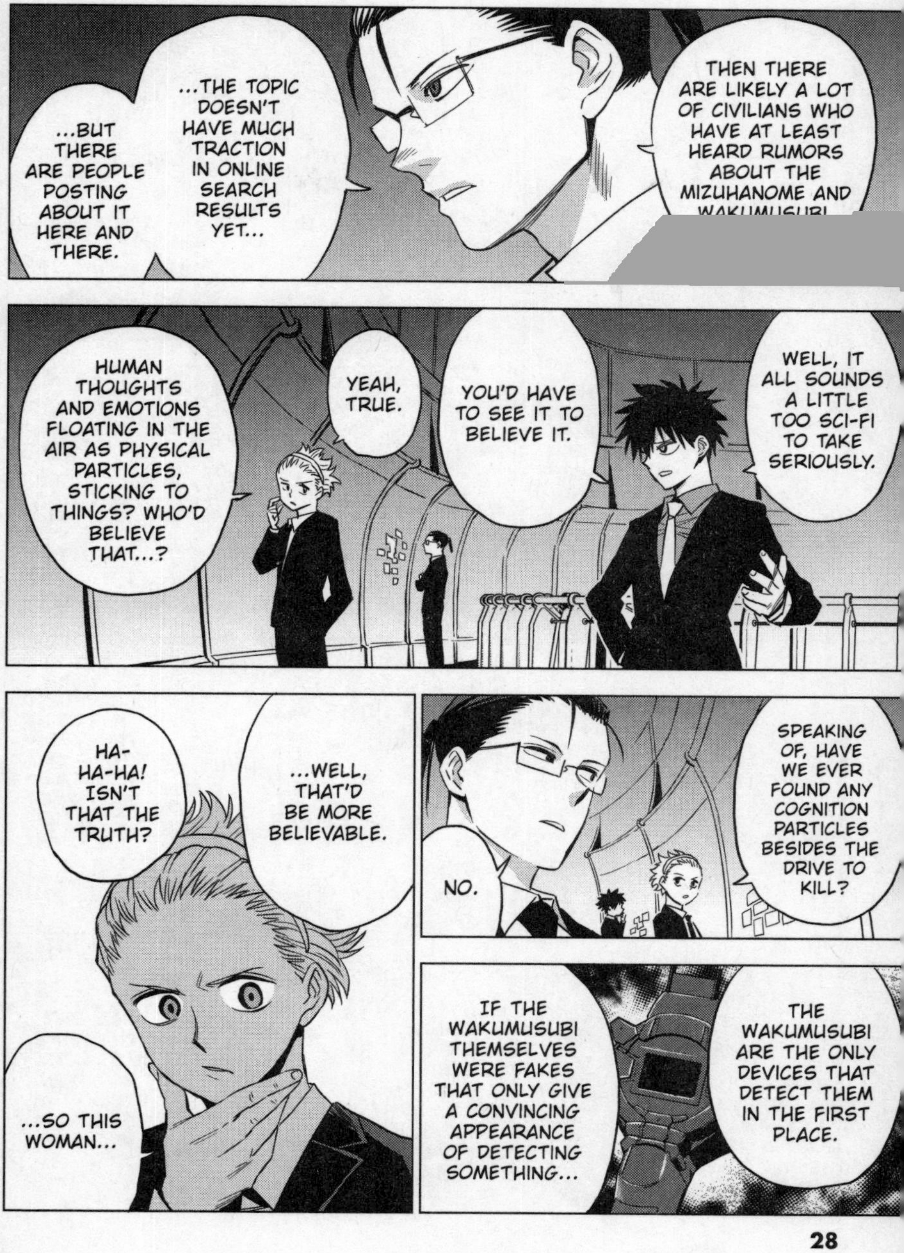
THEN THERE ARE LIKELY A LOT OF CIVILIANS WHO HAVE AT LEAST HEARD RUMORS ABOUT THE MIZUHANOME AND WAKUMUSUBI
...THE TOPIC DOESN'T HAVE MUCH TRACTION IN ONLINE SEARCH RESULTS YET...
...BUT THERE ARE PEOPLE POSTING ABOUT IT HERE AND THERE.
WELL, IT ALL SOUNDS A LITTLE TOO SCI-FI TO TAKE SERIOUSLY.
YOU'D HAVE TO SEE IT TO BELIEVE IT.
YEAH, TRUE.
HUMAN THOUGHTS AND EMOTIONS FLOATING IN THE AIR AS PHYSICAL PARTICLES, STICKING TO THINGS? WHO'D BELIEVE THAT...?
SPEAKING OF, HAVE WE EVER FOUND ANY COGNITION PARTICLES BESIDES THE DRIVE TO KILL?
NO.
THE WAKUMUSUBI ARE THE ONLY DEVICES THAT DETECT THEM IN THE FIRST PLACE.
IF THE WAKUMUSUBI THEMSELVES WERE FAKES THAT ONLY GIVE A CONVINCING APPEARANCE OF DETECTING SOMETHING...
...WELL, THAT'D BE MORE BELIEVABLE.
HA-HA-HA! ISN'T THAT THE TRUTH?
...SO THIS WOMAN...

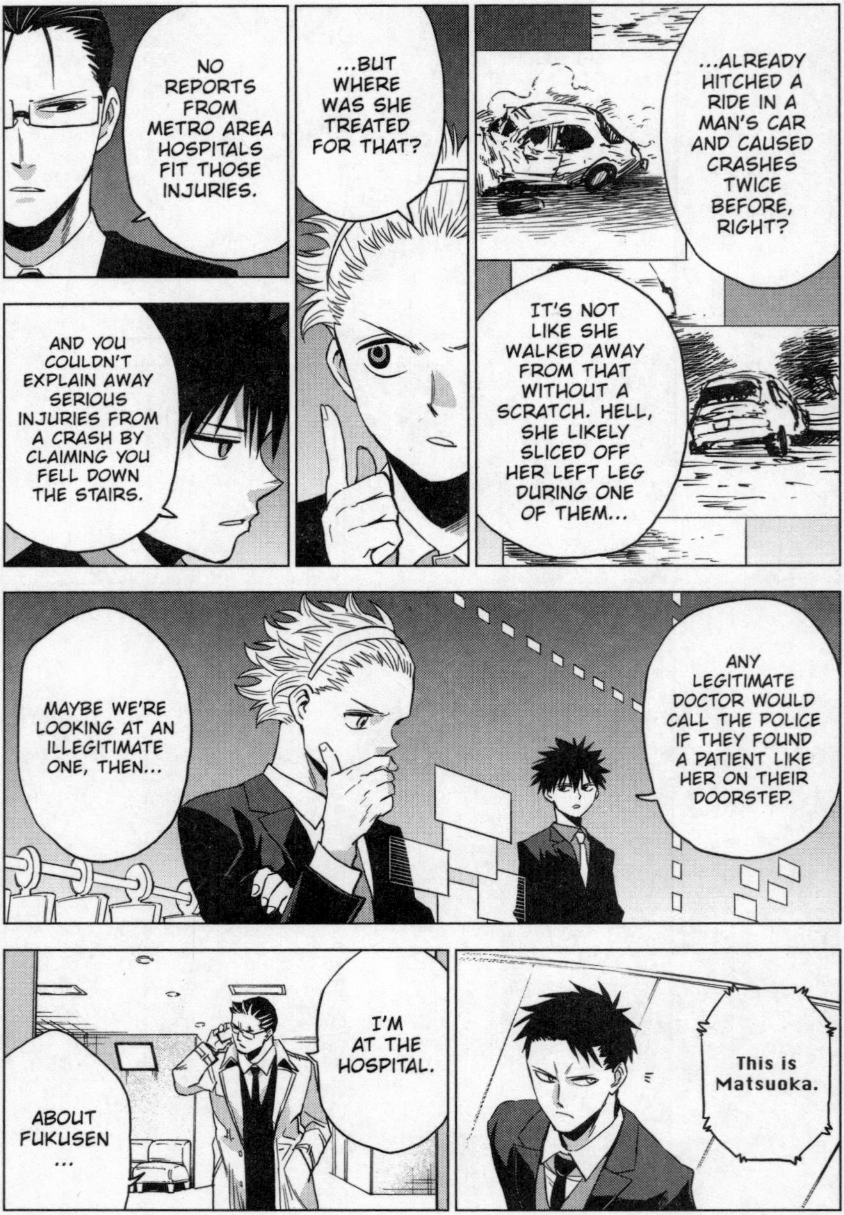
...ALREADY HITCHED A RIDE IN A MAN'S CAR AND CAUSED CRASHES TWICE BEFORE, RIGHT?
IT'S NOT LIKE SHE WALKED AWAY FROM THAT WITHOUT A SCRATCH. HELL, SHE LIKELY SLICED OFF HER LEFT LEG DURING ONE OF THEM...
...BUT WHERE WAS SHE TREATED FOR THAT?
NO REPORTS FROM METRO AREA HOSPITALS FIT THOSE INJURIES.
AND YOU COULDN'T EXPLAIN AWAY SERIOUS INJURIES FROM A CRASH BY CLAIMING YOU FELL DOWN THE STAIRS.
ANY LEGITIMATE DOCTOR WOULD CALL THE POLICE IF THEY FOUND A PATIENT LIKE HER ON THEIR DOORSTEP.
MAYBE WE'RE LOOKING AT AN ILLEGITIMATE ONE, THEN...
This is Matsuoka.
I'M AT THE HOSPITAL.
ABOUT FUKUSEN ...

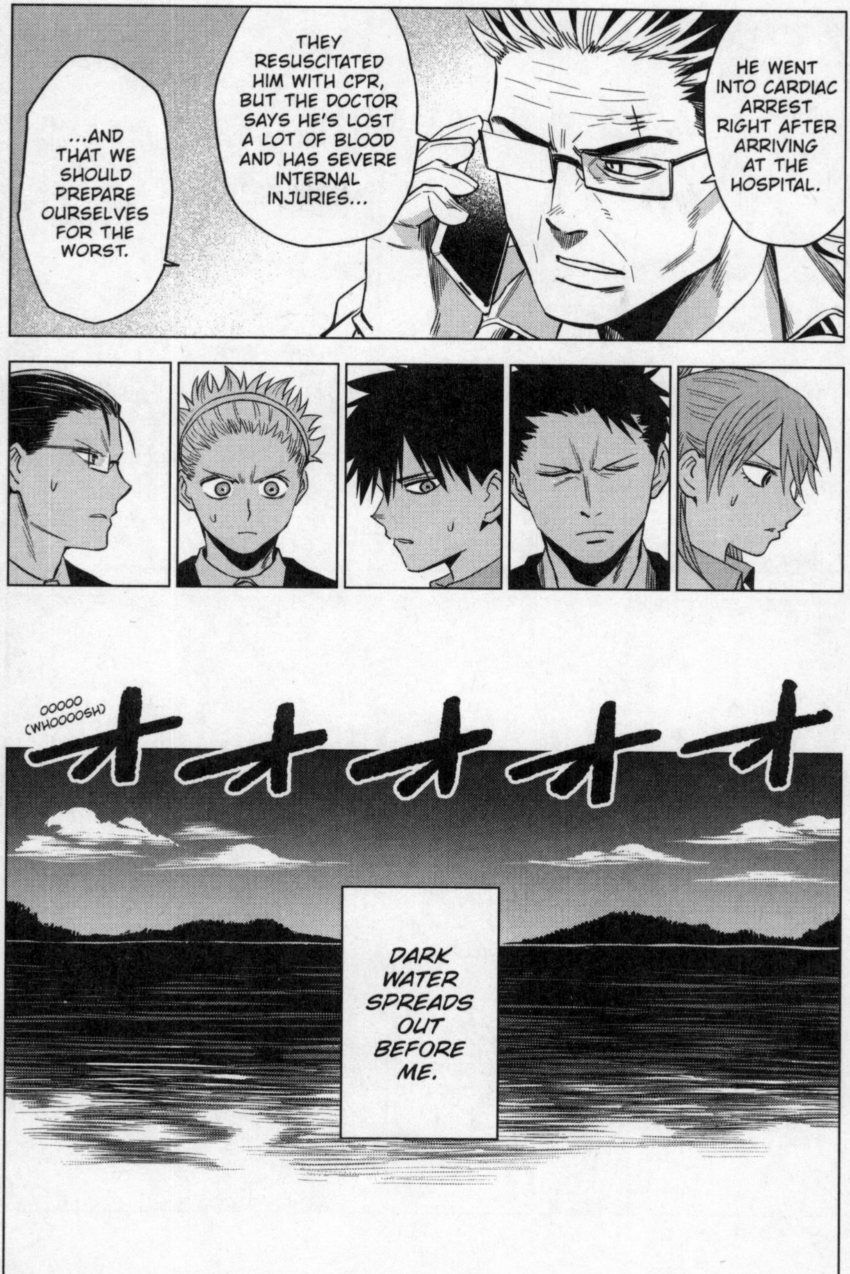
HE WENT INTO CARDIAC ARREST RIGHT AFTER ARRIVING AT THE HOSPITAL.
THEY RESUSCITATED HIM WITH CPR, BUT THE DOCTOR SAYS HE'S LOST A LOT OF BLOOD AND HAS SEVERE INTERNAL INJURIES...
...AND THAT WE SHOULD PREPARE OURSELVES FOR THE WORST.
OOOOO (WHOOOOSH)
DARK WATER SPREADS OUT BEFORE ME.

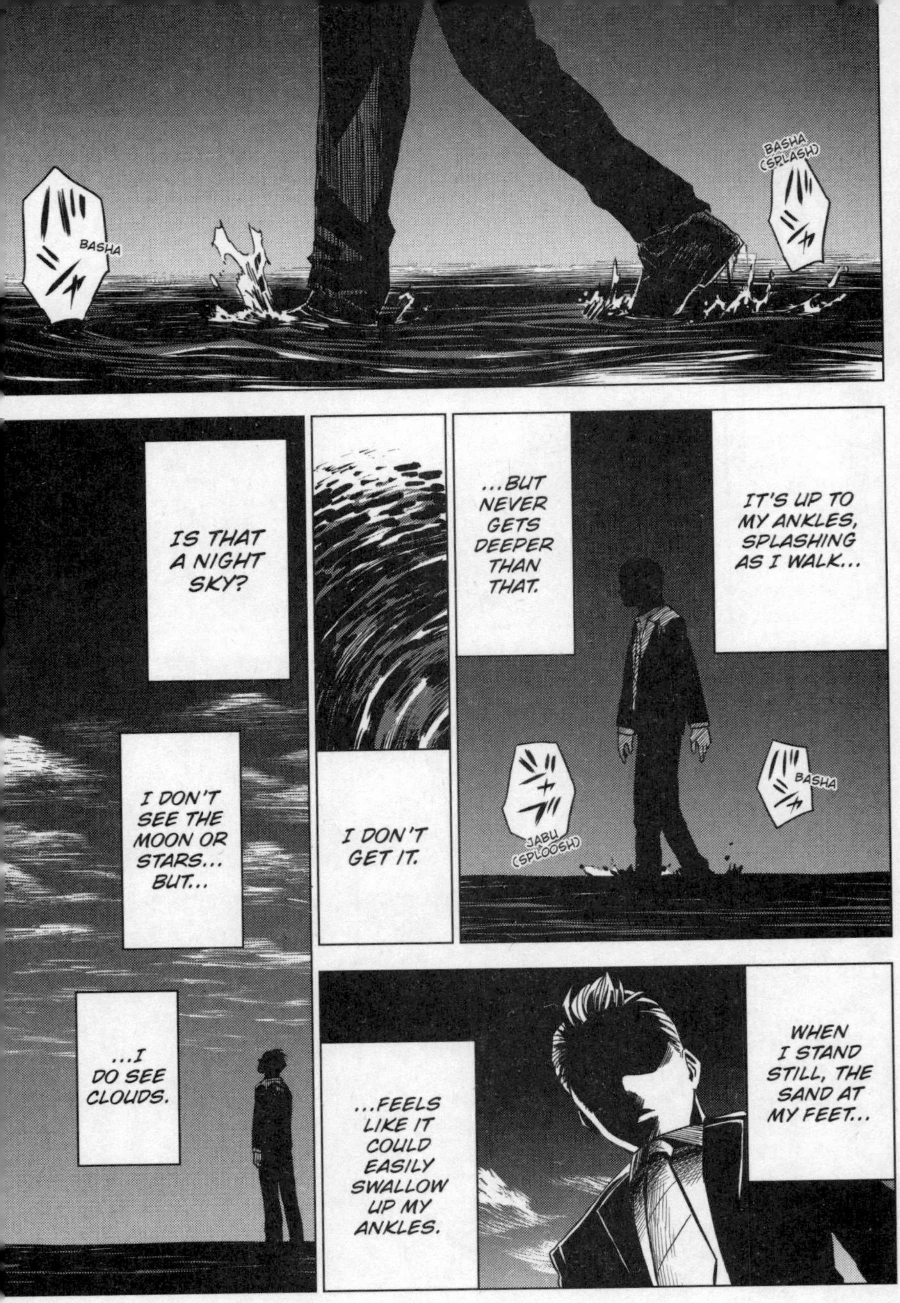
BASHA (SPLASH)
BASHA
IT'S UP TO MY ANKLES, SPLASHING AS I WALK...
...BUT NEVER GETS DEEPER THAN THAT.
BASHA
JABU (SPLOOSH)
I DON'T GET IT.
WHEN I STAND STILL, THE SAND AT MY FEET...
...FEELS LIKE IT COULD EASILY SWALLOW UP MY ANKLES.
IS THAT A NIGHT SKY?
I DON'T SEE THE MOON OR STARS... BUT...
...I DO SEE CLOUDS.

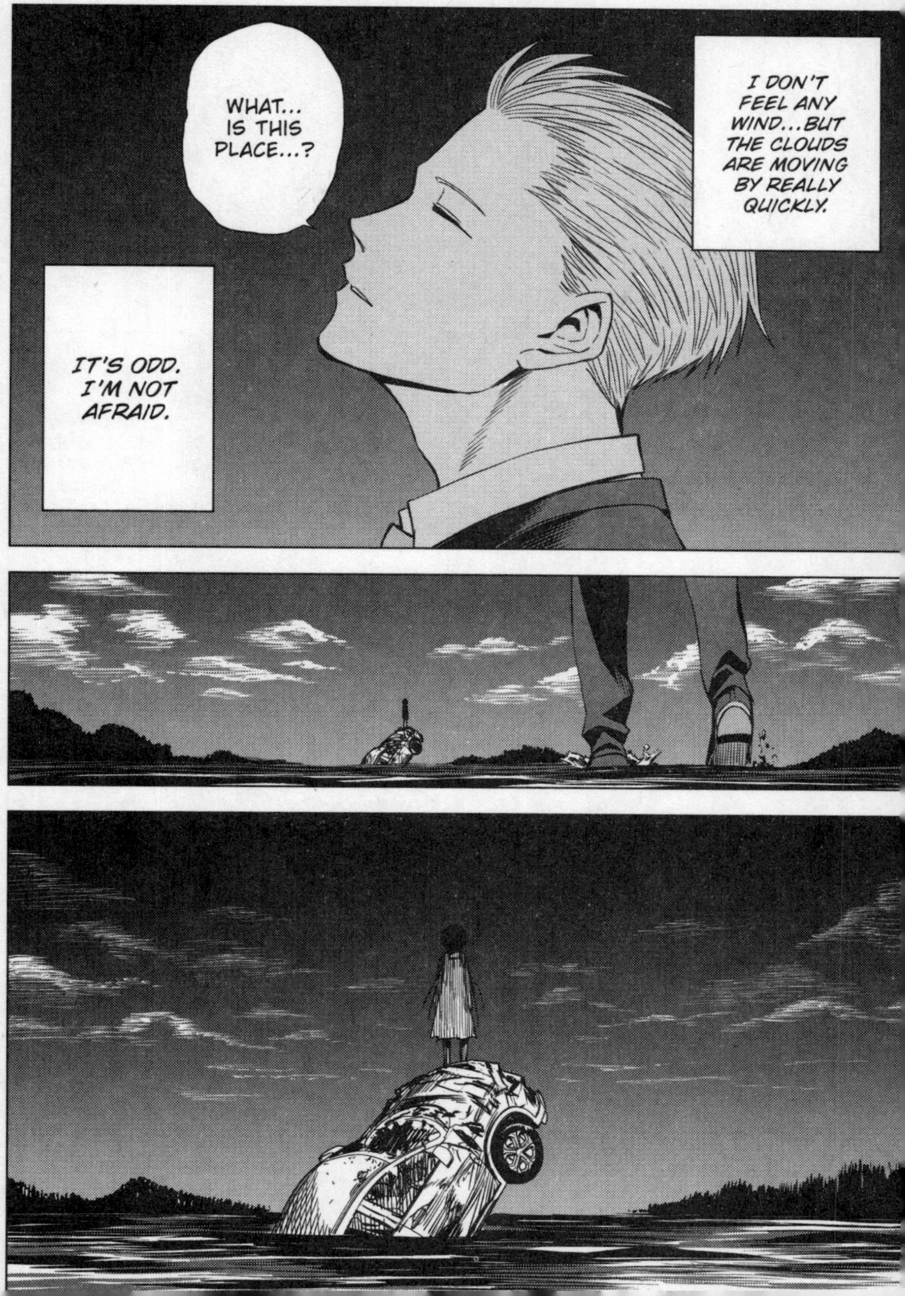
I DON'T FEEL ANY WIND...BUT THE CLOUDS ARE MOVING BY REALLY QUICKLY.
WHAT... IS THIS PLACE...?
IT'S ODD. I'M NOT AFRAID.

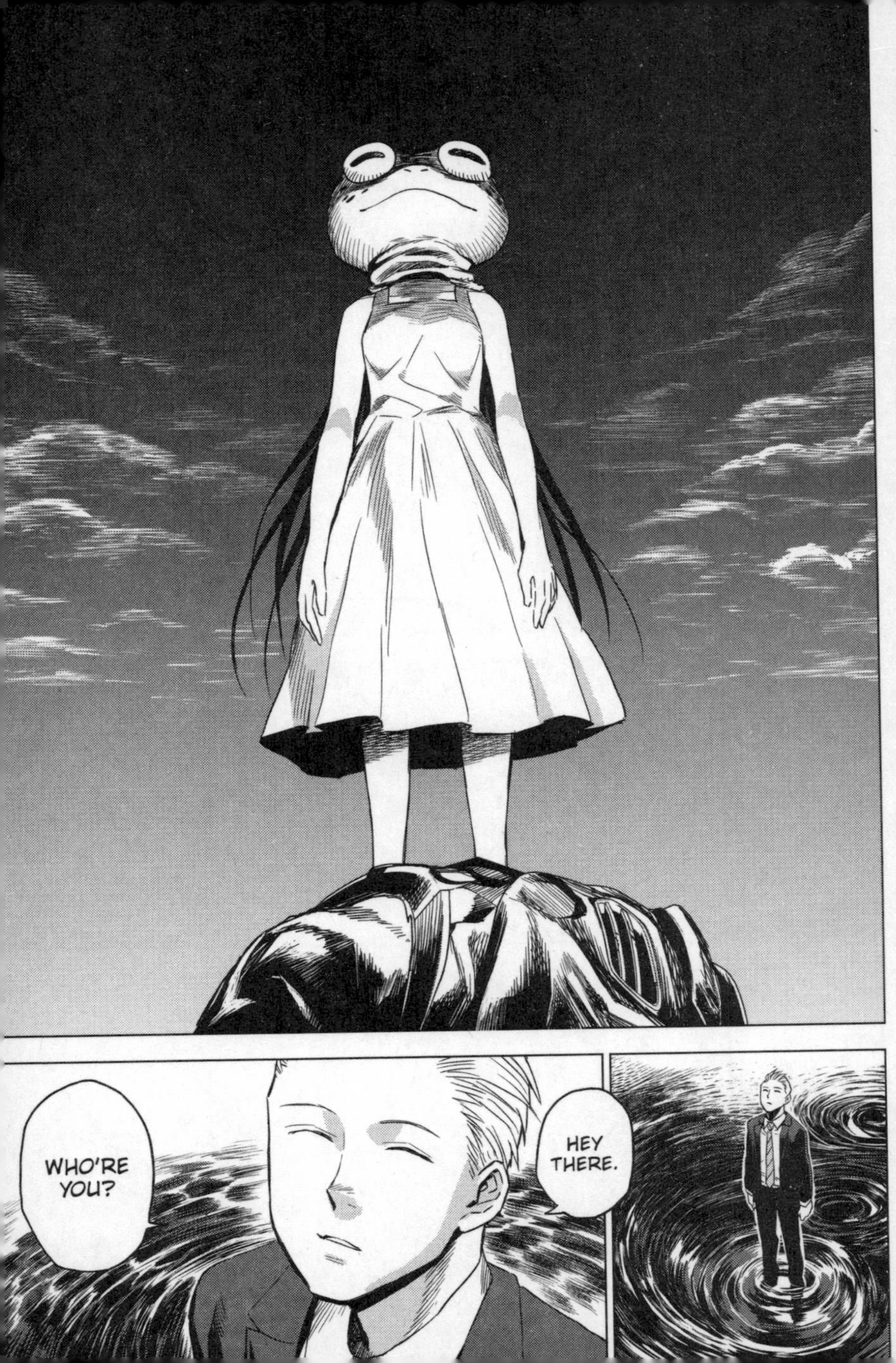
HEY THERE.
WHO'RE YOU?

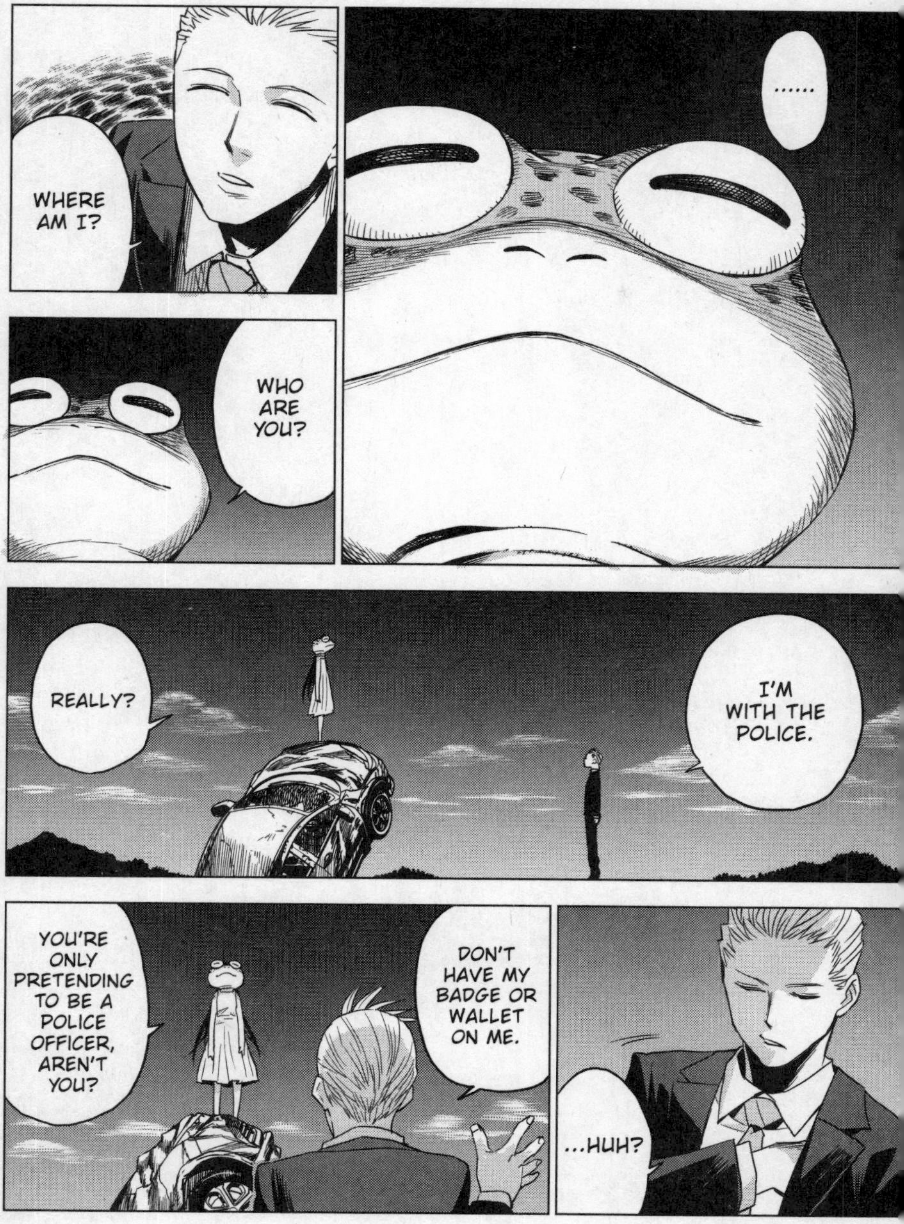
......
WHERE AM I?
WHO ARE YOU?
I'M WITH THE POLICE.
REALLY?
...HUH?
DON'T HAVE MY BADGE OR WALLET ON ME.
YOU'RE ONLY PRETENDING TO BE A POLICE OFFICER, AREN'T YOU?

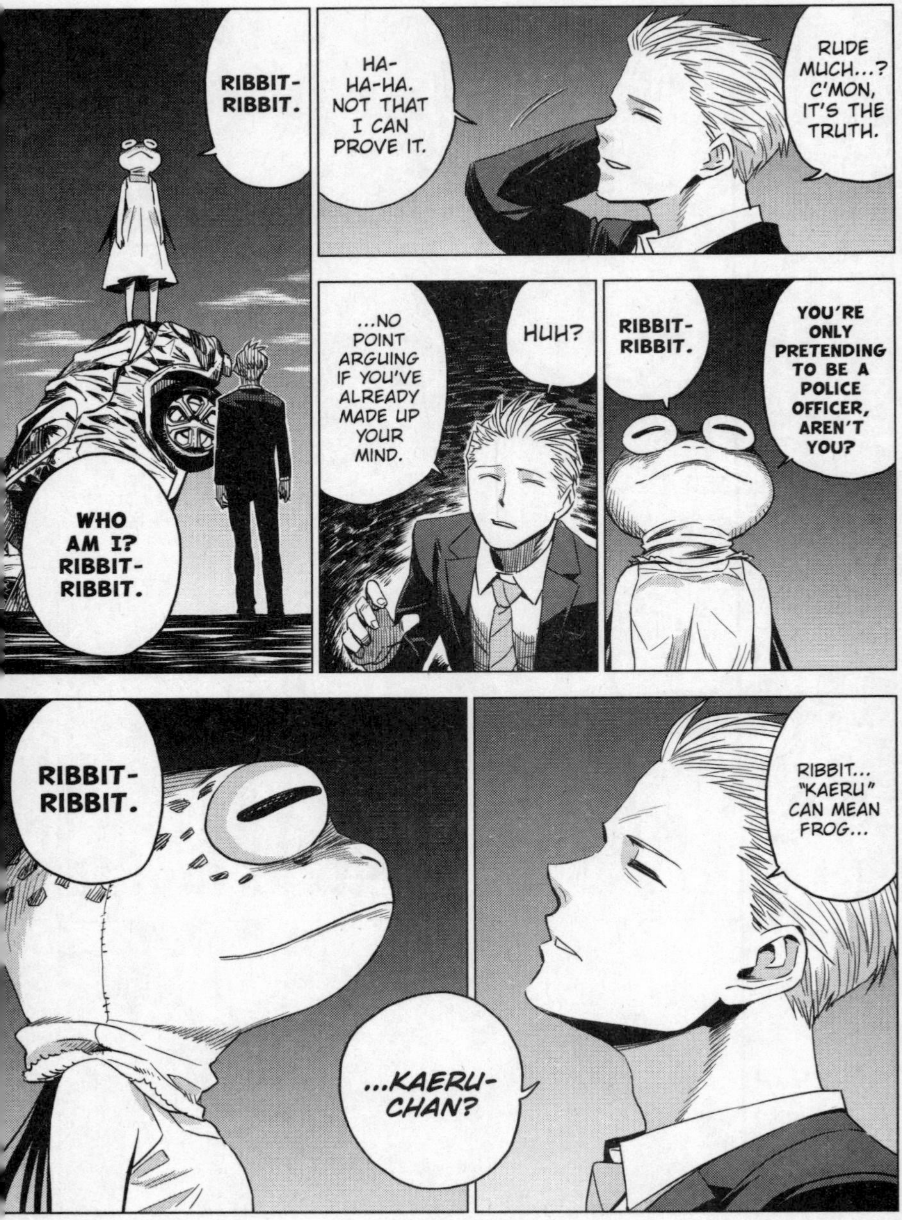
RUDE MUCH...? C'MON, IT'S THE TRUTH.
HA-HA-HA. NOT THAT I CAN PROVE IT.
YOU'RE ONLY PRETENDING TO BE A POLICE OFFICER, AREN'T YOU?
RIBBIT-RIBBIT.
HUH?
...NO POINT ARGUING IF YOU'VE ALREADY MADE UP YOUR MIND.
RIBBIT-RIBBIT.
WHO AM I? RIBBIT-RIBBIT.
RIBBIT... "KAERU" CAN MEAN FROG...
...KAERU-CHAN?
RIBBIT-RIBBIT.

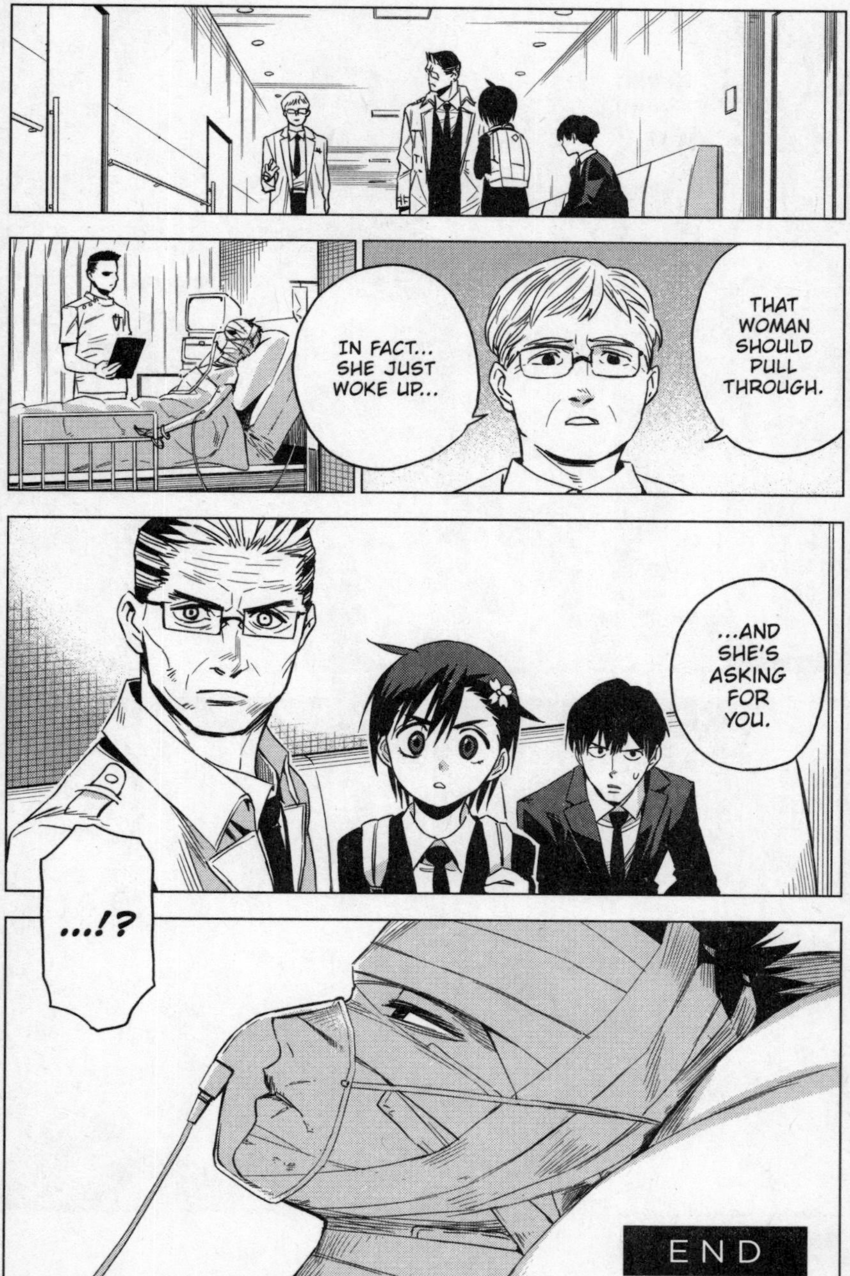
THAT WOMAN SHOULD PULL THROUGH.
IN FACT... SHE JUST WOKE UP...
...AND SHE'S ASKING FOR YOU.
...!?
END

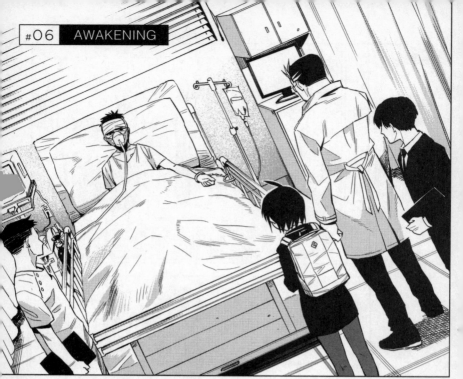

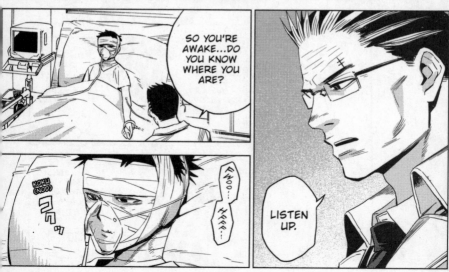

SO YOU'RE AWAKE...DO YOU KNOW WHERE YOU ARE?

KOKU (NOD)

FWOO--

LISTEN UP.

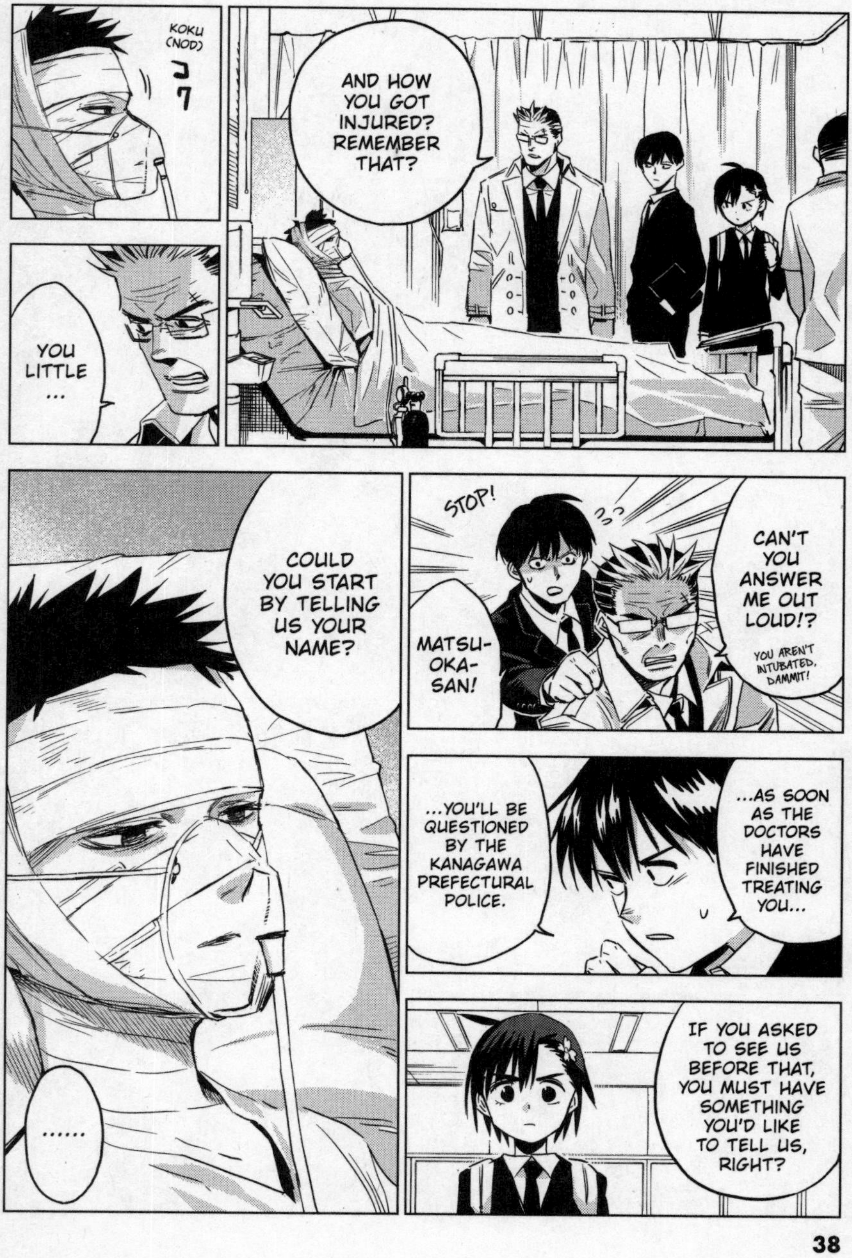
AND HOW YOU GOT INJURED? REMEMBER THAT?
KOKU (NOD)
コク
YOU LITTLE ...
CAN'T YOU ANSWER ME OUT LOUD!?
YOU AREN'T INTUBATED, DAMMIT!
STOP!
MATSU-OKA-SAN!
...AS SOON AS THE DOCTORS HAVE FINISHED TREATING YOU...
...YOU'LL BE QUESTIONED BY THE KANAGAWA PREFECTURAL POLICE.
IF YOU ASKED TO SEE US BEFORE THAT, YOU MUST HAVE SOMETHING YOU'D LIKE TO TELL US, RIGHT?
COULD YOU START BY TELLING US YOUR NAME?
......

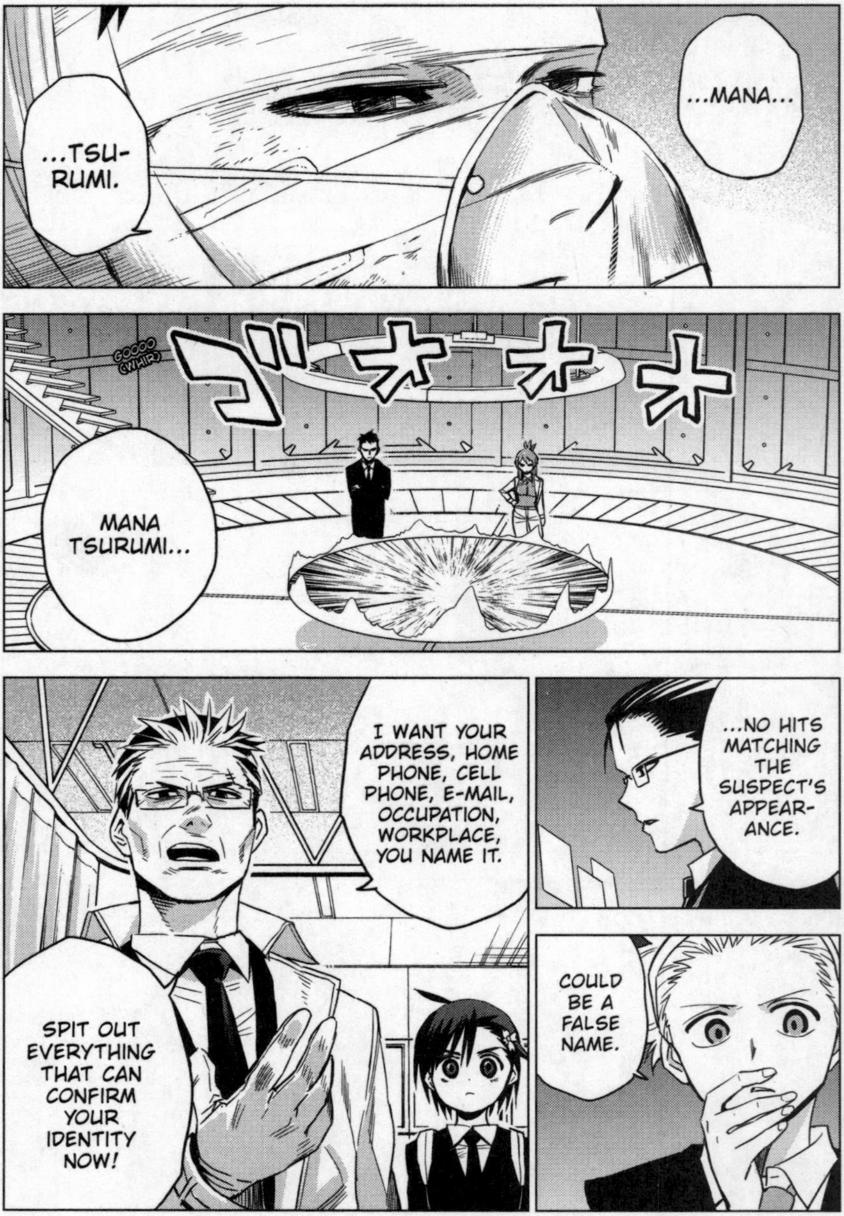
...MANA...
...TSU-RUMI.
ゴオオオ
GOOOO (WHIR)
MANA TSURUMI...
...NO HITS MATCHING THE SUSPECT'S APPEAR-ANCE.
COULD BE A FALSE NAME.
I WANT YOUR ADDRESS, HOME PHONE, CELL PHONE, E-MAIL, OCCUPATION, WORKPLACE, YOU NAME IT.
SPIT OUT EVERYTHING THAT CAN CONFIRM YOUR IDENTITY NOW!

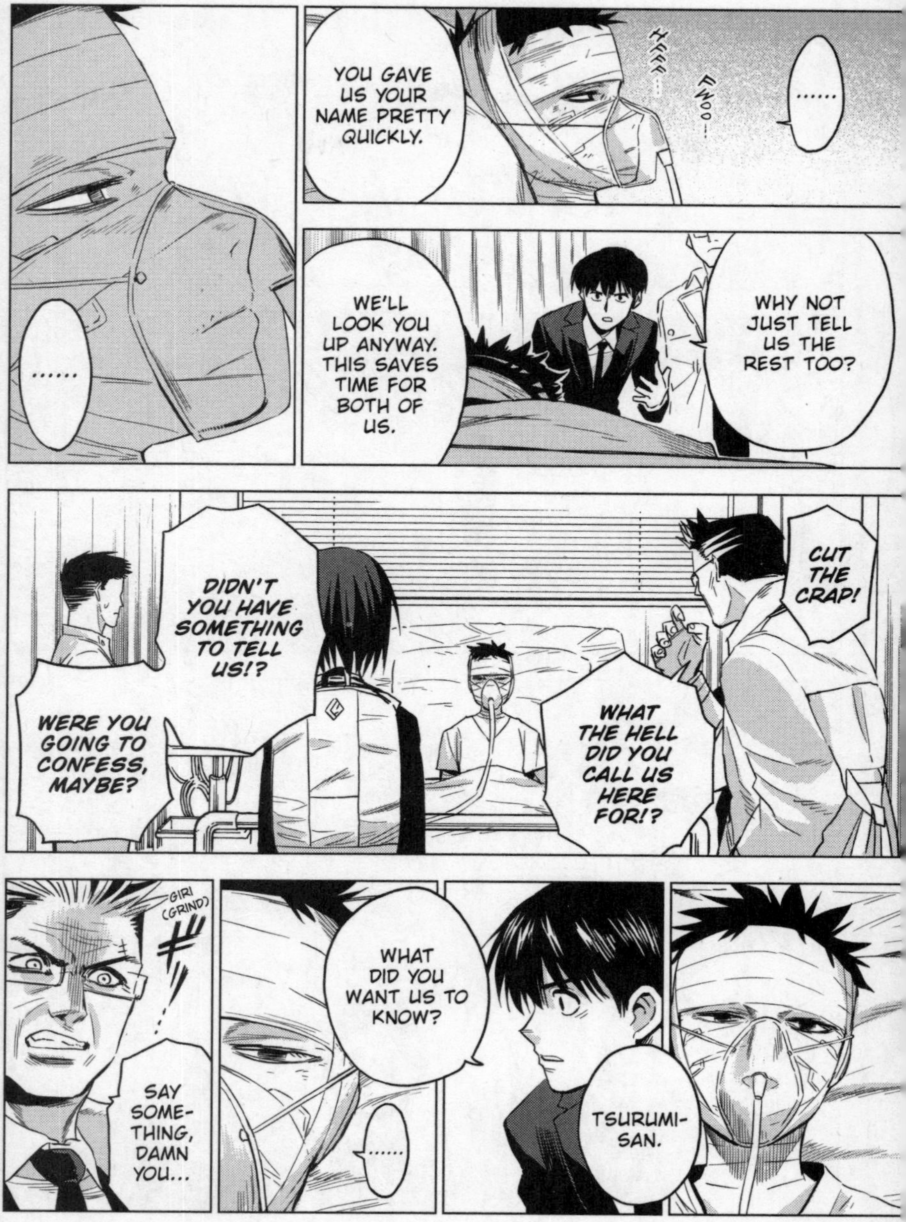
......
HFFF...
FWOO...
YOU GAVE US YOUR NAME PRETTY QUICKLY.
WHY NOT JUST TELL US THE REST TOO?
WE'LL LOOK YOU UP ANYWAY. THIS SAVES TIME FOR BOTH OF US.
......
CUT THE CRAP!
WHAT THE HELL DID YOU CALL US HERE FOR!?
DIDN'T YOU HAVE SOMETHING TO TELL US!?
WERE YOU GOING TO CONFESS, MAYBE?
TSURUMI-SAN.
WHAT DID YOU WANT US TO KNOW?
......
GIRI (GRIND)
SAY SOME-THING, DAMN YOU...

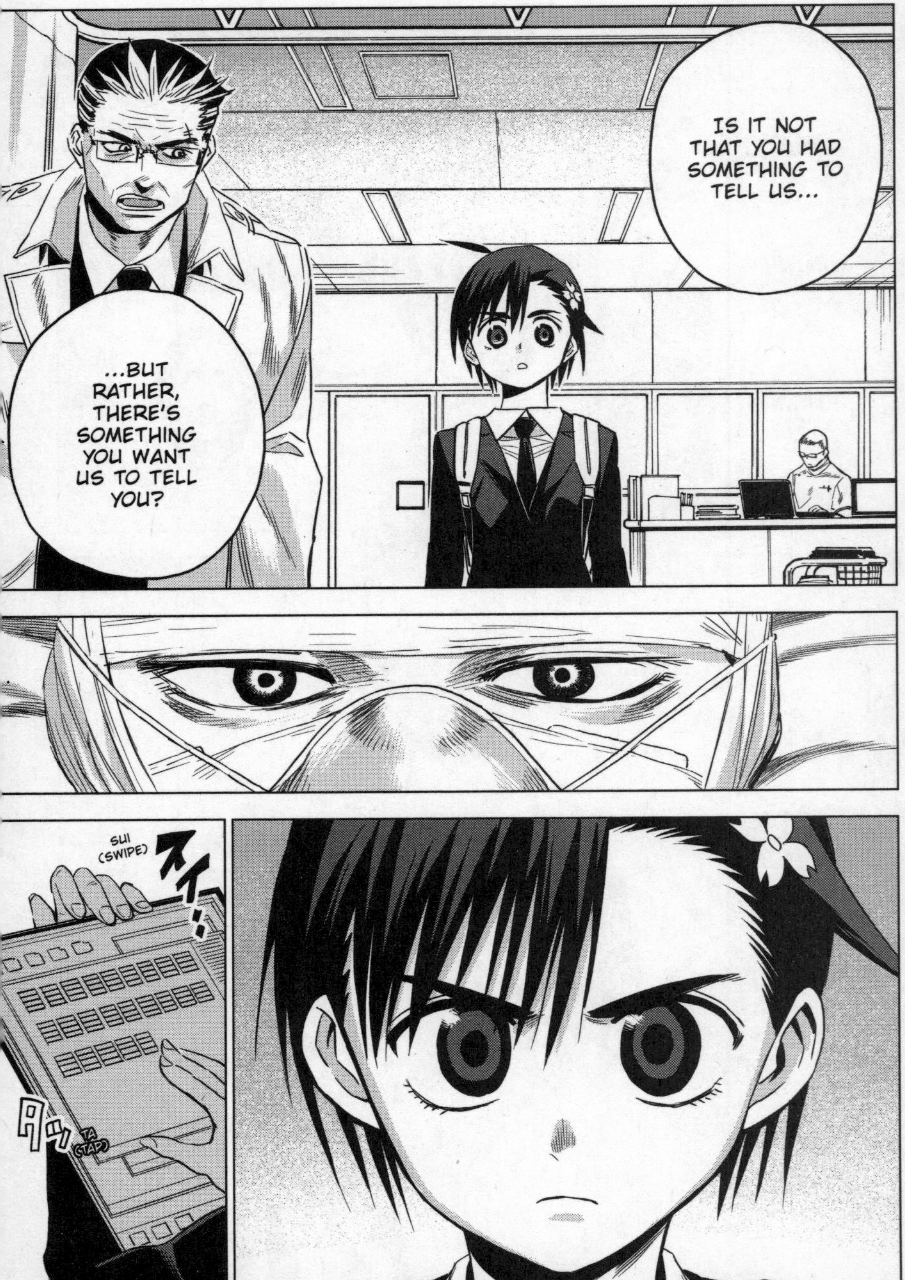
IS IT NOT THAT YOU HAD SOMETHING TO TELL US...
...BUT RATHER, THERE'S SOMETHING YOU WANT US TO TELL YOU?
SUI (SWIPE)
TA (TAP)

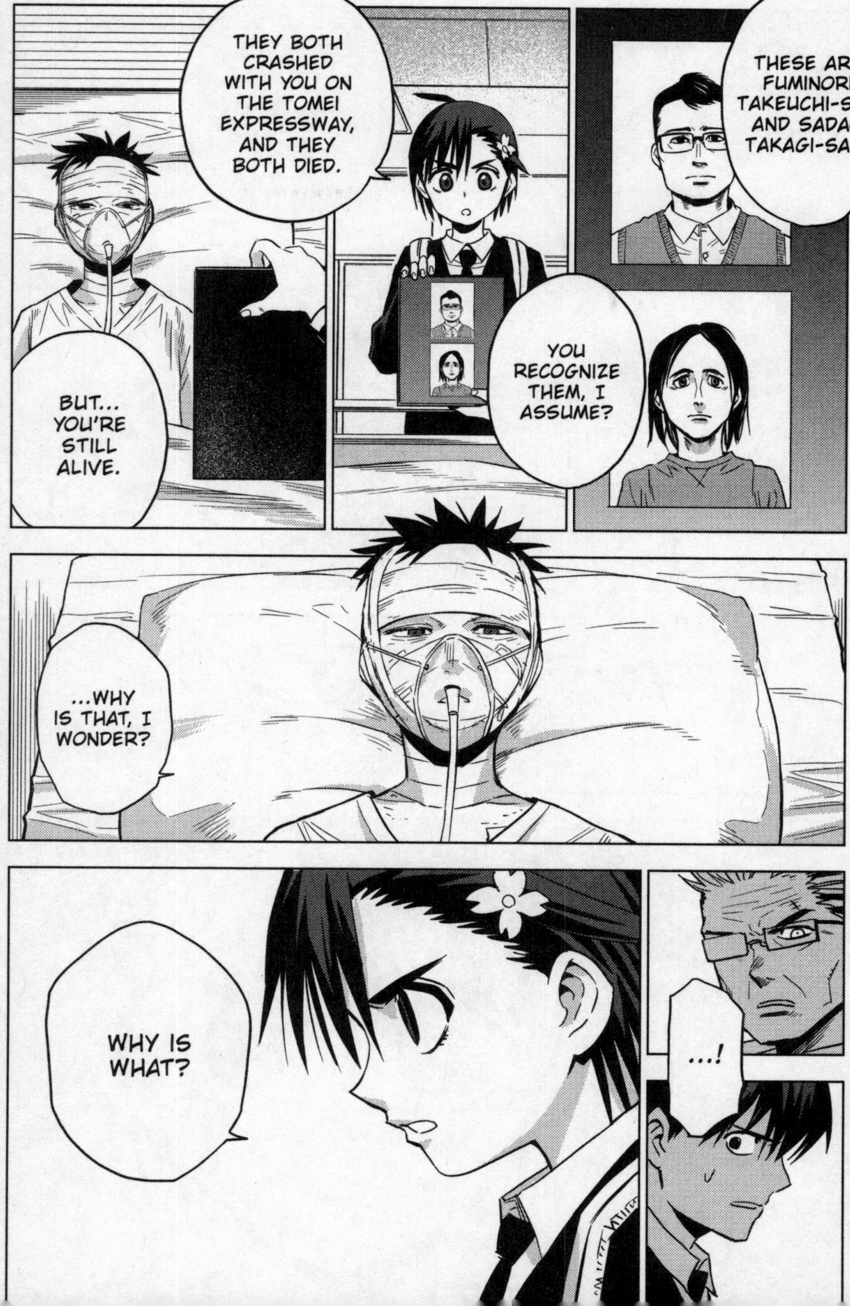
THESE ARE FUMINORI TAKEUCHI-SAN AND SADAO TAKAGI-SAN.
YOU RECOGNIZE THEM, I ASSUME?
THEY BOTH CRASHED WITH YOU ON THE TOMEI EXPRESSWAY, AND THEY BOTH DIED.
BUT... YOU'RE STILL ALIVE.
...WHY IS THAT, I WONDER?
...!
WHY IS WHAT?

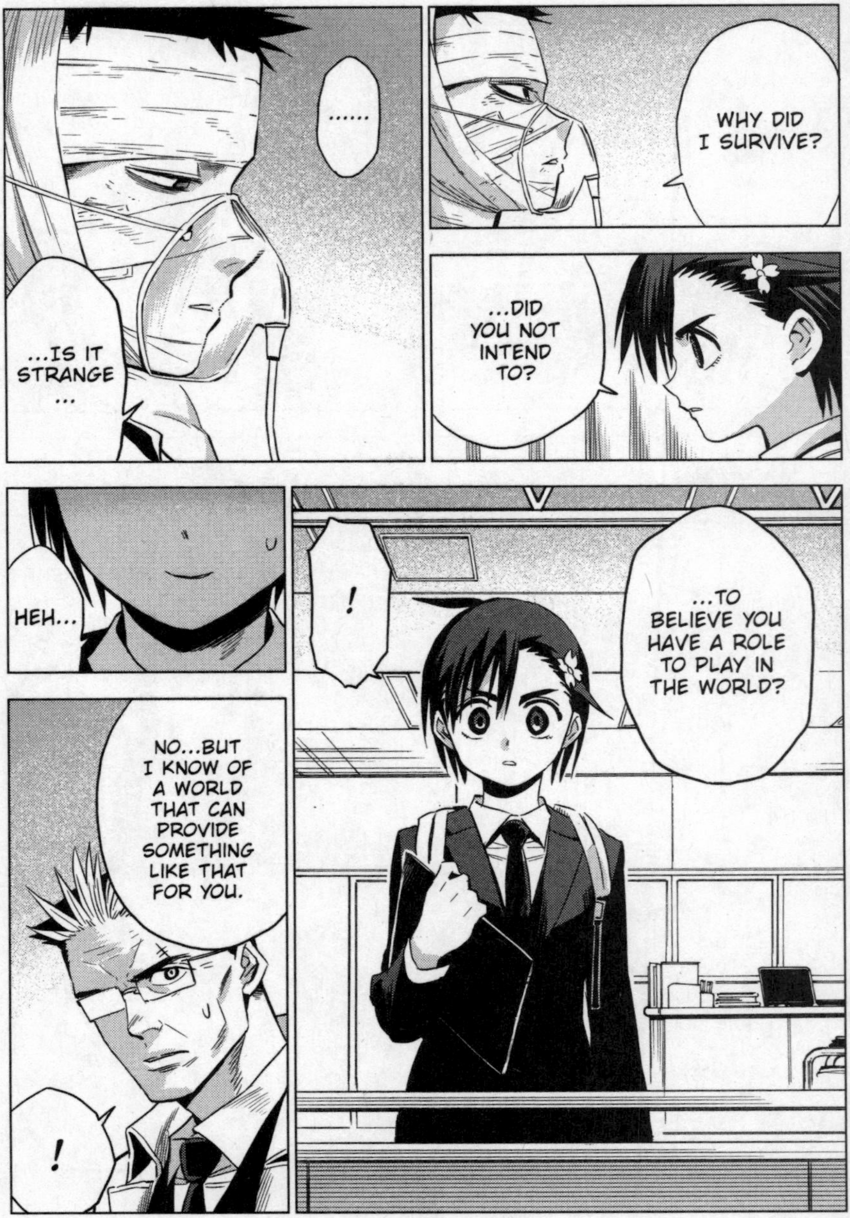
WHY DID I SURVIVE?
...DID YOU NOT INTEND TO?
......
...IS IT STRANGE ...
...TO BELIEVE YOU HAVE A ROLE TO PLAY IN THE WORLD?
!
HEH...
NO...BUT I KNOW OF A WORLD THAT CAN PROVIDE SOMETHING LIKE THAT FOR YOU.
!

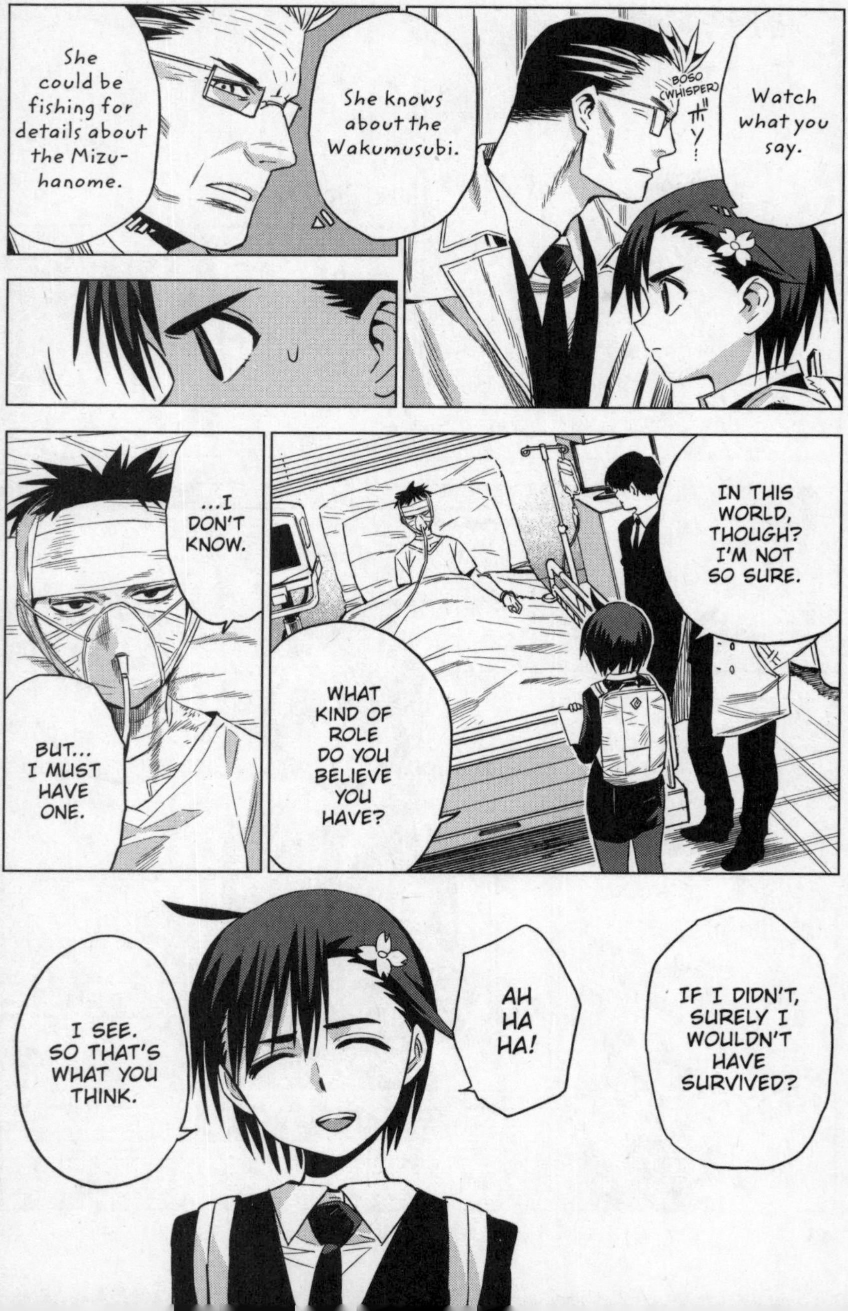
BOSO (WHISPER)
Watch what you say.
She knows about the Wakumusubi.
She could be fishing for details about the Mizu-hanome.
IN THIS WORLD, THOUGH? I'M NOT SO SURE.
WHAT KIND OF ROLE DO YOU BELIEVE YOU HAVE?
...I DON'T KNOW.
BUT... I MUST HAVE ONE.
IF I DIDN'T, SURELY I WOULDN'T HAVE SURVIVED?
AH HA HA!
I SEE. SO THAT'S WHAT YOU THINK.

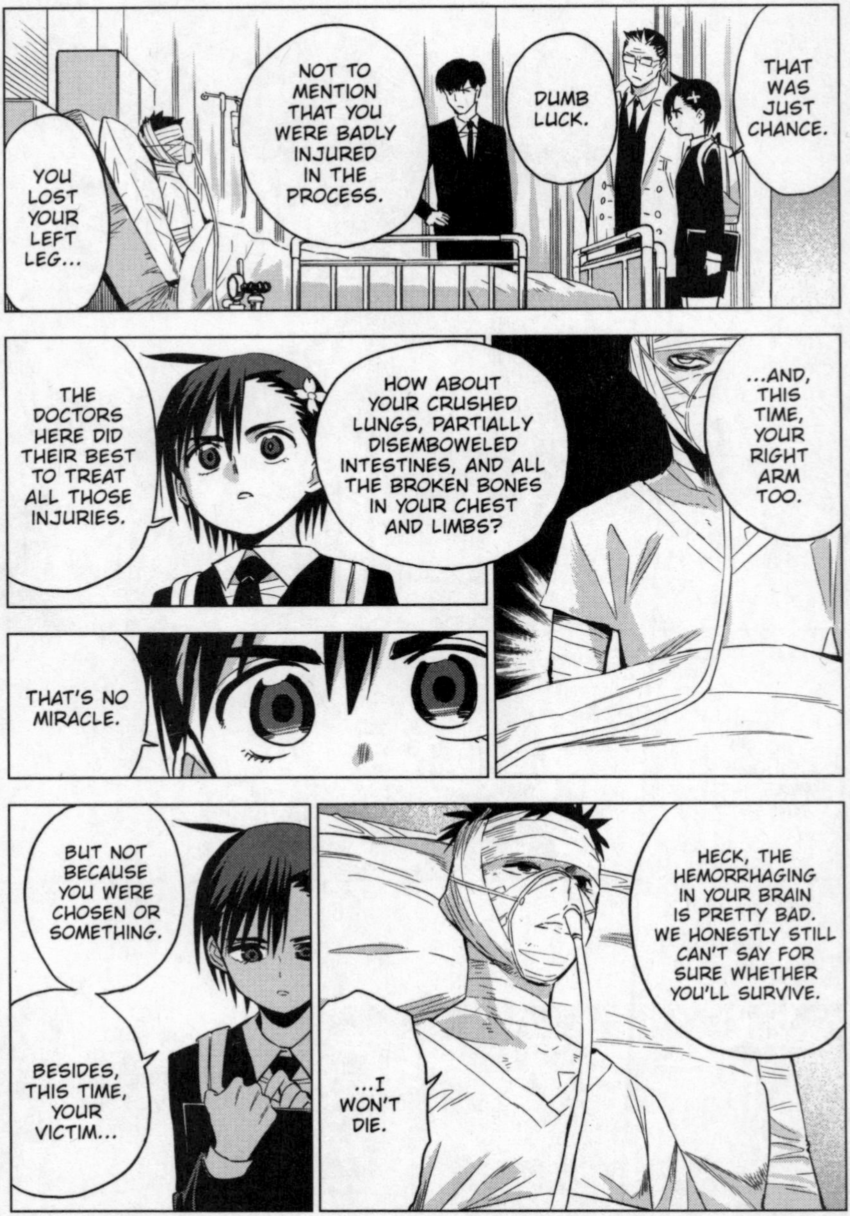
THAT WAS JUST CHANCE.
DUMB LUCK.
NOT TO MENTION THAT YOU WERE BADLY INJURED IN THE PROCESS.
YOU LOST YOUR LEFT LEG...
...AND, THIS TIME, YOUR RIGHT ARM TOO.
HOW ABOUT YOUR CRUSHED LUNGS, PARTIALLY DISEMBOWELED INTESTINES, AND ALL THE BROKEN BONES IN YOUR CHEST AND LIMBS?
THE DOCTORS HERE DID THEIR BEST TO TREAT ALL THOSE INJURIES.
THAT'S NO MIRACLE.
HECK, THE HEMORRHAGING IN YOUR BRAIN IS PRETTY BAD. WE HONESTLY STILL CAN'T SAY FOR SURE WHETHER YOU'LL SURVIVE.
...I WON'T DIE.
BUT NOT BECAUSE YOU WERE CHOSEN OR SOMETHING.
BESIDES, THIS TIME, YOUR VICTIM...

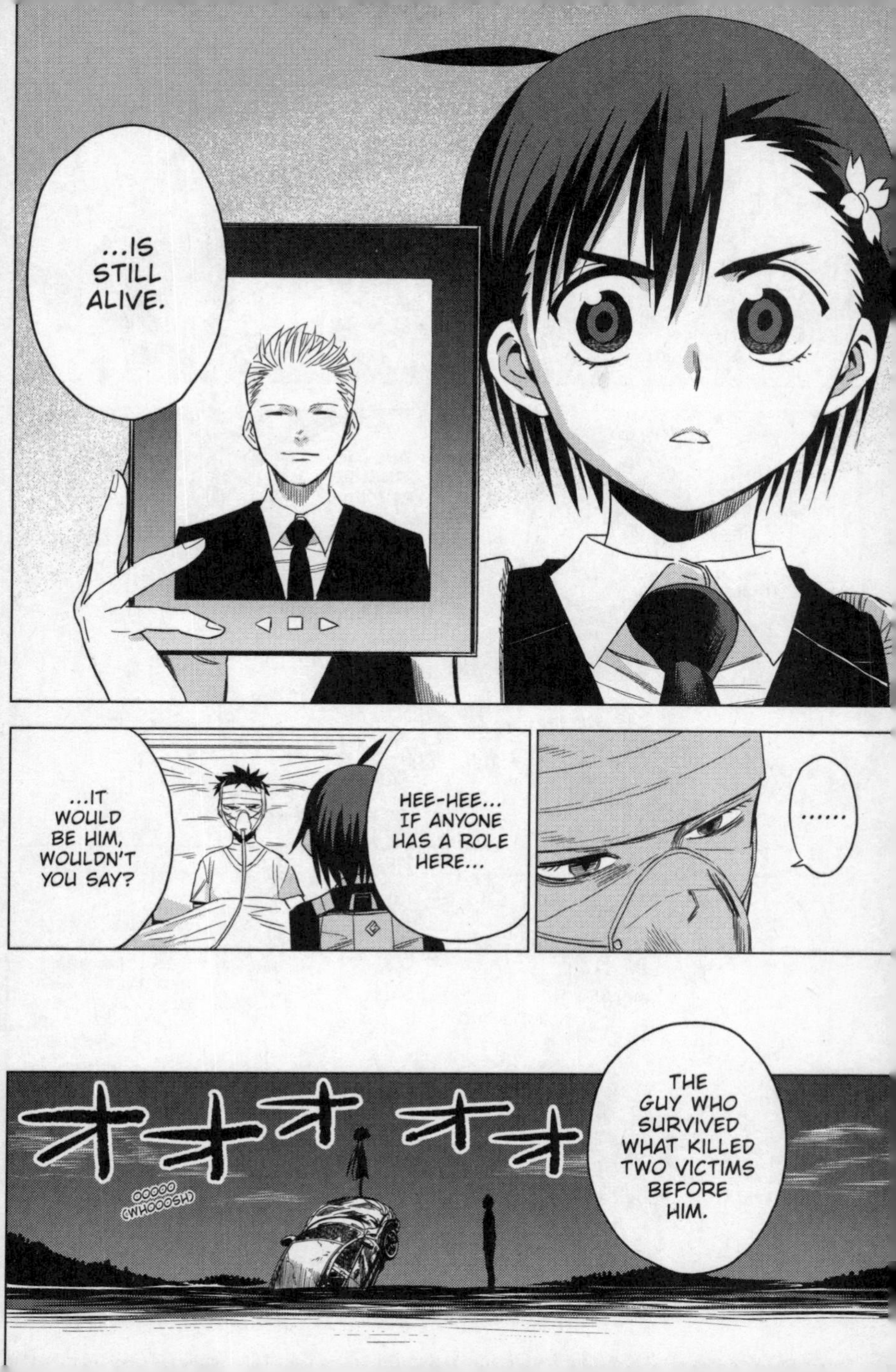
...IS STILL ALIVE.
......
HEE-HEE... IF ANYONE HAS A ROLE HERE...
...IT WOULD BE HIM, WOULDN'T YOU SAY?
THE GUY WHO SURVIVED WHAT KILLED TWO VICTIMS BEFORE HIM.
オオオオオ
OOOOO (WHOOOSH)

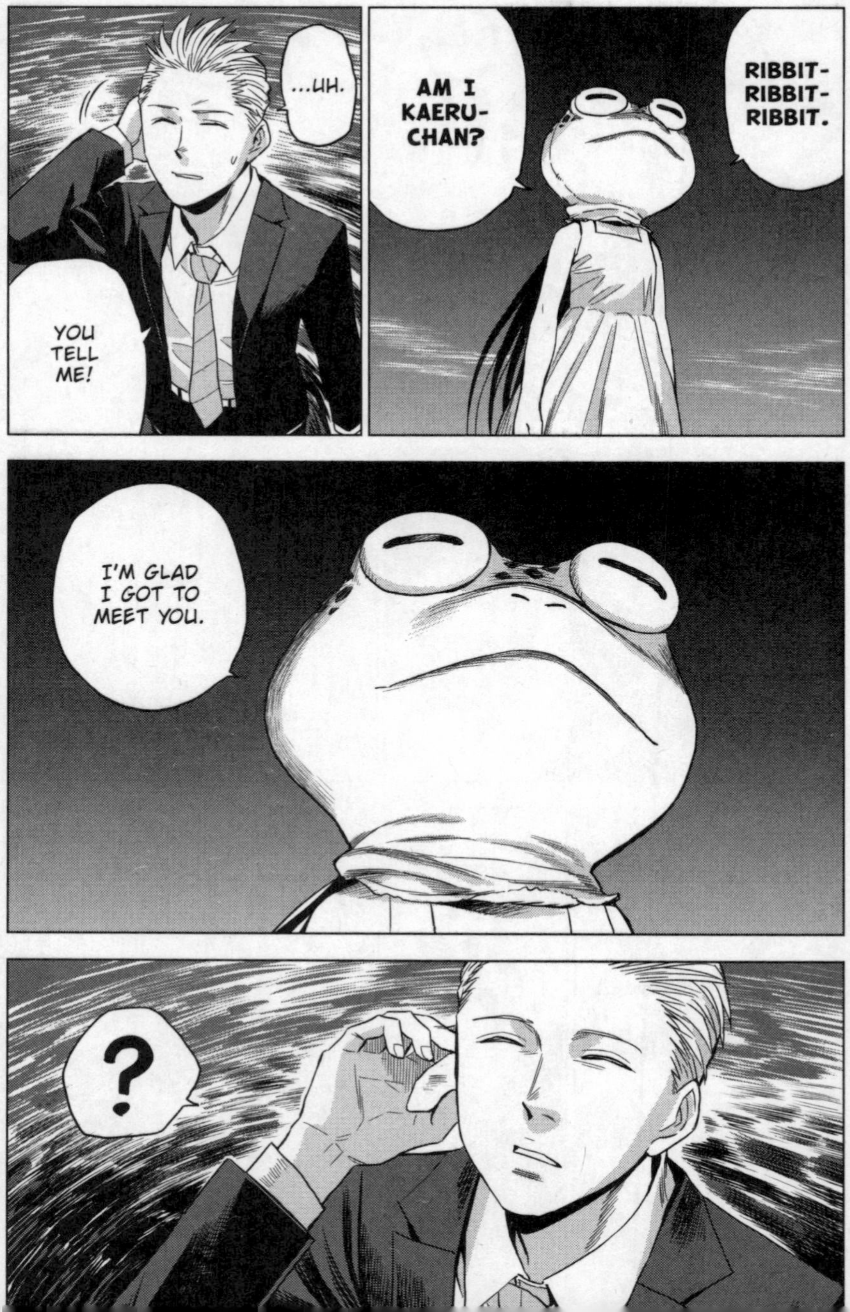
RIBBIT-RIBBIT-RIBBIT.
AM I KAERU-CHAN?
...UH.
YOU TELL ME!
I'M GLAD I GOT TO MEET YOU.
?

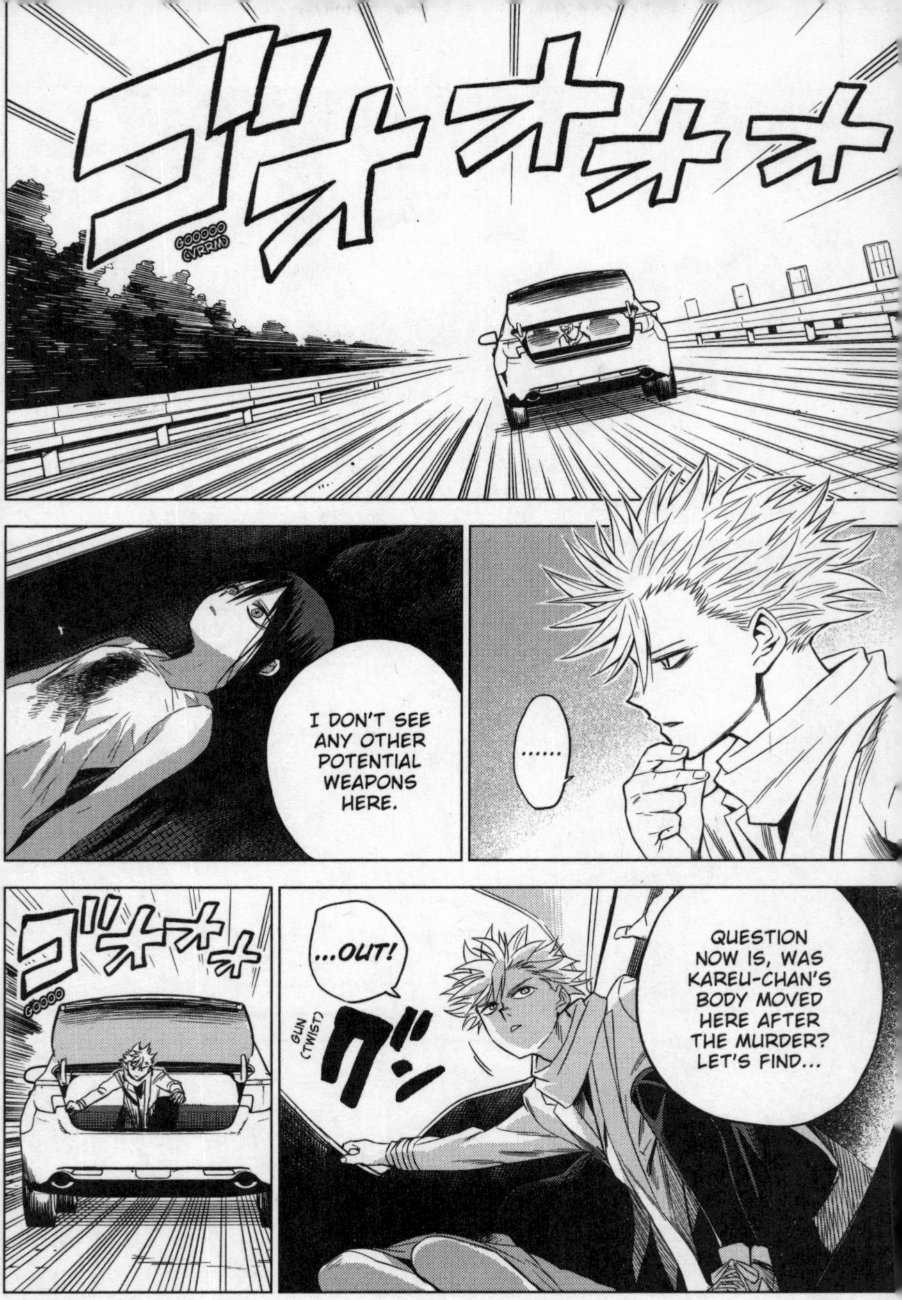
GOOOOO (VRRM)
......
I DON'T SEE ANY OTHER POTENTIAL WEAPONS HERE.
QUESTION NOW IS, WAS KAREU-CHAN'S BODY MOVED HERE AFTER THE MURDER? LET'S FIND...
...OUT!
GUN (TWIST)
GOOOO

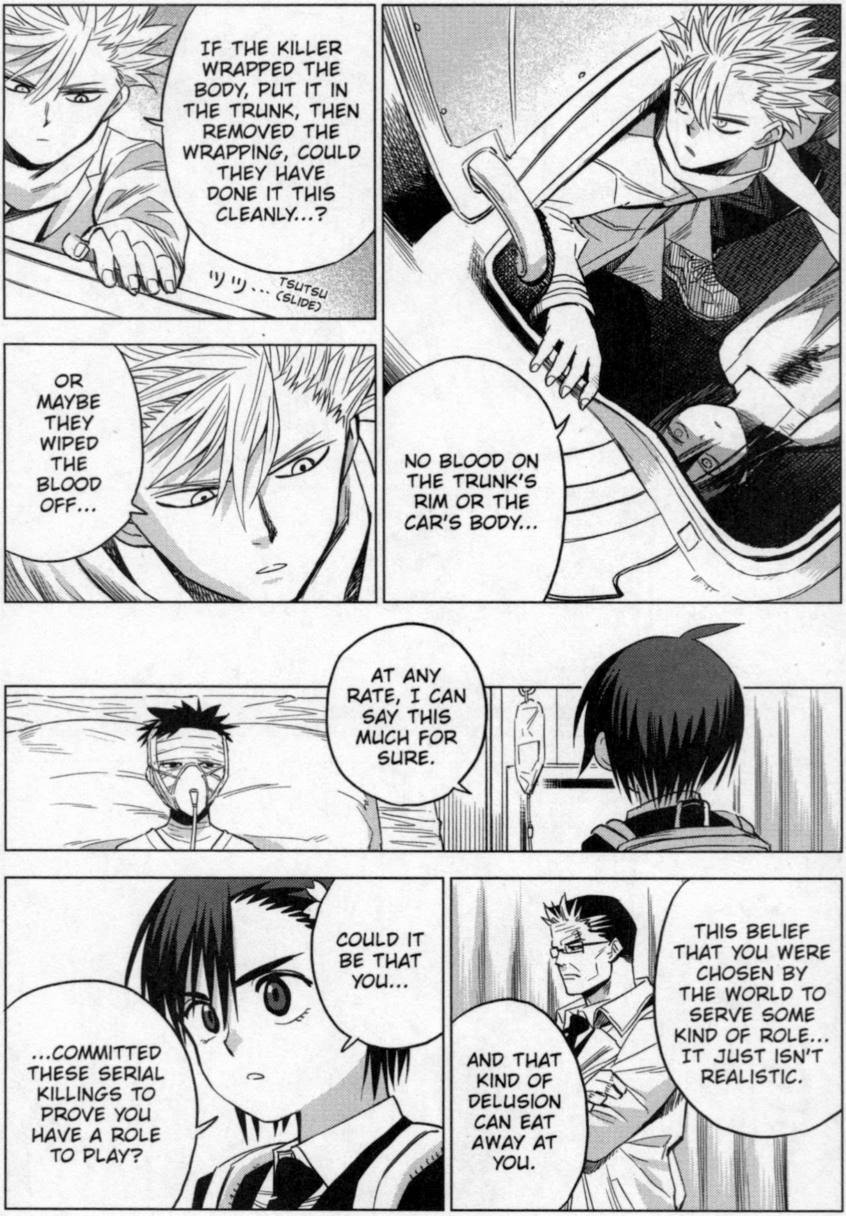
NO BLOOD ON THE TRUNK'S RIM OR THE CAR'S BODY...
IF THE KILLER WRAPPED THE BODY, PUT IT IN THE TRUNK, THEN REMOVED THE WRAPPING, COULD THEY HAVE DONE IT THIS CLEANLY...?
ツツ... TSUTSU (SLIDE)
OR MAYBE THEY WIPED THE BLOOD OFF...
AT ANY RATE, I CAN SAY THIS MUCH FOR SURE.
THIS BELIEF THAT YOU WERE CHOSEN BY THE WORLD TO SERVE SOME KIND OF ROLE... IT JUST ISN'T REALISTIC.
AND THAT KIND OF DELUSION CAN EAT AWAY AT YOU.
COULD IT BE THAT YOU...
...COMMITTED THESE SERIAL KILLINGS TO PROVE YOU HAVE A ROLE TO PLAY?

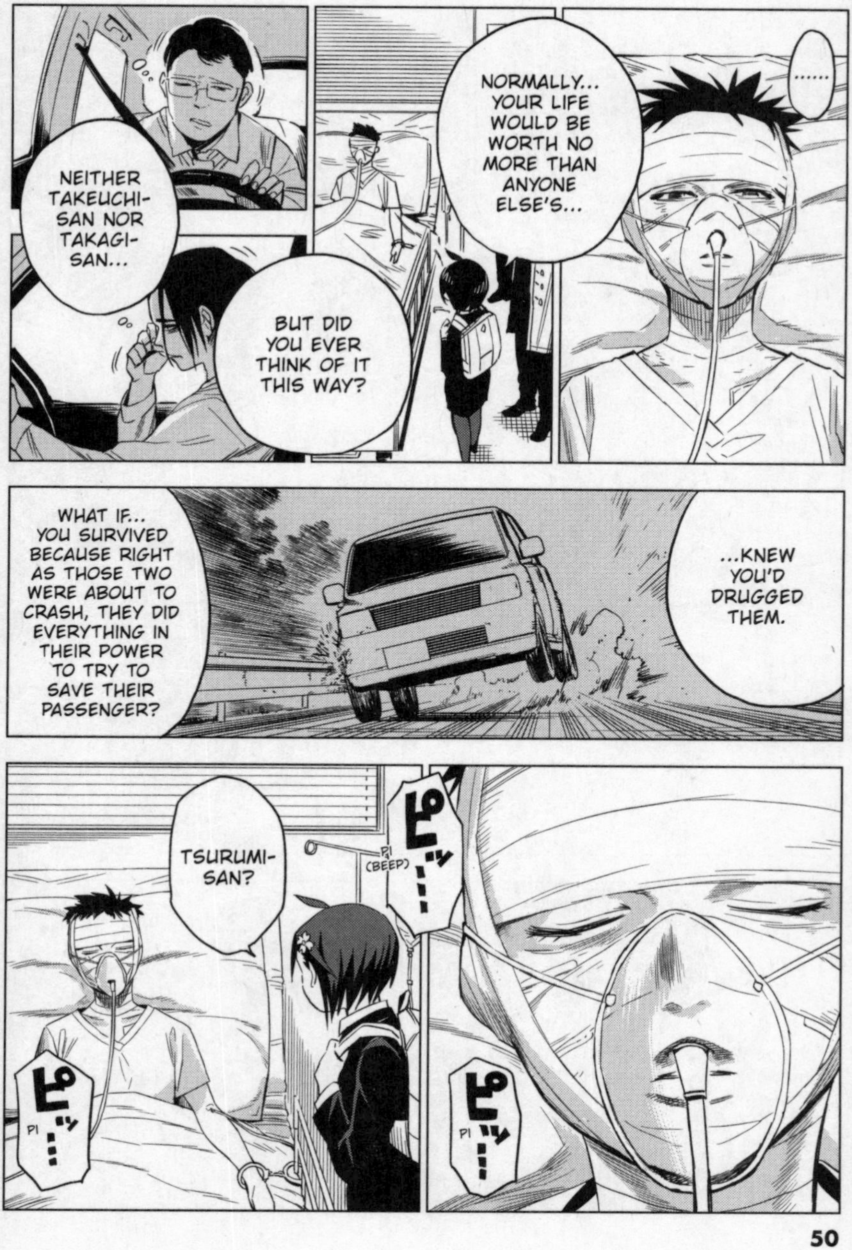
......
NORMALLY... YOUR LIFE WOULD BE WORTH NO MORE THAN ANYONE ELSE'S...
NEITHER TAKEUCHI-SAN NOR TAKAGI-SAN...
BUT DID YOU EVER THINK OF IT THIS WAY?
WHAT IF... YOU SURVIVED BECAUSE RIGHT AS THOSE TWO WERE ABOUT TO CRASH, THEY DID EVERYTHING IN THEIR POWER TO TRY TO SAVE THEIR PASSENGER?
...KNEW YOU'D DRUGGED THEM.
ピッ…
PI (BEEP)
ピッ…
PI
TSURUMI-SAN?
ピッ…
PI

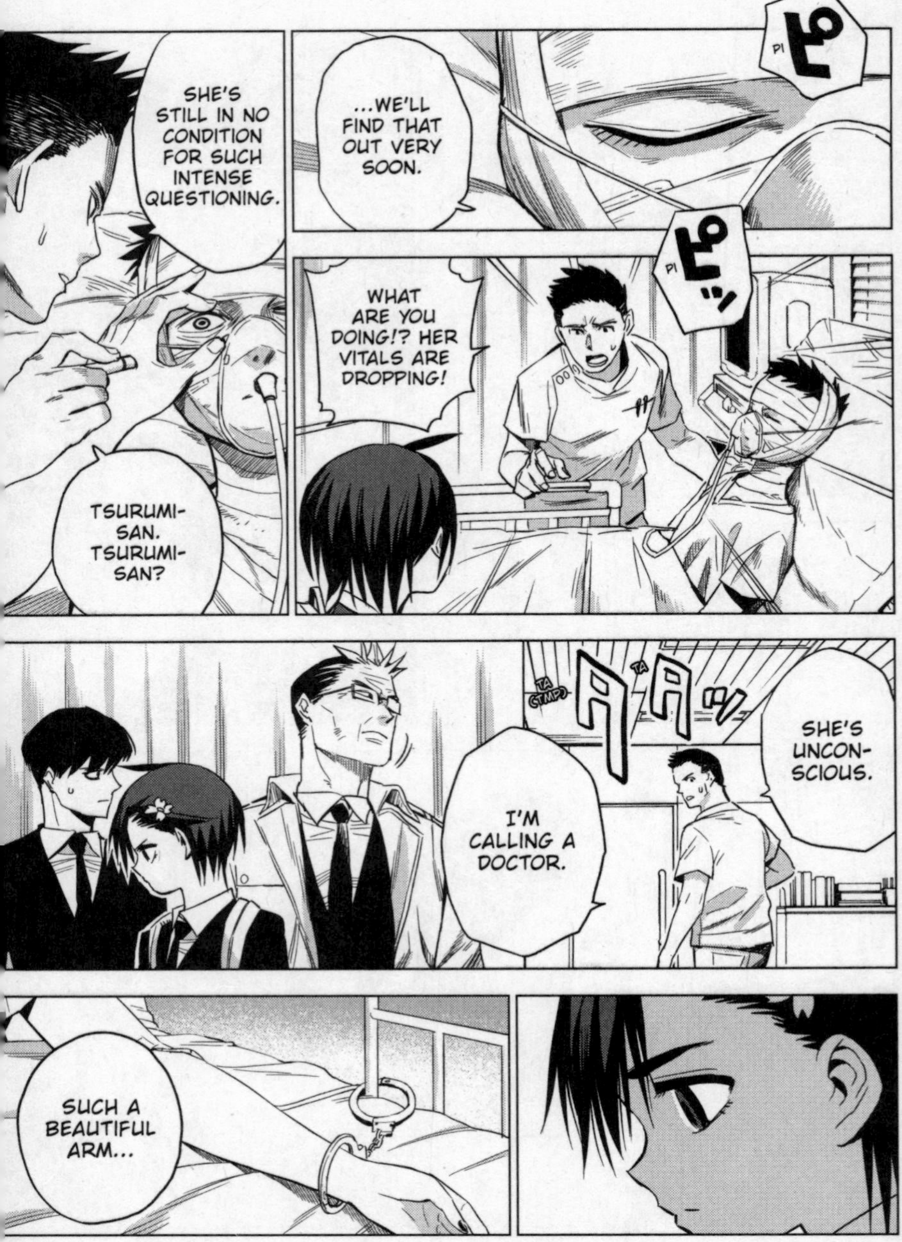
PI
...WE'LL FIND THAT OUT VERY SOON.
PI
WHAT ARE YOU DOING!? HER VITALS ARE DROPPING!
SHE'S STILL IN NO CONDITION FOR SUCH INTENSE QUESTIONING.
TSURUMI-SAN. TSURUMI-SAN?
SHE'S UNCONSCIOUS.
TA
TA (STMP)
I'M CALLING A DOCTOR.
SUCH A BEAUTIFUL ARM...

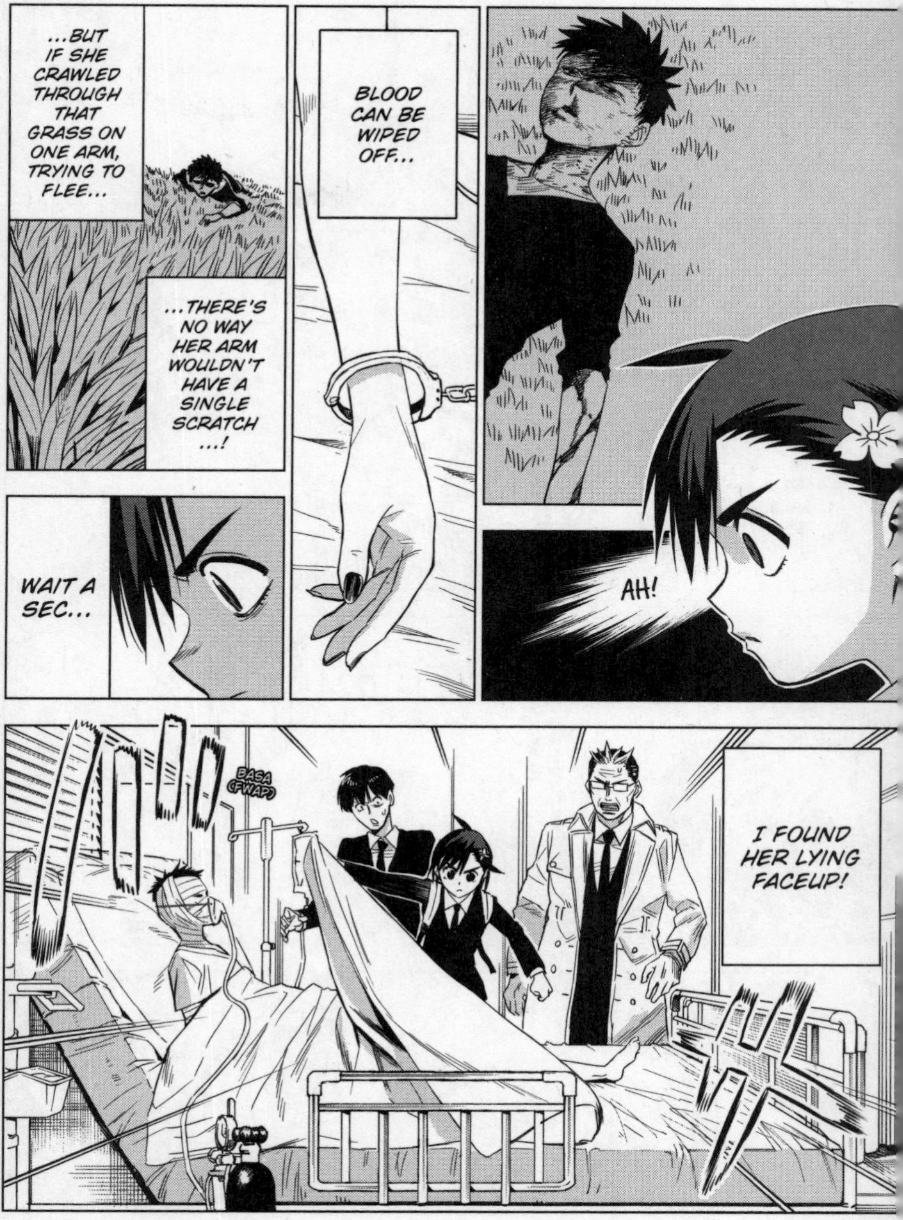
AH!
BLOOD CAN BE WIPED OFF...
...BUT IF SHE CRAWLED THROUGH THAT GRASS ON ONE ARM, TRYING TO FLEE...
...THERE'S NO WAY HER ARM WOULDN'T HAVE A SINGLE SCRATCH ...!
WAIT A SEC...
I FOUND HER LYING FACEUP!
BASA (FWAP)

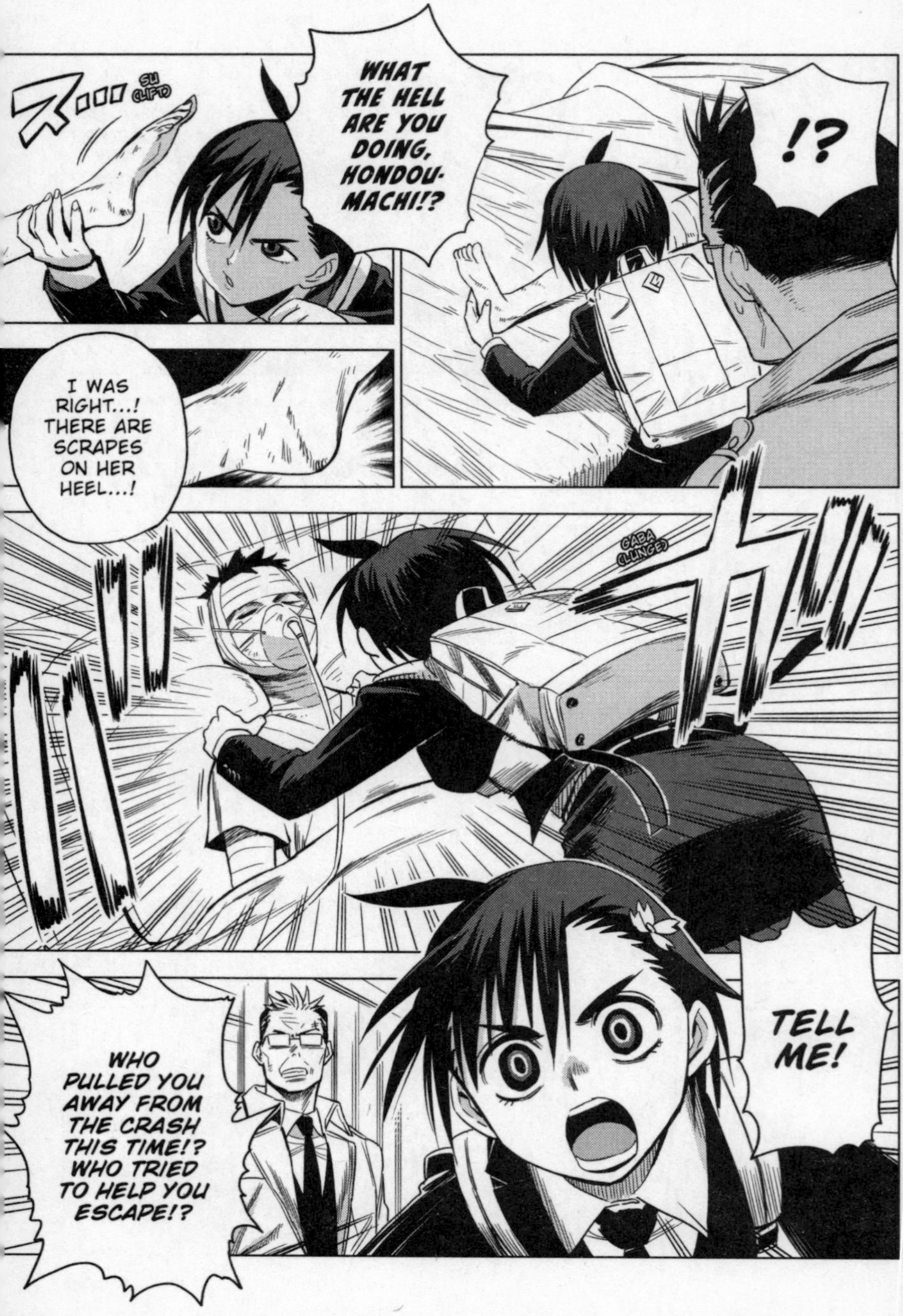
!?
WHAT THE HELL ARE YOU DOING, HONDOUMACHI!?
SU (LIFT)
I WAS RIGHT...! THERE ARE SCRAPES ON HER HEEL...!
GABA (LUNGE)
TELL ME!
WHO PULLED YOU AWAY FROM THE CRASH THIS TIME!? WHO TRIED TO HELP YOU ESCAPE!?

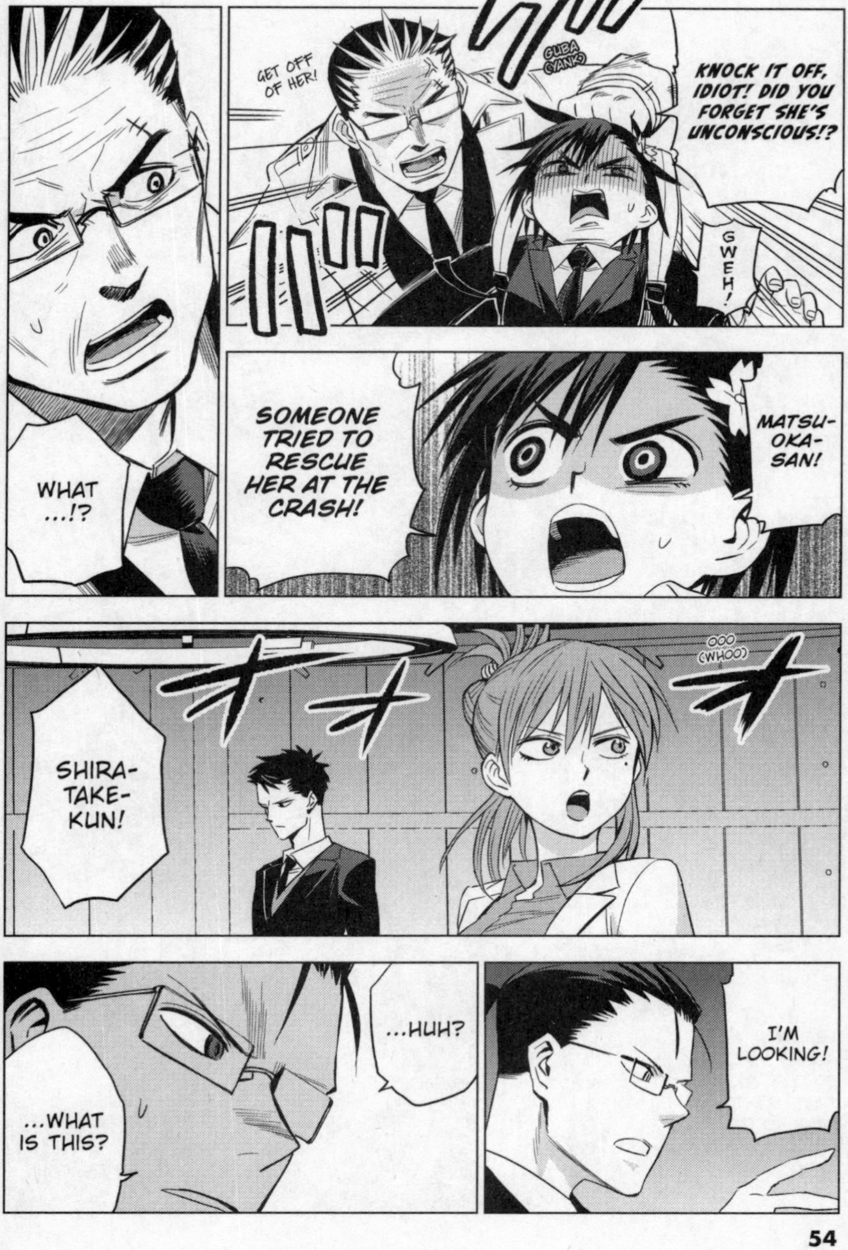
KNOCK IT OFF, IDIOT! DID YOU FORGET SHE'S UNCONSCIOUS!?
GUBA (GYANK)
GWEH!
GET OFF OF HER!
MATSU-OKA-SAN!
SOMEONE TRIED TO RESCUE HER AT THE CRASH!
WHAT ...!?
OOO (WHOO)
SHIRA-TAKE-KUN!
I'M LOOKING!
...HUH?
...WHAT IS THIS?

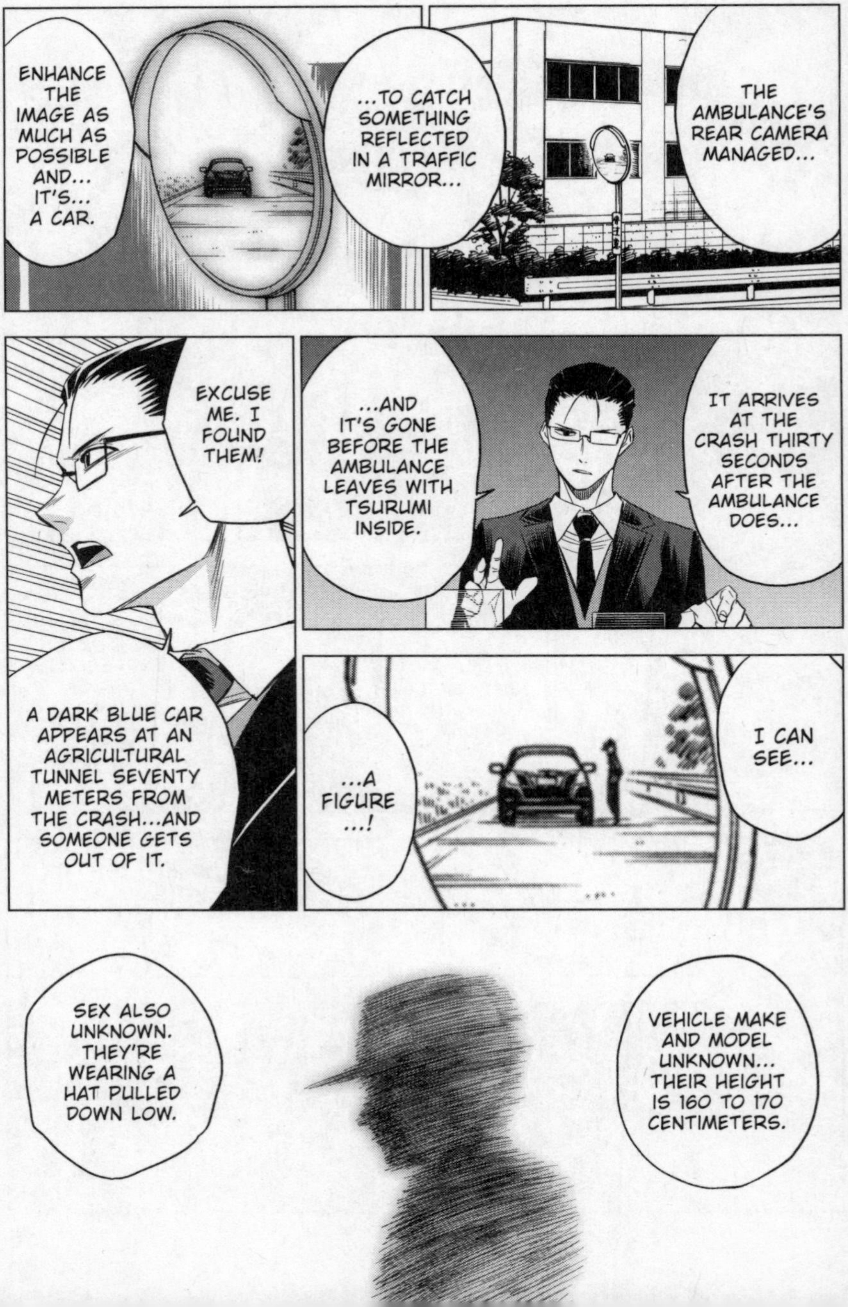
THE AMBULANCE'S REAR CAMERA MANAGED...
...TO CATCH SOMETHING REFLECTED IN A TRAFFIC MIRROR...
ENHANCE THE IMAGE AS MUCH AS POSSIBLE AND... IT'S... A CAR.
IT ARRIVES AT THE CRASH THIRTY SECONDS AFTER THE AMBULANCE DOES...
...AND IT'S GONE BEFORE THE AMBULANCE LEAVES WITH TSURUMI INSIDE.
I CAN SEE...
...A FIGURE ...!
EXCUSE ME. I FOUND THEM!
A DARK BLUE CAR APPEARS AT AN AGRICULTURAL TUNNEL SEVENTY METERS FROM THE CRASH...AND SOMEONE GETS OUT OF IT.
VEHICLE MAKE AND MODEL UNKNOWN... THEIR HEIGHT IS 160 TO 170 CENTIMETERS.
SEX ALSO UNKNOWN. THEY'RE WEARING A HAT PULLED DOWN LOW.

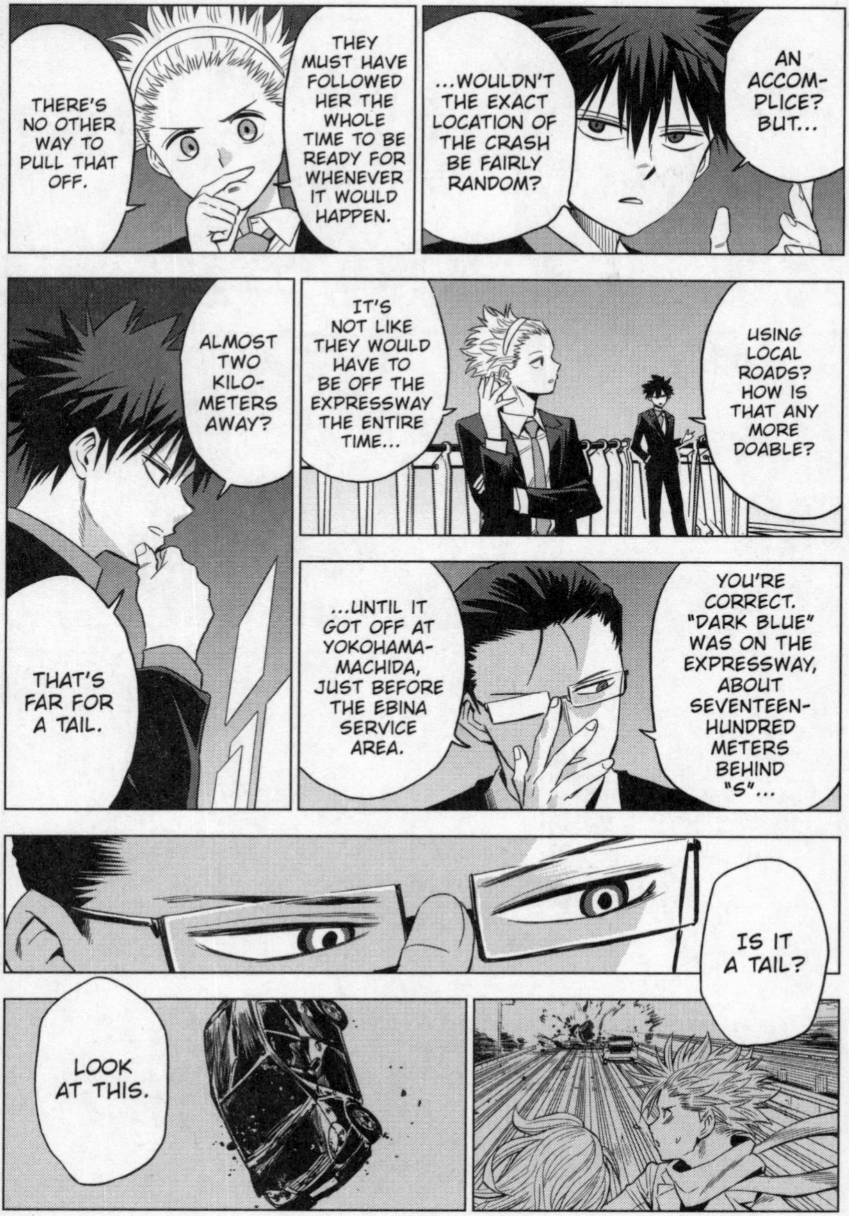
AN ACCOMPLICE? BUT...
...WOULDN'T THE EXACT LOCATION OF THE CRASH BE FAIRLY RANDOM?
THEY MUST HAVE FOLLOWED HER THE WHOLE TIME TO BE READY FOR WHENEVER IT WOULD HAPPEN.
THERE'S NO OTHER WAY TO PULL THAT OFF.
USING LOCAL ROADS? HOW IS THAT ANY MORE DOABLE?
IT'S NOT LIKE THEY WOULD HAVE TO BE OFF THE EXPRESSWAY THE ENTIRE TIME...
YOU'RE CORRECT. "DARK BLUE" WAS ON THE EXPRESSWAY, ABOUT SEVENTEEN-HUNDRED METERS BEHIND "S"...
...UNTIL IT GOT OFF AT YOKOHAMA-MACHIDA, JUST BEFORE THE EBINA SERVICE AREA.
ALMOST TWO KILO-METERS AWAY?
THAT'S FAR FOR A TAIL.
IS IT A TAIL?
LOOK AT THIS.

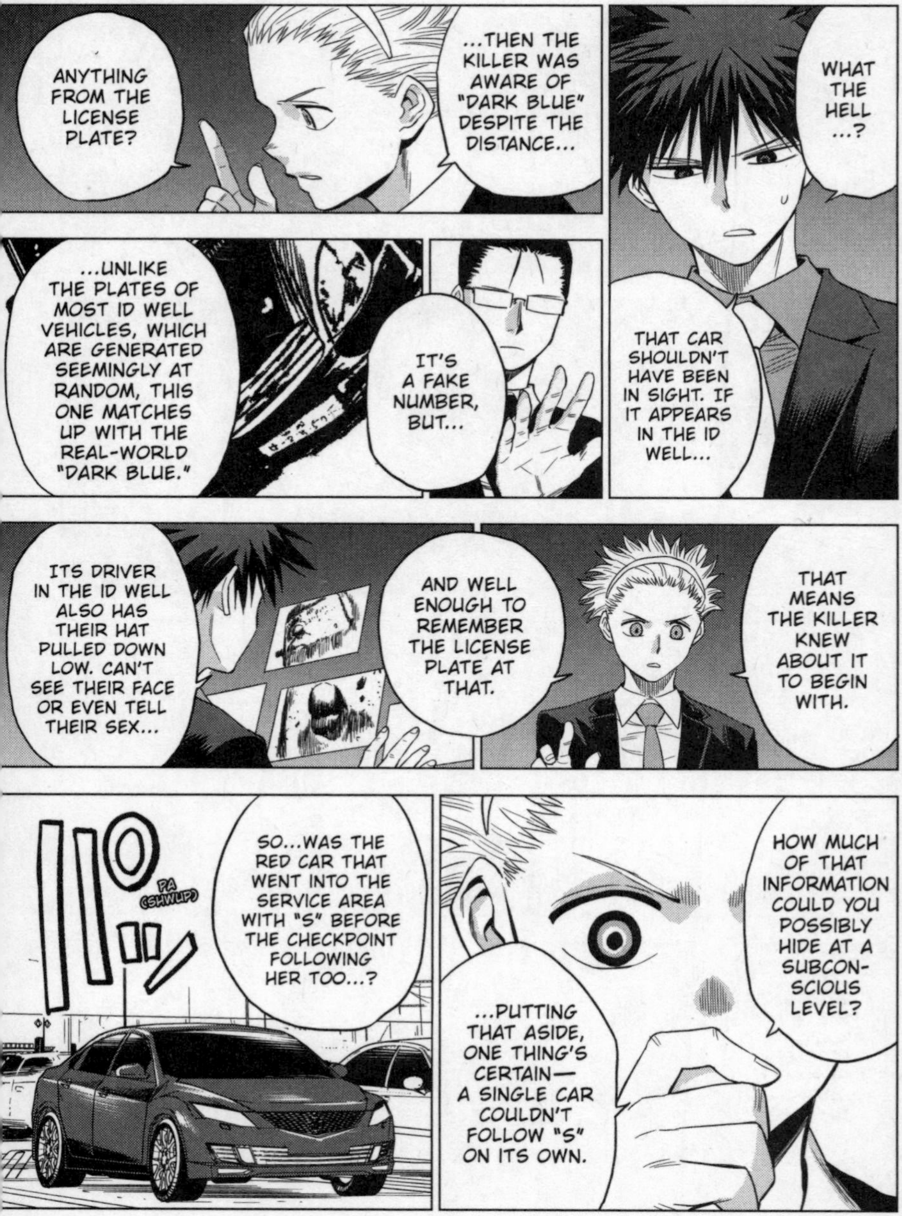
WHAT THE HELL ...?
THAT CAR SHOULDN'T HAVE BEEN IN SIGHT. IF IT APPEARS IN THE ID WELL...
...THEN THE KILLER WAS AWARE OF "DARK BLUE" DESPITE THE DISTANCE...
ANYTHING FROM THE LICENSE PLATE?
IT'S A FAKE NUMBER, BUT...
...UNLIKE THE PLATES OF MOST ID WELL VEHICLES, WHICH ARE GENERATED SEEMINGLY AT RANDOM, THIS ONE MATCHES UP WITH THE REAL-WORLD "DARK BLUE."
THAT MEANS THE KILLER KNEW ABOUT IT TO BEGIN WITH.
AND WELL ENOUGH TO REMEMBER THE LICENSE PLATE AT THAT.
ITS DRIVER IN THE ID WELL ALSO HAS THEIR HAT PULLED DOWN LOW. CAN'T SEE THEIR FACE OR EVEN TELL THEIR SEX...
HOW MUCH OF THAT INFORMATION COULD YOU POSSIBLY HIDE AT A SUBCON-SCIOUS LEVEL?
...PUTTING THAT ASIDE, ONE THING'S CERTAIN—A SINGLE CAR COULDN'T FOLLOW "S" ON ITS OWN.
SO...WAS THE RED CAR THAT WENT INTO THE SERVICE AREA WITH "S" BEFORE THE CHECKPOINT FOLLOWING HER TOO...?
PA (SHWUP)

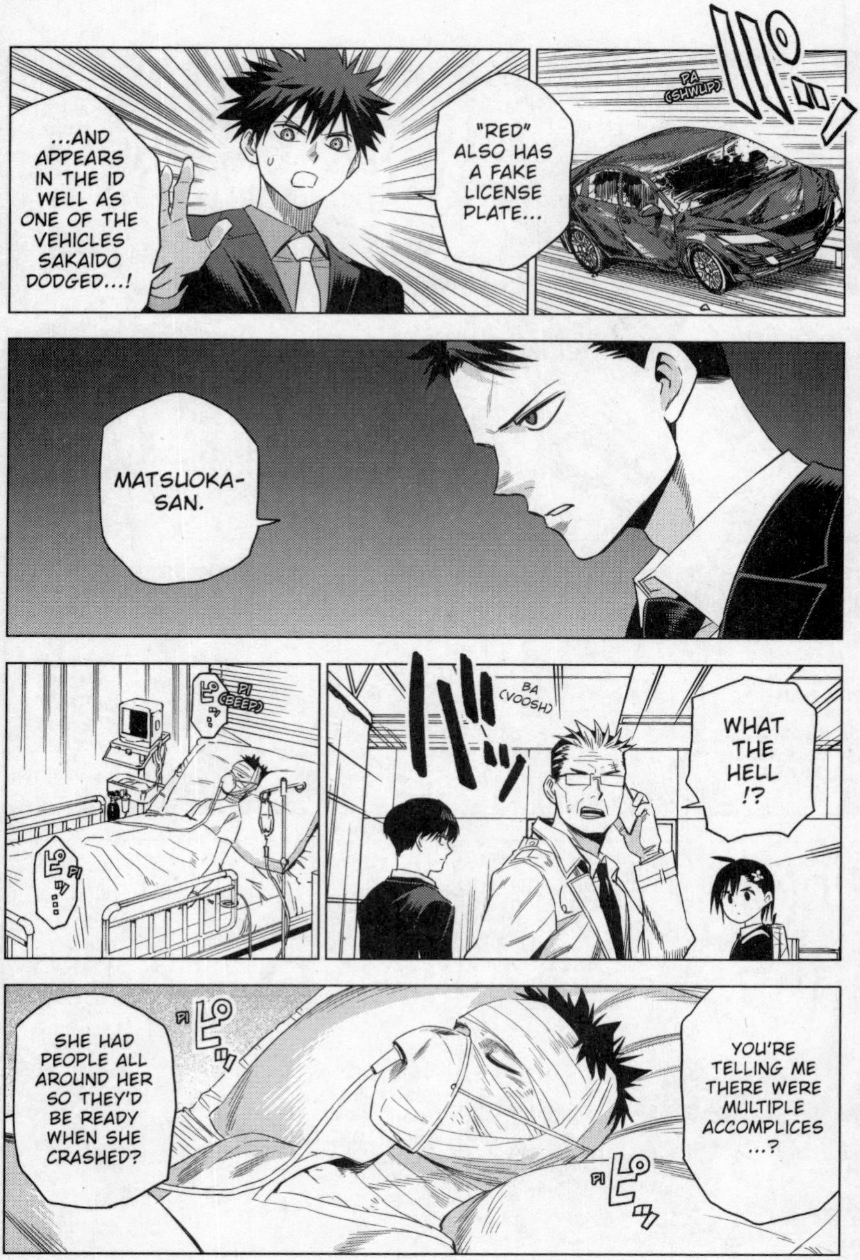
PA (SHWUP)
"RED" ALSO HAS A FAKE LICENSE PLATE...
...AND APPEARS IN THE ID WELL AS ONE OF THE VEHICLES SAKAIDO DODGED...!
MATSUOKA-SAN.
BA (VOOSH)
WHAT THE HELL!?
PI (BEEP)
PI
YOU'RE TELLING ME THERE WERE MULTIPLE ACCOMPLICES...?
PI
PI
SHE HAD PEOPLE ALL AROUND HER SO THEY'D BE READY WHEN SHE CRASHED?

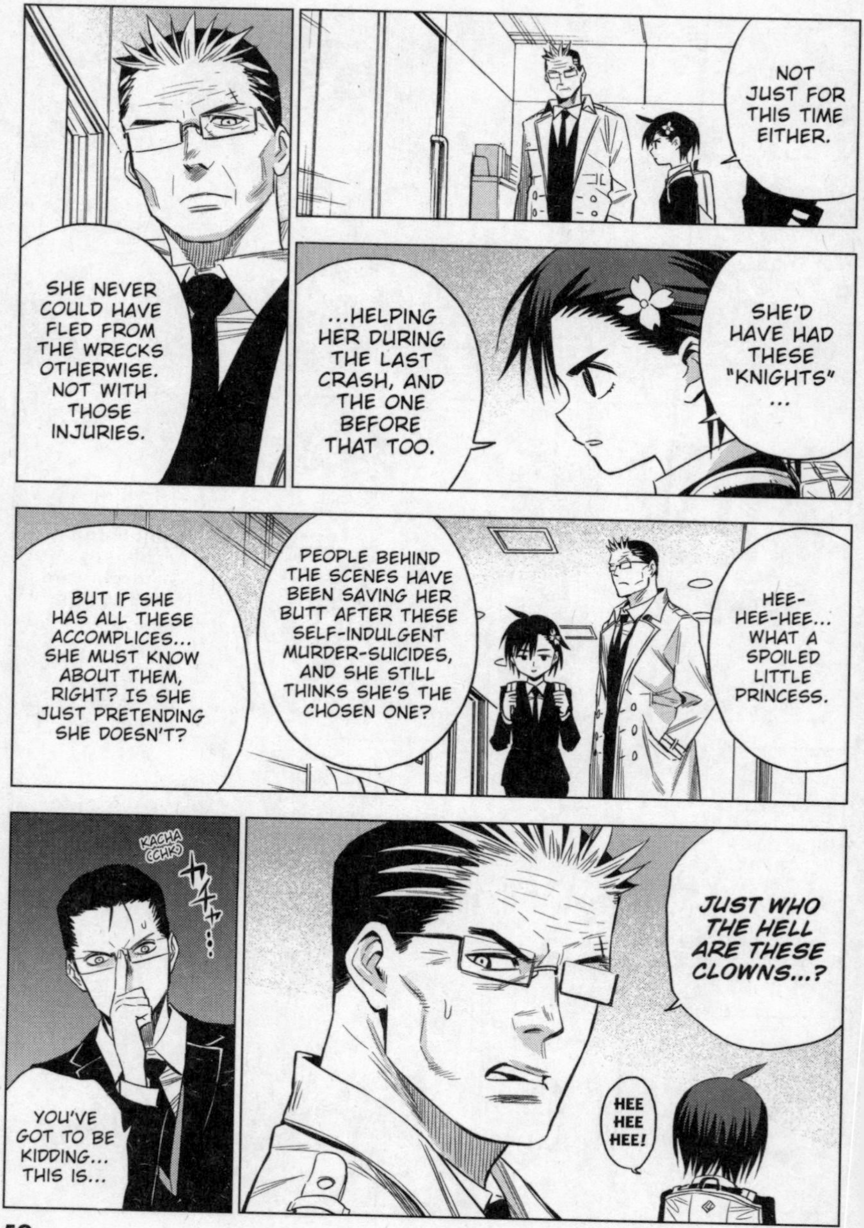
NOT JUST FOR THIS TIME EITHER.
SHE'D HAVE HAD THESE "KNIGHTS"...
...HELPING HER DURING THE LAST CRASH, AND THE ONE BEFORE THAT TOO.
SHE NEVER COULD HAVE FLED FROM THE WRECKS OTHERWISE. NOT WITH THOSE INJURIES.
HEE-HEE-HEE... WHAT A SPOILED LITTLE PRINCESS.
PEOPLE BEHIND THE SCENES HAVE BEEN SAVING HER BUTT AFTER THESE SELF-INDULGENT MURDER-SUICIDES, AND SHE STILL THINKS SHE'S THE CHOSEN ONE?
BUT IF SHE HAS ALL THESE ACCOMPLICES... SHE MUST KNOW ABOUT THEM, RIGHT? IS SHE JUST PRETENDING SHE DOESN'T?
JUST WHO THE HELL ARE THESE CLOWNS...?
HEE HEE HEE!
KACHA (CHK)
YOU'VE GOT TO BE KIDDING... THIS IS...

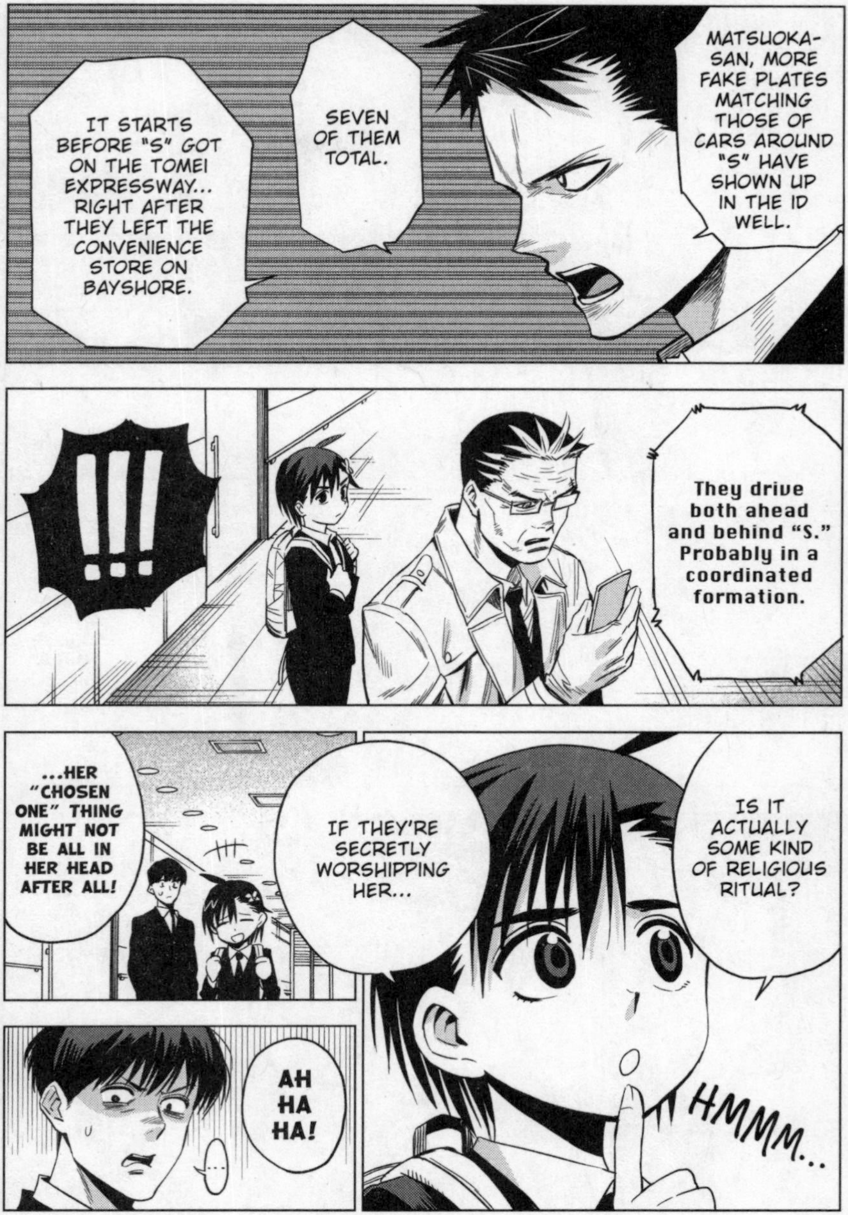
MATSUOKA-SAN, MORE FAKE PLATES MATCHING THOSE OF CARS AROUND "S" HAVE SHOWN UP IN THE ID WELL.
SEVEN OF THEM TOTAL.
IT STARTS BEFORE "S" GOT ON THE TOMEI EXPRESSWAY... RIGHT AFTER THEY LEFT THE CONVENIENCE STORE ON BAYSHORE.
They drive both ahead and behind "S." Probably in a coordinated formation.
!!!
IS IT ACTUALLY SOME KIND OF RELIGIOUS RITUAL?
IF THEY'RE SECRETLY WORSHIPPING HER...
HMMM...
...HER "CHOSEN ONE" THING MIGHT NOT BE ALL IN HER HEAD AFTER ALL!
AH HA HA!
...

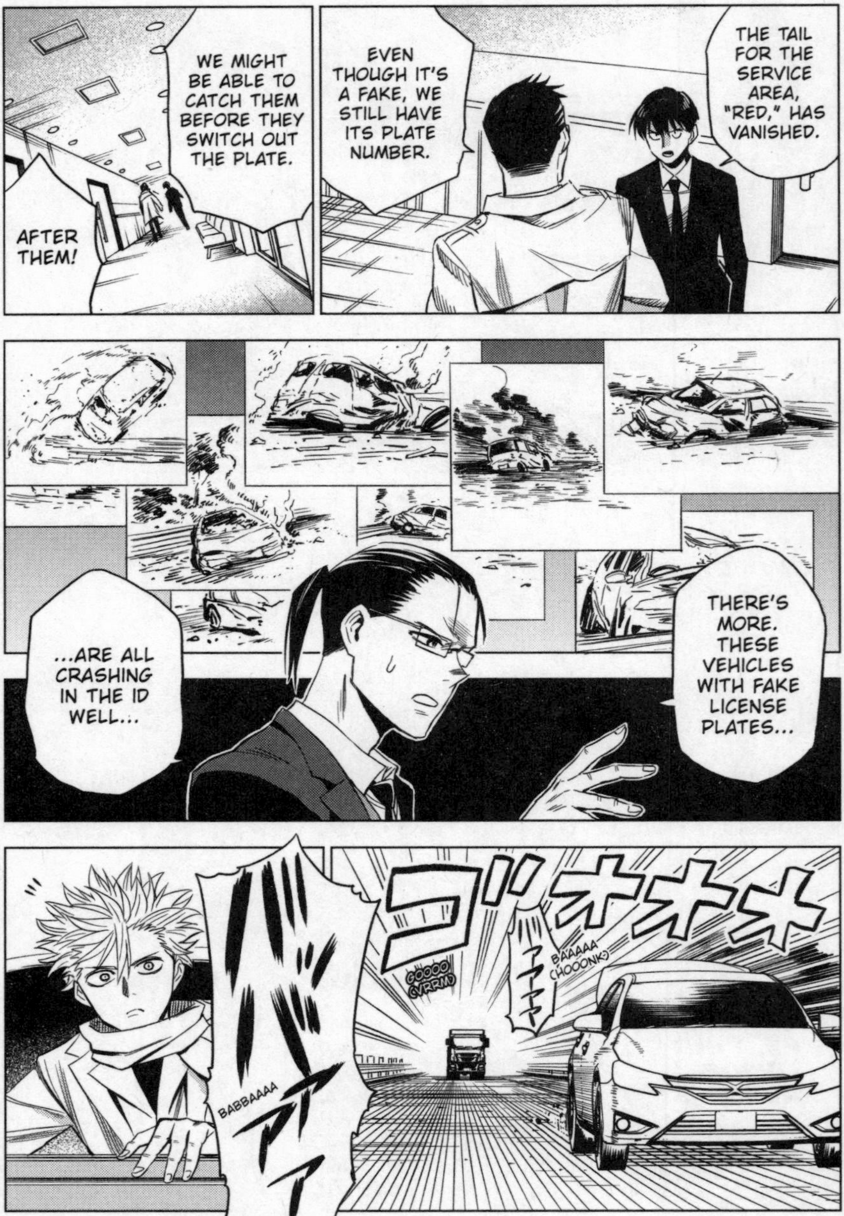
THE TAIL FOR THE SERVICE AREA, "RED," HAS VANISHED.
EVEN THOUGH IT'S A FAKE, WE STILL HAVE ITS PLATE NUMBER.
WE MIGHT BE ABLE TO CATCH THEM BEFORE THEY SWITCH OUT THE PLATE.
AFTER THEM!
THERE'S MORE. THESE VEHICLES WITH FAKE LICENSE PLATES...
...ARE ALL CRASHING IN THE ID WELL...
GOOOO (VRRM)
BAAAAA (HOOONK)
BABBAAAA

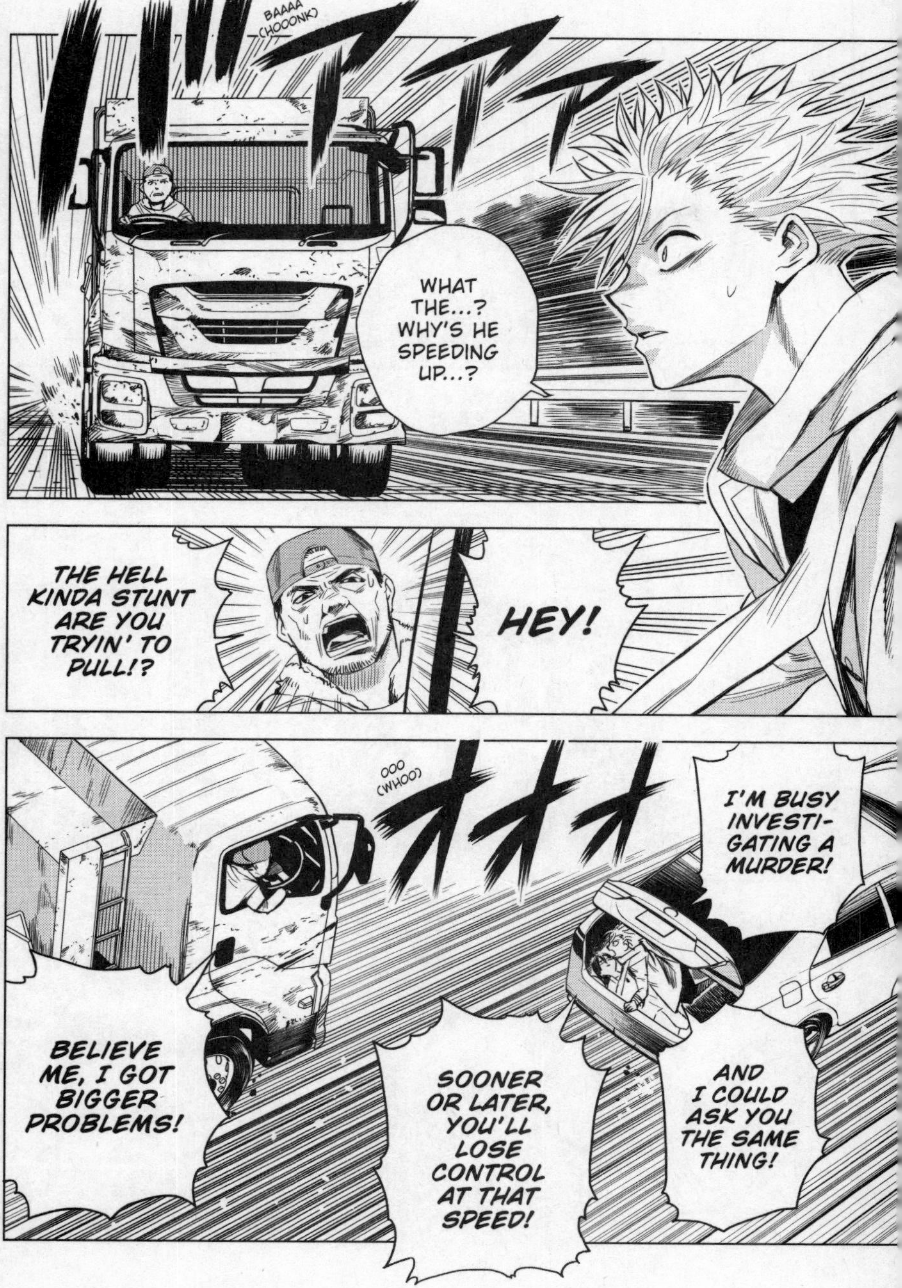
BAAAA (HOOONK)
WHAT THE...? WHY'S HE SPEEDING UP...?
HEY!
THE HELL KINDA STUNT ARE YOU TRYIN' TO PULL!?
I'M BUSY INVESTI-GATING A MURDER!
OOO (WHOO)
AND I COULD ASK YOU THE SAME THING!
SOONER OR LATER, YOU'LL LOSE CONTROL AT THAT SPEED!
BELIEVE ME, I GOT BIGGER PROBLEMS!

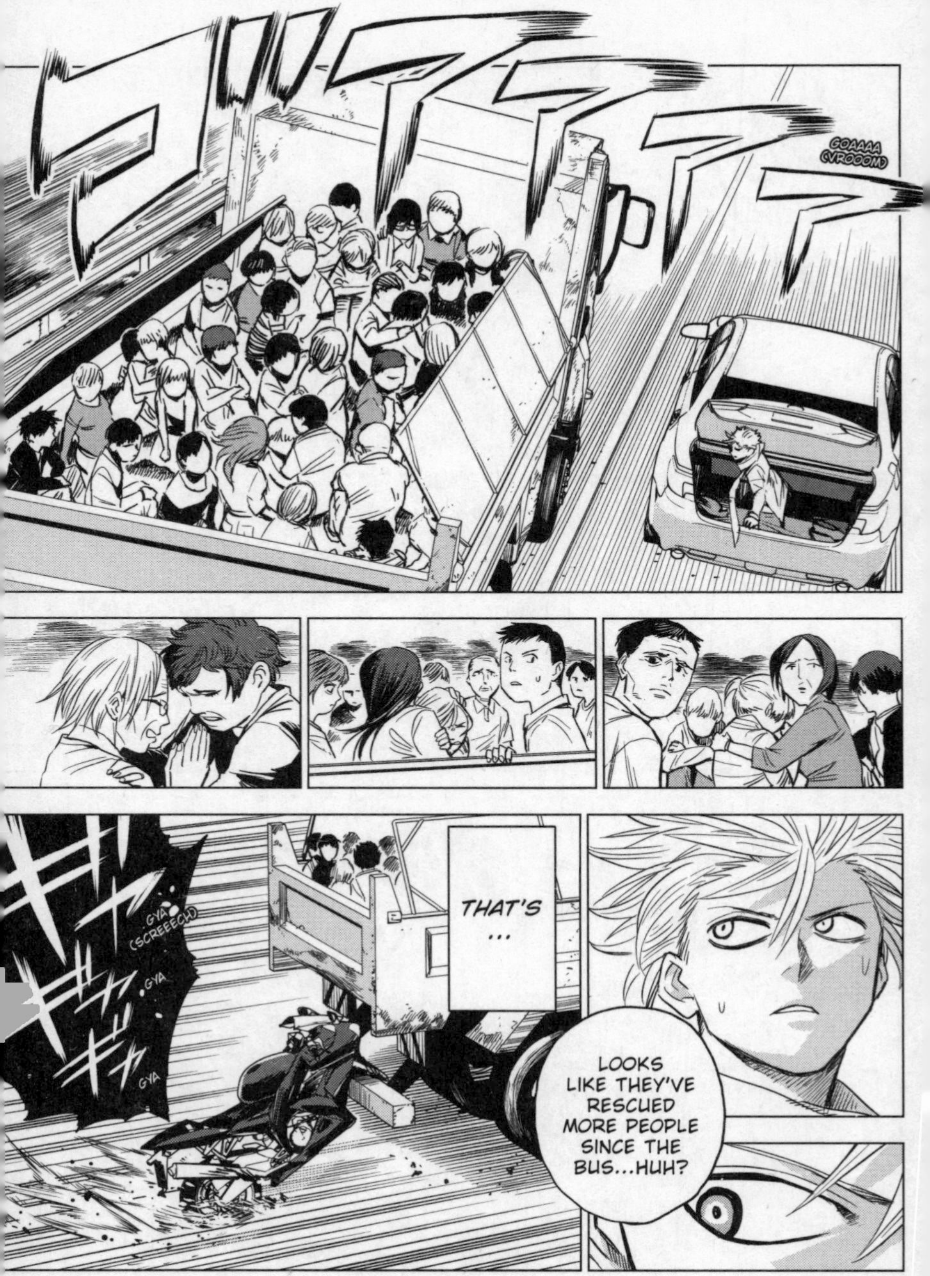
GOAAAA
(VROOOM)
LOOKS LIKE THEY'VE RESCUED MORE PEOPLE SINCE THE BUS...HUH?
THAT'S ...
GYA
(SCREEECH)
GYA
GYA

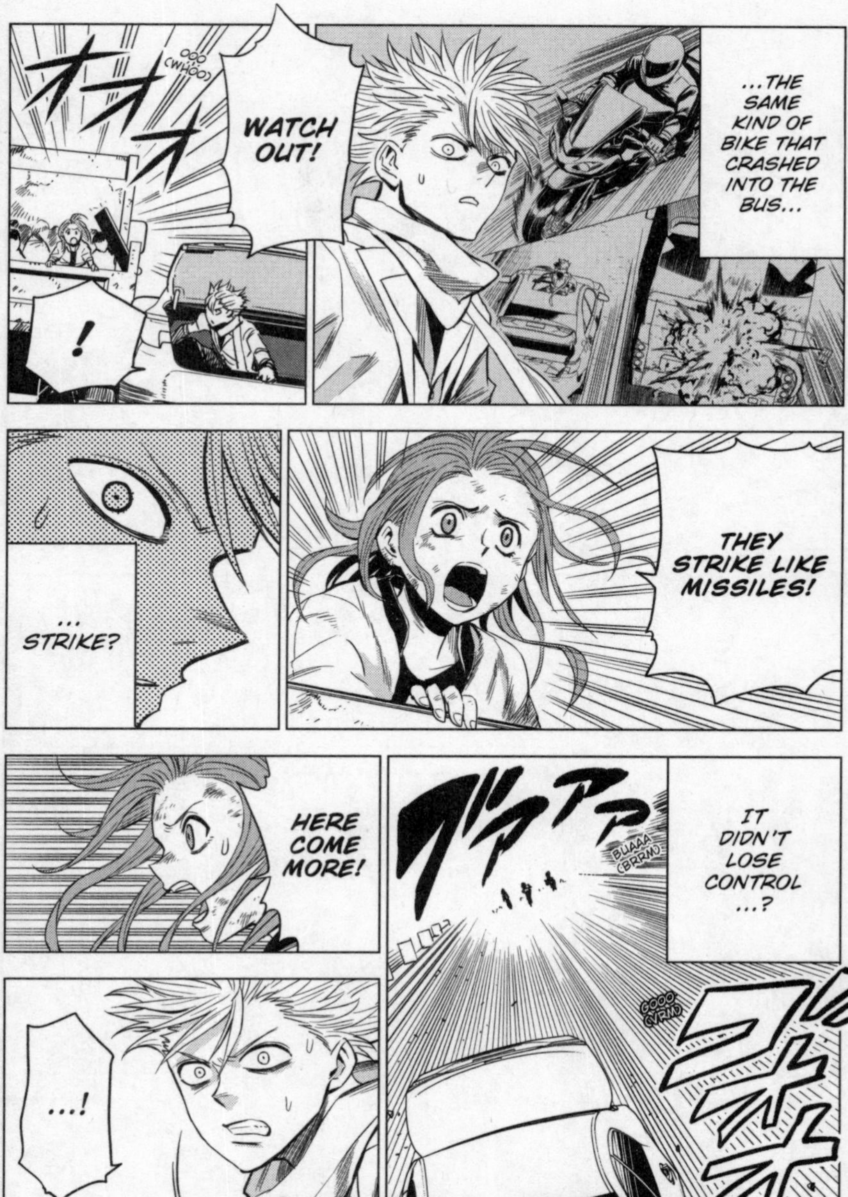
...THE SAME KIND OF BIKE THAT CRASHED INTO THE BUS...
OOO (WHOOO)
WATCH OUT!
!
THEY STRIKE LIKE MISSILES!
... STRIKE?
IT DIDN'T LOSE CONTROL ...?
BUAAA (BRRM)
HERE COME MORE!
GOOO (VRM)
...!

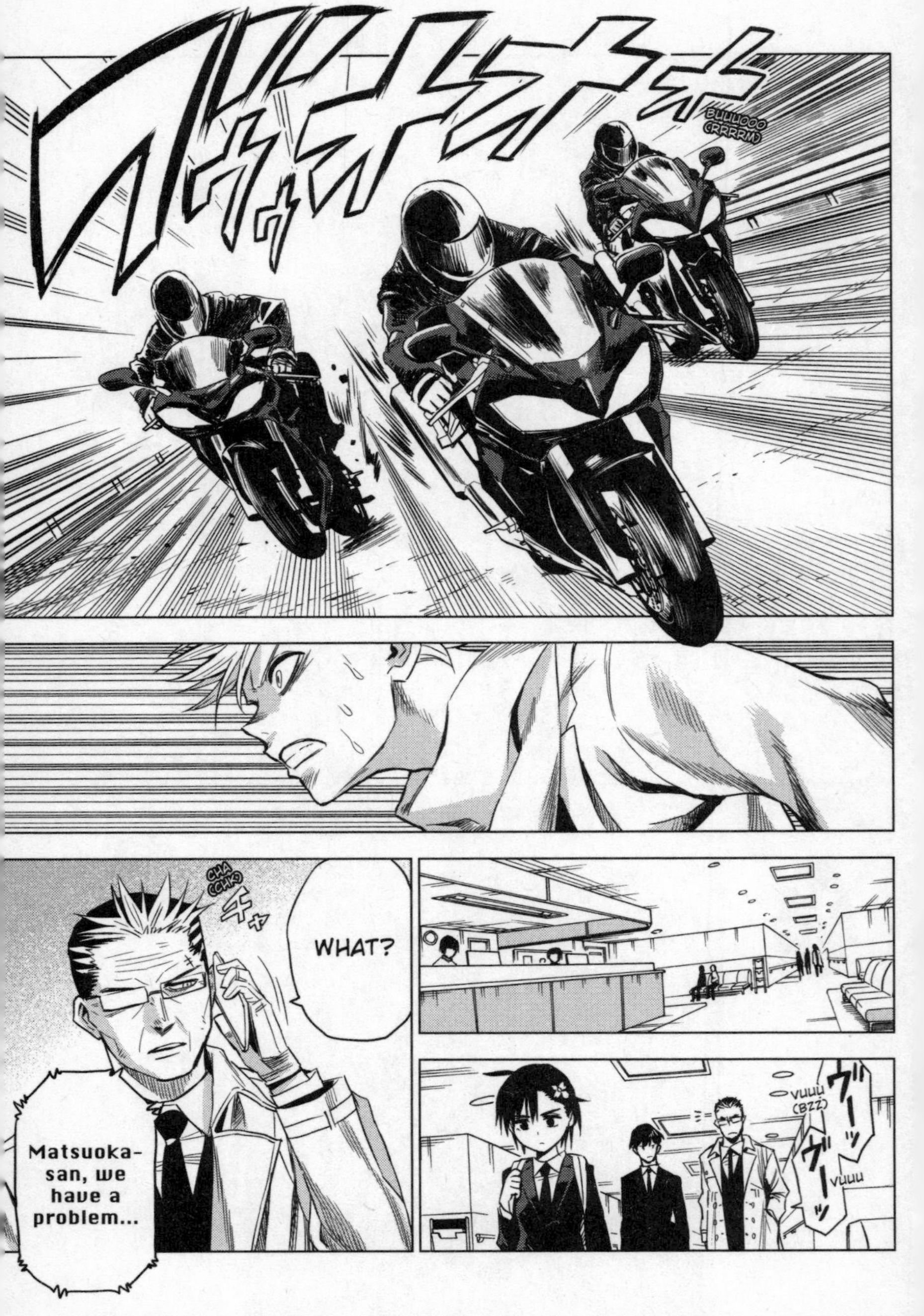
BUUUOOO (RRRRM)
VUUU (BZZ)
ヴーッ
ヴーッ
VUUU
CHA (CHK)
チャ
WHAT?
Matsuoka-san, we have a problem...

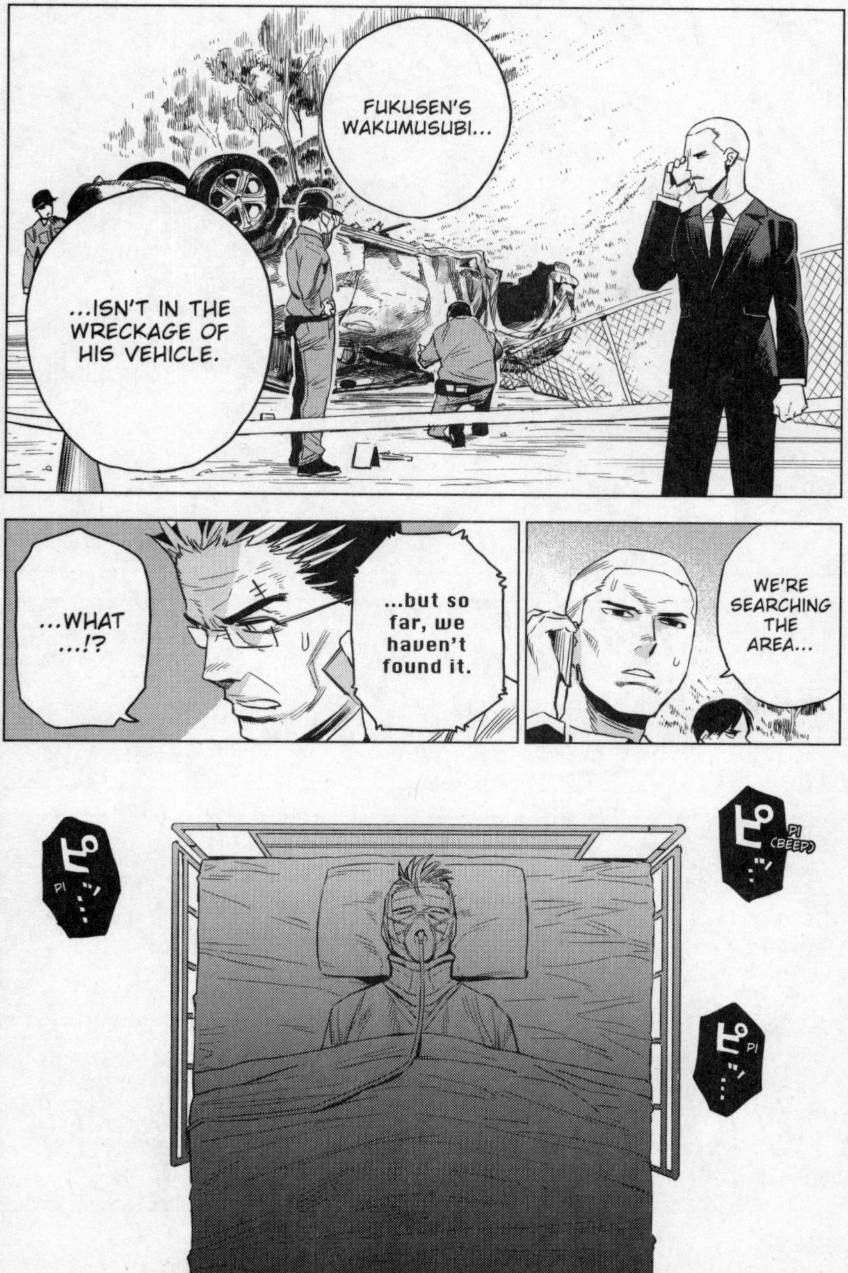
FUKUSEN'S WAKUMUSUBI...
...ISN'T IN THE WRECKAGE OF HIS VEHICLE.
WE'RE SEARCHING THE AREA...
...but so far, we haven't found it.
...WHAT ...!?
PI (BEEP)
PI
PI

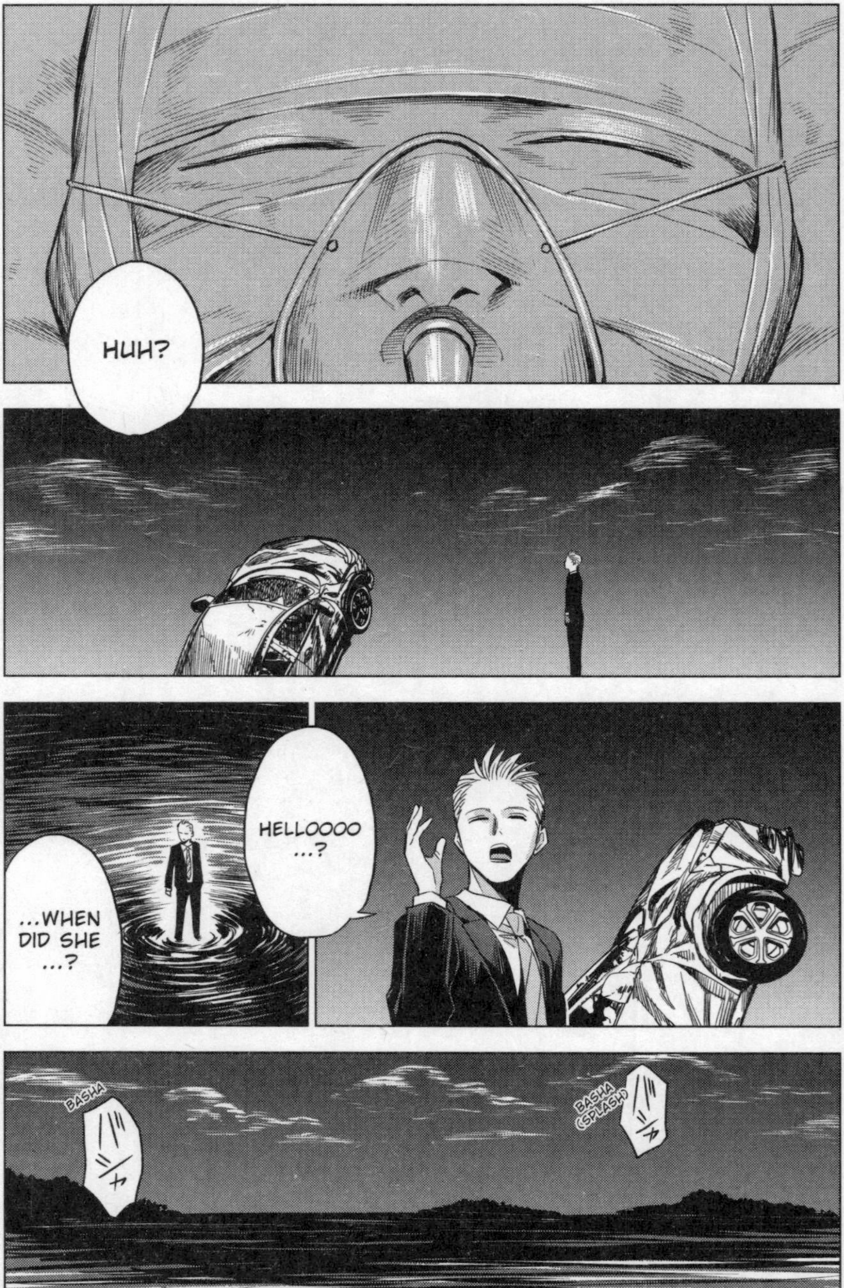
HUH?
HELLOOOO ...?
...WHEN DID SHE ...?
BASHA (SPLASH)
BASHA

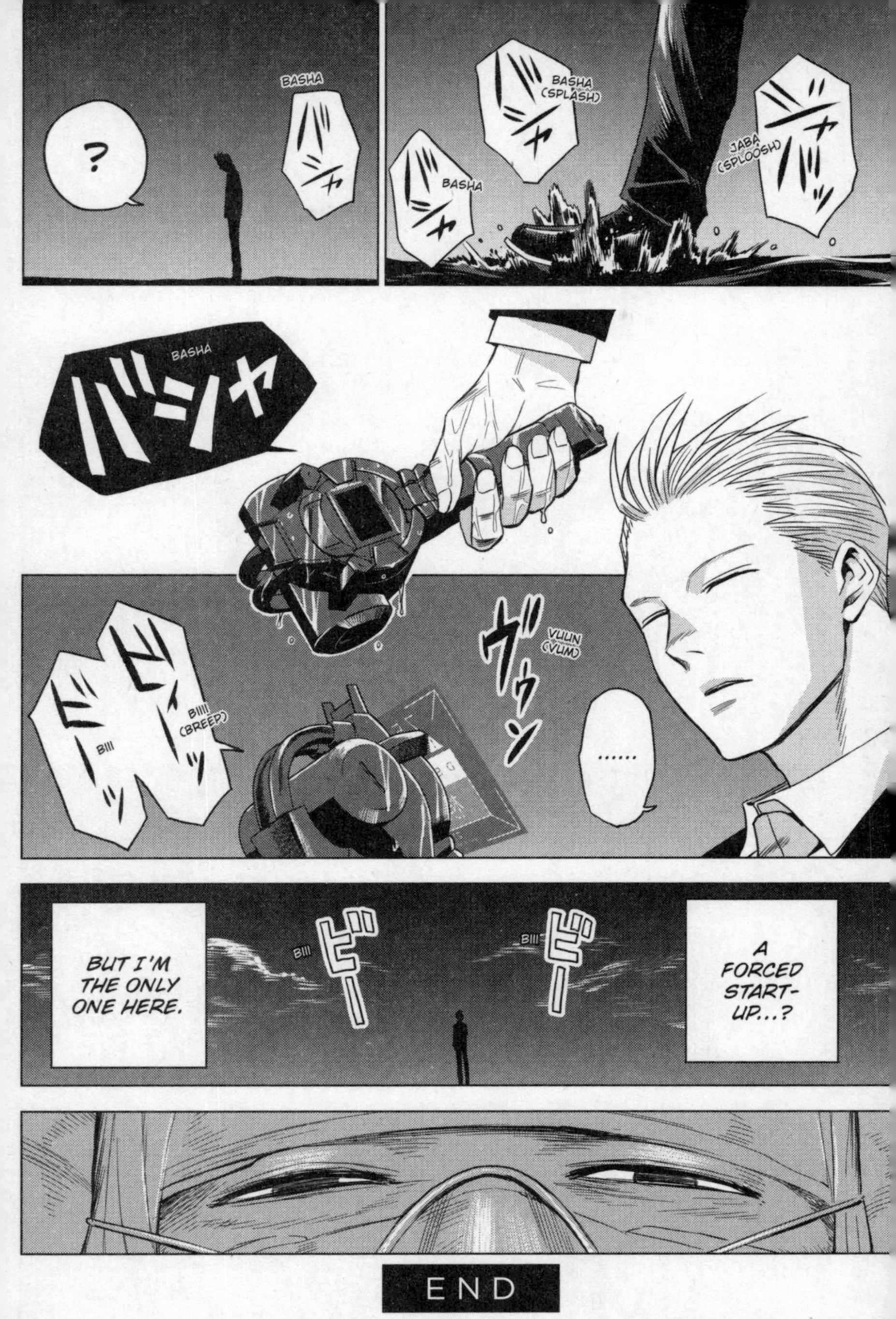

ジャバッ
JABA (SPLOOSH)
バシャ
BASHA (SPLASH)
バシャ
BASHA
バシャ
BASHA
?
バシャ
BASHA
......
ヴゥン
VUUN (VUM)
ビィィッ
BIIII (BREEP)
ビーッ
BIII
A FORCED START-UP...?
ビー
BIII
ビー
BIII
BUT I'M THE ONLY ONE HERE.

END

#07 MERGE

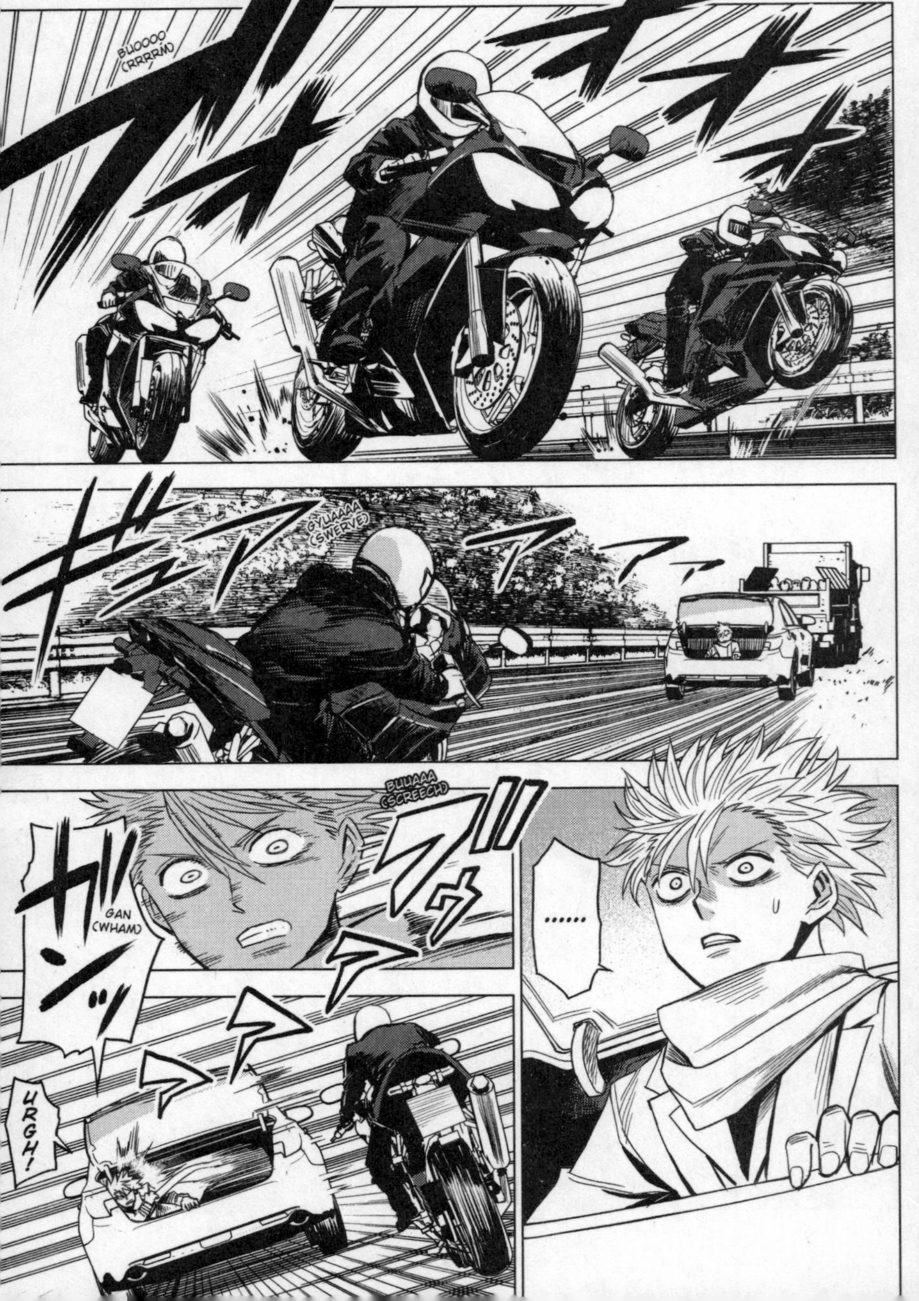
BUOOOO (RRRRRM)
GYUAAAA (SWERVE)
......
BUUAAA (SCREECH)
GAN (WHAM)
URGH!

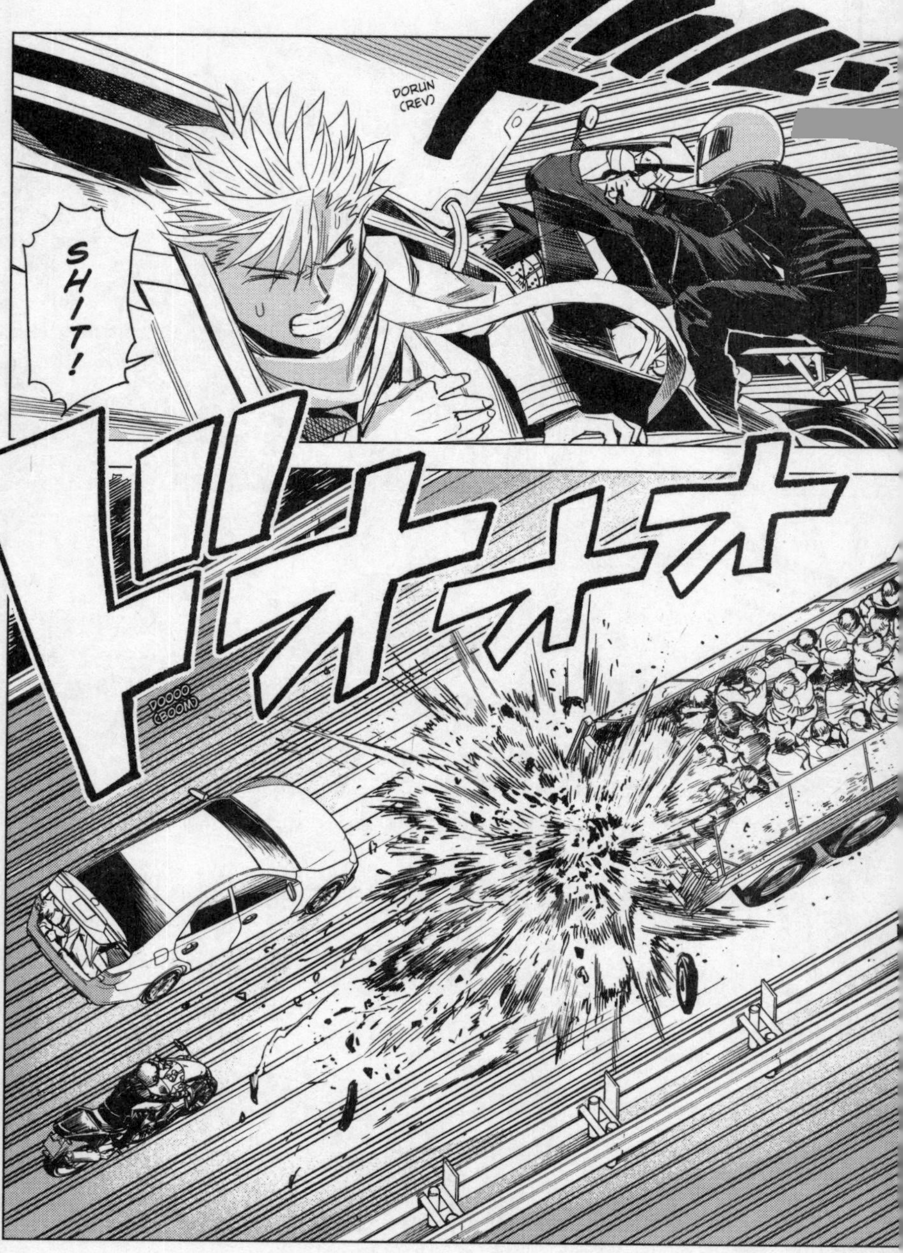
DORUN
(REV)
SHIT!
DOOOO
(BOOM)

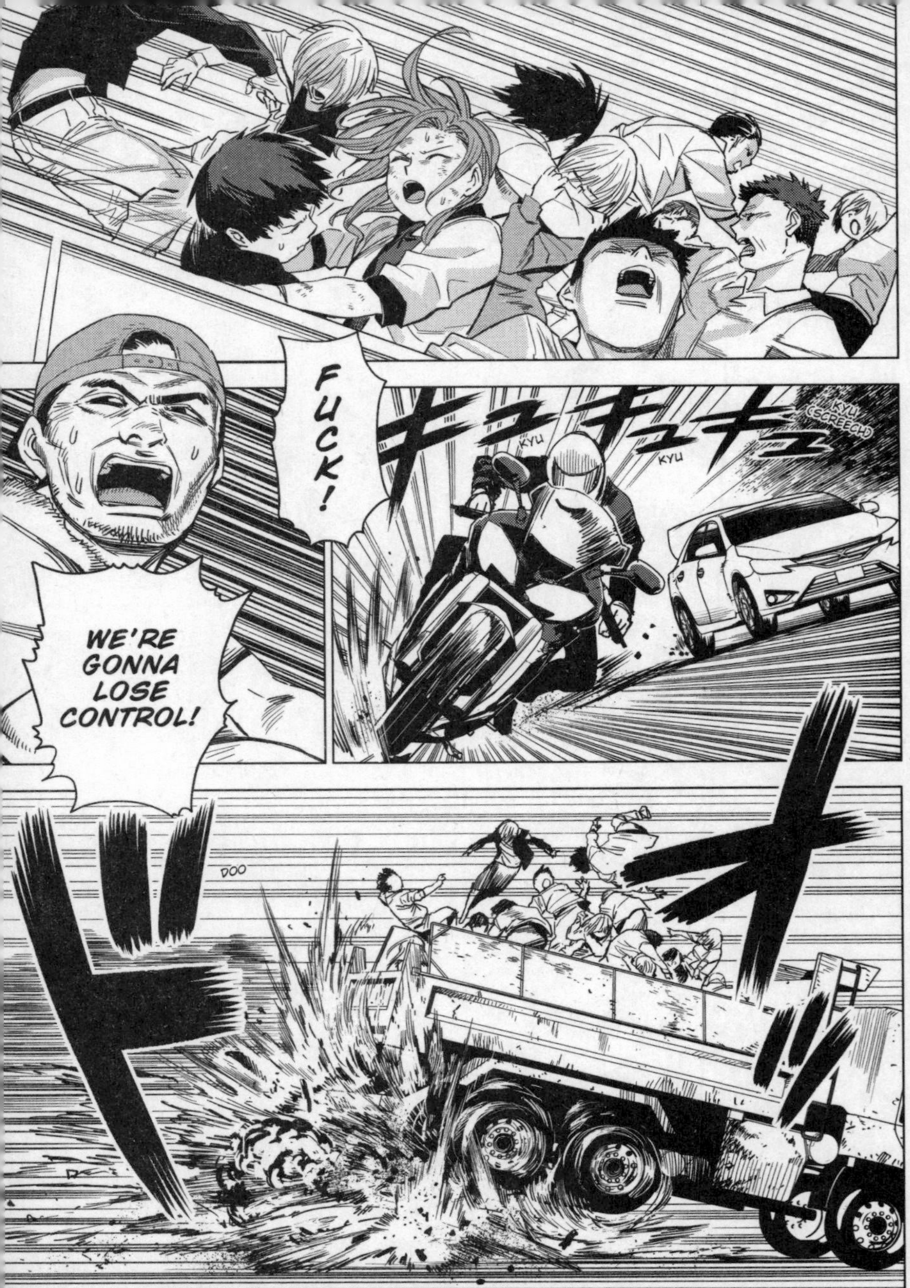
KYU KYU (SCREECH)
KYU
KYU
FUCK!
WE'RE GONNA LOSE CONTROL!
DOO

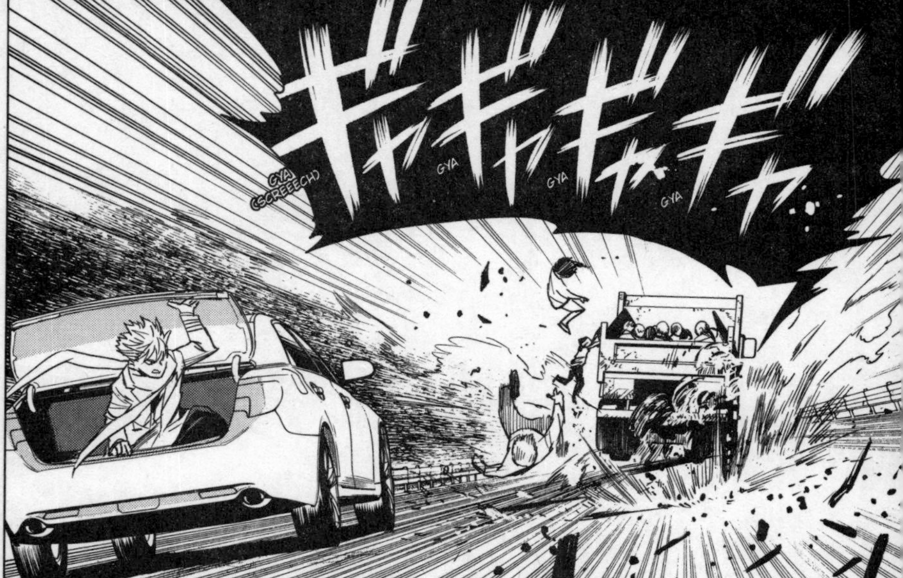
GYA
GYA
GYA
GYA (SCREEECH)

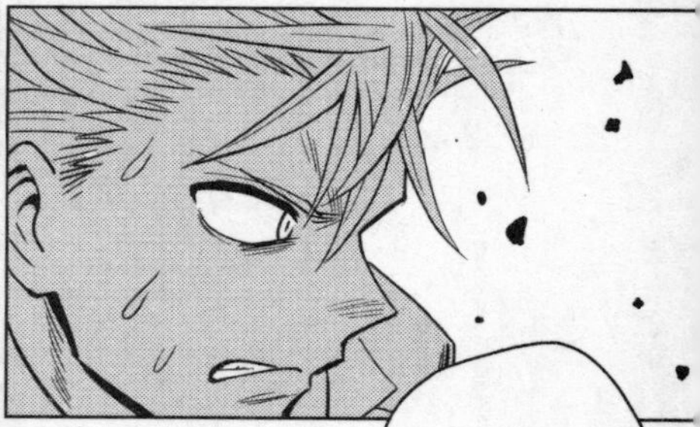

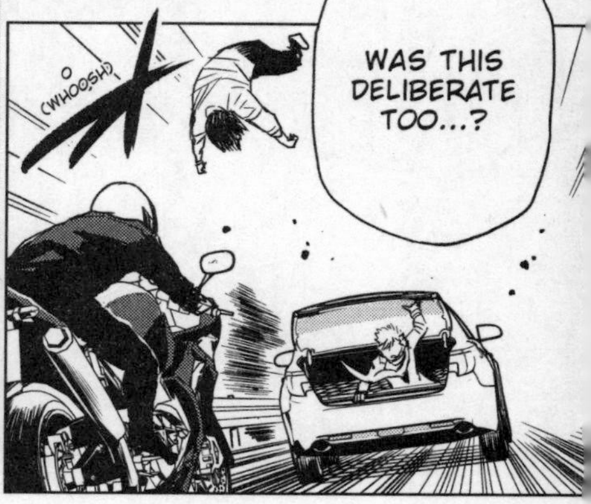
WAS THIS DELIBERATE TOO...?
O (WHOOSH)

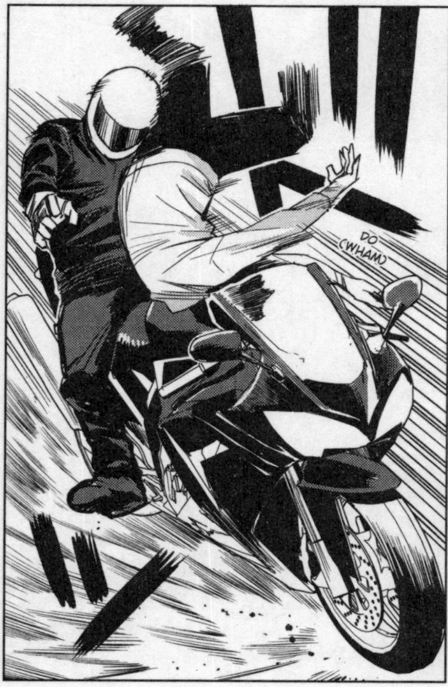
DO (WHAM)

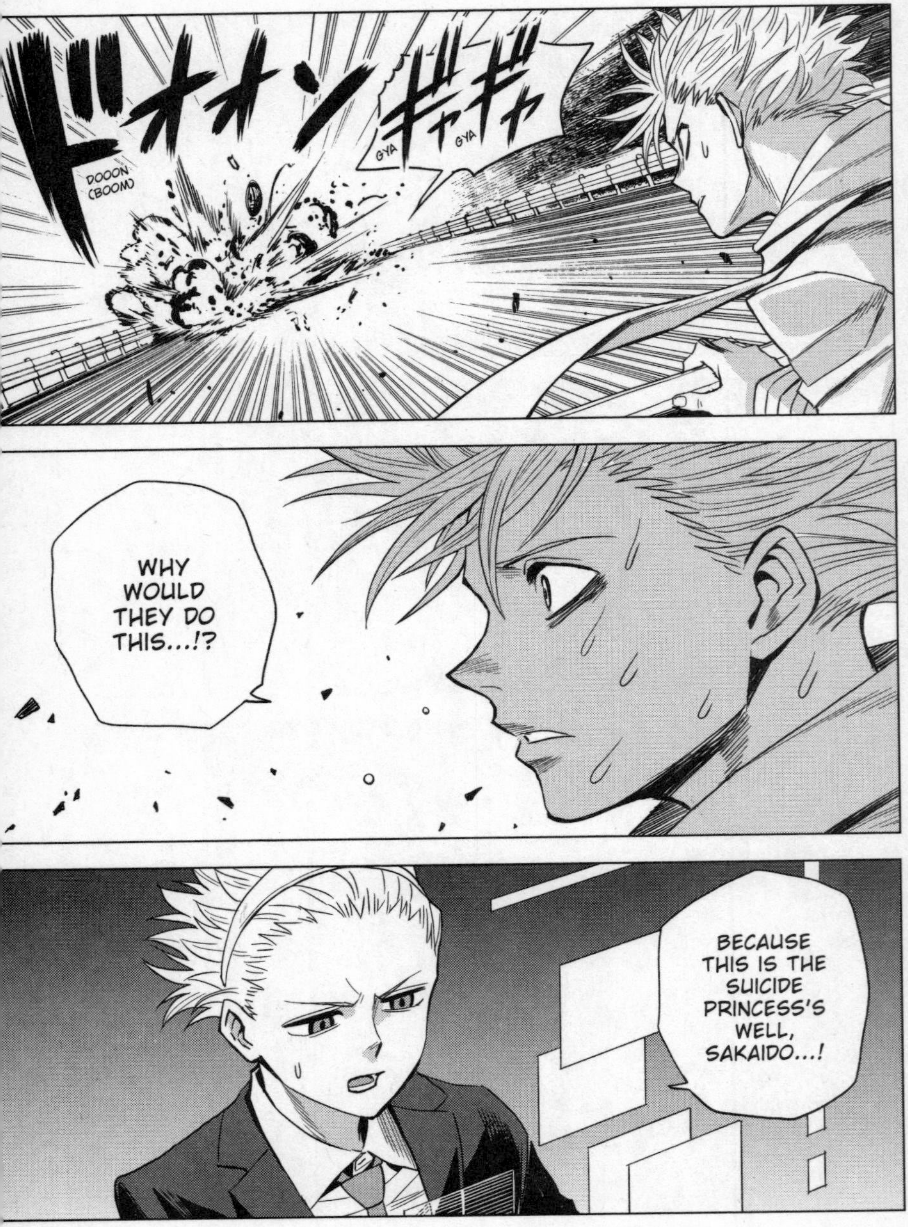
ギャギャ
GYA GYA
ドオオン
DOOON (BOOM)
WHY WOULD THEY DO THIS...!?
BECAUSE THIS IS THE SUICIDE PRINCESS'S WELL, SAKAIDO...!

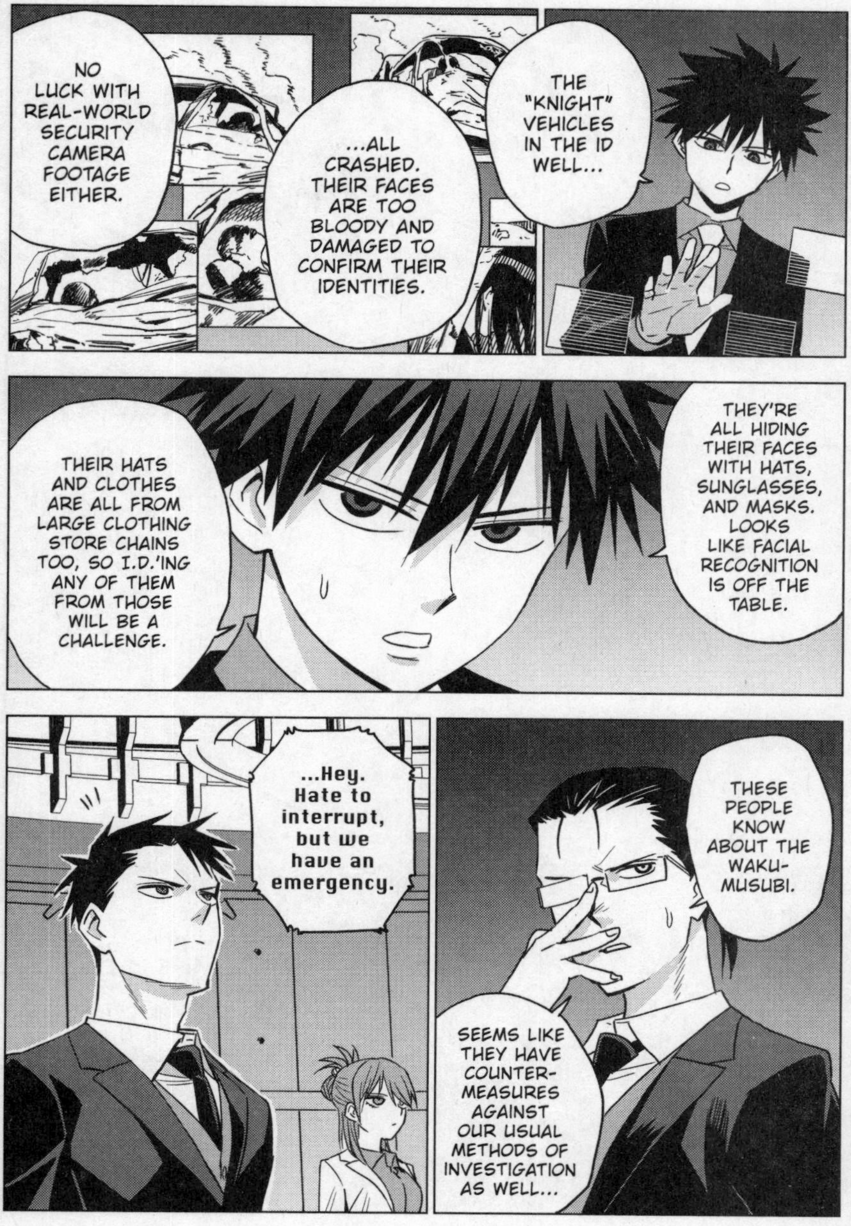
THE "KNIGHT" VEHICLES IN THE ID WELL...
...ALL CRASHED. THEIR FACES ARE TOO BLOODY AND DAMAGED TO CONFIRM THEIR IDENTITIES.
NO LUCK WITH REAL-WORLD SECURITY CAMERA FOOTAGE EITHER.
THEY'RE ALL HIDING THEIR FACES WITH HATS, SUNGLASSES, AND MASKS. LOOKS LIKE FACIAL RECOGNITION IS OFF THE TABLE.
THEIR HATS AND CLOTHES ARE ALL FROM LARGE CLOTHING STORE CHAINS TOO, SO I.D.'ING ANY OF THEM FROM THOSE WILL BE A CHALLENGE.
THESE PEOPLE KNOW ABOUT THE WAKU-MUSUBI.
SEEMS LIKE THEY HAVE COUNTER-MEASURES AGAINST OUR USUAL METHODS OF INVESTIGATION AS WELL...
...Hey. Hate to interrupt, but we have an emergency.

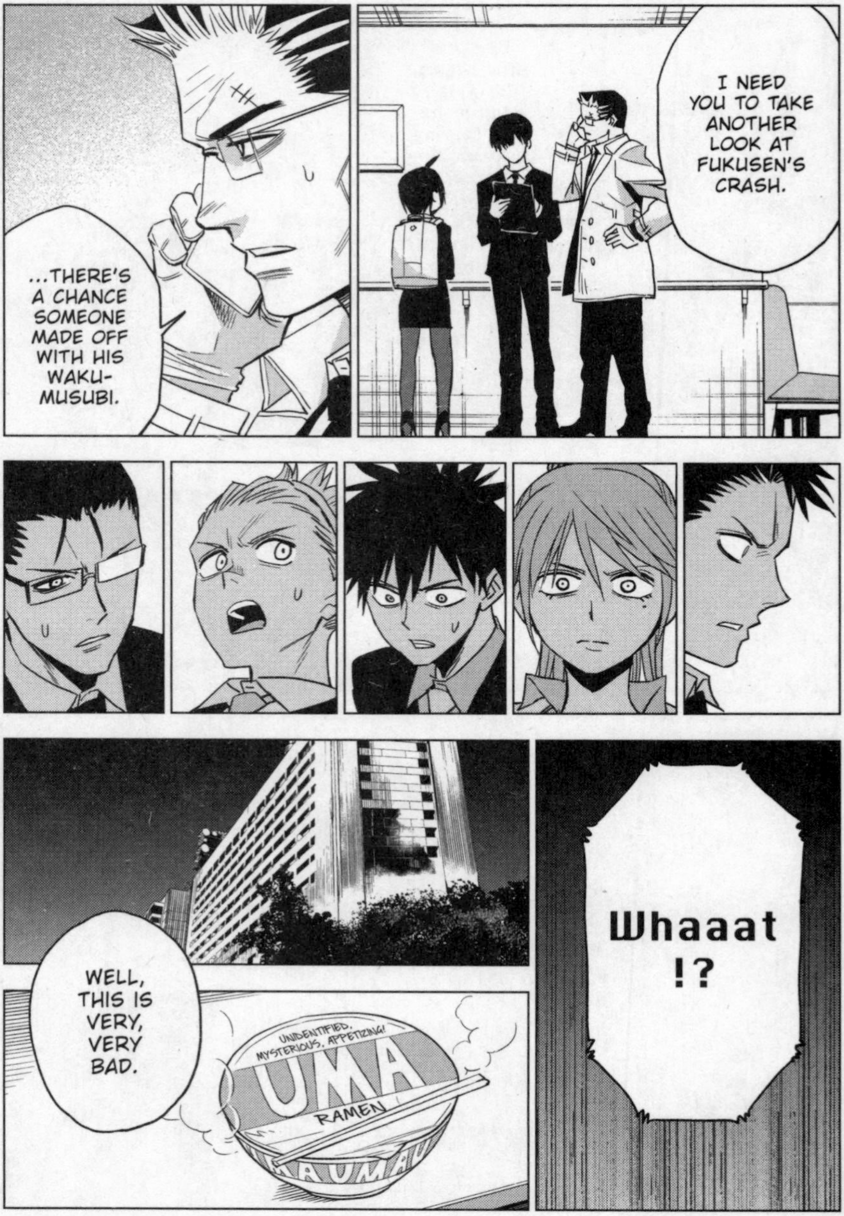
I NEED YOU TO TAKE ANOTHER LOOK AT FUKUSEN'S CRASH.
...THERE'S A CHANCE SOMEONE MADE OFF WITH HIS WAKU-MUSUBI.
Whaaat !?
WELL, THIS IS VERY, VERY BAD.
UNIDENTIFIED. MYSTERIOUS. APPETIZING!
UMA
RAMEN

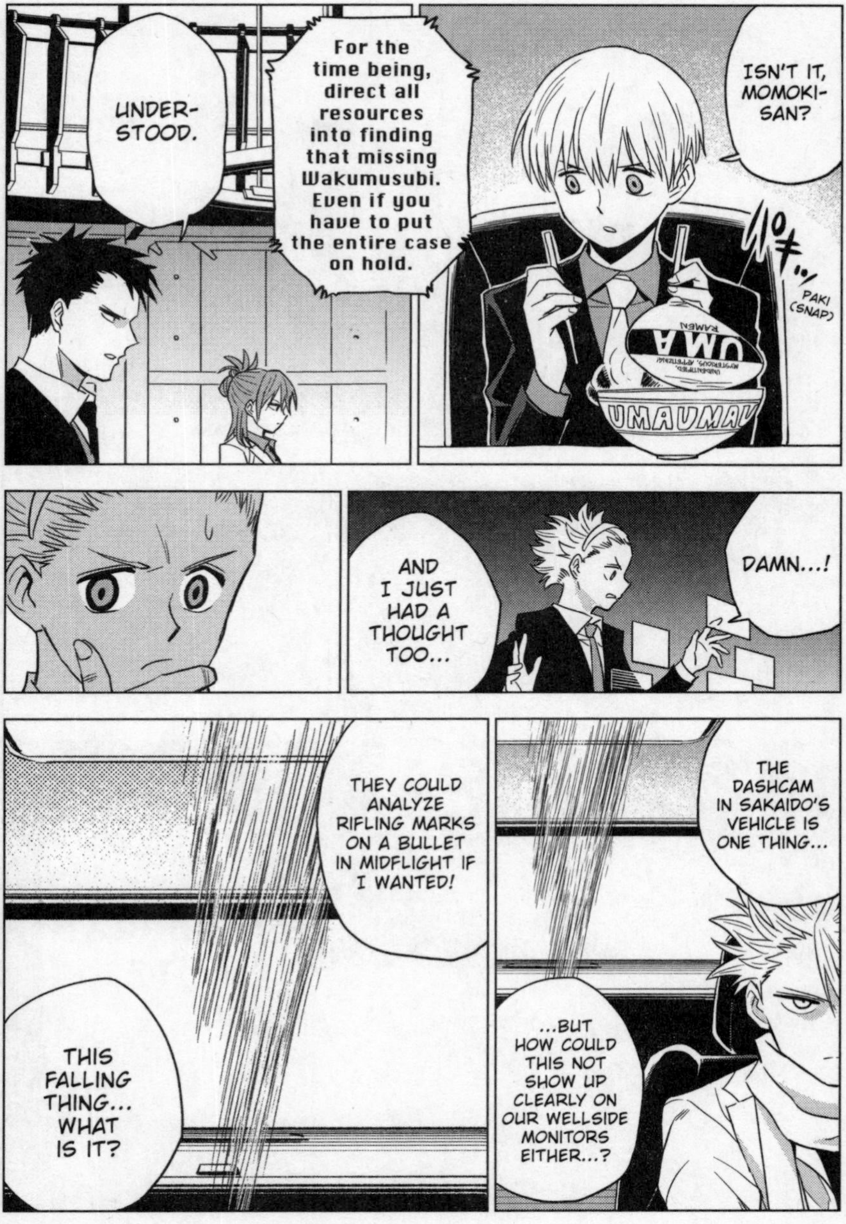
ISN'T IT, MOMOKI-SAN?
PAKI (SNAP)
UMA
RAMEN
UMAUMAU
For the time being, direct all resources into finding that missing Wakumusubi. Even if you have to put the entire case on hold.
UNDER-STOOD.
DAMN...!
AND I JUST HAD A THOUGHT TOO...
THE DASHCAM IN SAKAIDO'S VEHICLE IS ONE THING...
...BUT HOW COULD THIS NOT SHOW UP CLEARLY ON OUR WELLSIDE MONITORS EITHER...?
THEY COULD ANALYZE RIFLING MARKS ON A BULLET IN MIDFLIGHT IF I WANTED!
THIS FALLING THING... WHAT IS IT?

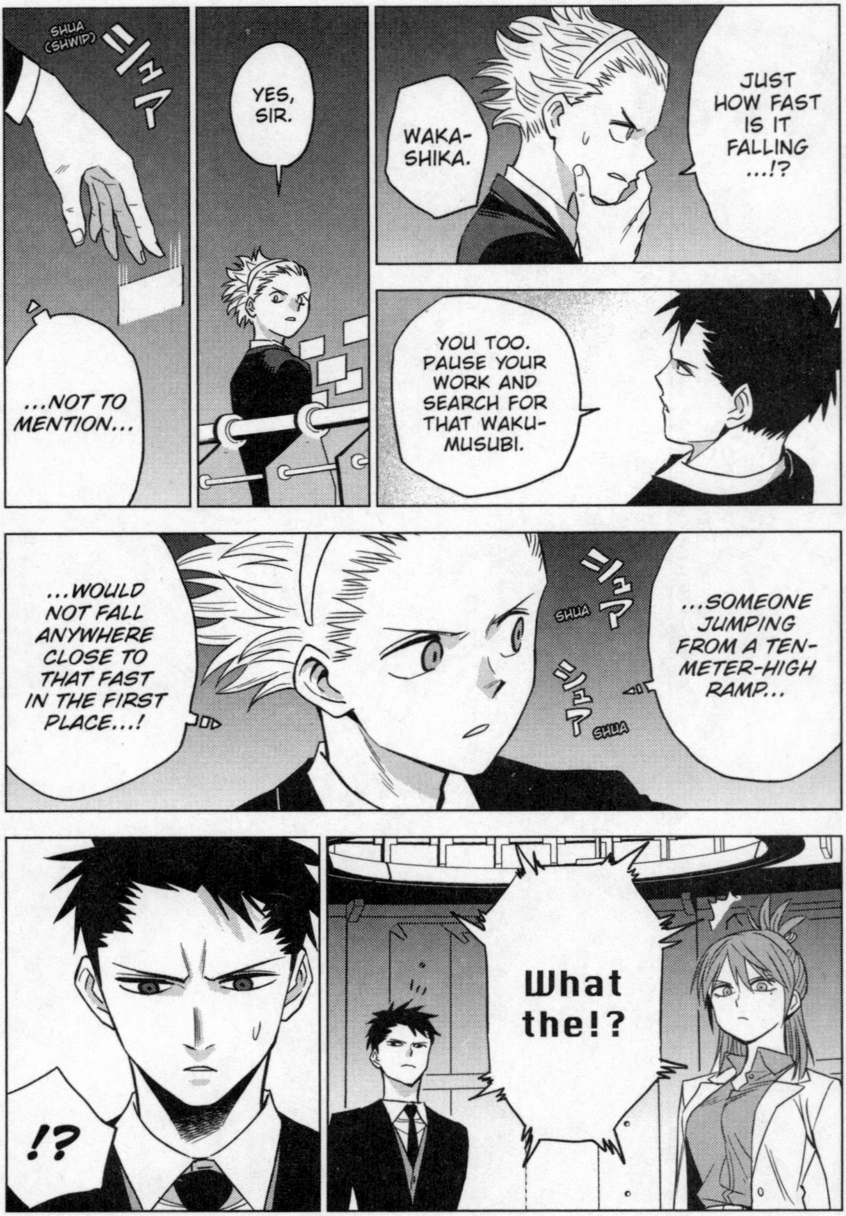
JUST HOW FAST IS IT FALLING ...!?
WAKA-SHIKA.
YOU TOO. PAUSE YOUR WORK AND SEARCH FOR THAT WAKU-MUSUBI.
YES, SIR.
シュア
SHUA (SHWIP)
...NOT TO MENTION...
...SOMEONE JUMPING FROM A TEN-METER-HIGH RAMP...
シュア
SHUA
シュア
SHUA
...WOULD NOT FALL ANYWHERE CLOSE TO THAT FAST IN THE FIRST PLACE...!
What the!?
!?

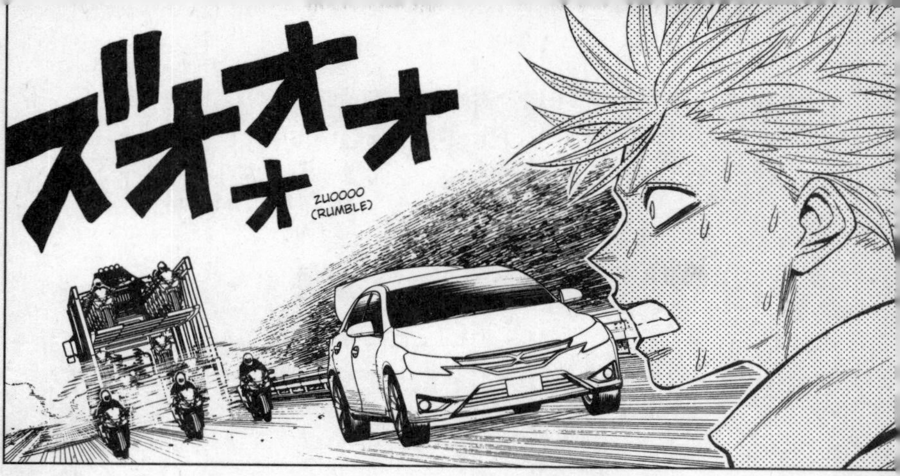
ズオオォォ
ZUOOOO (RUMBLE)
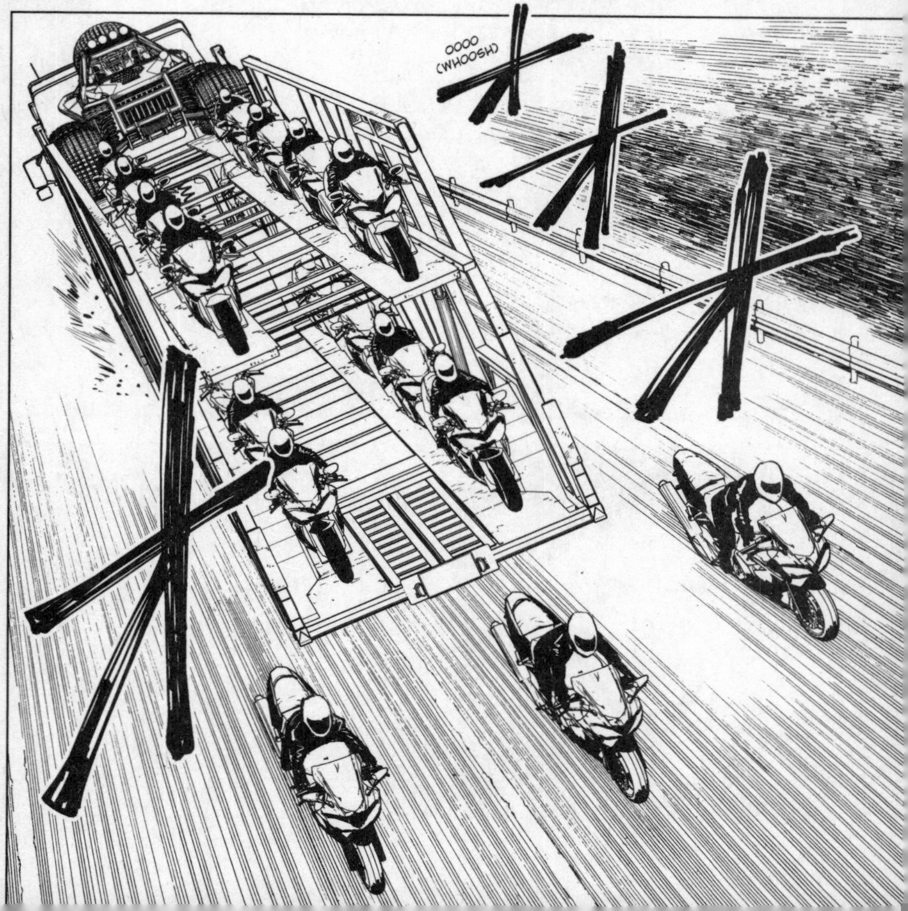
オオオオ
OOOO (WHOOSH)

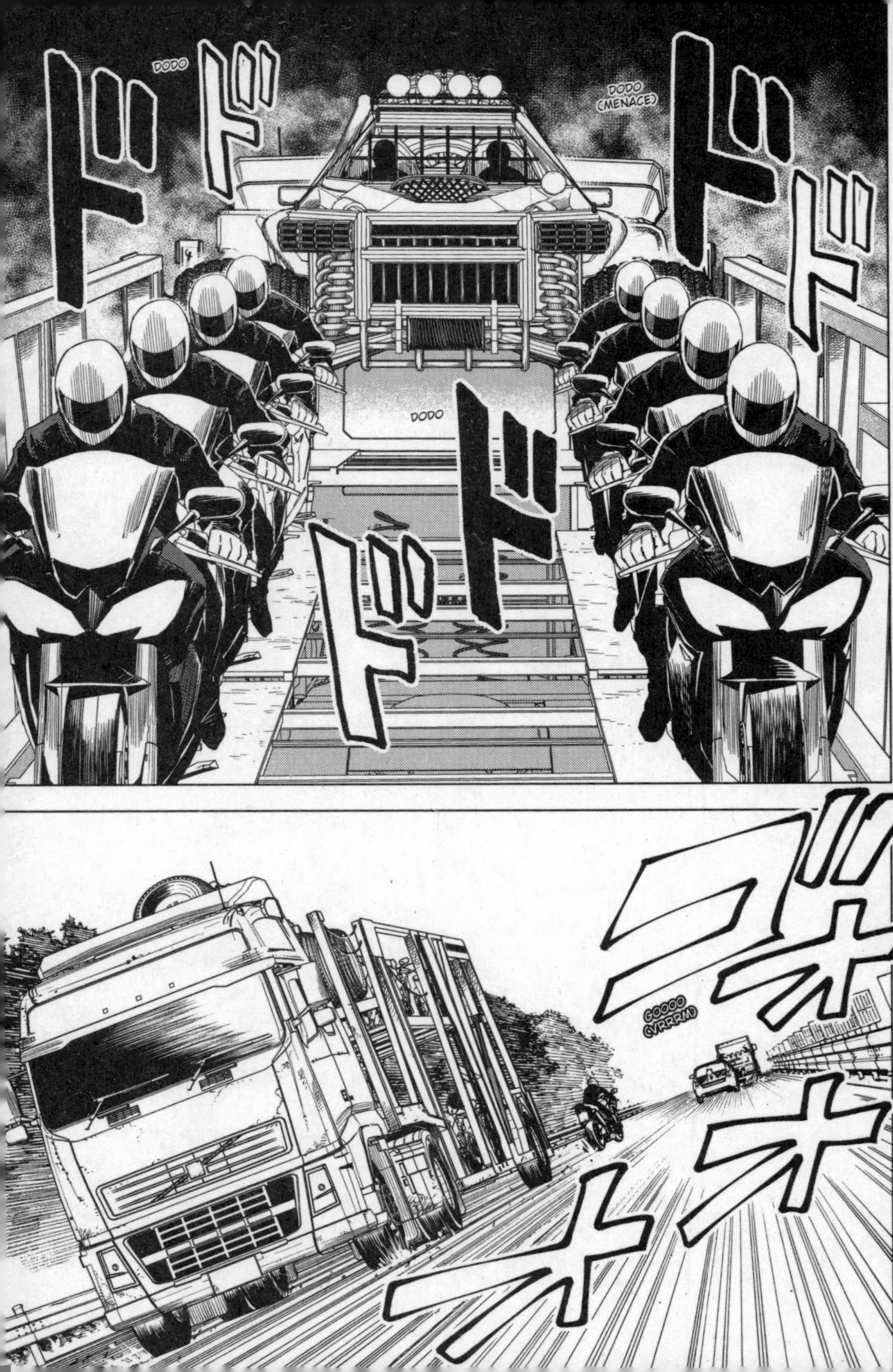
ドドドド
DODO (MENACE)
ドドドド
DODO
ドドドド
DODO
ゴオオオ
GOOOO (VRRRM)

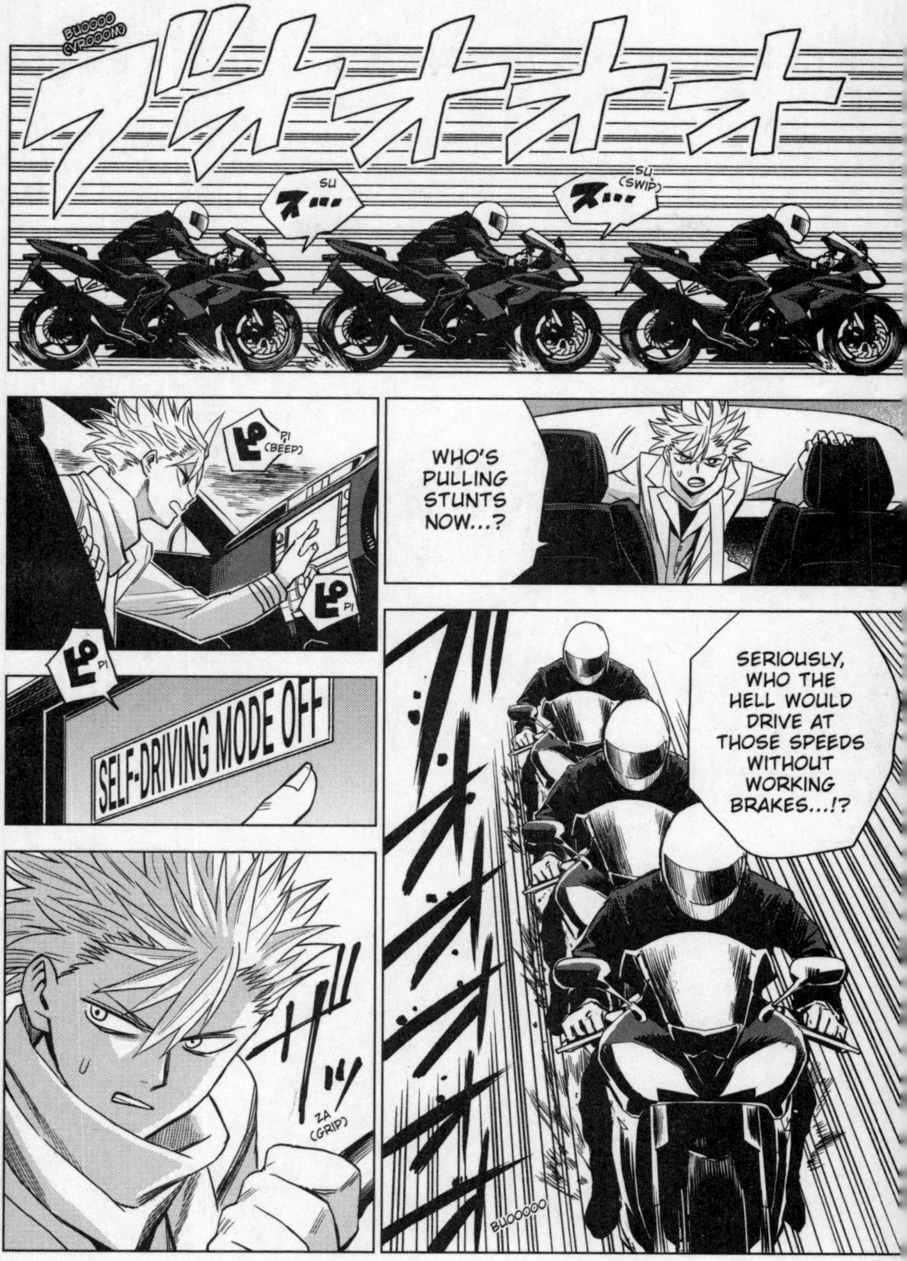
BUOOOO (VROOOM)
SU (SWIP)
SU
WHO'S PULLING STUNTS NOW...?
SERIOUSLY, WHO THE HELL WOULD DRIVE AT THOSE SPEEDS WITHOUT WORKING BRAKES...!?
BUOOOO
PI (BEEP)
PI
PI
SELF-DRIVING MODE OFF
ZA (GRIP)

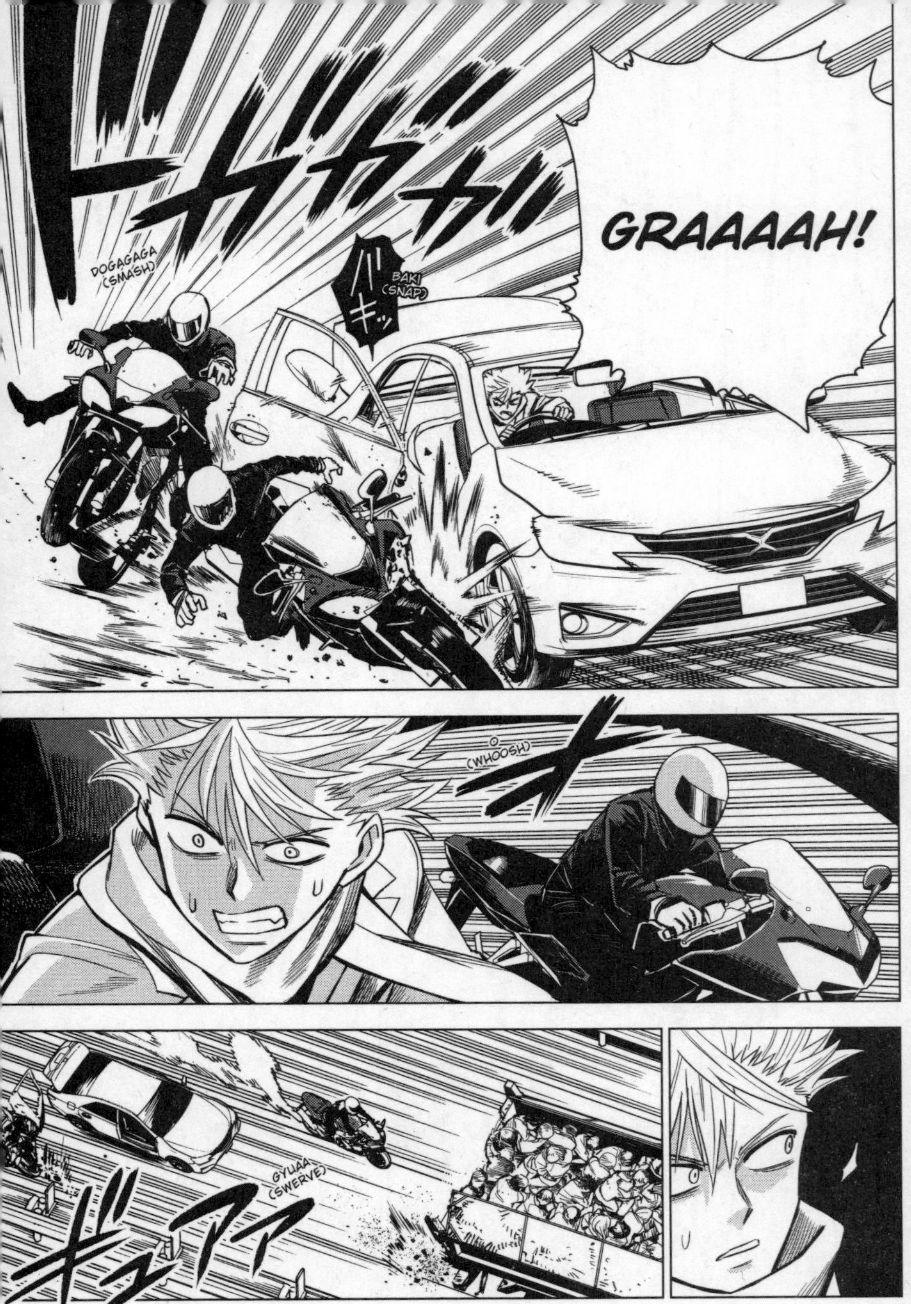
GRAAAAH!
BAKI (SNAP)
DOGAGAGA (SMASH)
O (WHOOSH)
GYUAA (SWERVE)

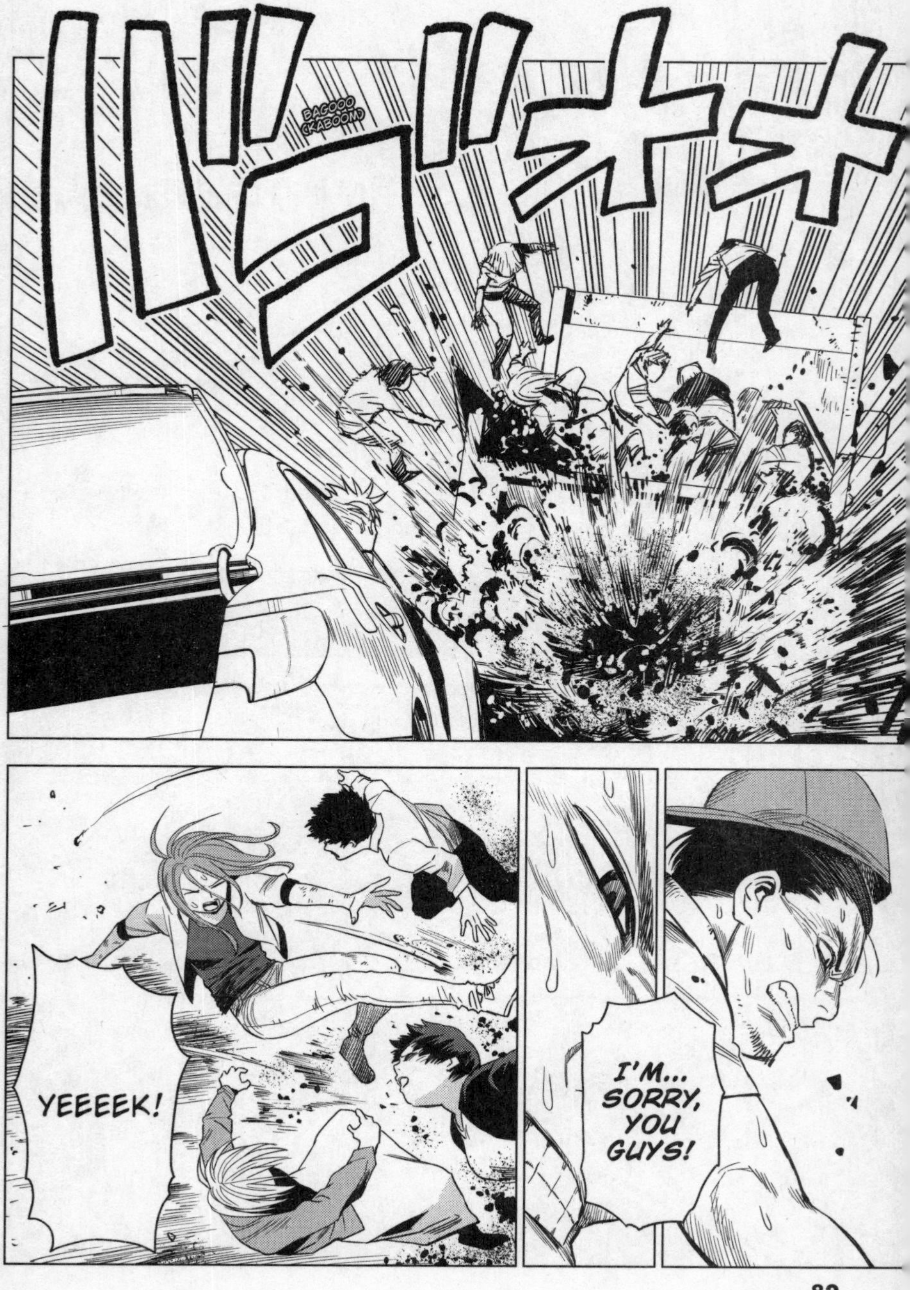
BAGOOO (KABOOM)
I'M... SORRY, YOU GUYS!
YEEEEK!

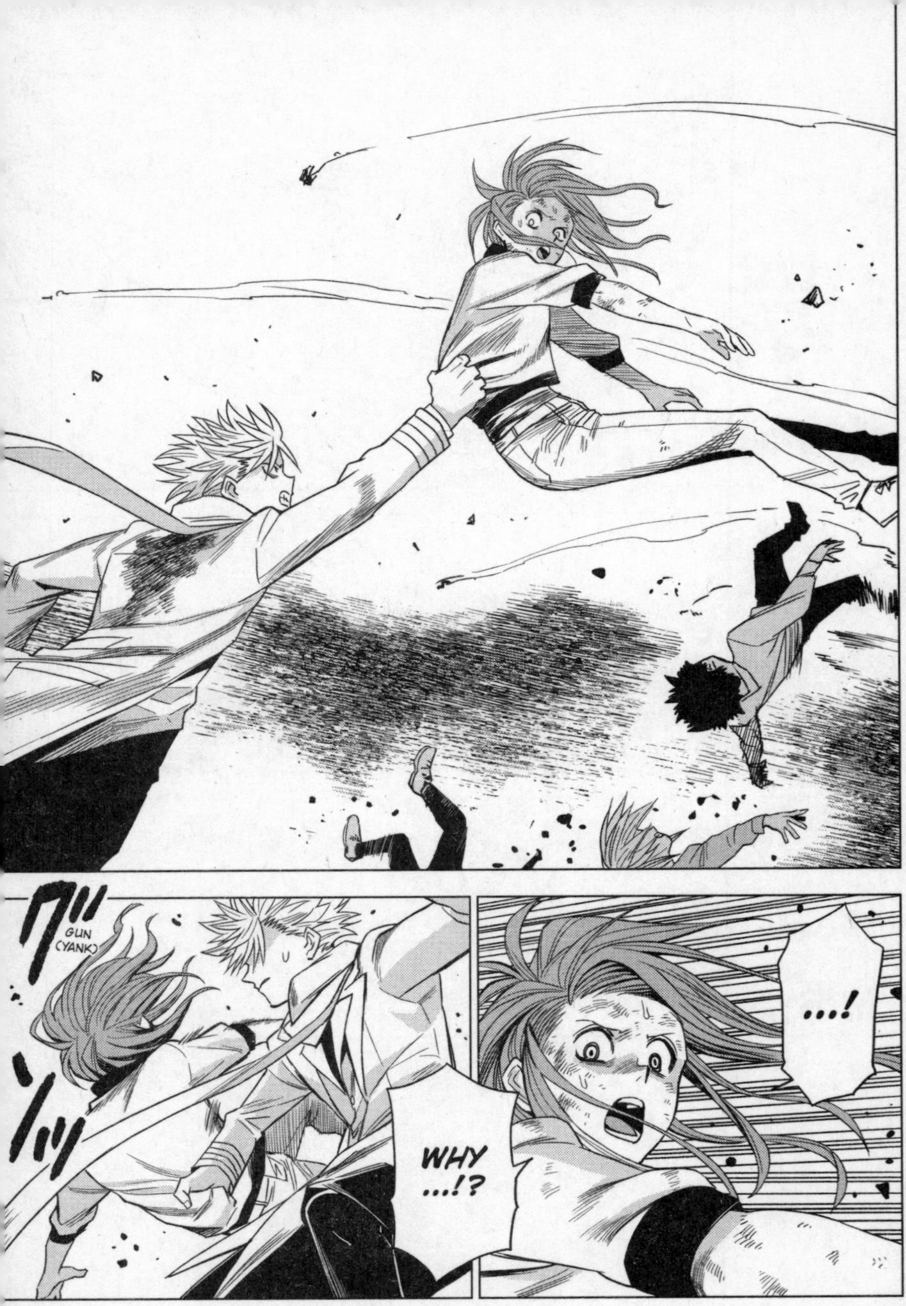
...!
WHY ...!?
GUN (YANK)

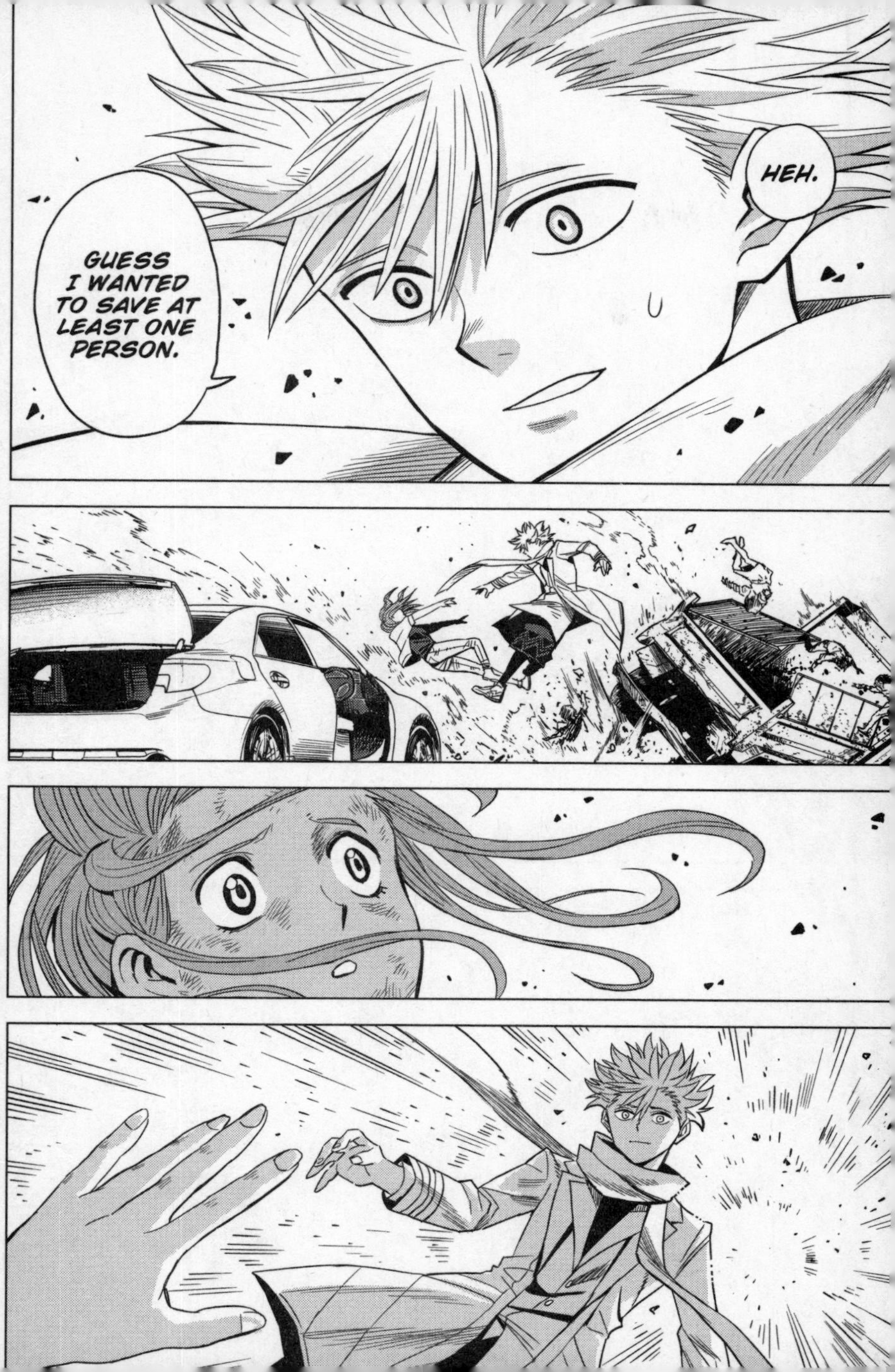
HEH.
GUESS I WANTED TO SAVE AT LEAST ONE PERSON.

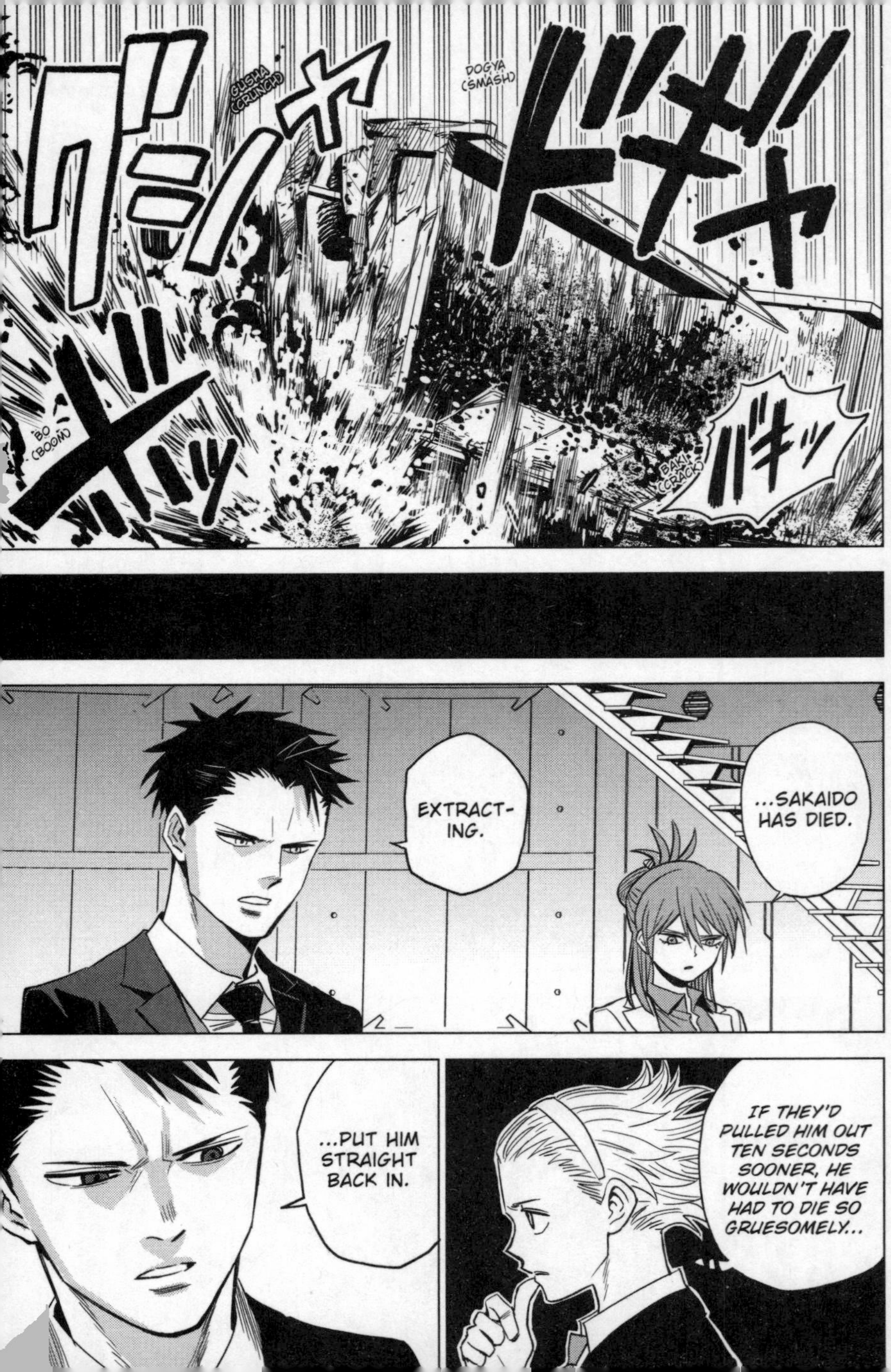
ドギャ
DOGYA (SMASH)
グシャ
GUSHA (CRUNCH)
バキッ
BAKI (CRACK)
ボッ
BO (BOOM)
...SAKAIDO HAS DIED.
EXTRACT-ING.
IF THEY'D PULLED HIM OUT TEN SECONDS SOONER, HE WOULDN'T HAVE HAD TO DIE SO GRUESOMELY...
...PUT HIM STRAIGHT BACK IN.

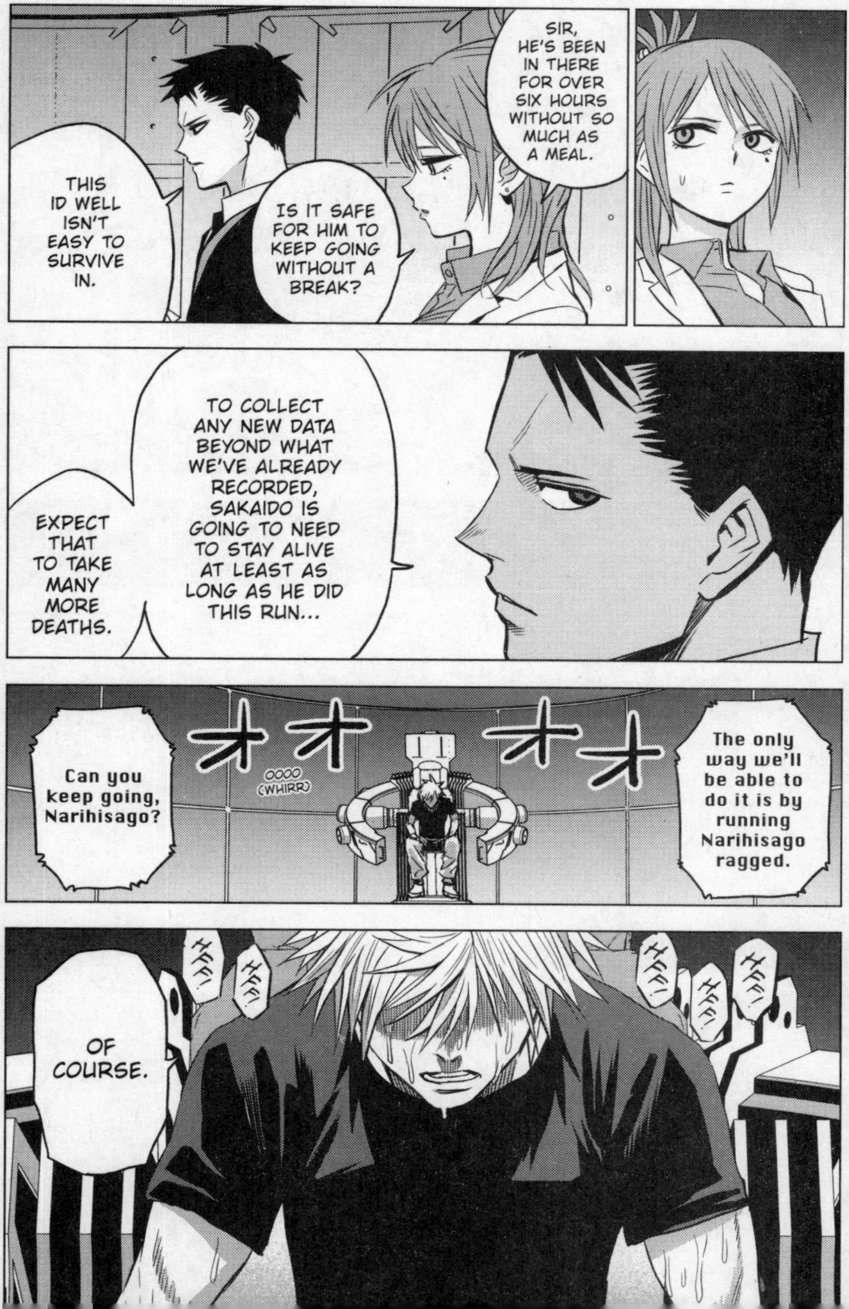
SIR, HE'S BEEN IN THERE FOR OVER SIX HOURS WITHOUT SO MUCH AS A MEAL.
IS IT SAFE FOR HIM TO KEEP GOING WITHOUT A BREAK?
THIS ID WELL ISN'T EASY TO SURVIVE IN.
TO COLLECT ANY NEW DATA BEYOND WHAT WE'VE ALREADY RECORDED, SAKAIDO IS GOING TO NEED TO STAY ALIVE AT LEAST AS LONG AS HE DID THIS RUN...
EXPECT THAT TO TAKE MANY MORE DEATHS.
The only way we'll be able to do it is by running Narihisago ragged.
オオ
オオ
OOOO (WHIRR)
Can you keep going, Narihisago?
OF COURSE.

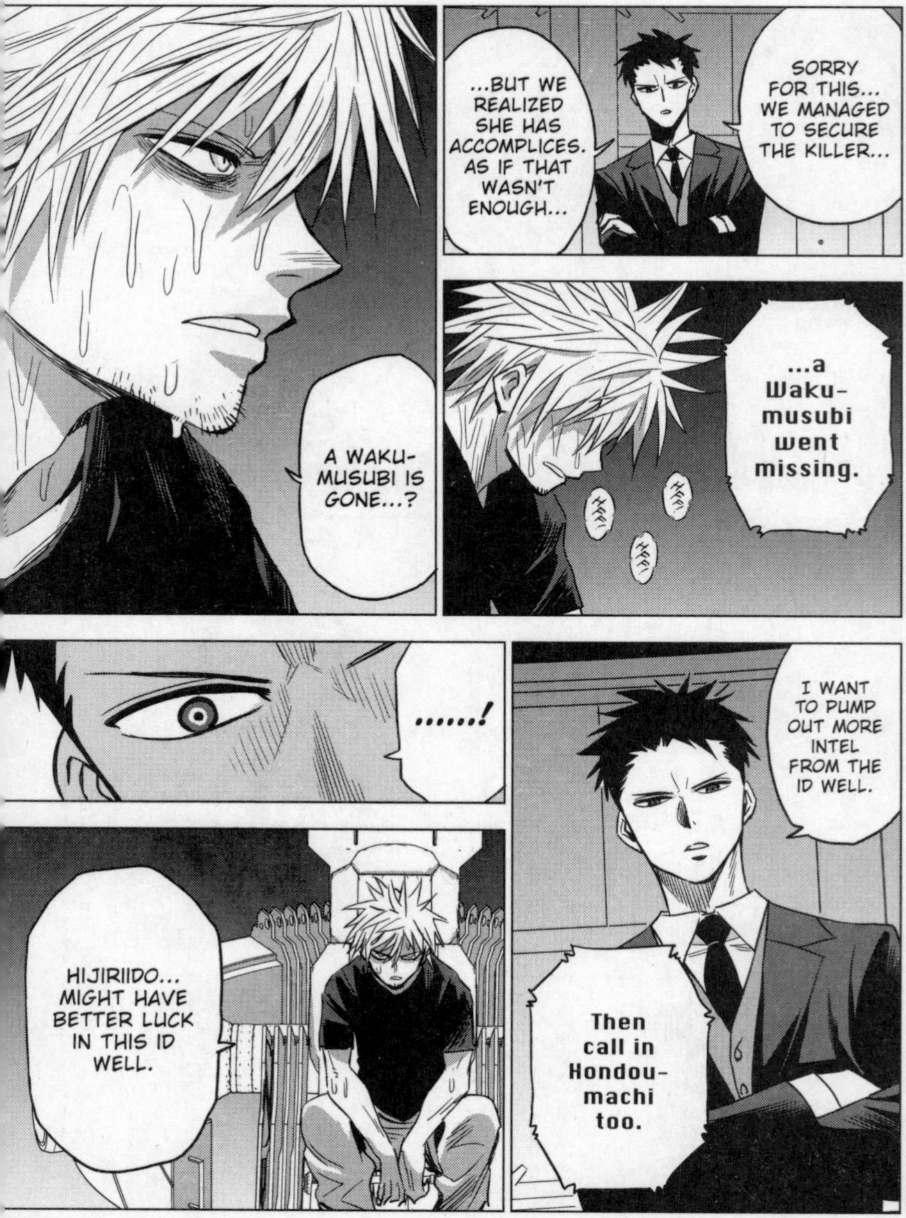
SORRY FOR THIS... WE MANAGED TO SECURE THE KILLER...
...BUT WE REALIZED SHE HAS ACCOMPLICES. AS IF THAT WASN'T ENOUGH...
...a Waku-musubi went missing.
A WAKU-MUSUBI IS GONE...?
I WANT TO PUMP OUT MORE INTEL FROM THE ID WELL.
Then call in Hondou-machi too.
......!
HIJIRIIDO... MIGHT HAVE BETTER LUCK IN THIS ID WELL.

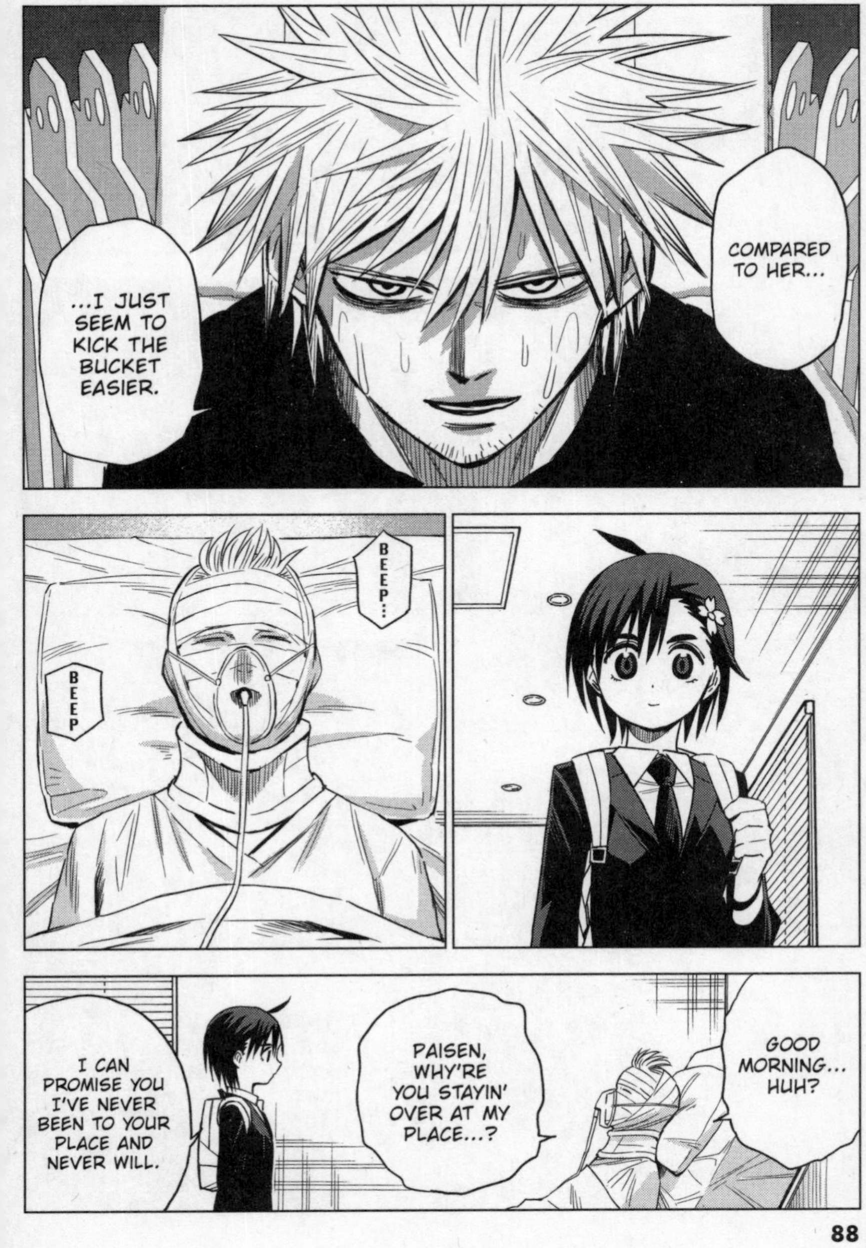
COMPARED TO HER...
...I JUST SEEM TO KICK THE BUCKET EASIER.
BEEP...
BEEP
GOOD MORNING... HUH?
PAISEN, WHY'RE YOU STAYIN' OVER AT MY PLACE...?
I CAN PROMISE YOU I'VE NEVER BEEN TO YOUR PLACE AND NEVER WILL.

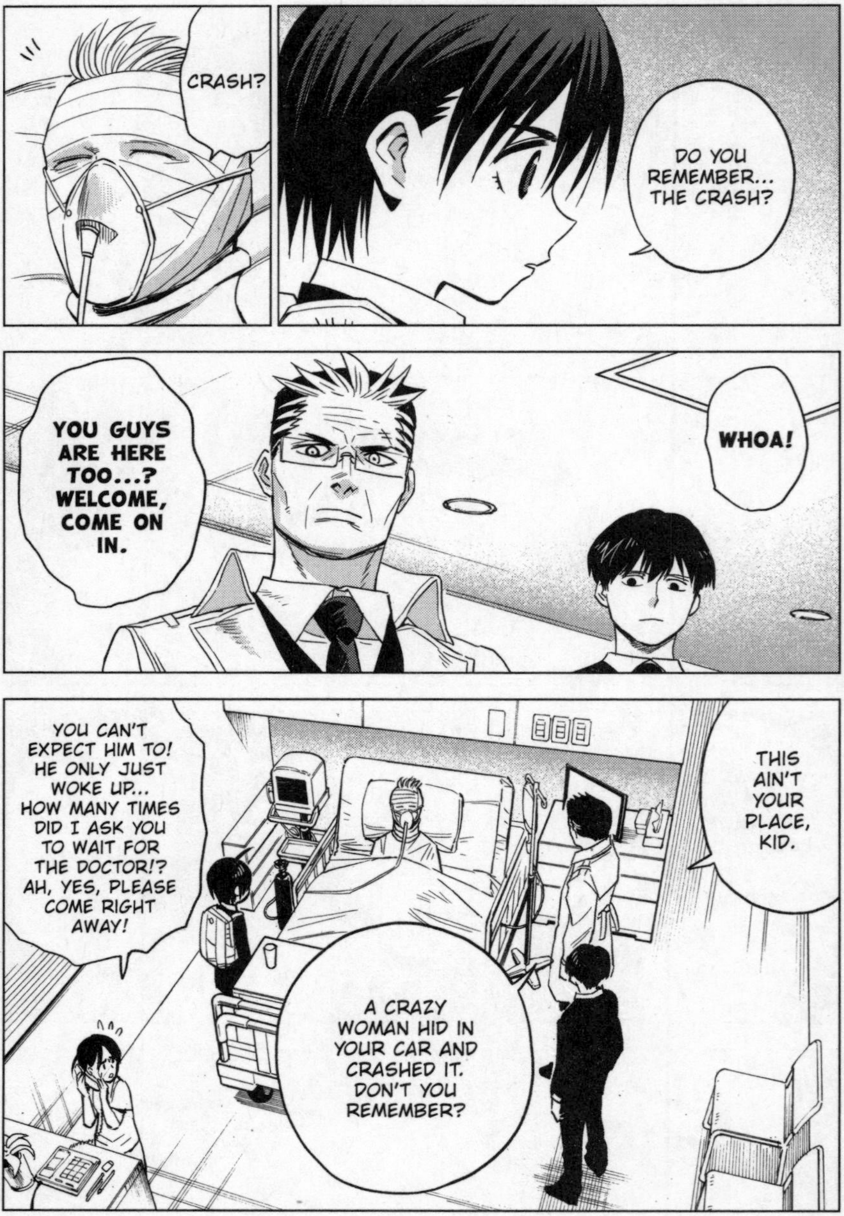
DO YOU REMEMBER... THE CRASH?
CRASH?
WHOA!
YOU GUYS ARE HERE TOO...? WELCOME, COME ON IN.
THIS AIN'T YOUR PLACE, KID.
YOU CAN'T EXPECT HIM TO! HE ONLY JUST WOKE UP... HOW MANY TIMES DID I ASK YOU TO WAIT FOR THE DOCTOR!? AH, YES, PLEASE COME RIGHT AWAY!
A CRAZY WOMAN HID IN YOUR CAR AND CRASHED IT. DON'T YOU REMEMBER?

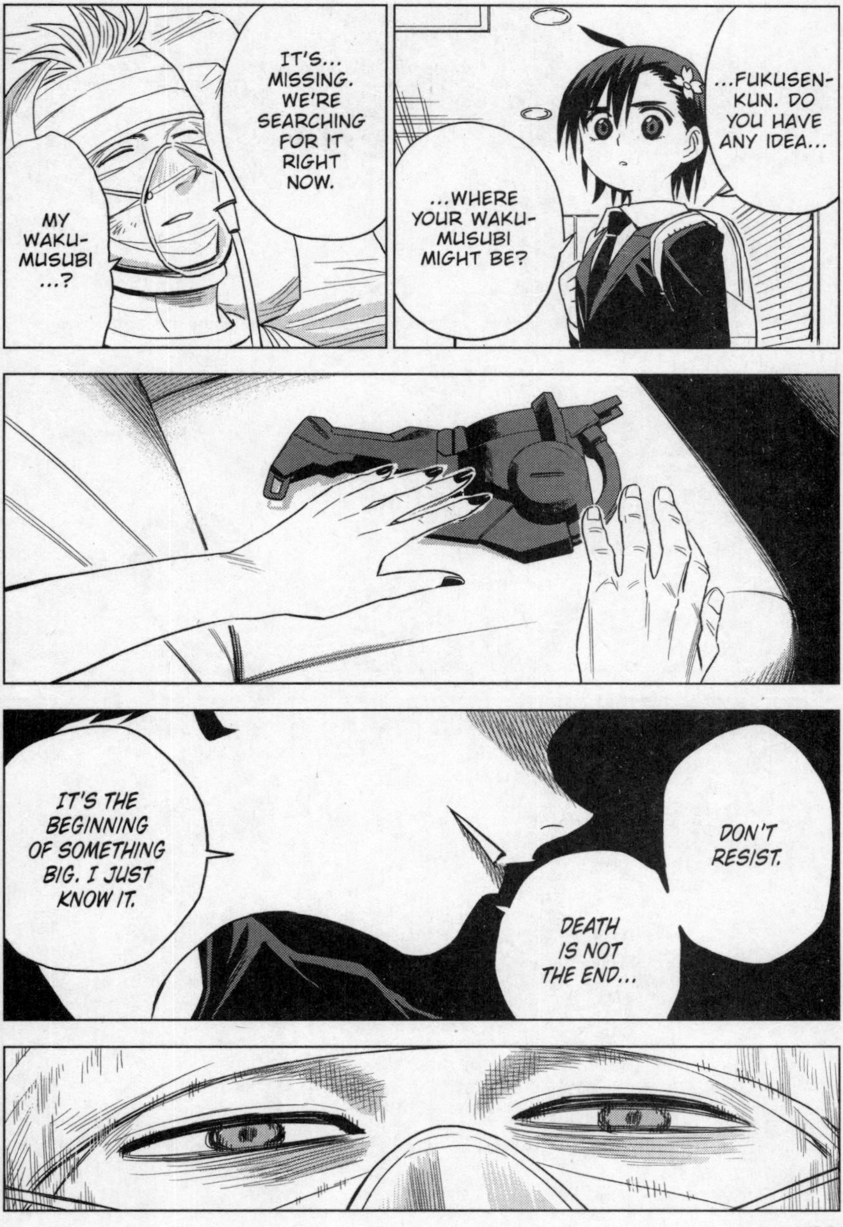
...FUKUSEN-KUN. DO YOU HAVE ANY IDEA...
...WHERE YOUR WAKU-MUSUBI MIGHT BE?
IT'S... MISSING. WE'RE SEARCHING FOR IT RIGHT NOW.
MY WAKU-MUSUBI ...?
DON'T RESIST.
DEATH IS NOT THE END...
IT'S THE BEGINNING OF SOMETHING BIG. I JUST KNOW IT.

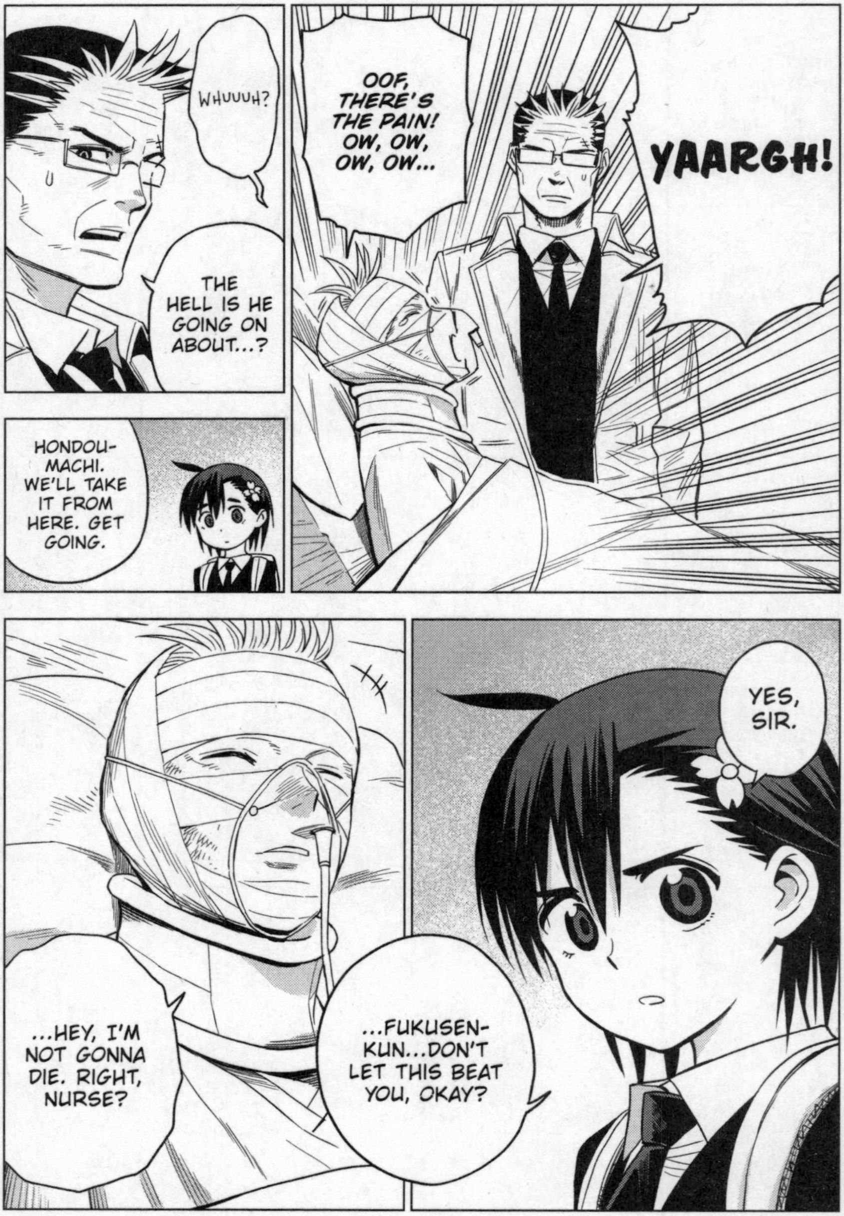
YAARGH!
OOF, THERE'S THE PAIN! OW, OW, OW, OW...
WHUUUH?
THE HELL IS HE GOING ON ABOUT...?
HONDOU-MACHI. WE'LL TAKE IT FROM HERE. GET GOING.
YES, SIR.
...FUKUSEN-KUN...DON'T LET THIS BEAT YOU, OKAY?
...HEY, I'M NOT GONNA DIE. RIGHT, NURSE?

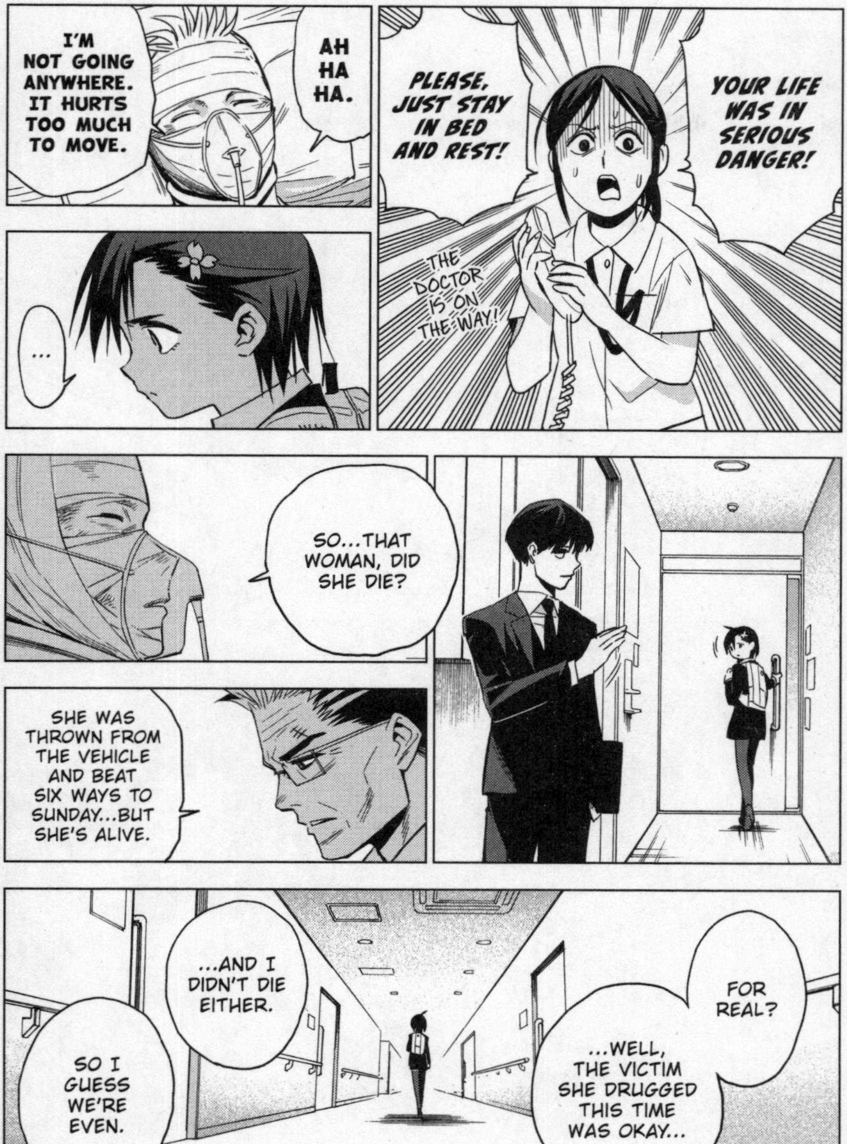
YOUR LIFE WAS IN SERIOUS DANGER!
PLEASE, JUST STAY IN BED AND REST!
THE DOCTOR IS ON THE WAY!
AH HA HA.
I'M NOT GOING ANYWHERE. IT HURTS TOO MUCH TO MOVE.
...
SO...THAT WOMAN, DID SHE DIE?
SHE WAS THROWN FROM THE VEHICLE AND BEAT SIX WAYS TO SUNDAY...BUT SHE'S ALIVE.
FOR REAL?
...WELL, THE VICTIM SHE DRUGGED THIS TIME WAS OKAY...
...AND I DIDN'T DIE EITHER.
SO I GUESS WE'RE EVEN.

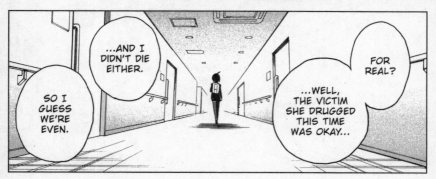

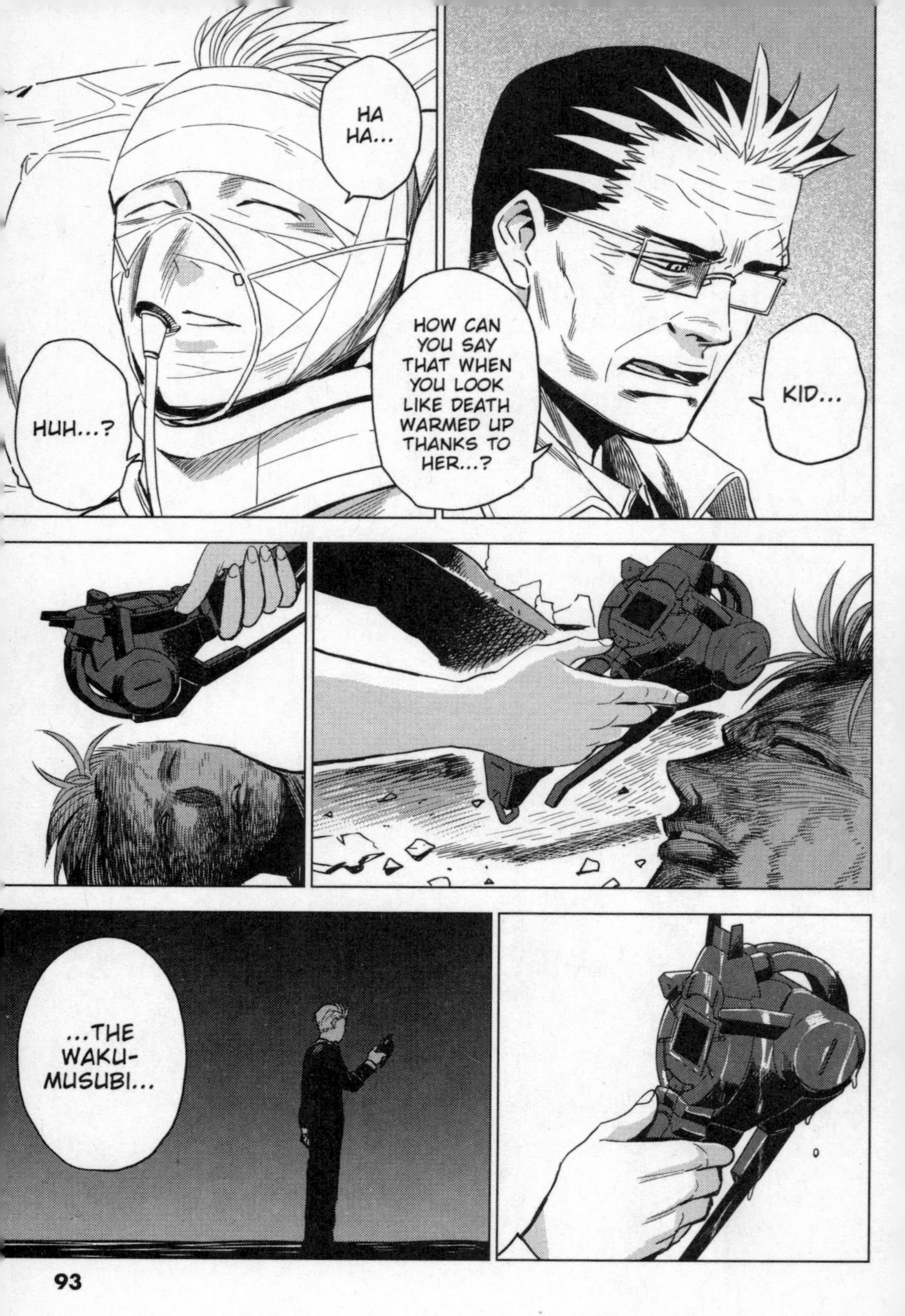
KID...
HOW CAN YOU SAY THAT WHEN YOU LOOK LIKE DEATH WARMED UP THANKS TO HER...?
HA HA...
HUH...?
...THE WAKU-MUSUBI...

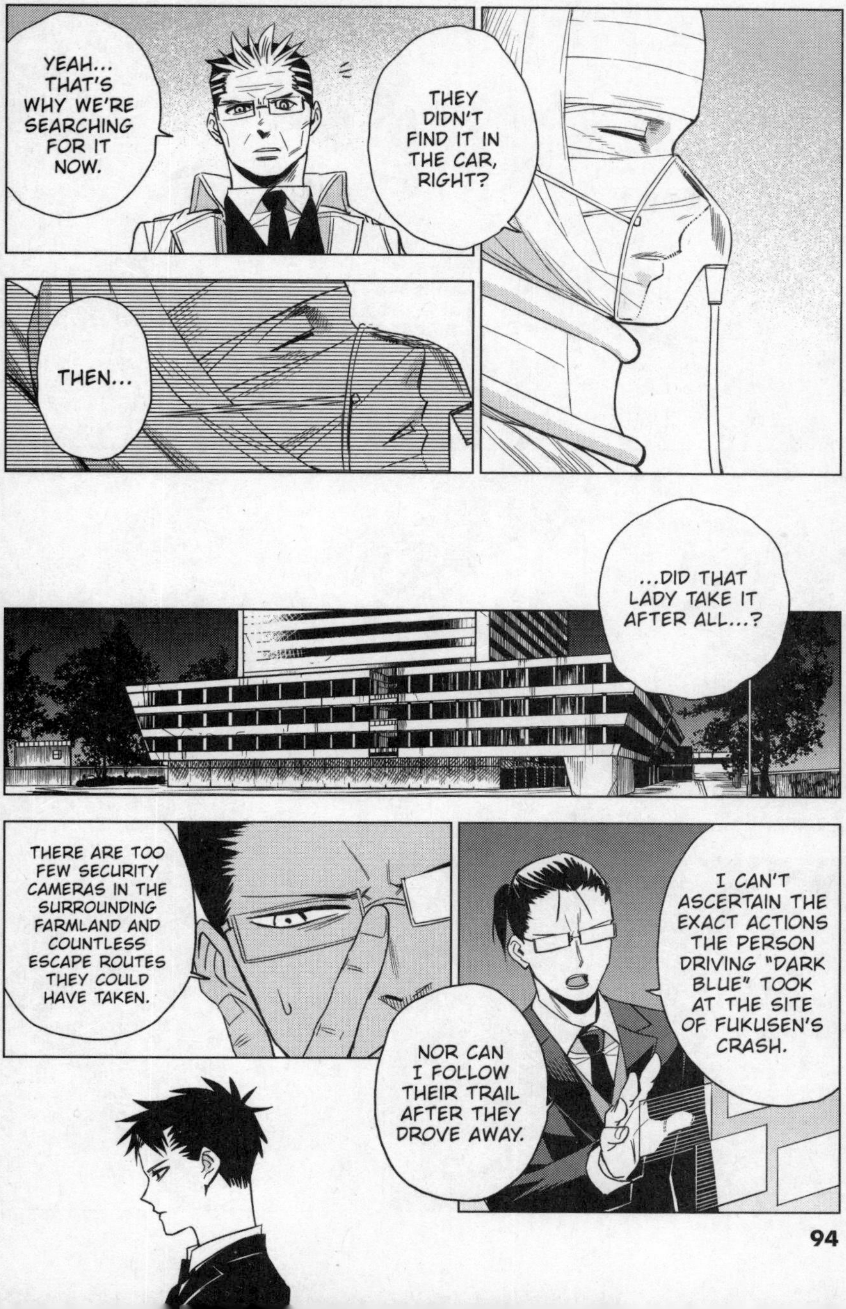
THEY DIDN'T FIND IT IN THE CAR, RIGHT?
YEAH... THAT'S WHY WE'RE SEARCHING FOR IT NOW.
THEN...
...DID THAT LADY TAKE IT AFTER ALL...?
I CAN'T ASCERTAIN THE EXACT ACTIONS THE PERSON DRIVING "DARK BLUE" TOOK AT THE SITE OF FUKUSEN'S CRASH.
NOR CAN I FOLLOW THEIR TRAIL AFTER THEY DROVE AWAY.
THERE ARE TOO FEW SECURITY CAMERAS IN THE SURROUNDING FARMLAND AND COUNTLESS ESCAPE ROUTES THEY COULD HAVE TAKEN.

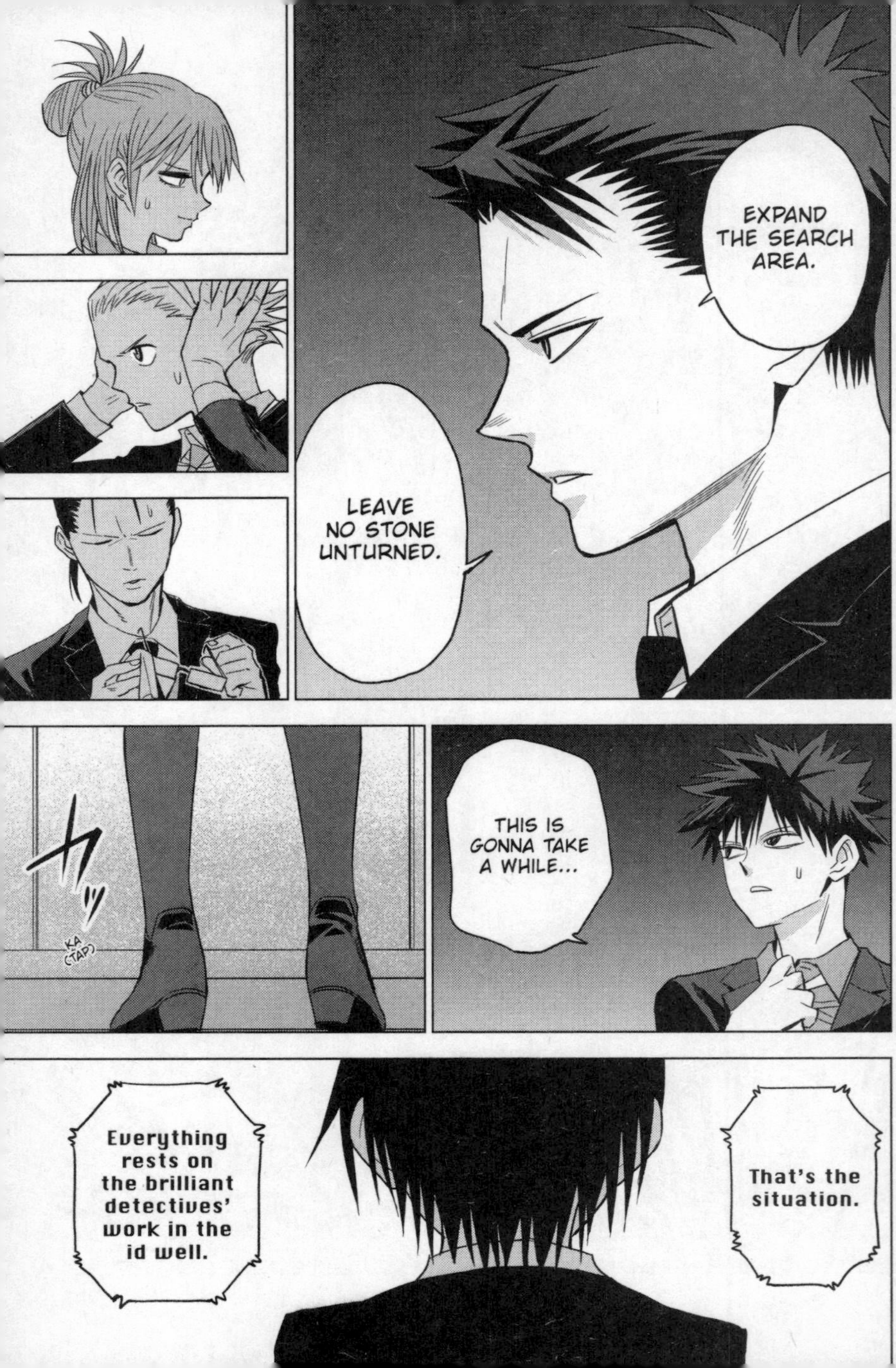
EXPAND THE SEARCH AREA.
LEAVE NO STONE UNTURNED.
THIS IS GONNA TAKE A WHILE...
カッ
KA (TAP)
Everything rests on the brilliant detectives' work in the id well.
That's the situation.

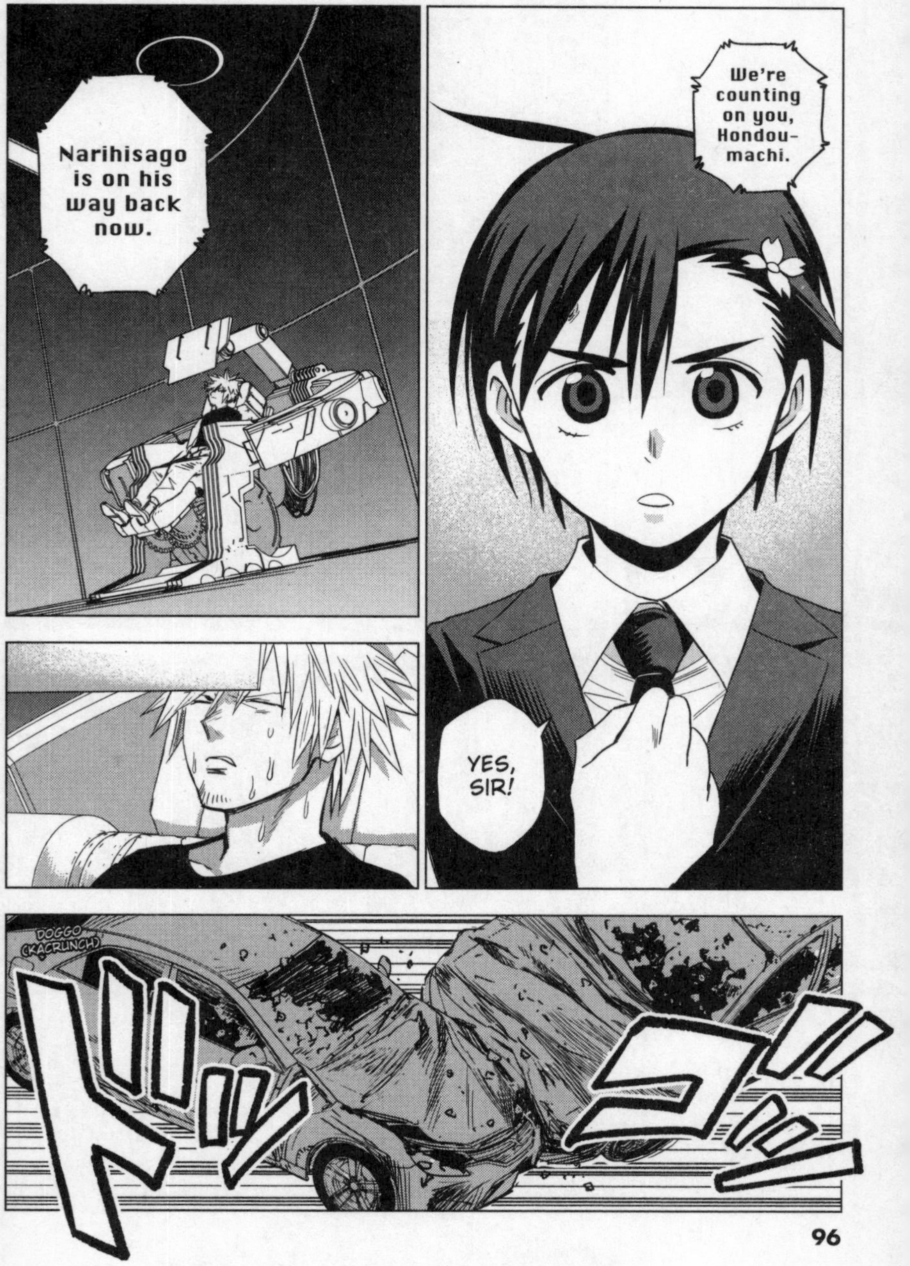
We're counting on you, Hondou-machi.
YES, SIR!
Narihisago is on his way back now.
DOGGO (KACRUNCH)

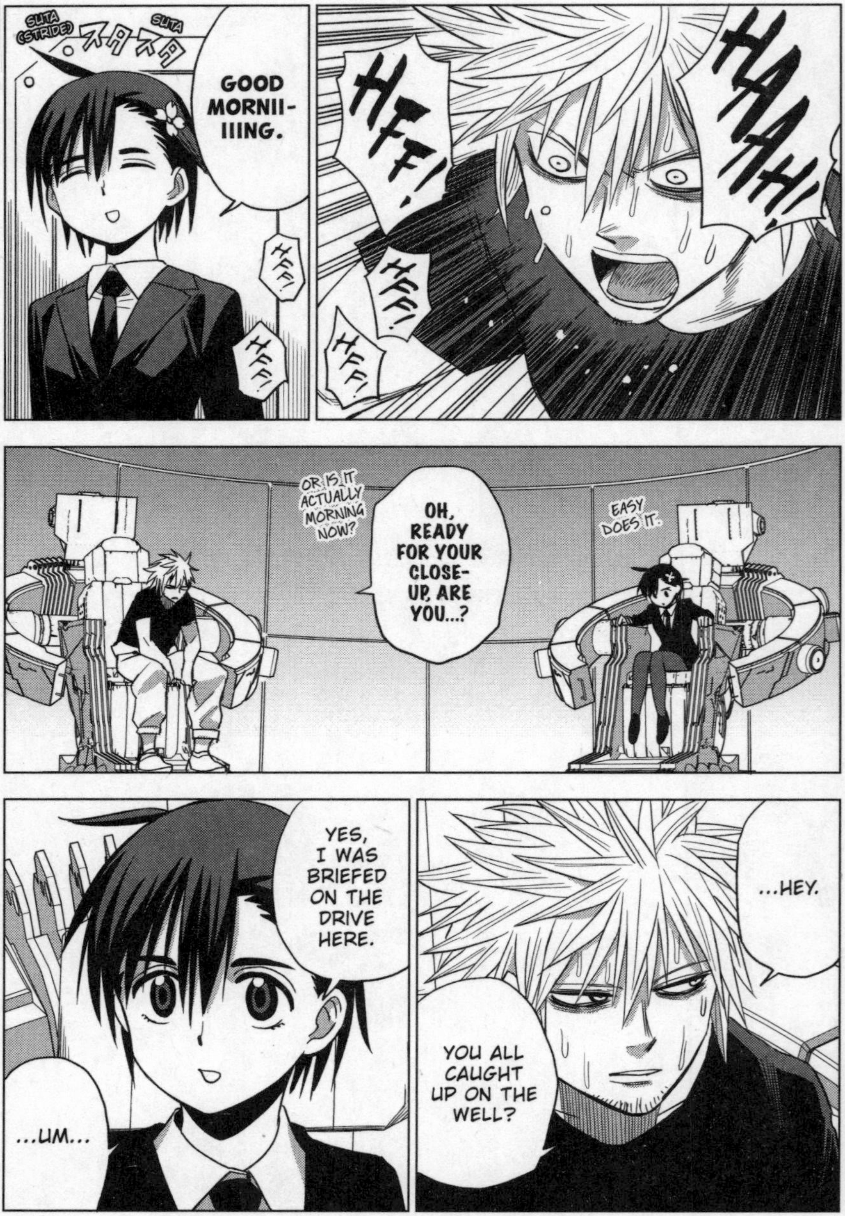
HAAH!
HFF!
HFF!
HFF!
GOOD MORNII-IIING.
SUTA (STRIDE) スタスタ SUTA
HFF!
HFF!
EASY DOES IT.
OH, READY FOR YOUR CLOSE-UP, ARE YOU...?
OR IS IT ACTUALLY MORNING NOW?
...HEY.
YOU ALL CAUGHT UP ON THE WELL?
YES, I WAS BRIEFED ON THE DRIVE HERE.
...UM...

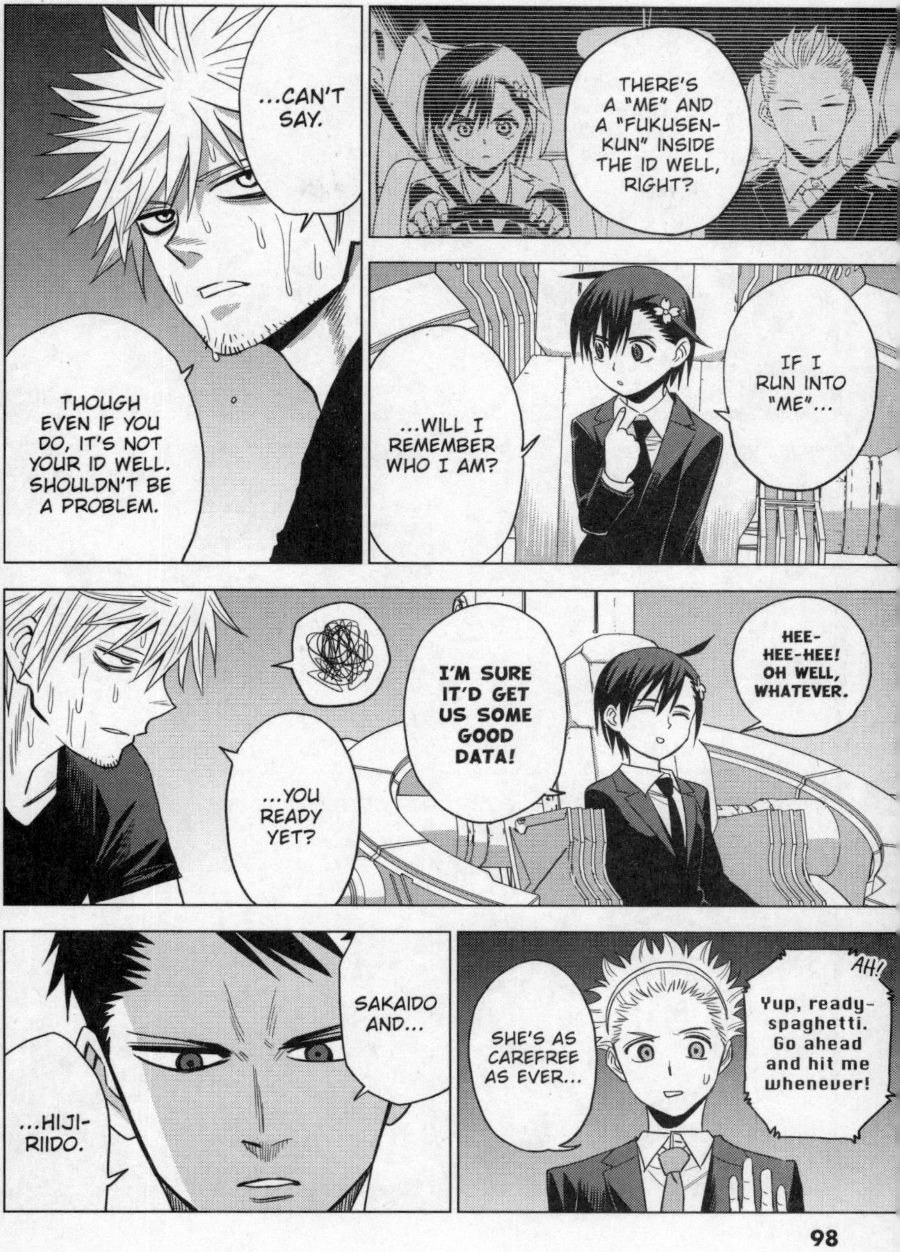
THERE'S A "ME" AND A "FUKUSEN-KUN" INSIDE THE ID WELL, RIGHT?
IF I RUN INTO "ME"...
...WILL I REMEMBER WHO I AM?
...CAN'T SAY.
THOUGH EVEN IF YOU DO, IT'S NOT YOUR ID WELL. SHOULDN'T BE A PROBLEM.
HEE-HEE-HEE! OH WELL, WHATEVER.
I'M SURE IT'D GET US SOME GOOD DATA!
...YOU READY YET?
AH!
Yup, ready-spaghetti. Go ahead and hit me whenever!
SHE'S AS CAREFREE AS EVER...
SAKAIDO AND...
...HIJI-RIIDO.

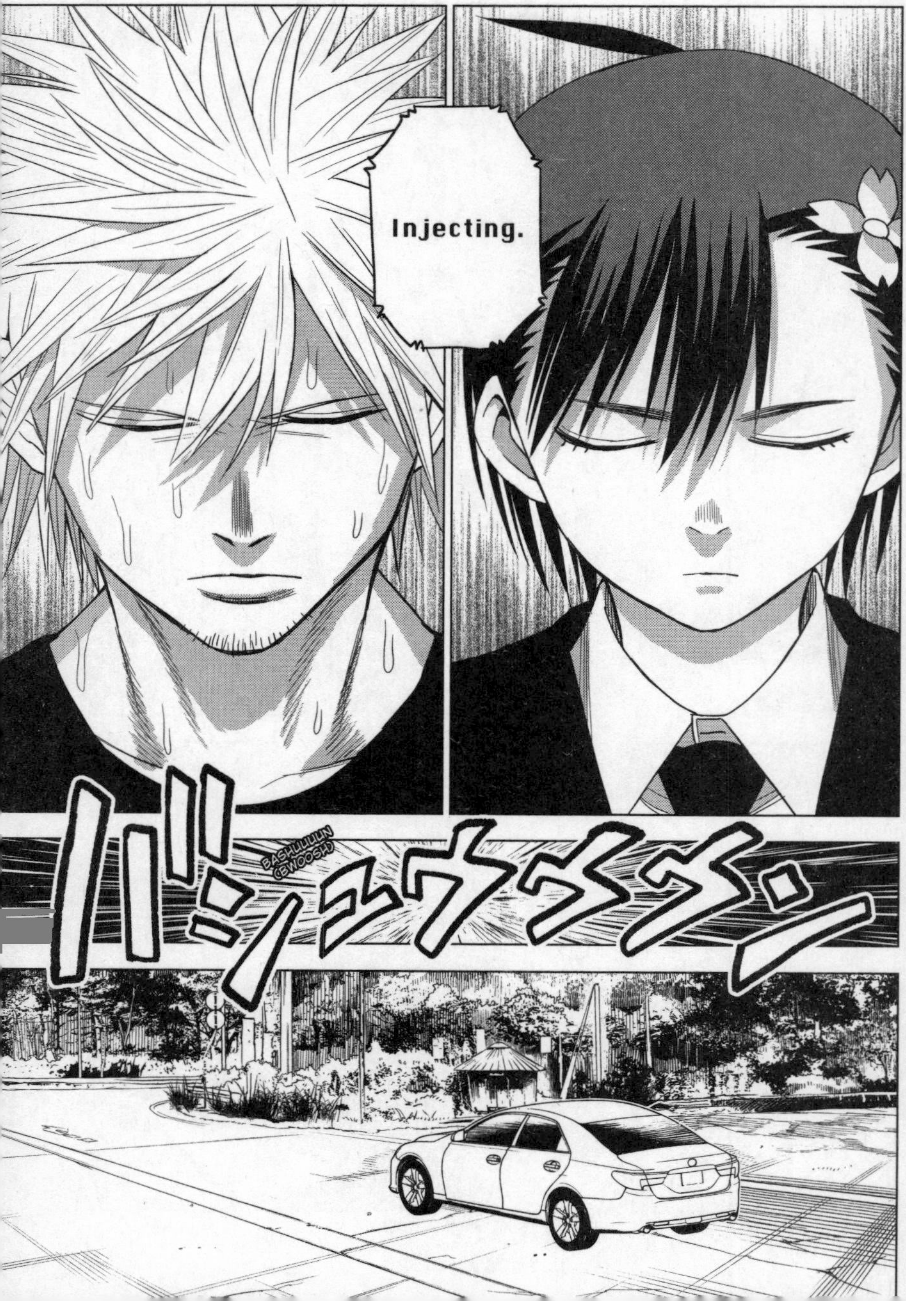
Injecting.
BASHUUUUN (BWOOSH)

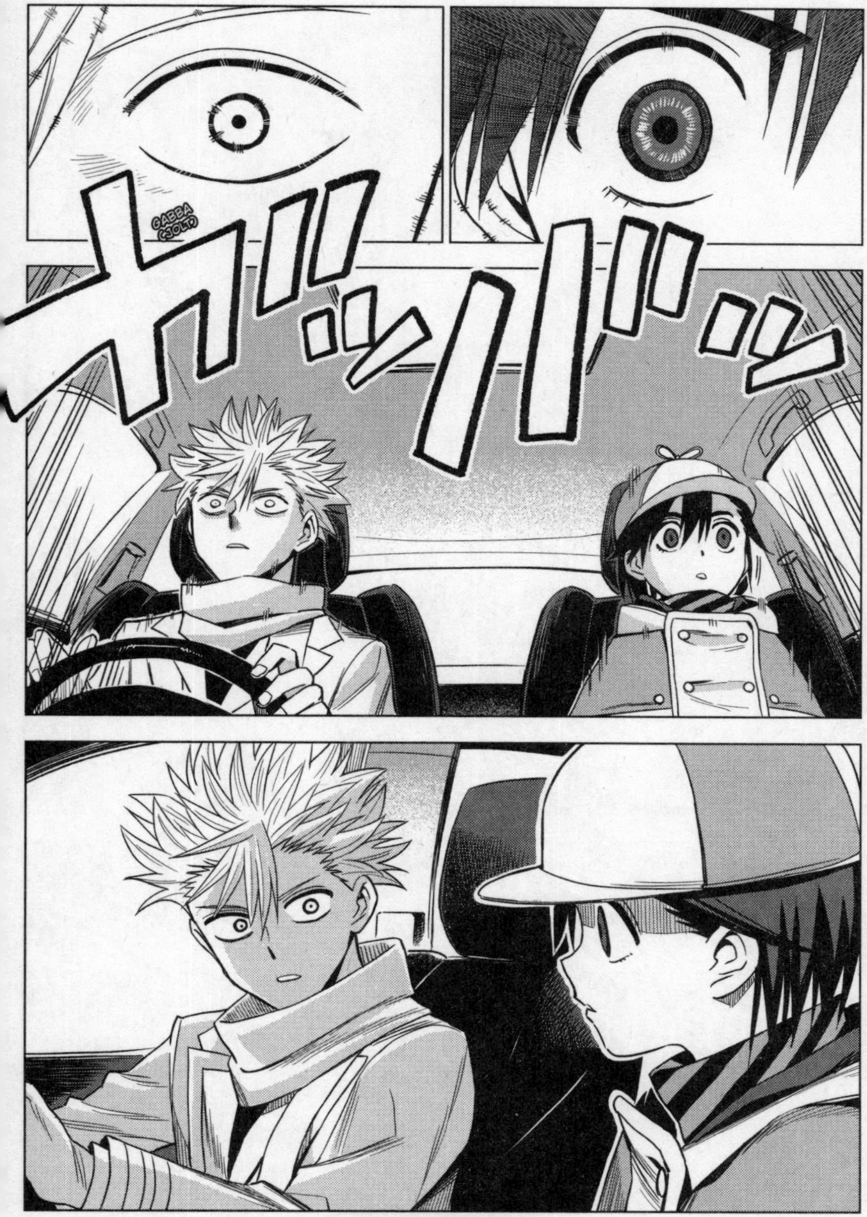
ガバッバッ
GABBA (JOLT)

END

#08 UNKNOWN

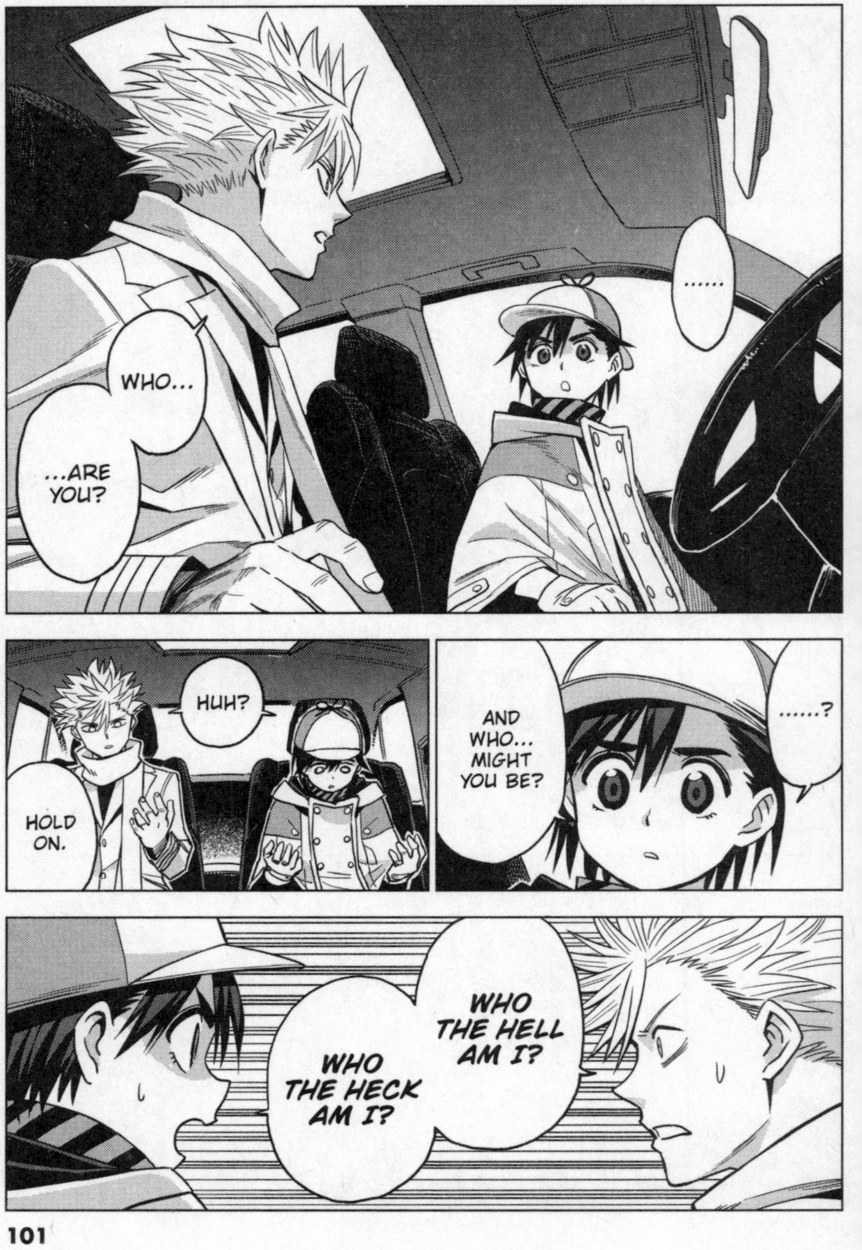
......
WHO...
...ARE YOU?
......?
AND WHO... MIGHT YOU BE?
HUH?
HOLD ON.
WHO THE HELL AM I?
WHO THE HECK AM I?

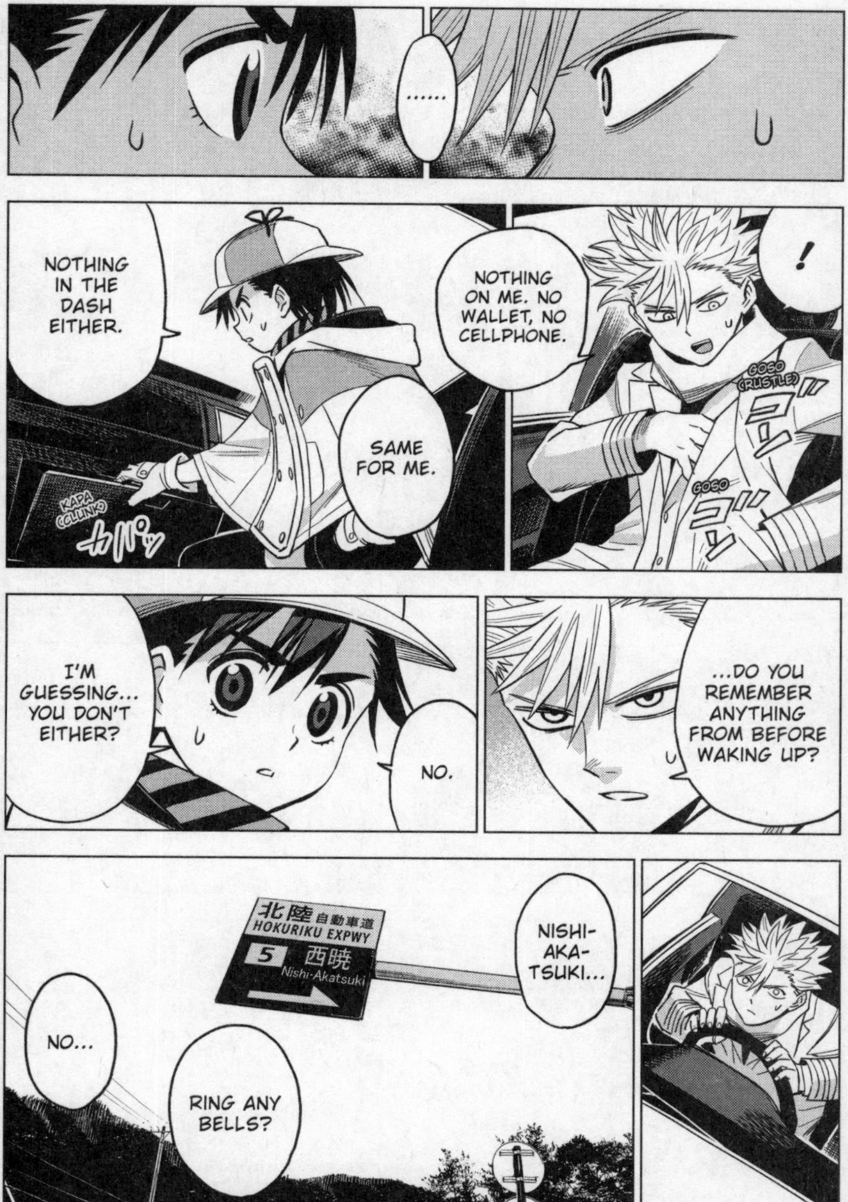
......
!
NOTHING ON ME. NO WALLET, NO CELLPHONE.
GOSO (RUSTLE)
GOSO
SAME FOR ME.
NOTHING IN THE DASH EITHER.
KAPA (CLUNK)
...DO YOU REMEMBER ANYTHING FROM BEFORE WAKING UP?
NO.
I'M GUESSING... YOU DON'T EITHER?
NISHI-AKATSUKI...
北陸自動車道
HOKURIKU EXPWY
5 西暁
Nishi-Akatsuki
RING ANY BELLS?
NO...

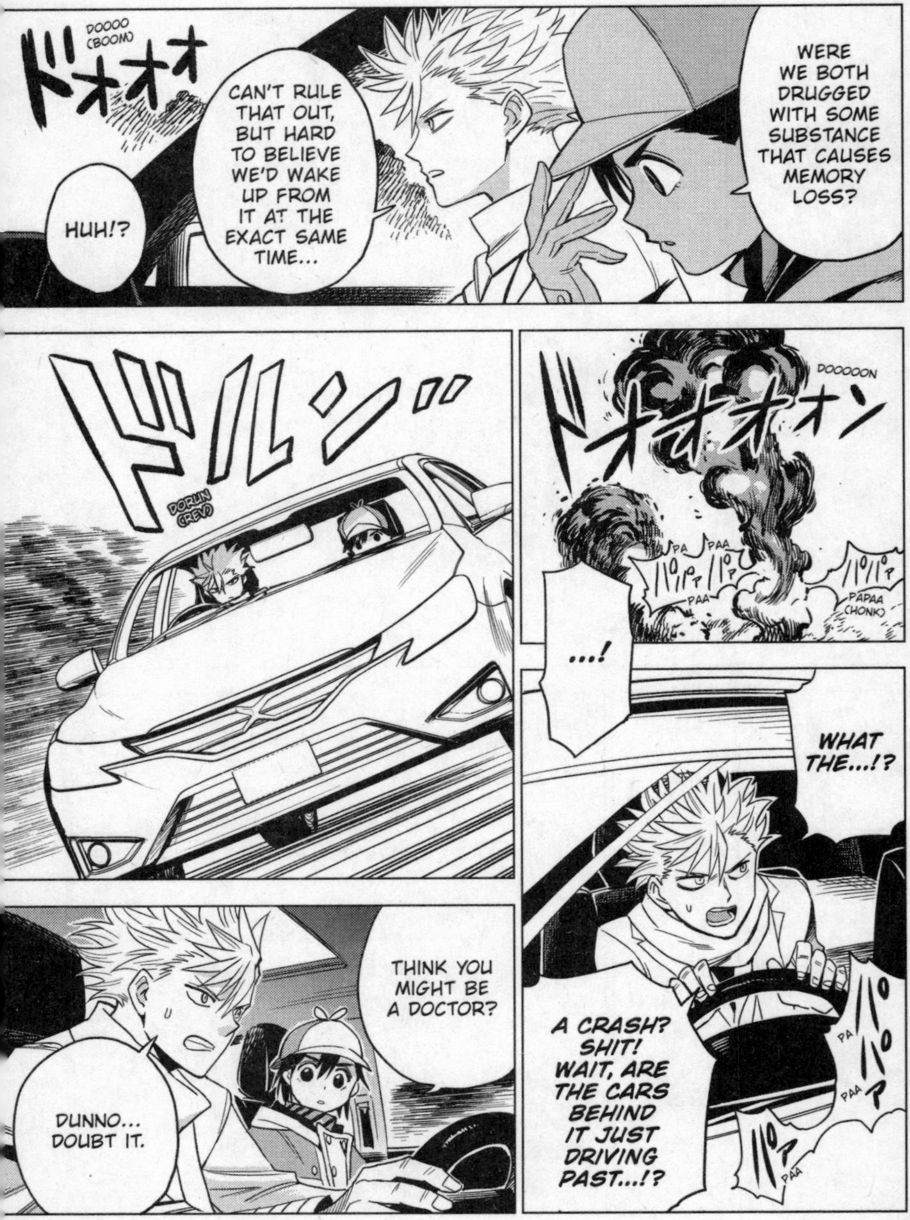
WERE WE BOTH DRUGGED WITH SOME SUBSTANCE THAT CAUSES MEMORY LOSS?
CAN'T RULE THAT OUT, BUT HARD TO BELIEVE WE'D WAKE UP FROM IT AT THE EXACT SAME TIME...
ドオオ
DOOOO (BOOM)
HUH!?
ドオオオオン
DOOOOON
PA
PAA
PAA
PAPAA (HONK)
ドルンッ
DORUN (REV)
...!
WHAT THE...!?
A CRASH? SHIT! WAIT, ARE THE CARS BEHIND IT JUST DRIVING PAST...!?
PA
PAA
PAA
THINK YOU MIGHT BE A DOCTOR?
DUNNO... DOUBT IT.

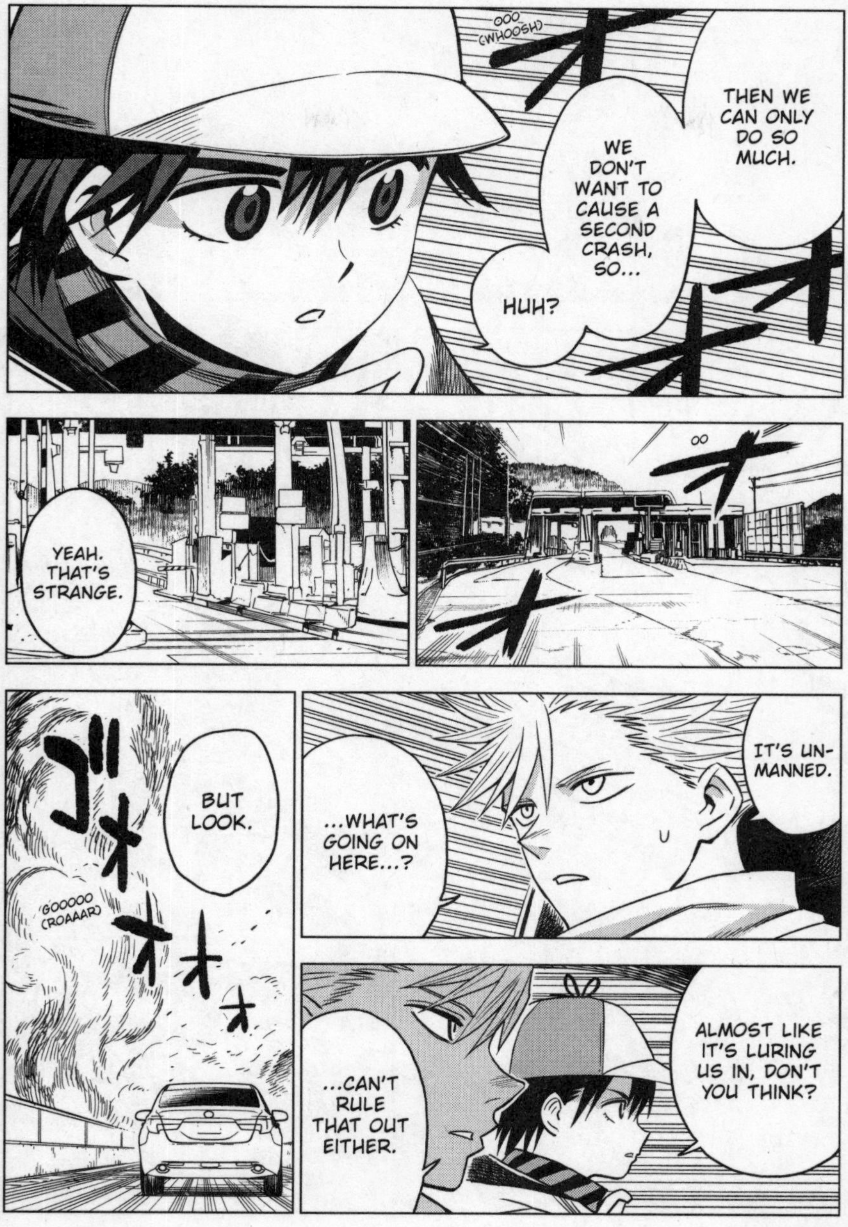
OOO (WHOOSH)
THEN WE CAN ONLY DO SO MUCH.
WE DON'T WANT TO CAUSE A SECOND CRASH, SO...
HUH?
OO
YEAH. THAT'S STRANGE.
IT'S UN-MANNED.
...WHAT'S GOING ON HERE...?
ALMOST LIKE IT'S LURING US IN, DON'T YOU THINK?
...CAN'T RULE THAT OUT EITHER.
BUT LOOK.
GOOOOO (ROAAAR)

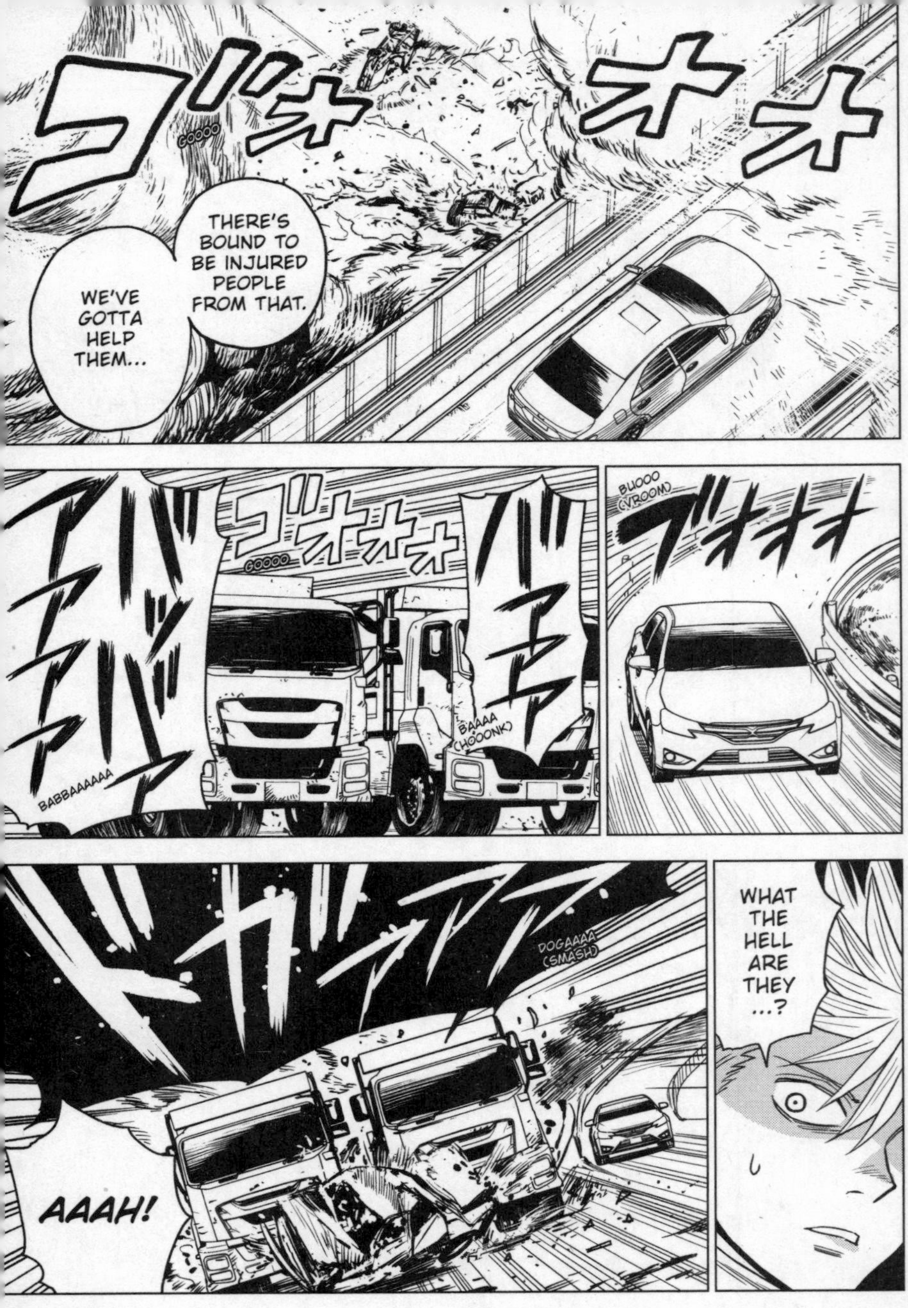
GOOOO
THERE'S BOUND TO BE INJURED PEOPLE FROM THAT.
WE'VE GOTTA HELP THEM...
BUOOO (VROOM)
GOOOO
BAAAA (HOOONK)
BABBAAAAAA
WHAT THE HELL ARE THEY ...?
DOGAAAA (SMASH)
AAAH!

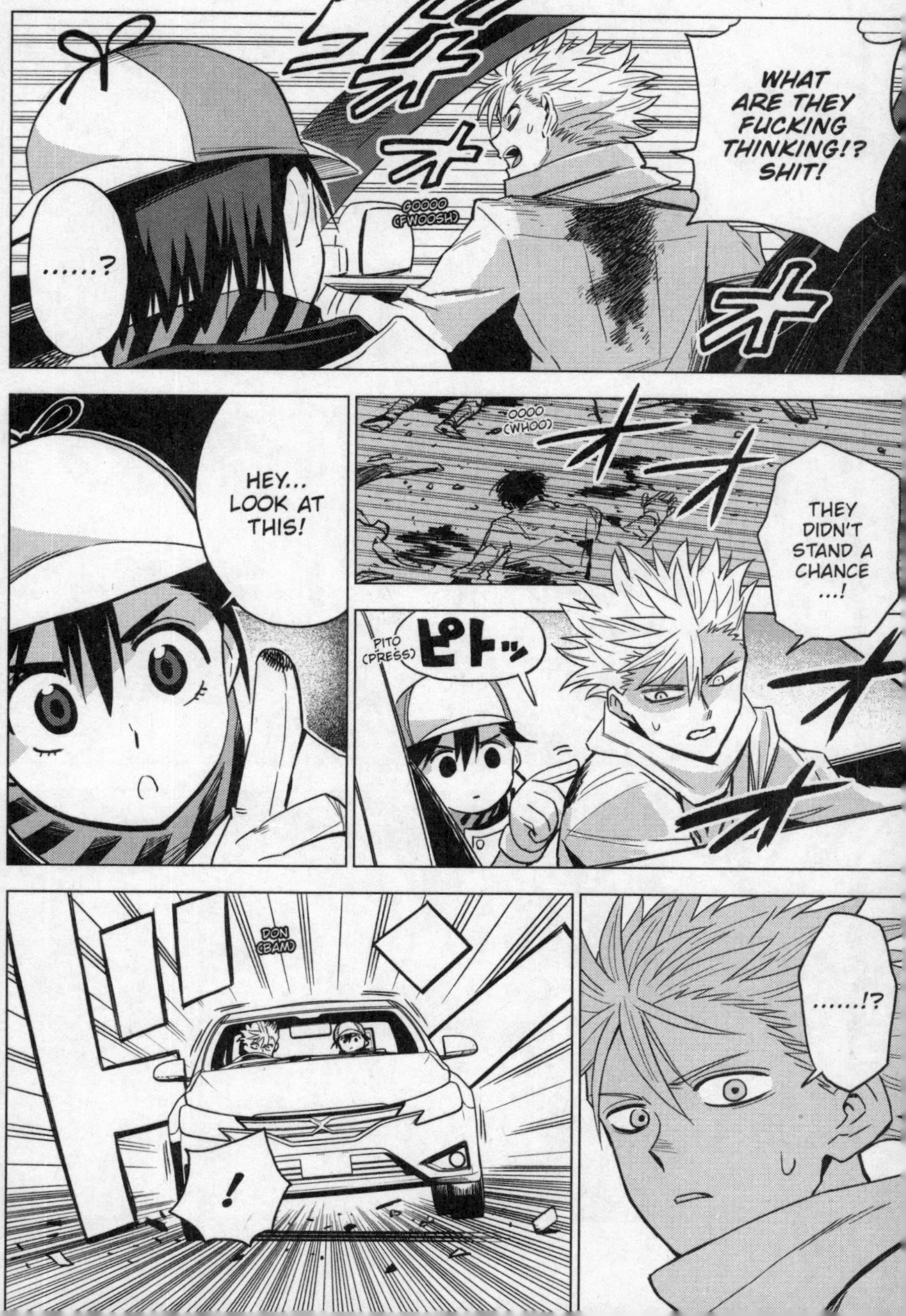
WHAT ARE THEY FUCKING THINKING!? SHIT!
GOOOO (FWOOSH)
......?
OOOO (WHOO)
THEY DIDN'T STAND A CHANCE ...!
PITO (PRESS)
HEY... LOOK AT THIS!
......!?
DON (BAM)
!

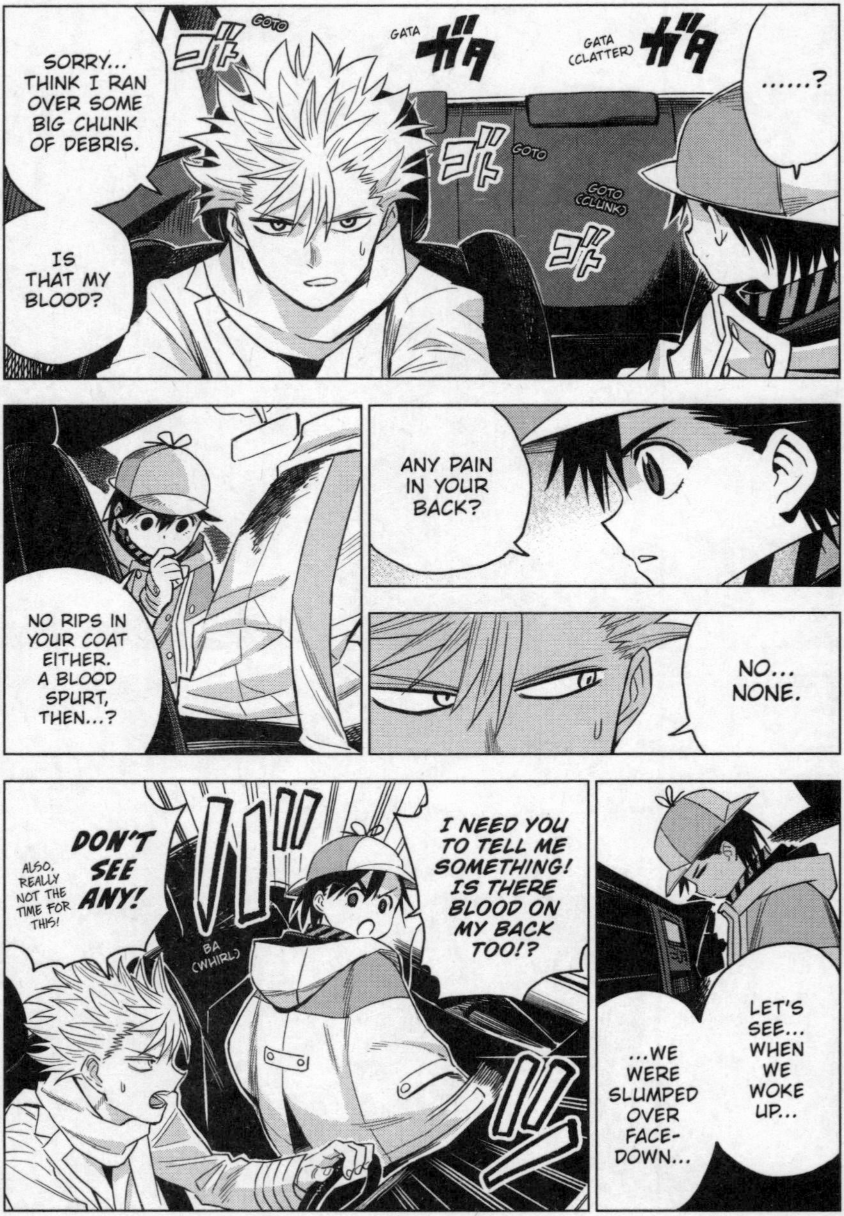
......?
GATA (CLATTER)
GATA
GOTO
SORRY... THINK I RAN OVER SOME BIG CHUNK OF DEBRIS.
GOTO
GOTO (CLUNK)
IS THAT MY BLOOD?
ANY PAIN IN YOUR BACK?
NO... NONE.
NO RIPS IN YOUR COAT EITHER. A BLOOD SPURT, THEN...?
LET'S SEE... WHEN WE WOKE UP...
...WE WERE SLUMPED OVER FACE-DOWN...
I NEED YOU TO TELL ME SOMETHING! IS THERE BLOOD ON MY BACK TOO!?
BA (WHIRL)
DON'T SEE ANY!
ALSO, REALLY NOT THE TIME FOR THIS!

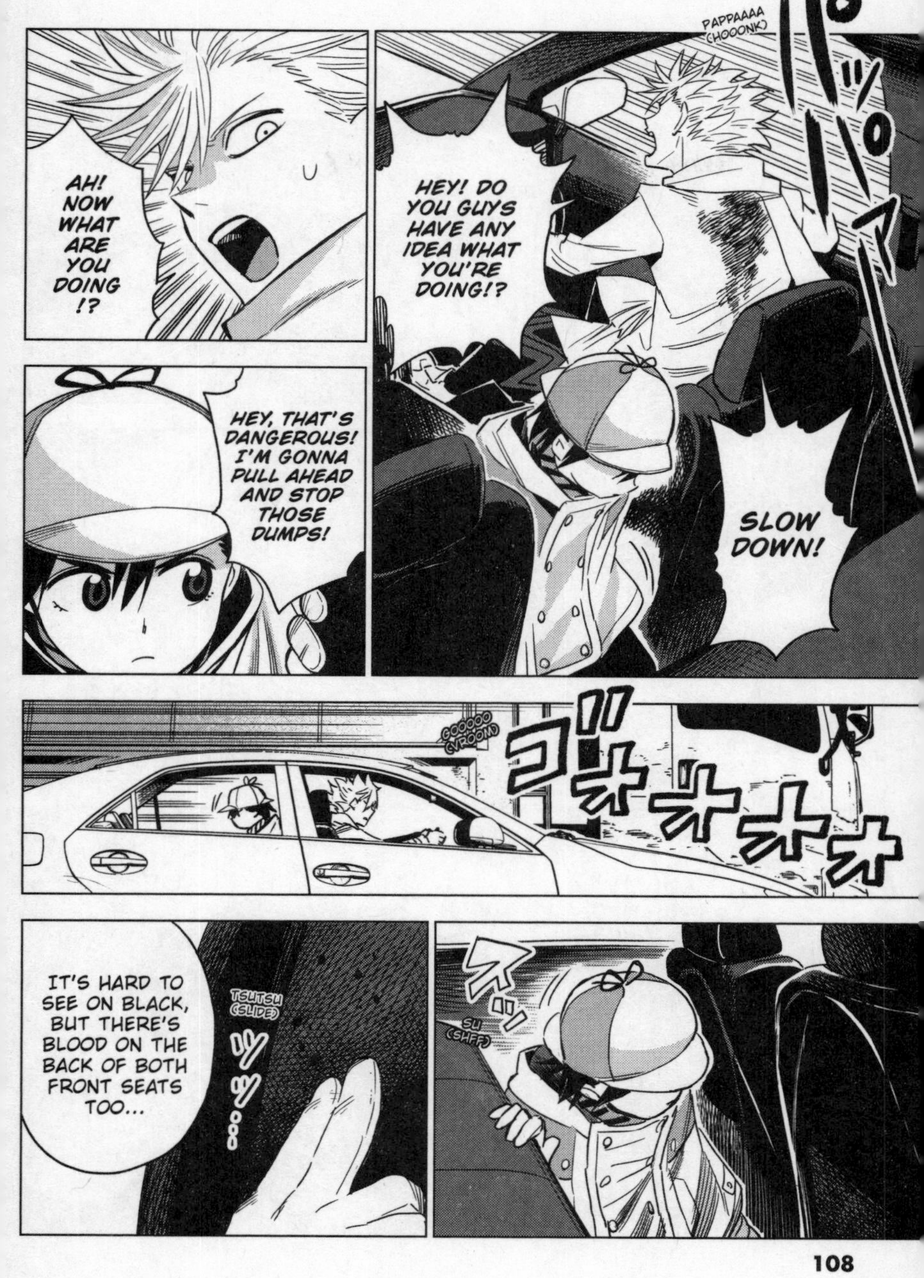
PAPPAAAA (HOOOONK)
HEY! DO YOU GUYS HAVE ANY IDEA WHAT YOU'RE DOING!?
SLOW DOWN!
AH! NOW WHAT ARE YOU DOING!?
HEY, THAT'S DANGEROUS! I'M GONNA PULL AHEAD AND STOP THOSE DUMPS!
GOOOOO (VROOM)
SU (SHFF)
TSUTSU (SLIDE)
IT'S HARD TO SEE ON BLACK, BUT THERE'S BLOOD ON THE BACK OF BOTH FRONT SEATS TOO...

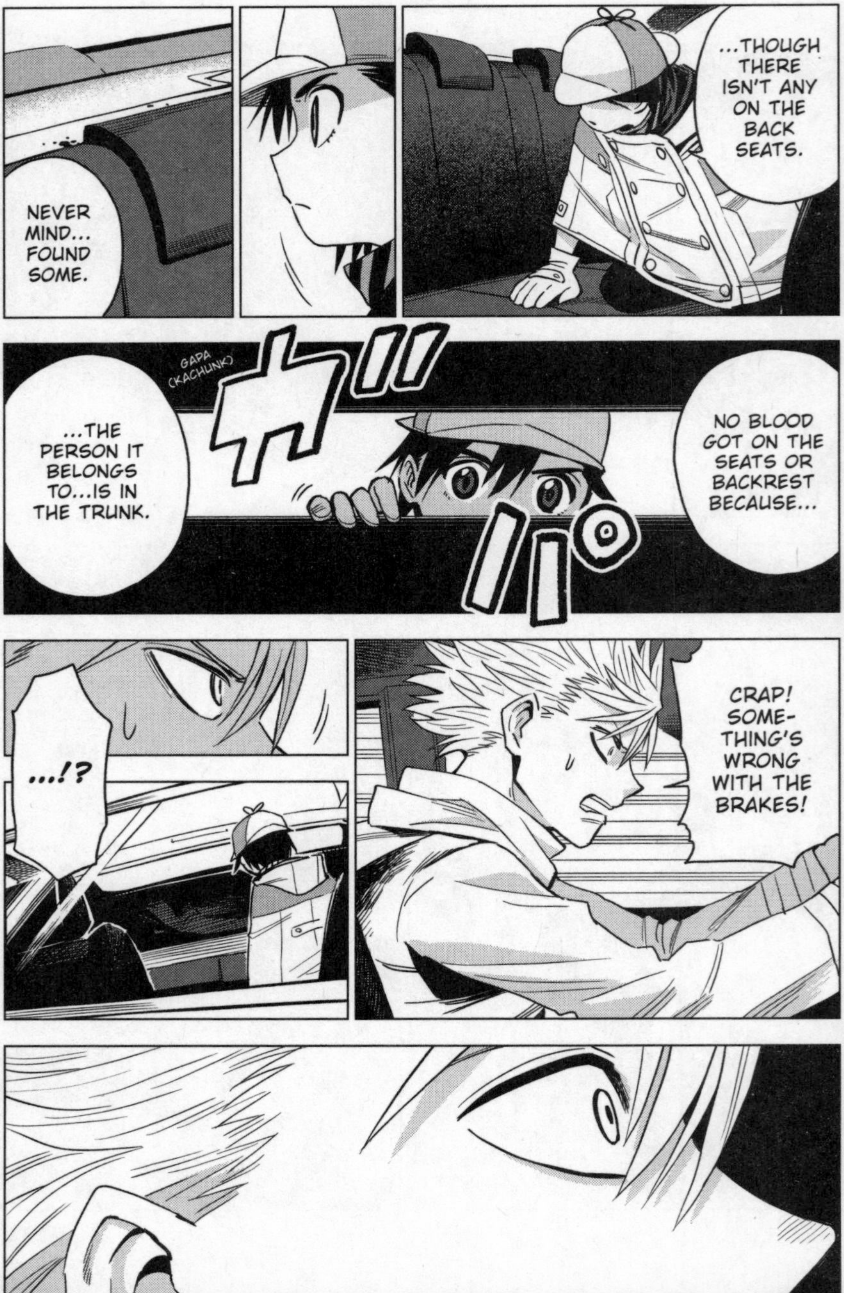
...THOUGH THERE ISN'T ANY ON THE BACK SEATS.
NEVER MIND... FOUND SOME.
NO BLOOD GOT ON THE SEATS OR BACKREST BECAUSE...
GAPA (KACHUNK)
...THE PERSON IT BELONGS TO...IS IN THE TRUNK.
CRAP! SOME-THING'S WRONG WITH THE BRAKES!
...!?

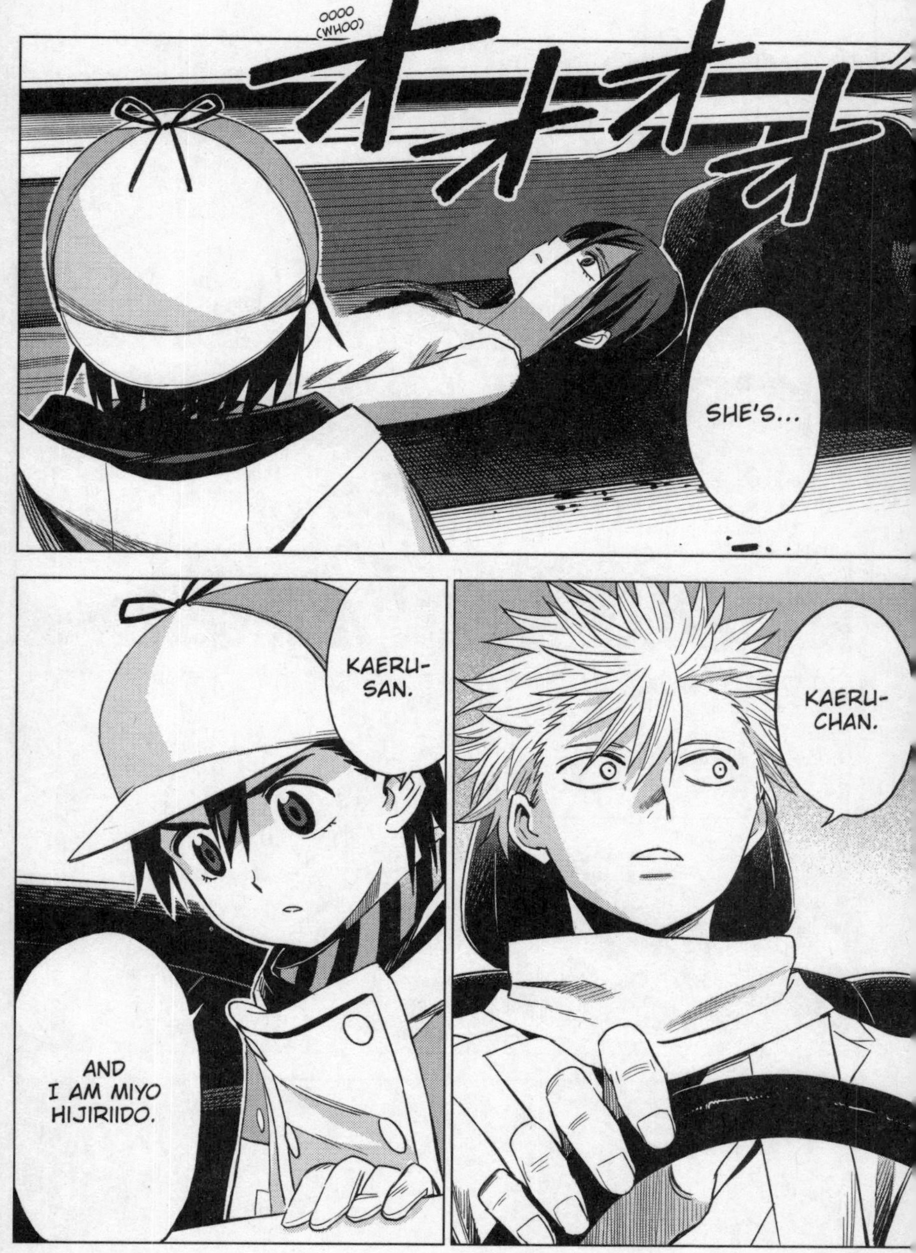
OOOO (WHOO)
オオオオ
SHE'S...
KAERU-CHAN.
KAERU-SAN.
AND I AM MIYO HIJIRIIDO.

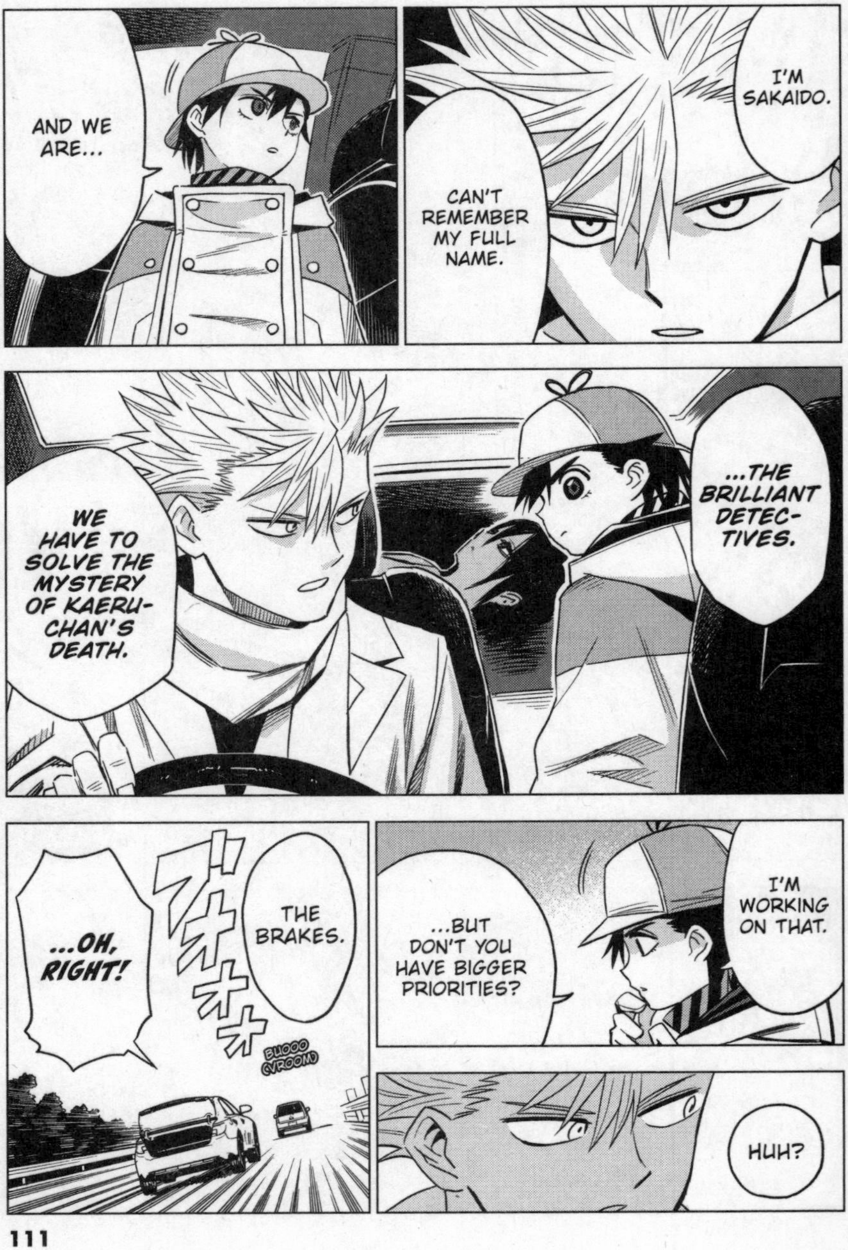
I'M SAKAIDO.
CAN'T REMEMBER MY FULL NAME.
AND WE ARE...
...THE BRILLIANT DETEC-TIVES.
WE HAVE TO SOLVE THE MYSTERY OF KAERU-CHAN'S DEATH.
I'M WORKING ON THAT.
...BUT DON'T YOU HAVE BIGGER PRIORITIES?
HUH?
THE BRAKES.
...OH, RIGHT!
BUOOO (VROOM)

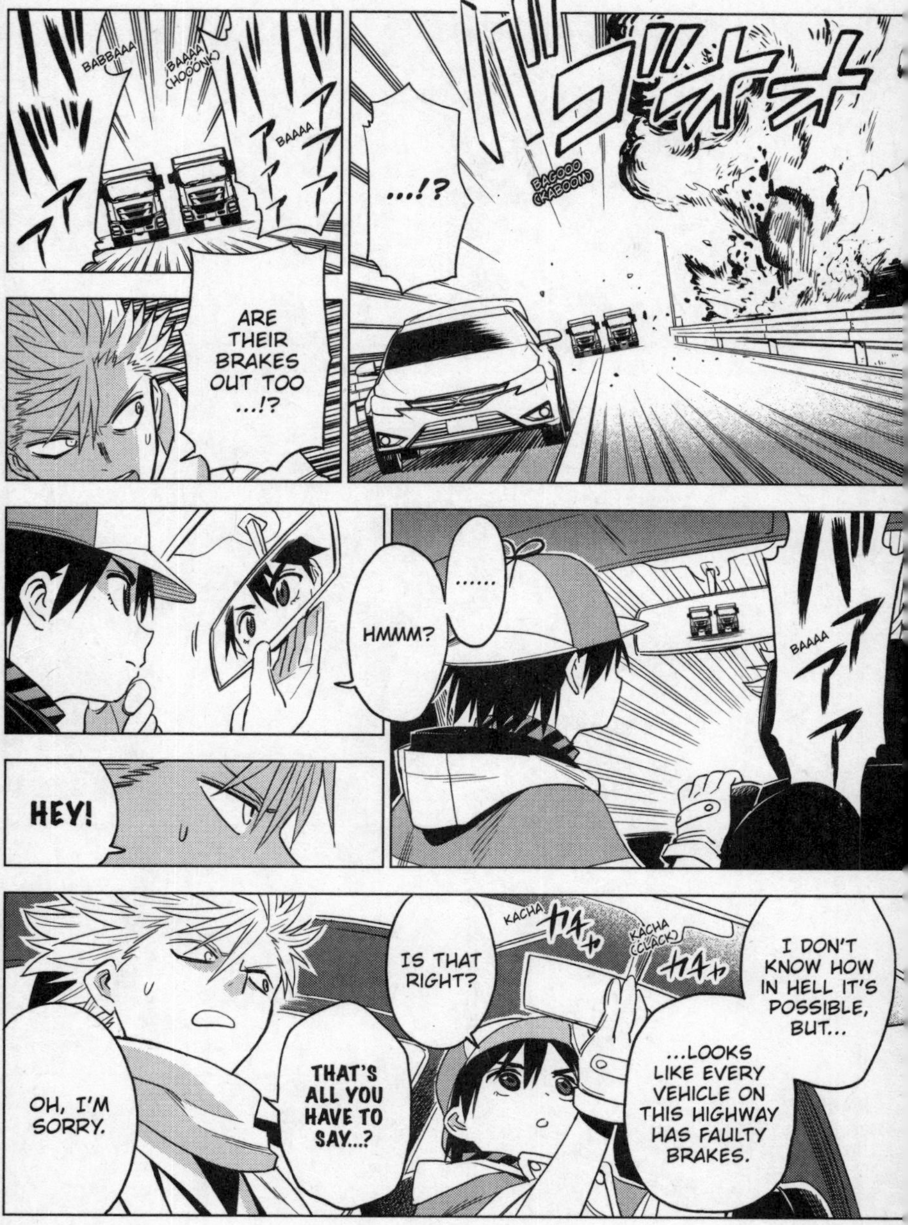
BAGOOO (KABOOM)
...!?
BABBAAA
BAAAA (HOOONK)
BAAAA
ARE THEIR BRAKES OUT TOO ...!?
BAAAA
......
HMMM?
HEY!
I DON'T KNOW HOW IN HELL IT'S POSSIBLE, BUT...
...LOOKS LIKE EVERY VEHICLE ON THIS HIGHWAY HAS FAULTY BRAKES.
KACHA
KACHA (CLACK)
IS THAT RIGHT?
THAT'S ALL YOU HAVE TO SAY...?
OH, I'M SORRY.

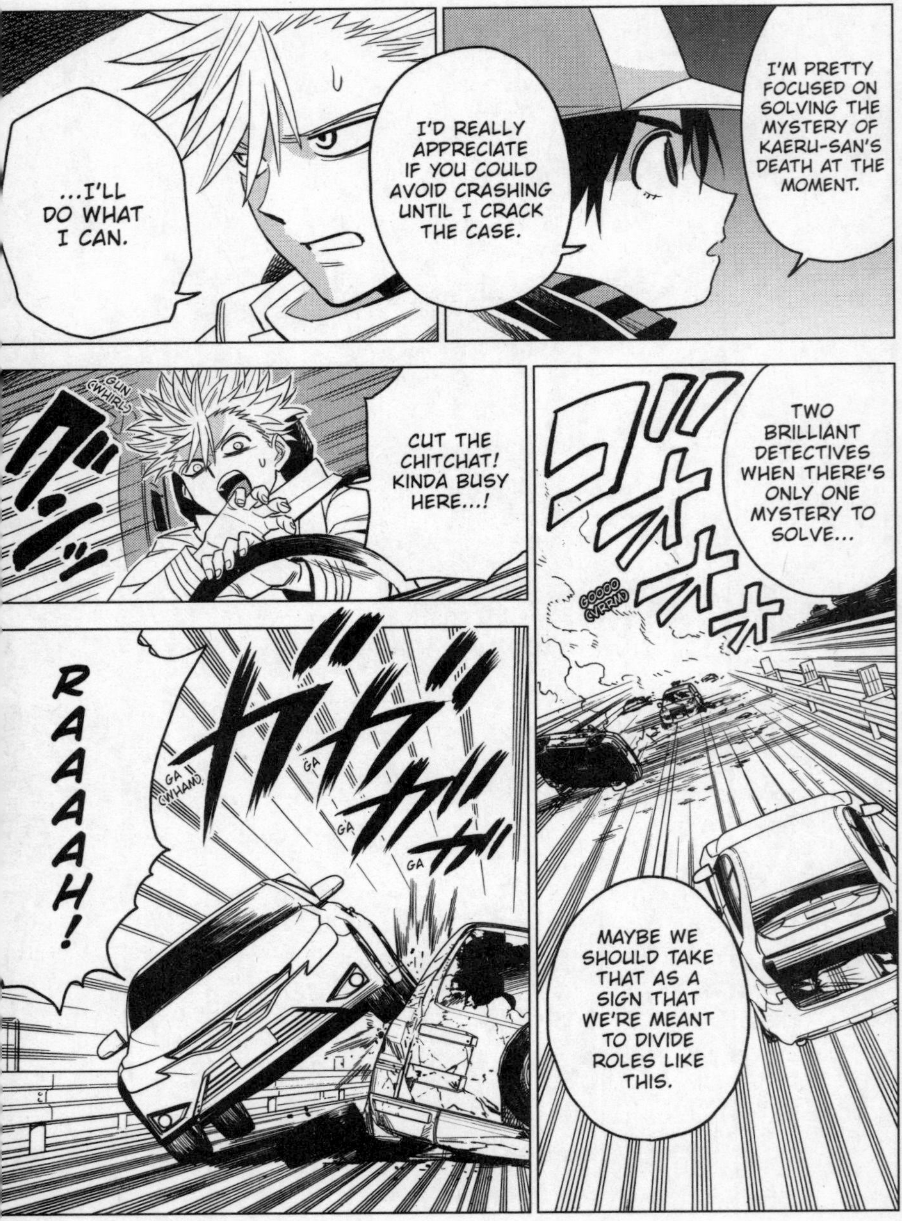
I'M PRETTY FOCUSED ON SOLVING THE MYSTERY OF KAERU-SAN'S DEATH AT THE MOMENT.
I'D REALLY APPRECIATE IF YOU COULD AVOID CRASHING UNTIL I CRACK THE CASE.
...I'LL DO WHAT I CAN.
TWO BRILLIANT DETECTIVES WHEN THERE'S ONLY ONE MYSTERY TO SOLVE...
GOOOO (VRRM)
MAYBE WE SHOULD TAKE THAT AS A SIGN THAT WE'RE MEANT TO DIVIDE ROLES LIKE THIS.
GUN (WHIRL)
CUT THE CHITCHAT! KINDA BUSY HERE...!
RAAAAAH!
GA (WHAM)
GA
GA
GA

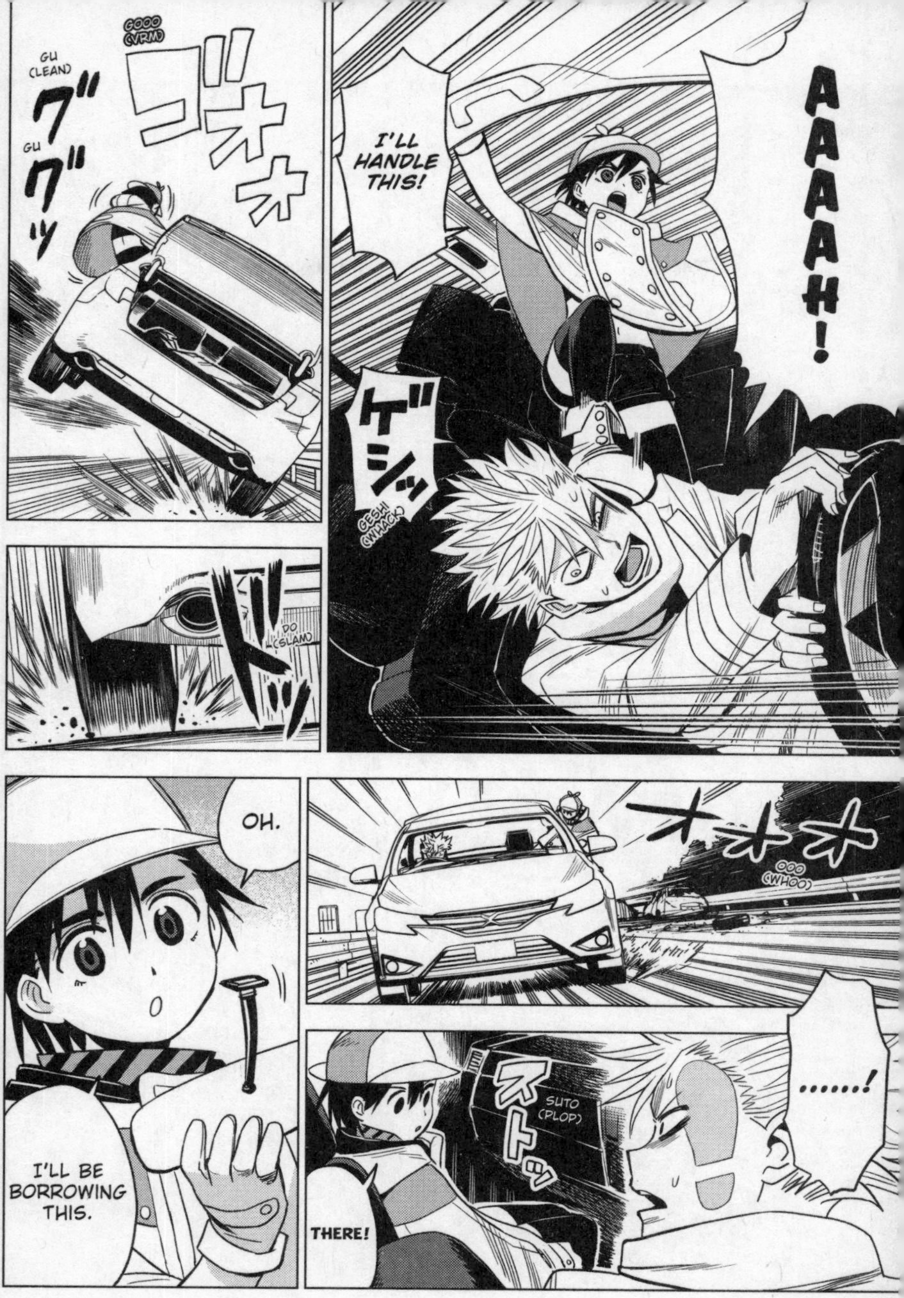
AAAAH!
I'LL HANDLE THIS!
ゲシッ
GESH! (WHACK)
ゴオォ
GOOO (VRM)
グ
GU (LEAN)
グッ
GU
DO (SLAM)
オォォ
OOO (WHOO)
......!
ストッ
SUTO (PLOP)
THERE!
OH.
I'LL BE BORROWING THIS.

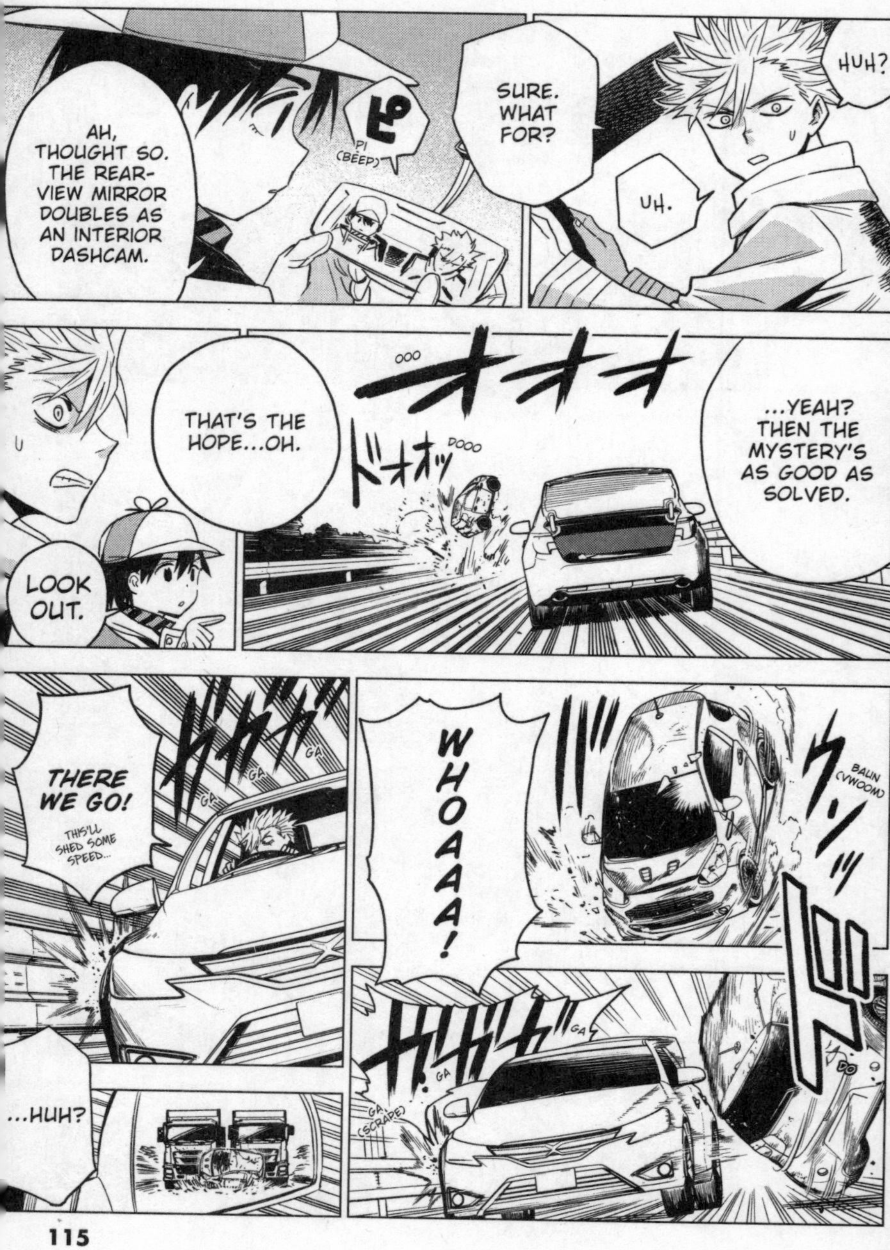
HUH?
UH.
SURE. WHAT FOR?
PI (BEEP)
AH, THOUGHT SO. THE REAR-VIEW MIRROR DOUBLES AS AN INTERIOR DASHCAM.
...YEAH? THEN THE MYSTERY'S AS GOOD AS SOLVED.
OOO
DOOO
THAT'S THE HOPE...OH.
LOOK OUT.
WHOAAAA!
BALIN (VWOOM)
DO
GA
GA
GA (SCRAPE)
GA
GA
GA
THERE WE GO!
THIS'LL SHED SOME SPEED...
...HUH?

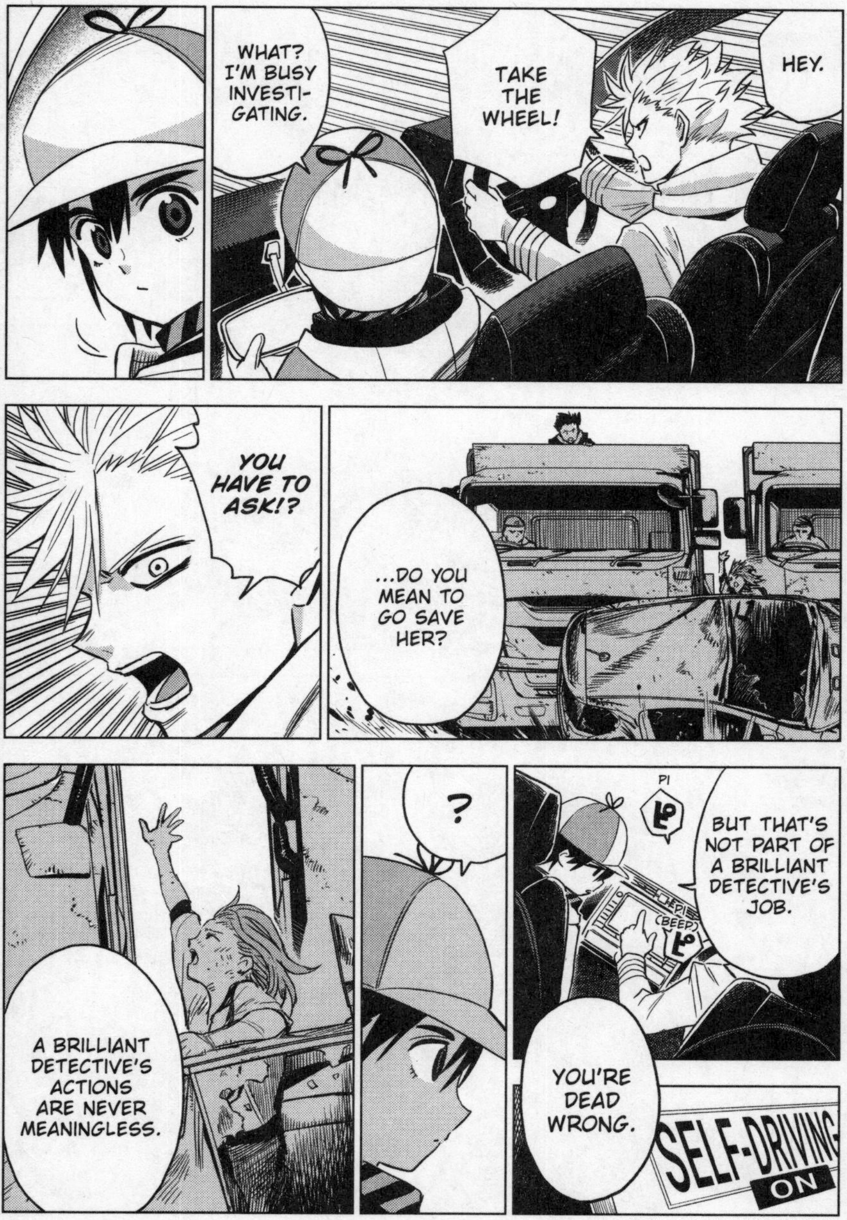
HEY.
TAKE THE WHEEL!
WHAT? I'M BUSY INVESTI-GATING.
...DO YOU MEAN TO GO SAVE HER?
YOU HAVE TO ASK!?
PI
BUT THAT'S NOT PART OF A BRILLIANT DETECTIVE'S JOB.
PI (BEEP)
SELF-DRIVING ON
?
YOU'RE DEAD WRONG.
A BRILLIANT DETECTIVE'S ACTIONS ARE NEVER MEANINGLESS.

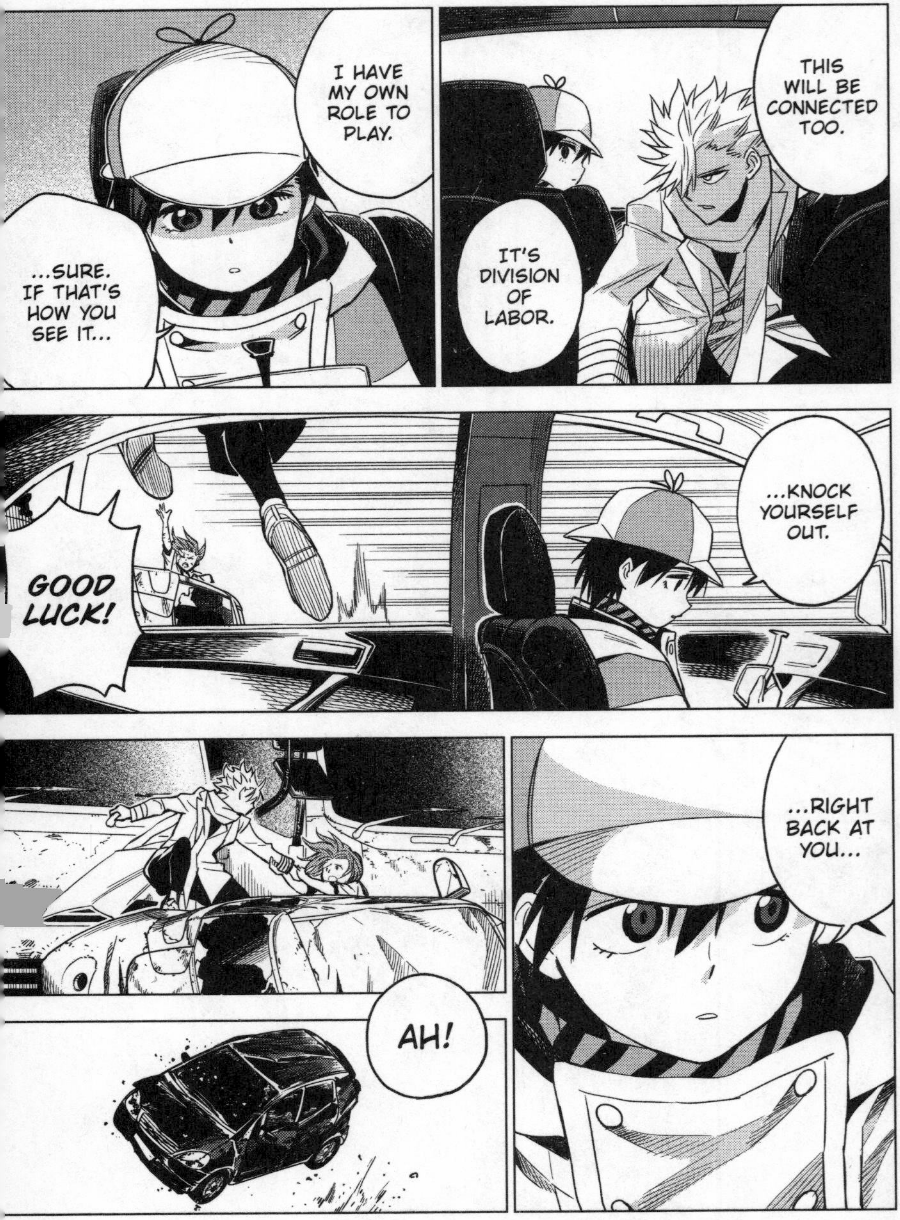
THIS WILL BE CONNECTED TOO.
IT'S DIVISION OF LABOR.
I HAVE MY OWN ROLE TO PLAY.
...SURE. IF THAT'S HOW YOU SEE IT...
...KNOCK YOURSELF OUT.
GOOD LUCK!
...RIGHT BACK AT YOU...
AH!

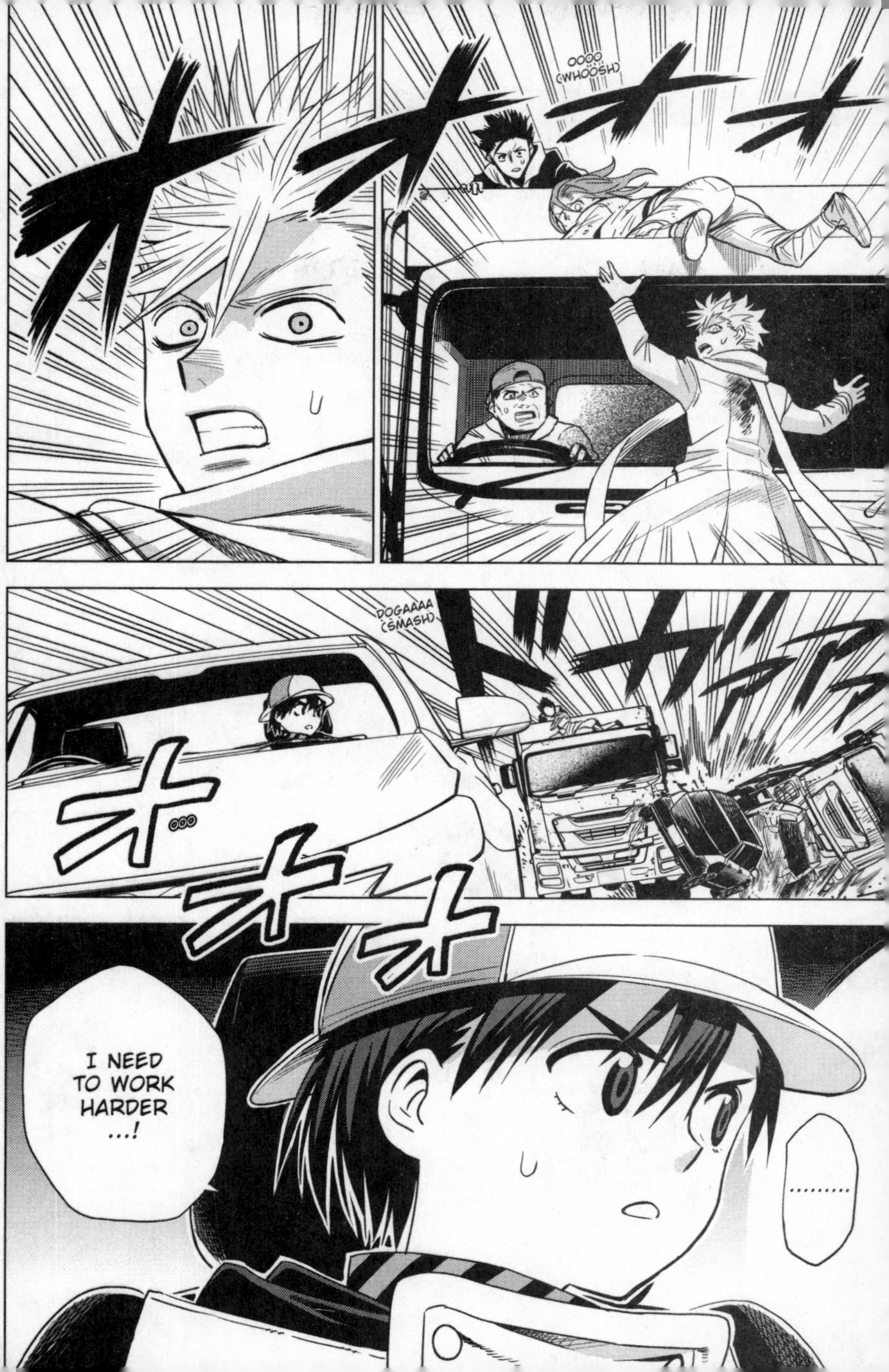

OOOO (WHOOSH)
DOGAAAA (SMASH)
I NEED TO WORK HARDER ...!
....

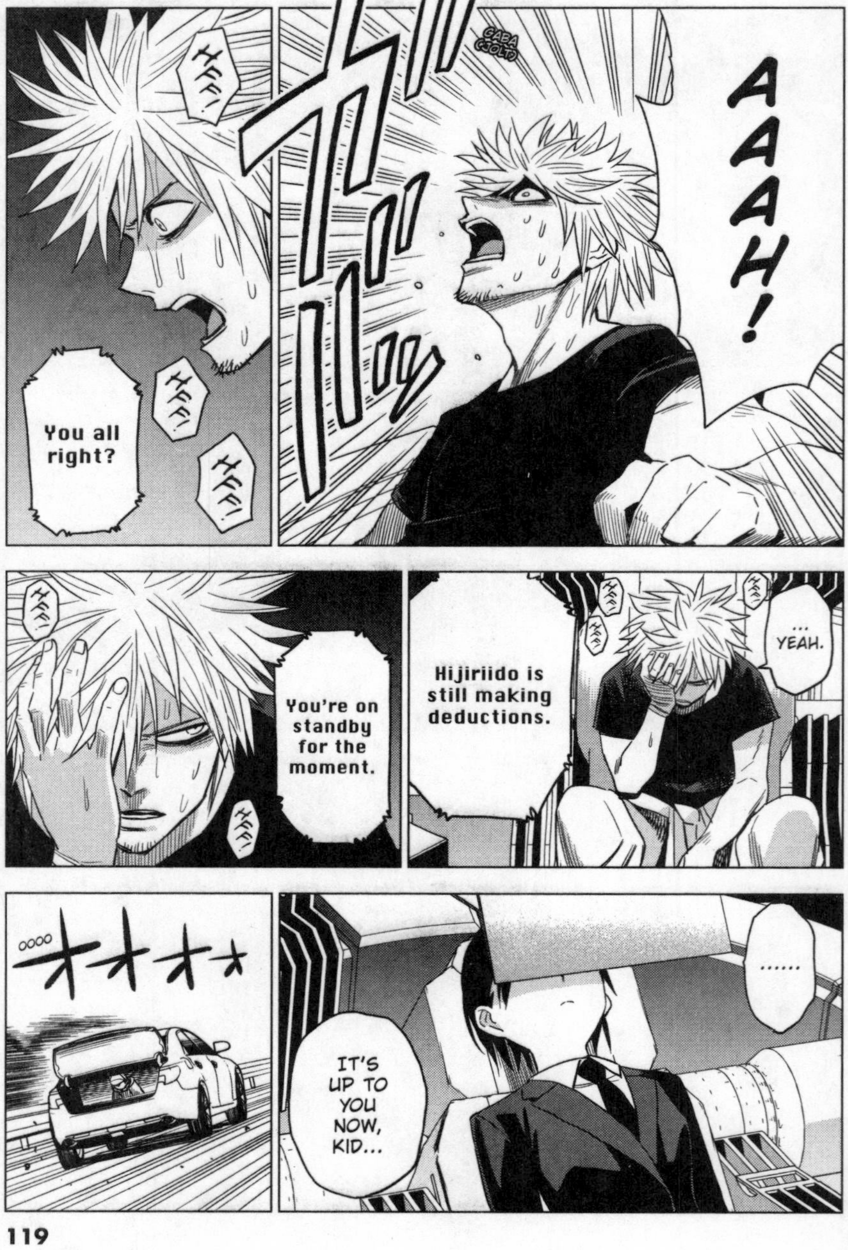
AAAH!
GABA (JOLT)
You all right?
...YEAH.
Hijiriido is still making deductions.
You're on standby for the moment.
......
IT'S UP TO YOU NOW, KID...
OOOO

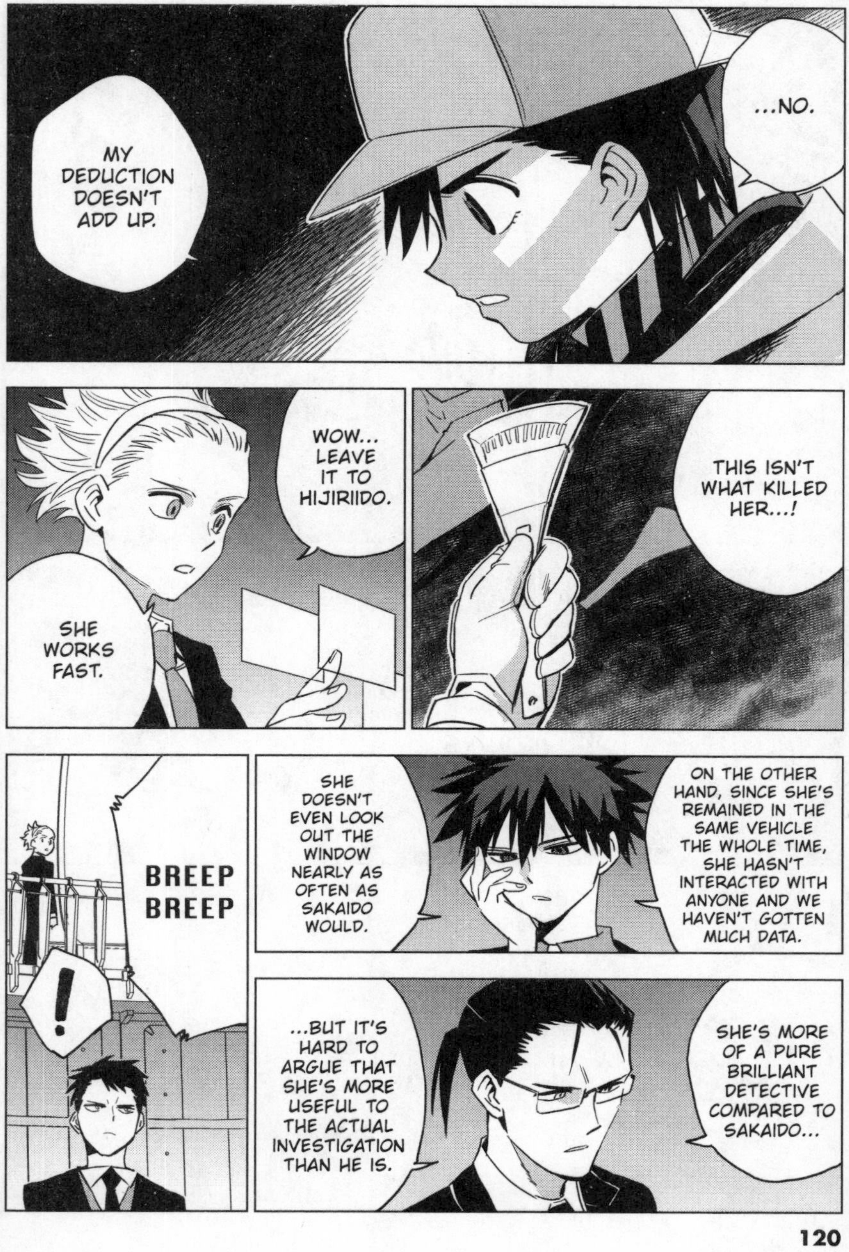
...NO.
MY DEDUCTION DOESN'T ADD UP.
THIS ISN'T WHAT KILLED HER...!
WOW... LEAVE IT TO HIJIRIIDO.
SHE WORKS FAST.
ON THE OTHER HAND, SINCE SHE'S REMAINED IN THE SAME VEHICLE THE WHOLE TIME, SHE HASN'T INTERACTED WITH ANYONE AND WE HAVEN'T GOTTEN MUCH DATA.
SHE DOESN'T EVEN LOOK OUT THE WINDOW NEARLY AS OFTEN AS SAKAIDO WOULD.
SHE'S MORE OF A PURE BRILLIANT DETECTIVE COMPARED TO SAKAIDO...
...BUT IT'S HARD TO ARGUE THAT SHE'S MORE USEFUL TO THE ACTUAL INVESTIGATION THAN HE IS.
BREEP BREEP
!

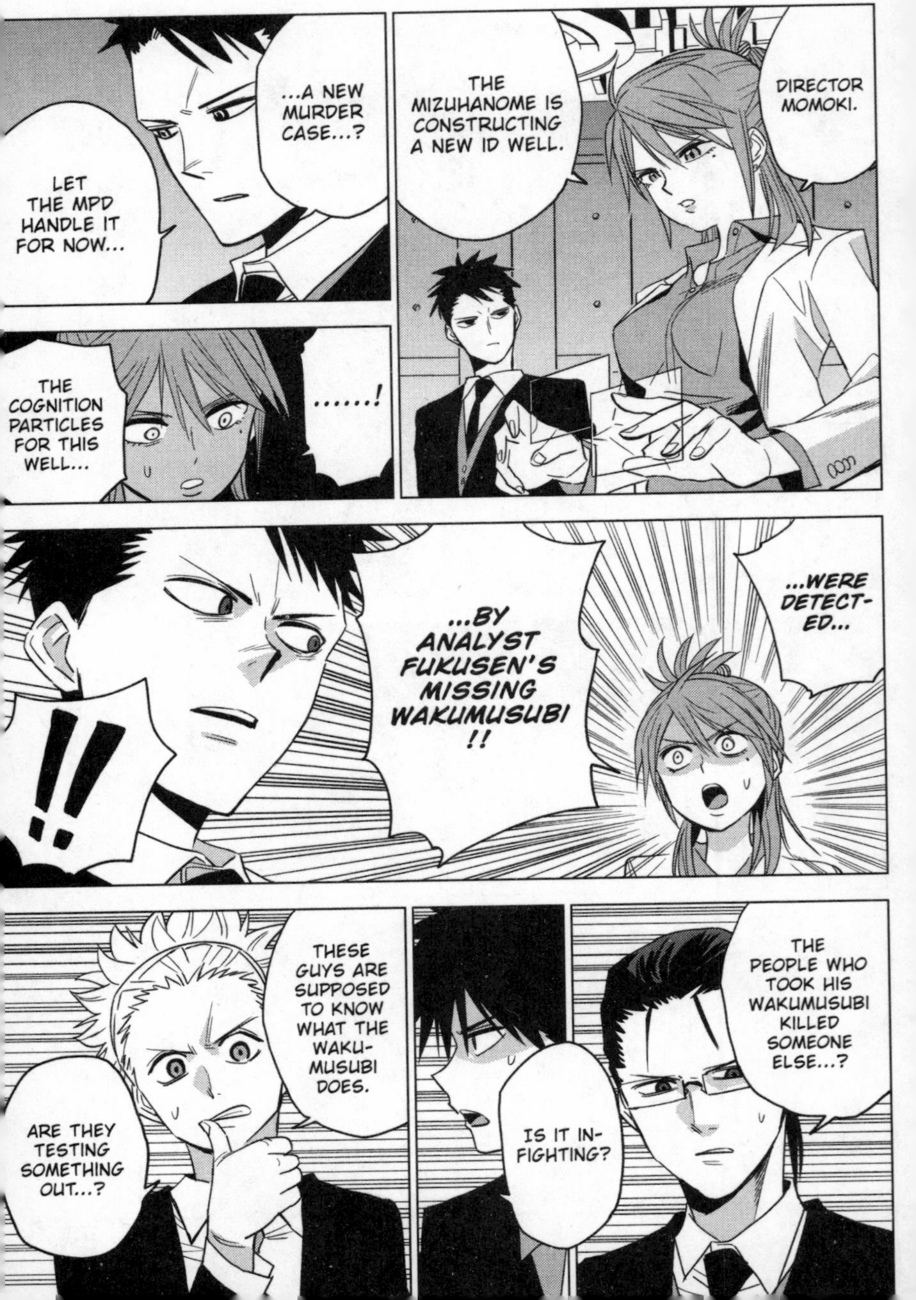
DIRECTOR MOMOKI.
THE MIZUHANOME IS CONSTRUCTING A NEW ID WELL.
...A NEW MURDER CASE...?
LET THE MPD HANDLE IT FOR NOW...
......!
THE COGNITION PARTICLES FOR THIS WELL...
...WERE DETECTED...
...BY ANALYST FUKUSEN'S MISSING WAKUMUSUBI !!
!!
THE PEOPLE WHO TOOK HIS WAKUMUSUBI KILLED SOMEONE ELSE...?
IS IT IN-FIGHTING?
THESE GUYS ARE SUPPOSED TO KNOW WHAT THE WAKU-MUSUBI DOES.
ARE THEY TESTING SOMETHING OUT...?

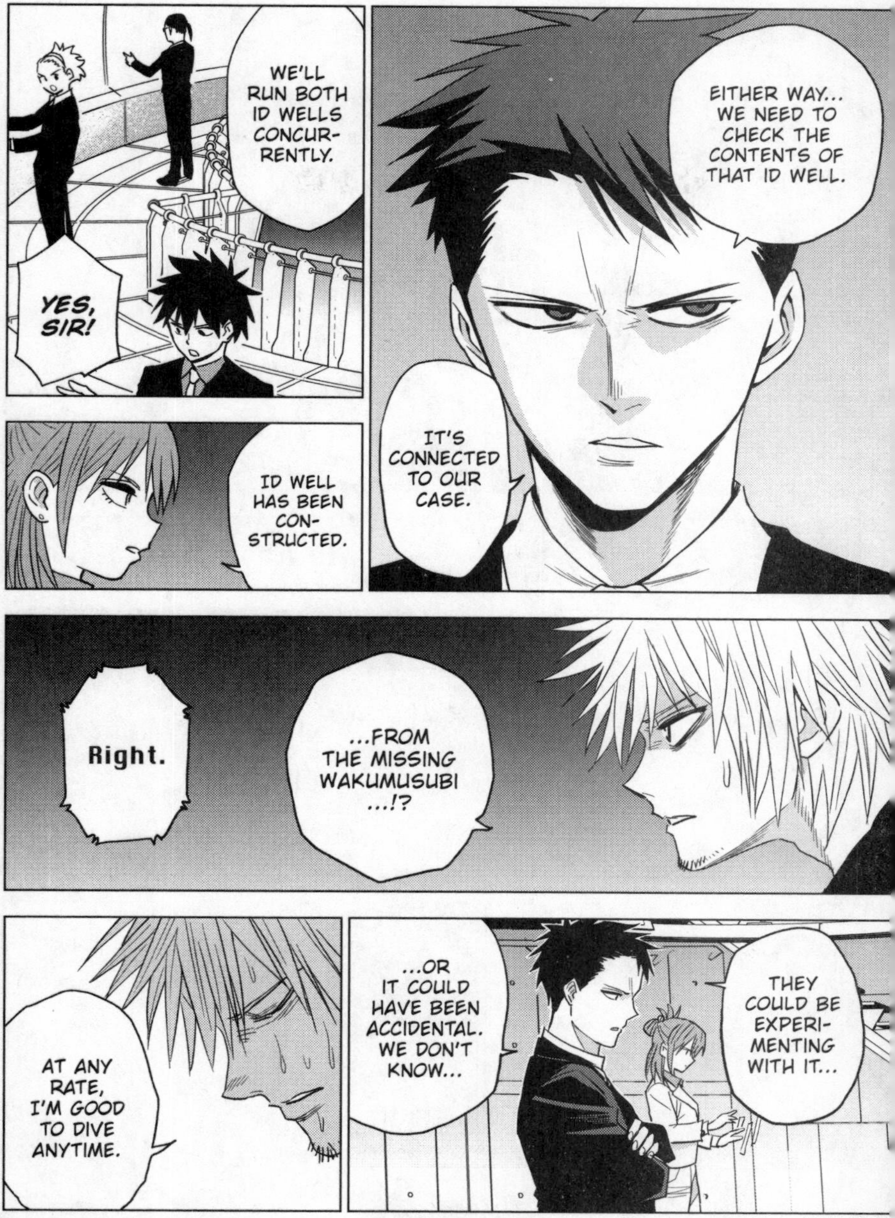
EITHER WAY... WE NEED TO CHECK THE CONTENTS OF THAT ID WELL.
IT'S CONNECTED TO OUR CASE.
WE'LL RUN BOTH ID WELLS CONCUR-RENTLY.
YES, SIR!
ID WELL HAS BEEN CON-STRUCTED.
...FROM THE MISSING WAKUMUSUBI ...!?
Right.
THEY COULD BE EXPERI-MENTING WITH IT...
...OR IT COULD HAVE BEEN ACCIDENTAL. WE DON'T KNOW...
AT ANY RATE, I'M GOOD TO DIVE ANYTIME.

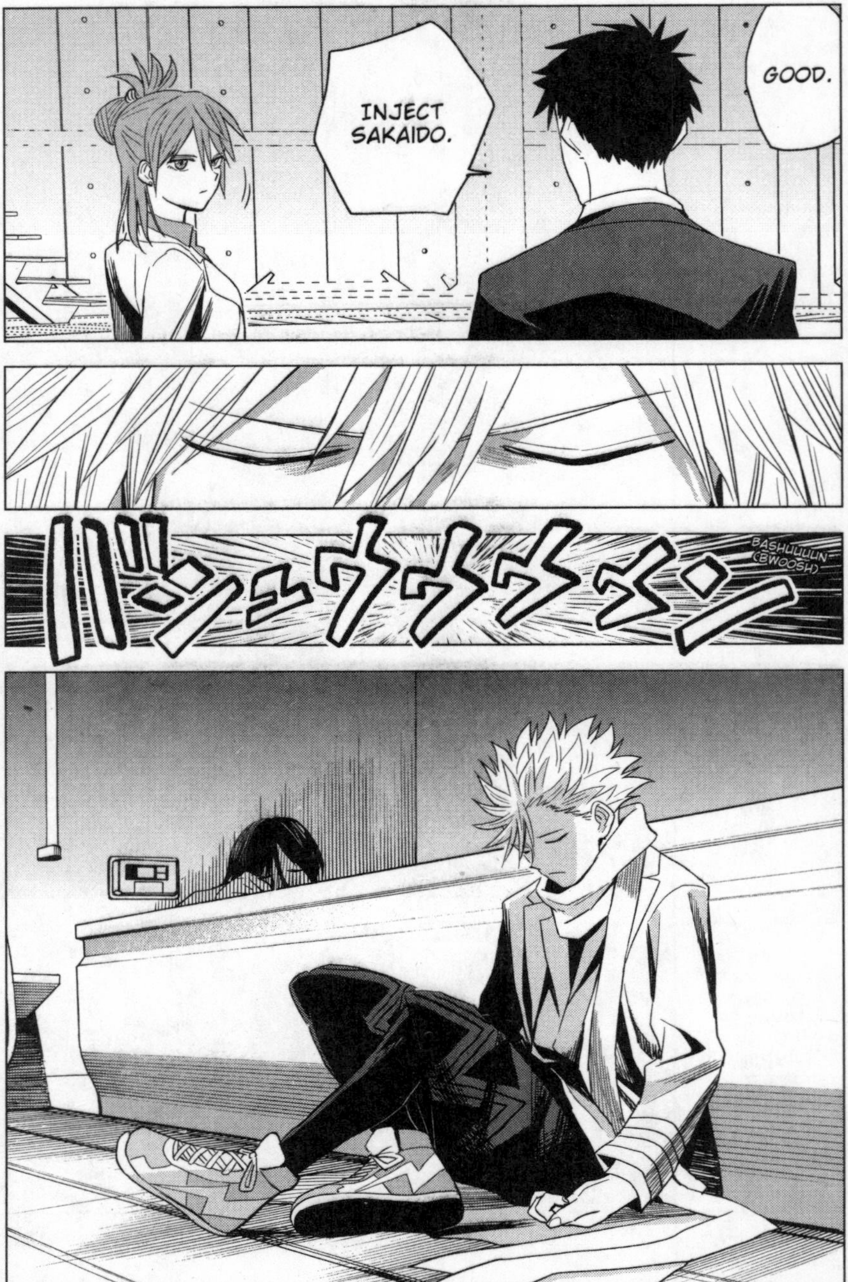
GOOD.
INJECT SAKAIDO.
バシュウウウゥン
BASHUUUUUN (BWOOSH)

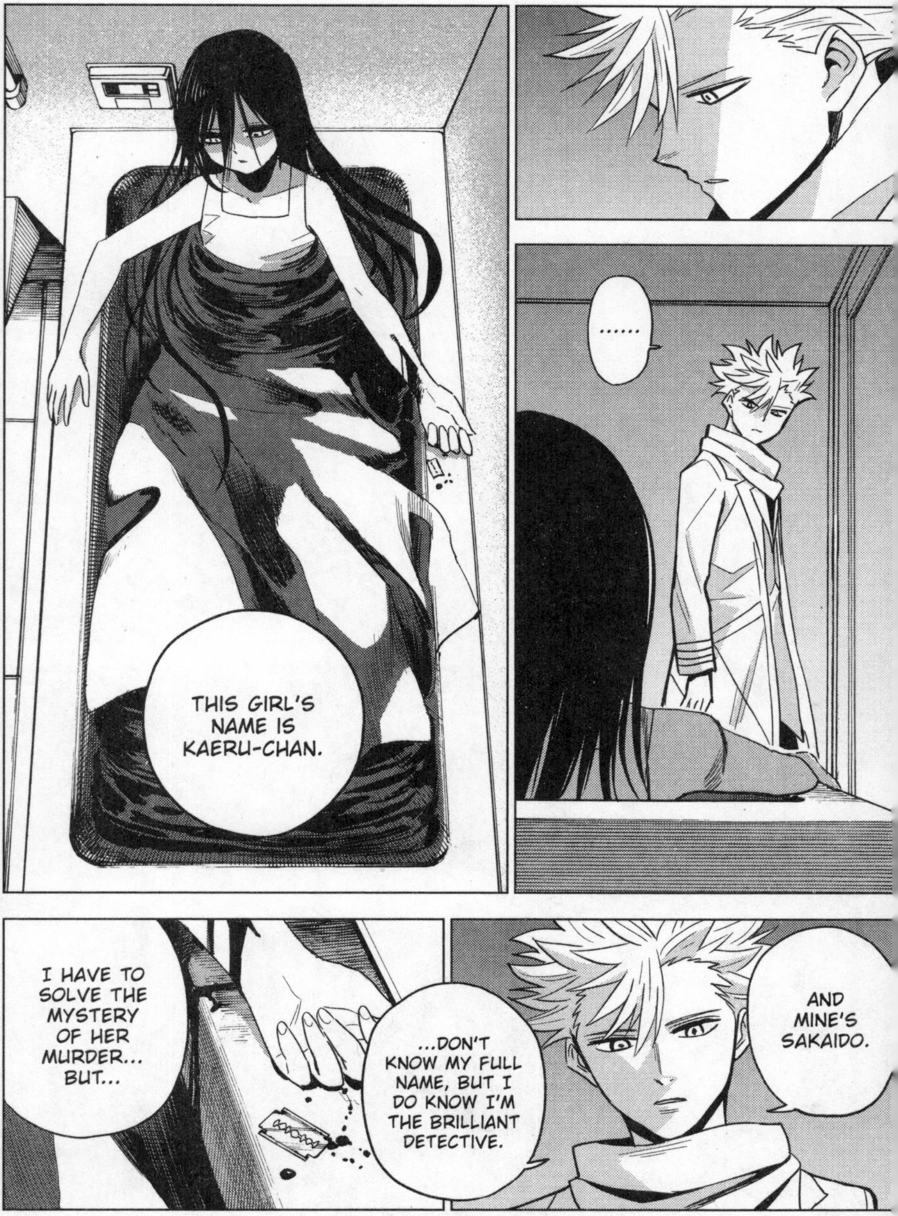
......
THIS GIRL'S NAME IS KAERU-CHAN.
AND MINE'S SAKAIDO.
...DON'T KNOW MY FULL NAME, BUT I DO KNOW I'M THE BRILLIANT DETECTIVE.
I HAVE TO SOLVE THE MYSTERY OF HER MURDER... BUT...

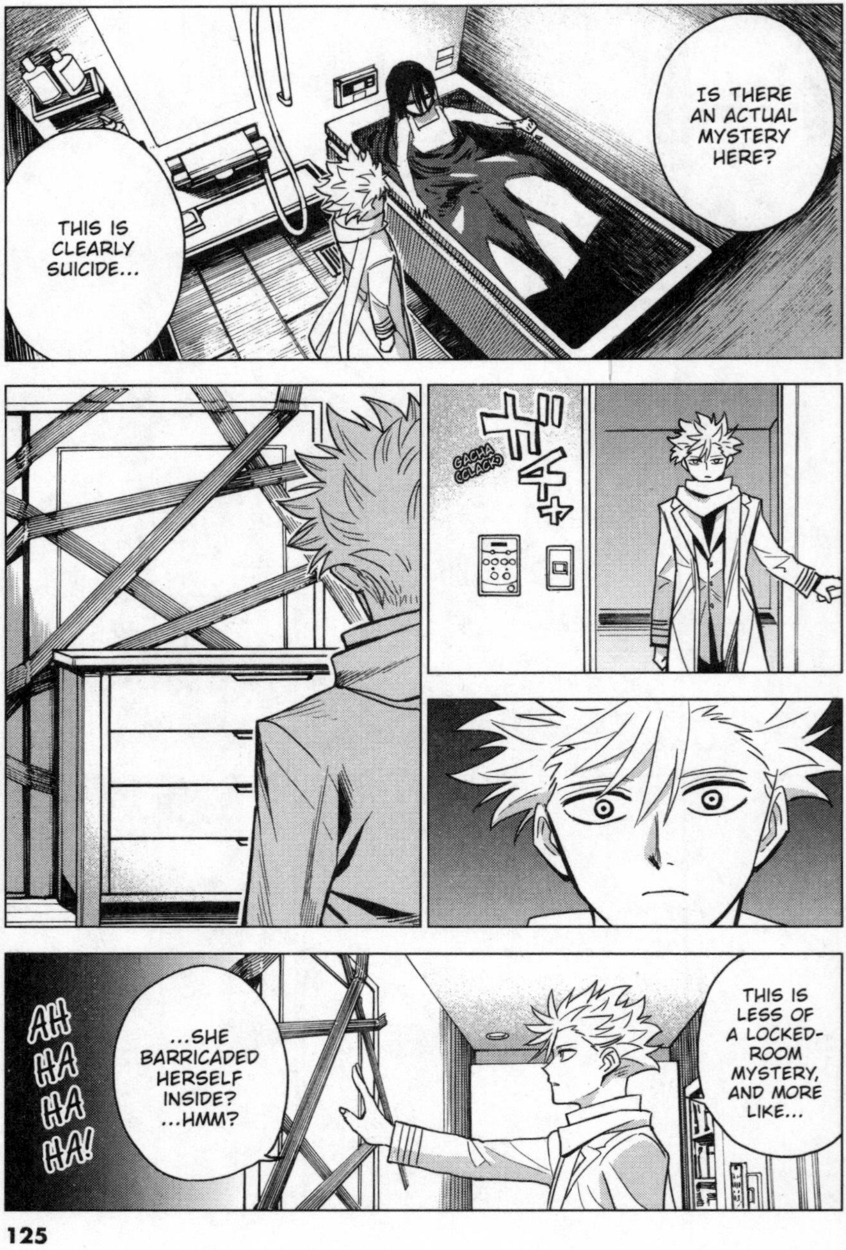
IS THERE AN ACTUAL MYSTERY HERE?
THIS IS CLEARLY SUICIDE...
GACHA (CLACK)
THIS IS LESS OF A LOCKED-ROOM MYSTERY, AND MORE LIKE...
...SHE BARRICADED HERSELF INSIDE? ...HMM?
AH HA HA HA!

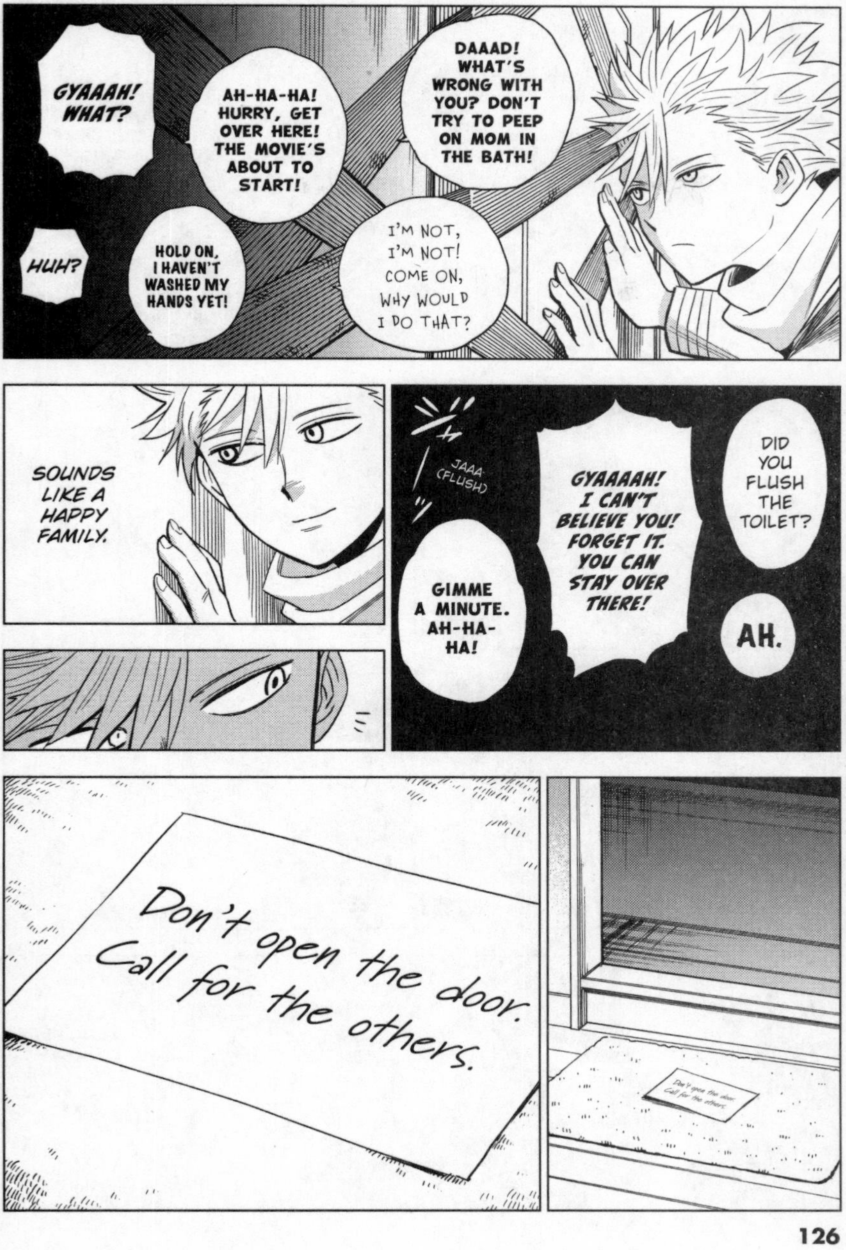
DAAAD! WHAT'S WRONG WITH YOU? DON'T TRY TO PEEP ON MOM IN THE BATH!
AH-HA-HA! HURRY, GET OVER HERE! THE MOVIE'S ABOUT TO START!
GYAAAH! WHAT?
I'M NOT, I'M NOT! COME ON, WHY WOULD I DO THAT?
HOLD ON, I HAVEN'T WASHED MY HANDS YET!
HUH?
DID YOU FLUSH THE TOILET?
GYAAAAH! I CAN'T BELIEVE YOU! FORGET IT. YOU CAN STAY OVER THERE!
JAAA (FLUSH)
AH.
GIMME A MINUTE. AH-HA-HA!
SOUNDS LIKE A HAPPY FAMILY.
Don't open the door. Call for the others.
Don't open the door. Call for the others.

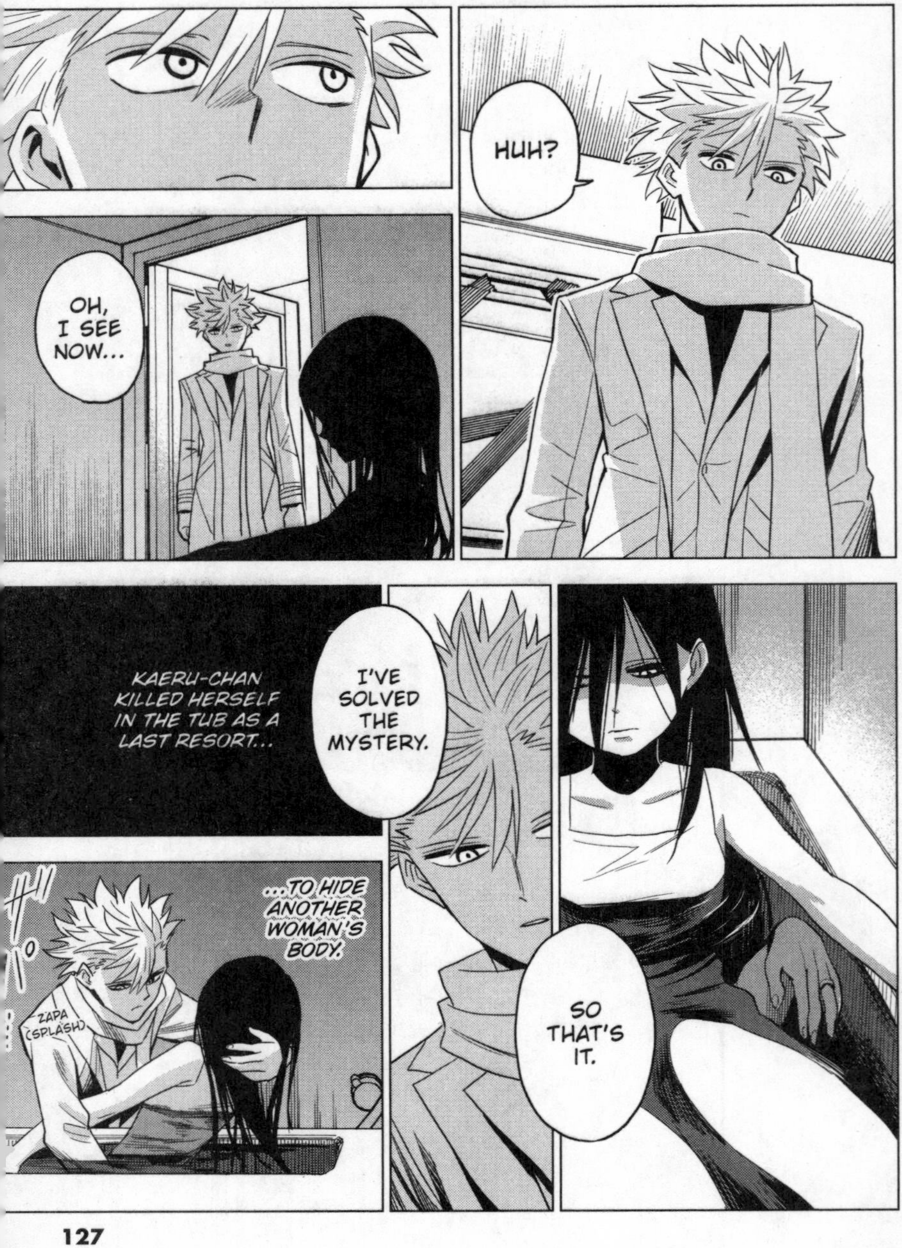
HUH?
OH, I SEE NOW...
SO THAT'S IT.
I'VE SOLVED THE MYSTERY.
KAERU-CHAN KILLED HERSELF IN THE TUB AS A LAST RESORT...
...TO HIDE ANOTHER WOMAN'S BODY.
ZAPA (SPLASH)

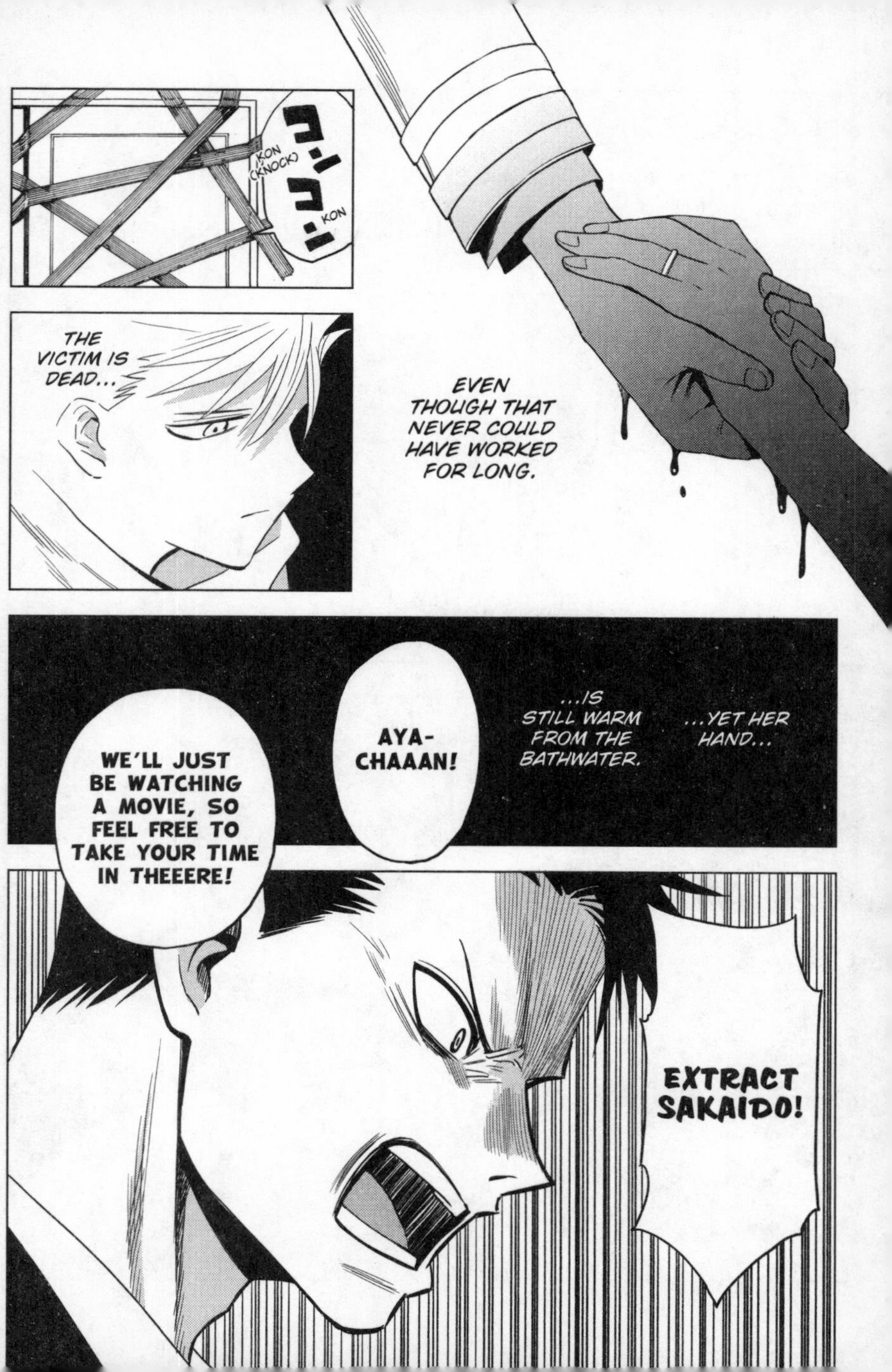
EVEN THOUGH THAT NEVER COULD HAVE WORKED FOR LONG.
KON (KNOCK)
KON
THE VICTIM IS DEAD...
...YET HER HAND...
...IS STILL WARM FROM THE BATHWATER.
AYA-CHAAAN!
WE'LL JUST BE WATCHING A MOVIE, SO FEEL FREE TO TAKE YOUR TIME IN THEEERE!
EXTRACT SAKAIDO!

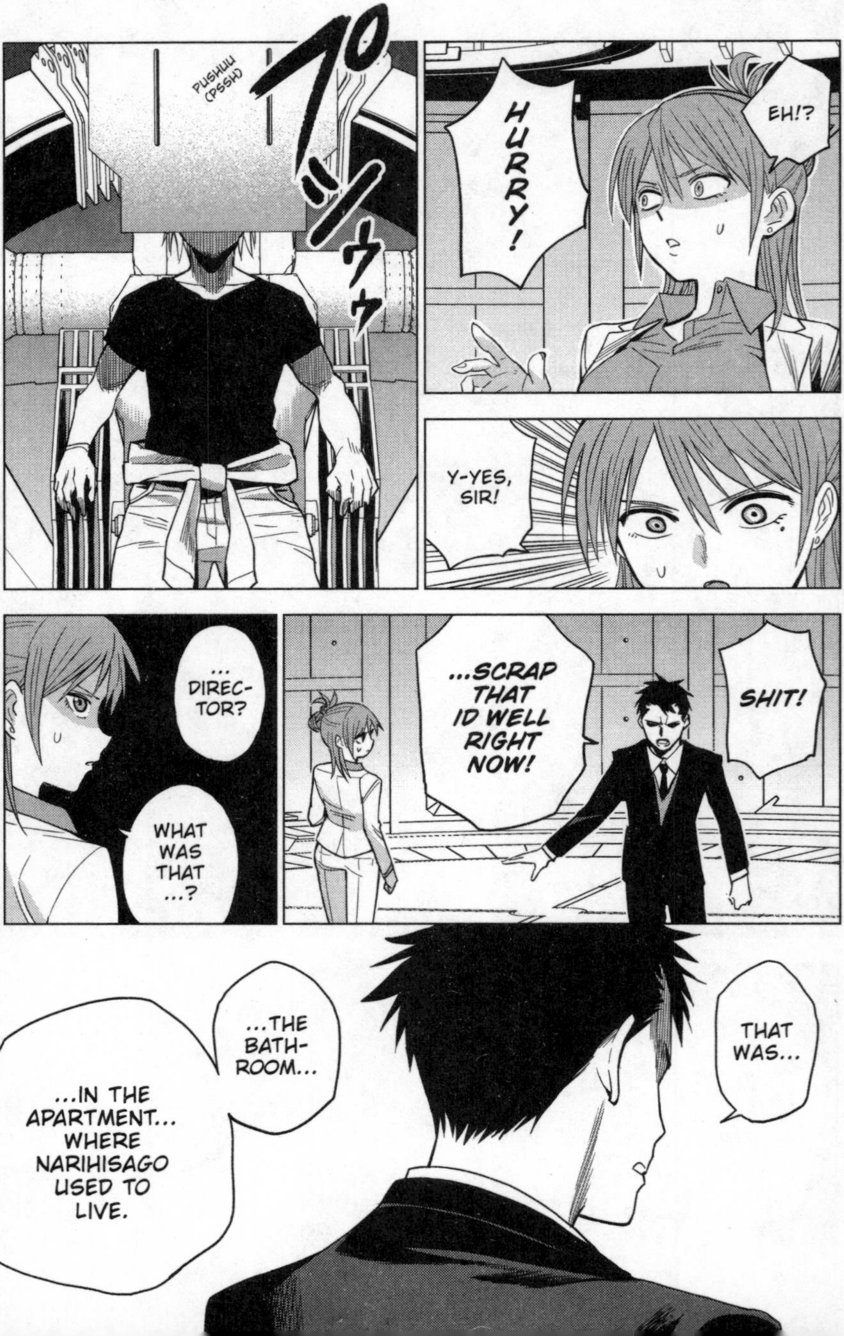
EH!?
HURRY!
Y-YES, SIR!
PUSHUU (PSSH)
SHIT!
...SCRAP THAT ID WELL RIGHT NOW!
...DIRECTOR?
WHAT WAS THAT ...?
THAT WAS...
...THE BATH-ROOM...
...IN THE APARTMENT... WHERE NARIHISAGO USED TO LIVE.

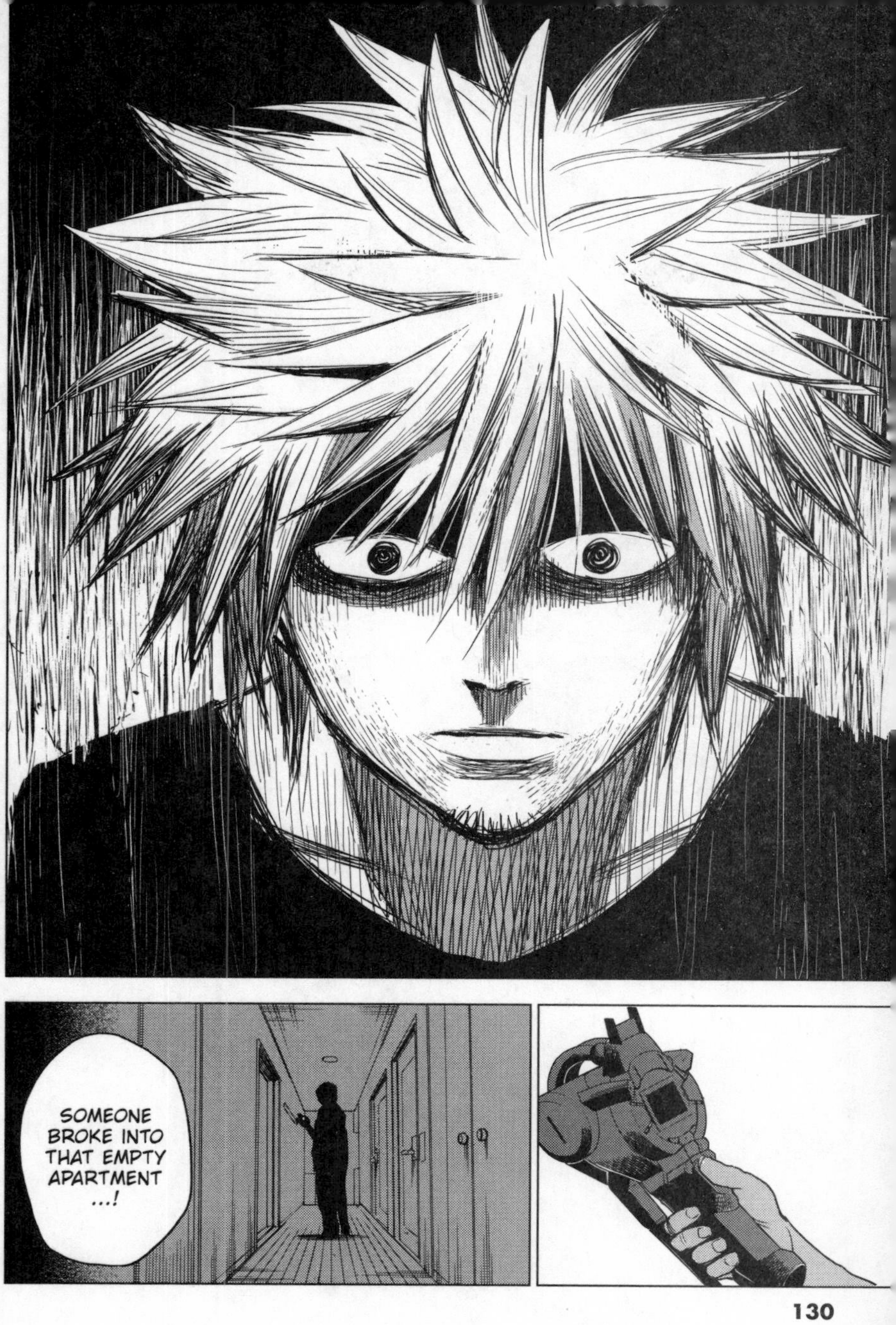
SOMEONE BROKE INTO THAT EMPTY APARTMENT ...!

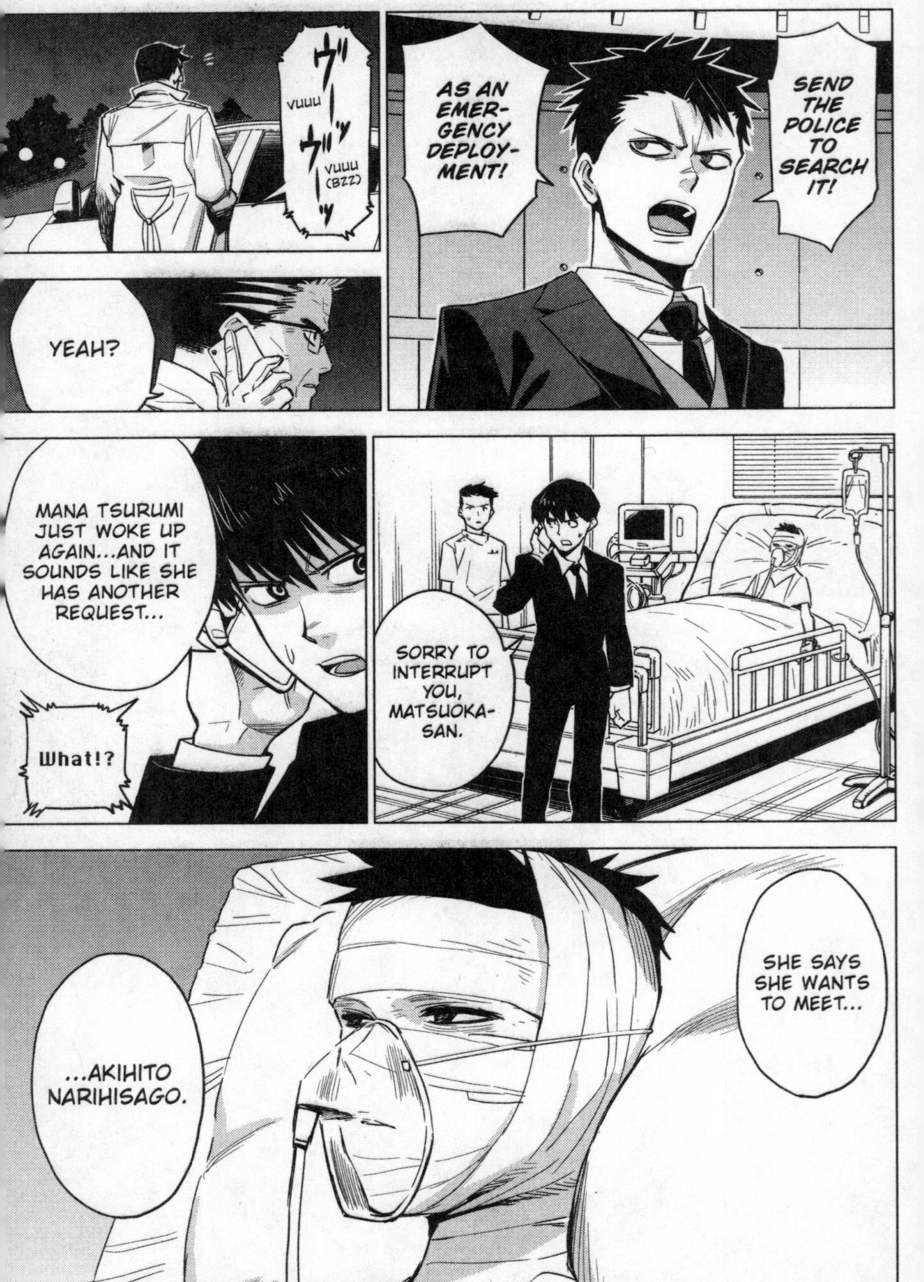
SEND THE POLICE TO SEARCH IT!
AS AN EMERGENCY DEPLOYMENT!
ヴーッ ヴーッ
VUUU VUUU (BZZ)
YEAH?
SORRY TO INTERRUPT YOU, MATSUOKA-SAN.
MANA TSURUMI JUST WOKE UP AGAIN...AND IT SOUNDS LIKE SHE HAS ANOTHER REQUEST...
What!?
SHE SAYS SHE WANTS TO MEET...
...AKIHITO NARIHISAGO.

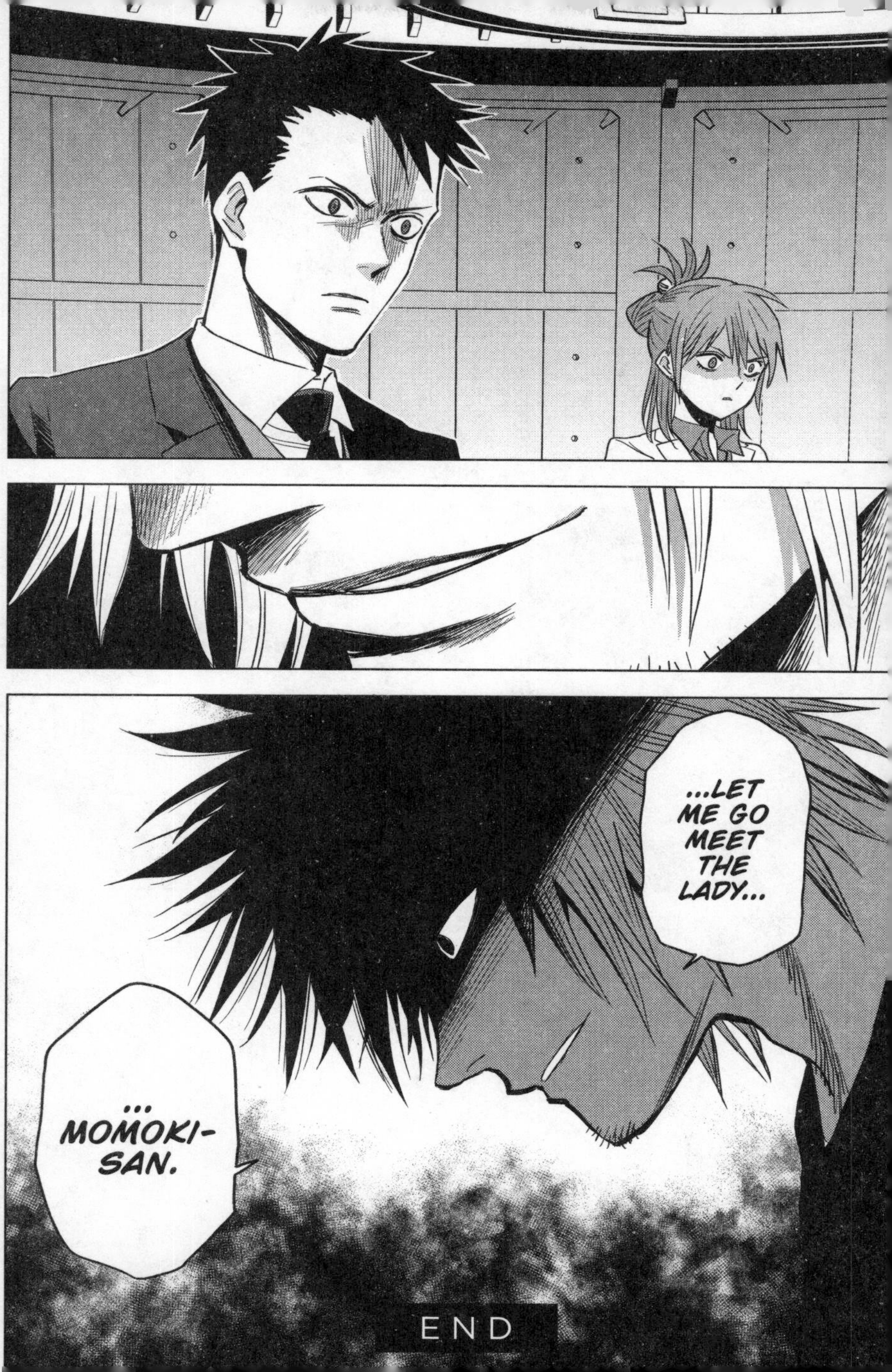
...LET ME GO MEET THE LADY...
... MOMOKI-SAN.
END

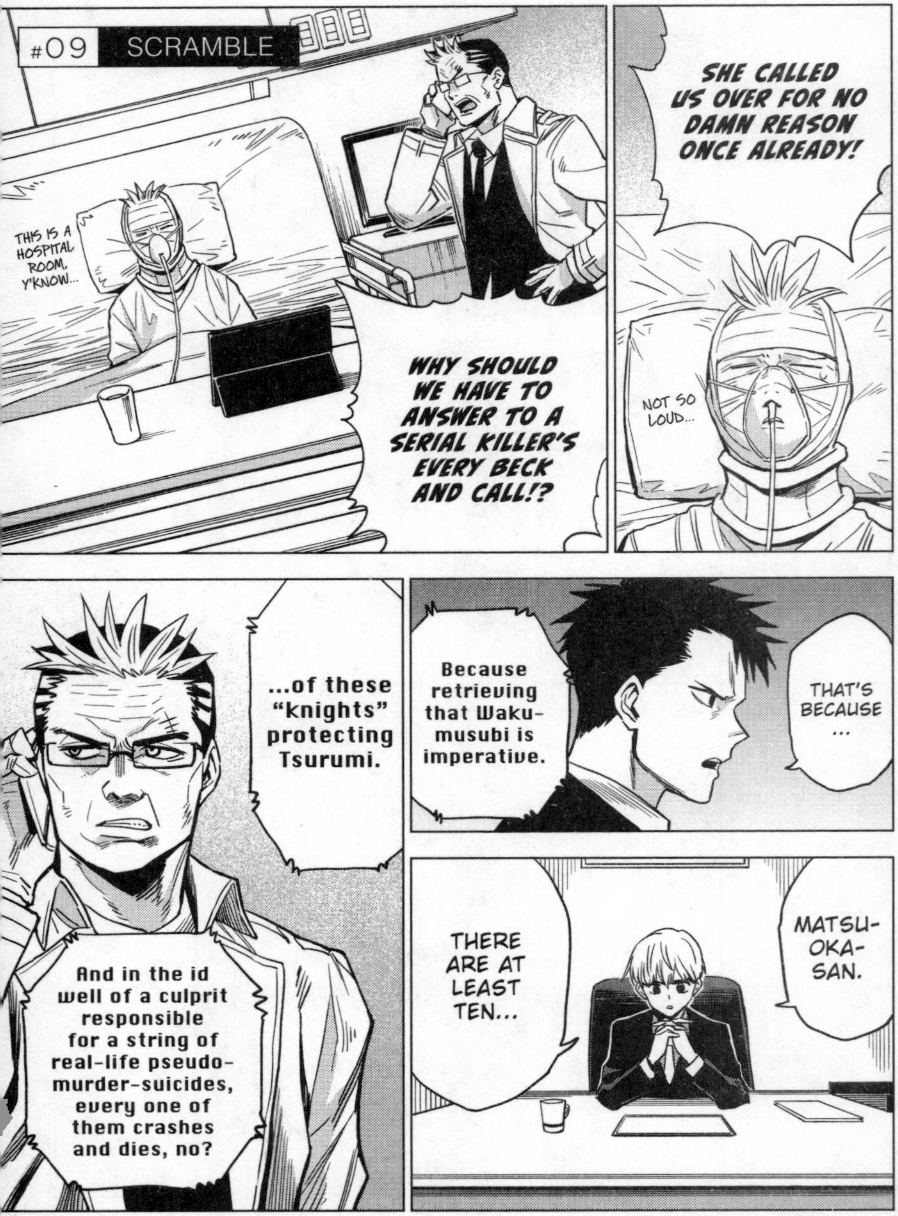

SHE CALLED US OVER FOR NO DAMN REASON ONCE ALREADY!
NOT SO LOUD...
#09 SCRAMBLE
WHY SHOULD WE HAVE TO ANSWER TO A SERIAL KILLER'S EVERY BECK AND CALL!?
THIS IS A HOSPITAL ROOM, Y'KNOW...
THAT'S BECAUSE ...
Because retrieving that Waku-musubi is imperative.
MATSU-OKA-SAN.
THERE ARE AT LEAST TEN...
...of these "knights" protecting Tsurumi.
And in the id well of a culprit responsible for a string of real-life pseudo-murder-suicides, every one of them crashes and dies, no?

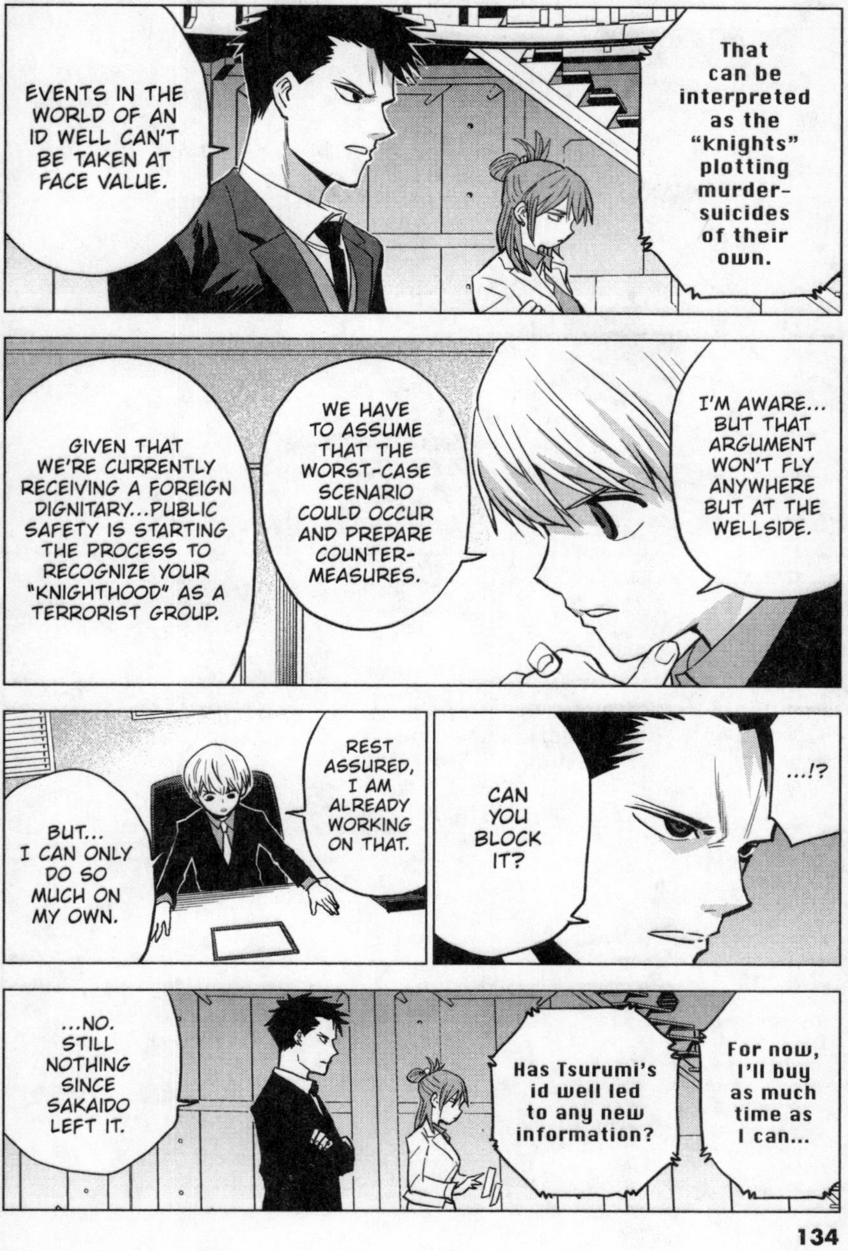
That can be interpreted as the "knights" plotting murder-suicides of their own.
EVENTS IN THE WORLD OF AN ID WELL CAN'T BE TAKEN AT FACE VALUE.
I'M AWARE... BUT THAT ARGUMENT WON'T FLY ANYWHERE BUT AT THE WELLSIDE.
WE HAVE TO ASSUME THAT THE WORST-CASE SCENARIO COULD OCCUR AND PREPARE COUNTER-MEASURES.
GIVEN THAT WE'RE CURRENTLY RECEIVING A FOREIGN DIGNITARY...PUBLIC SAFETY IS STARTING THE PROCESS TO RECOGNIZE YOUR "KNIGHTHOOD" AS A TERRORIST GROUP.
...!?
CAN YOU BLOCK IT?
REST ASSURED, I AM ALREADY WORKING ON THAT.
BUT... I CAN ONLY DO SO MUCH ON MY OWN.
For now, I'll buy as much time as I can...
Has Tsurumi's id well led to any new information?
...NO. STILL NOTHING SINCE SAKAIDO LEFT IT.

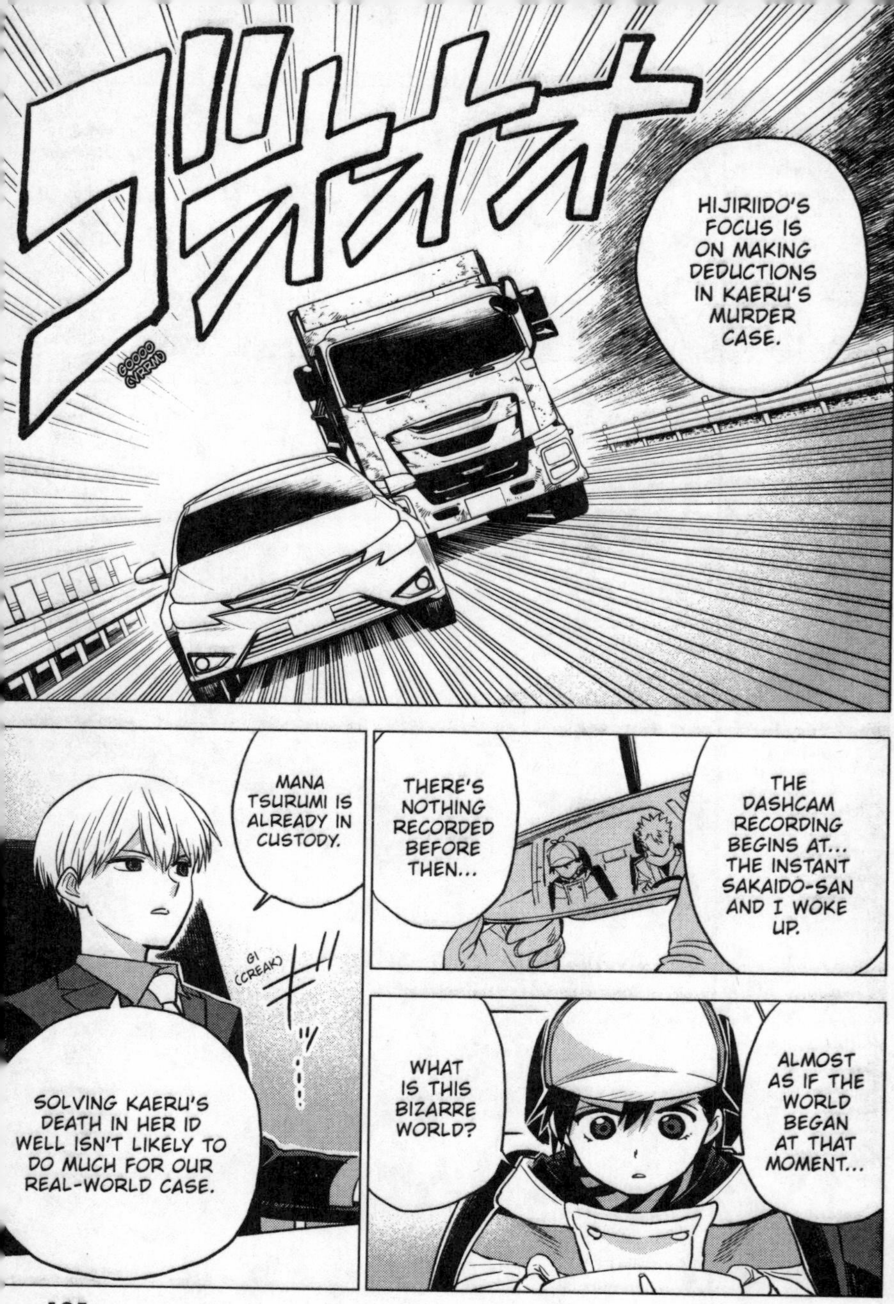
GOOOO VRRM
HIJIRIIDO'S FOCUS IS ON MAKING DEDUCTIONS IN KAERU'S MURDER CASE.
THE DASHCAM RECORDING BEGINS AT... THE INSTANT SAKAIDO-SAN AND I WOKE UP.
THERE'S NOTHING RECORDED BEFORE THEN...
ALMOST AS IF THE WORLD BEGAN AT THAT MOMENT...
WHAT IS THIS BIZARRE WORLD?
MANA TSURUMI IS ALREADY IN CUSTODY.
GI (CREAK)
SOLVING KAERU'S DEATH IN HER ID WELL ISN'T LIKELY TO DO MUCH FOR OUR REAL-WORLD CASE.

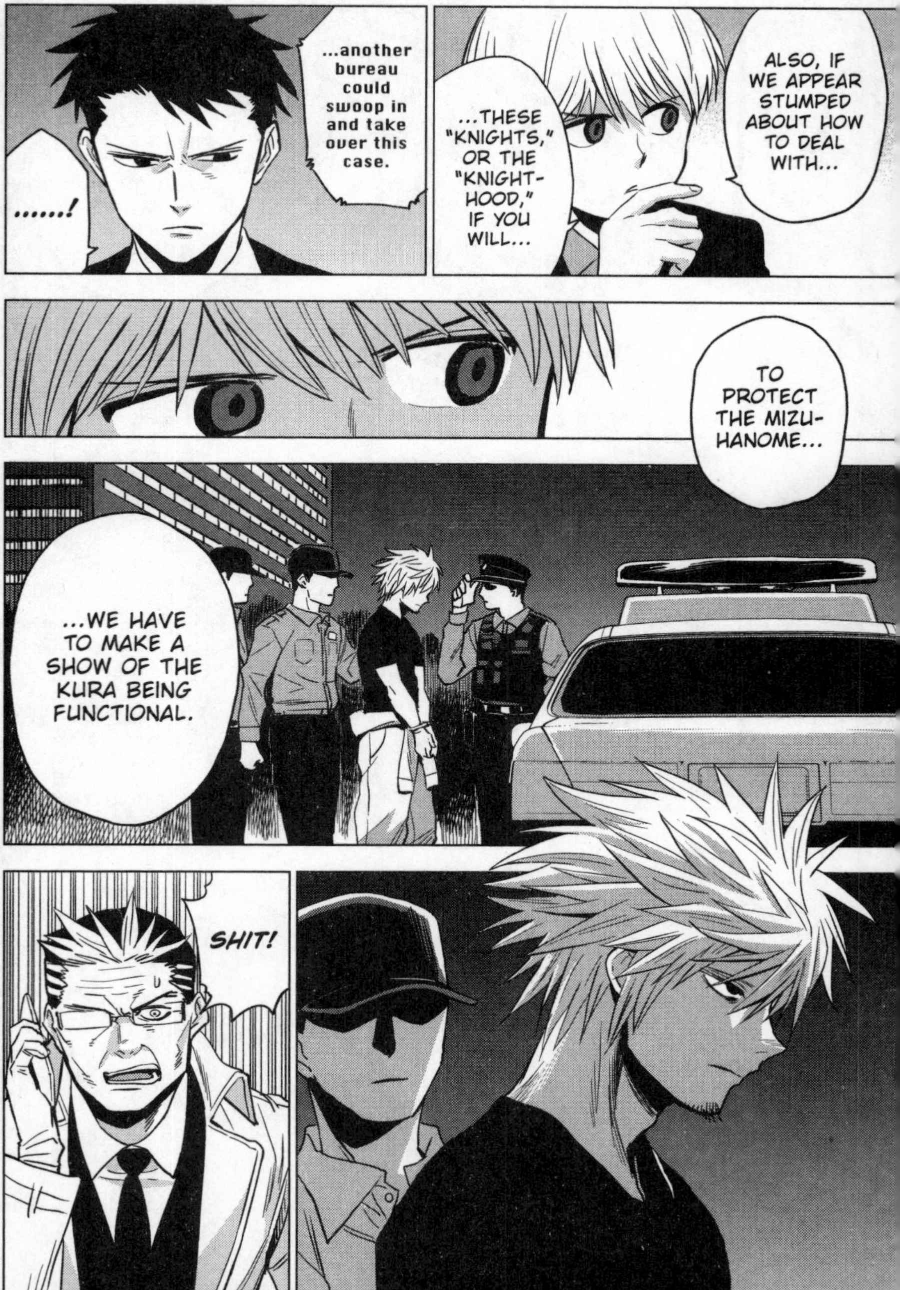
ALSO, IF WE APPEAR STUMPED ABOUT HOW TO DEAL WITH...
...THESE "KNIGHTS," OR THE "KNIGHTHOOD," IF YOU WILL...
...another bureau could swoop in and take over this case.
......!
TO PROTECT THE MIZUHANOME...
...WE HAVE TO MAKE A SHOW OF THE KURA BEING FUNCTIONAL.
SHIT!

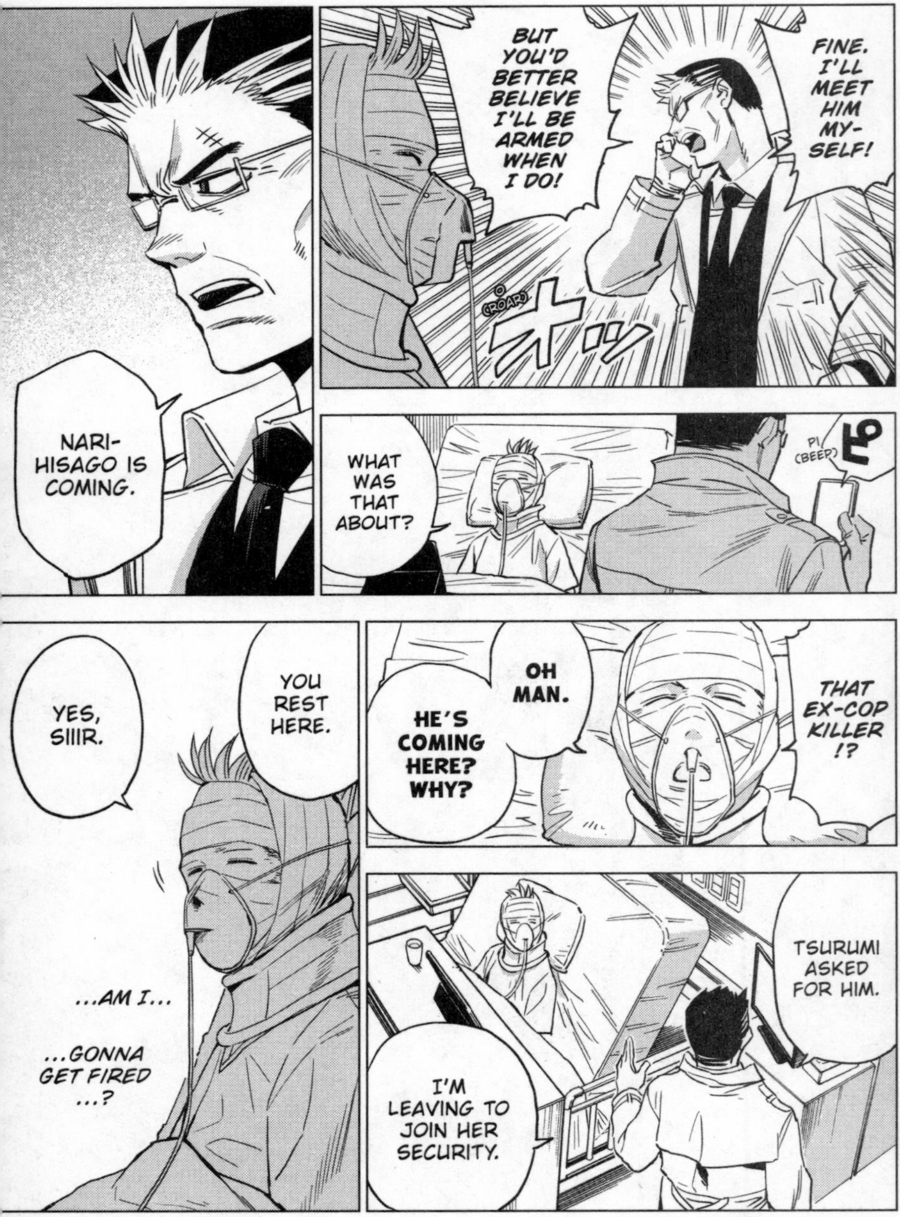
FINE. I'LL MEET HIM MY-SELF!
BUT YOU'D BETTER BELIEVE I'LL BE ARMED WHEN I DO!
O (ROAR)
PI (BEEP)
WHAT WAS THAT ABOUT?
NARI-HISAGO IS COMING.
THAT EX-COP KILLER !?
OH MAN.
HE'S COMING HERE? WHY?
TSURUMI ASKED FOR HIM.
I'M LEAVING TO JOIN HER SECURITY.
YOU REST HERE.
YES, SIIIR.
...AM I...
...GONNA GET FIRED ...?

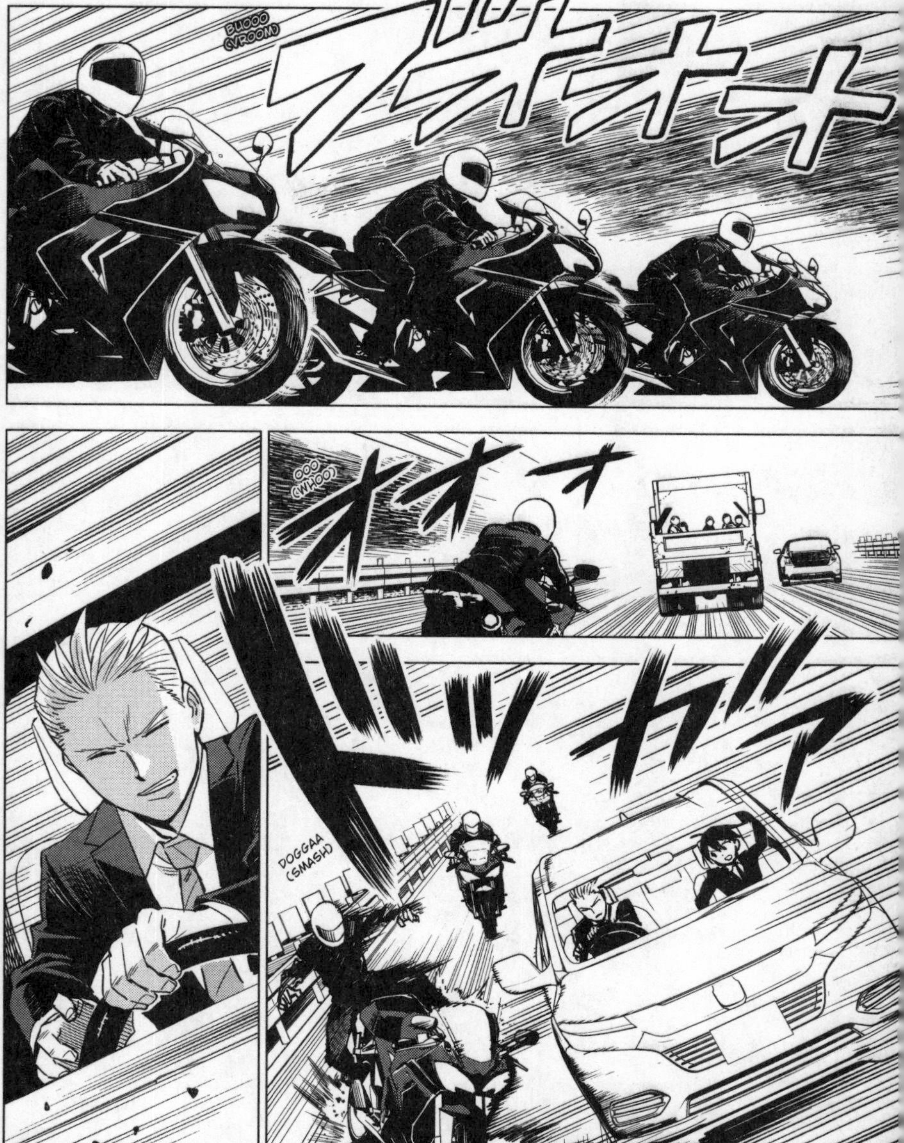
ブォオオ
BUOOO (VROOM)
オオォ
OOO (WHOO)
ドッガァ
DOGGAA (SMASH)

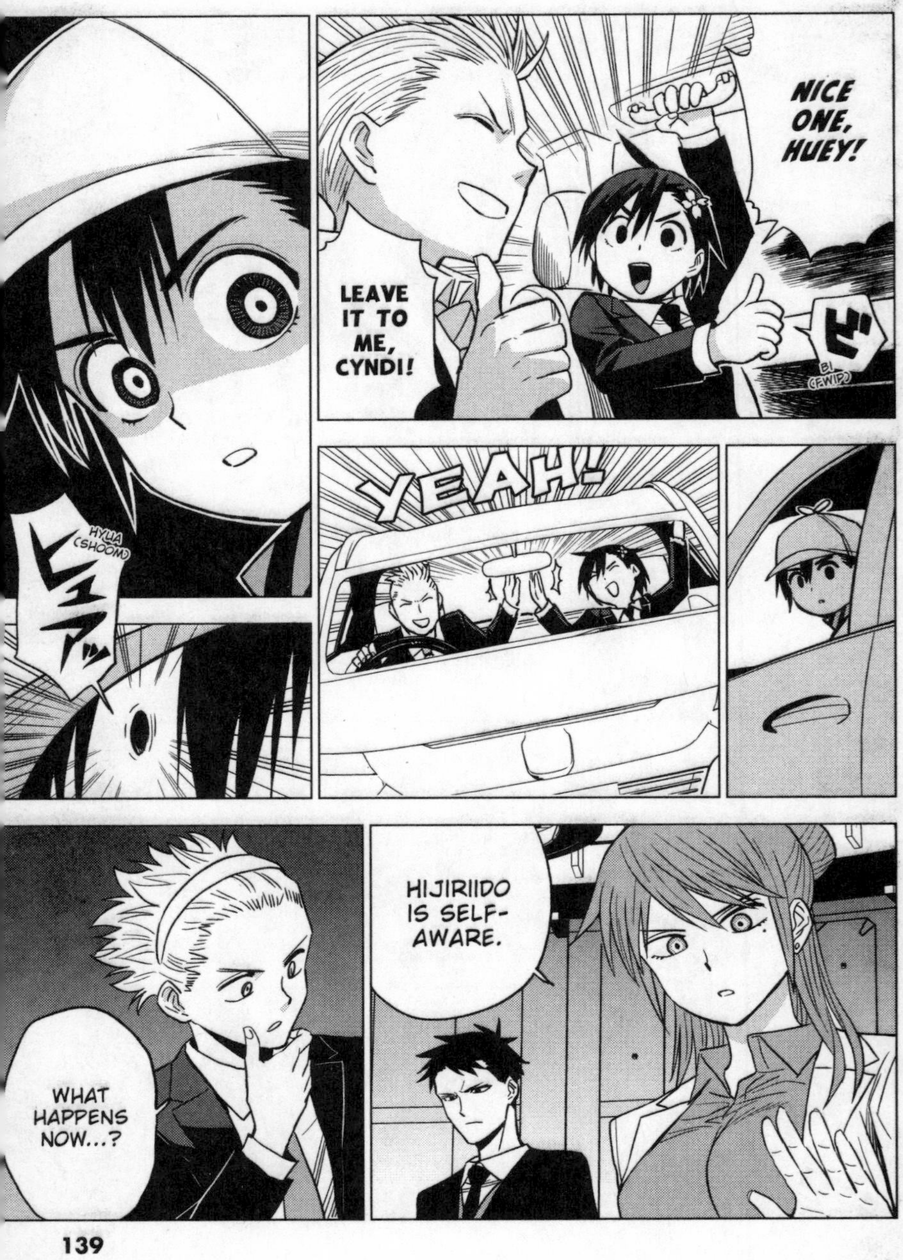
NICE ONE, HUEY!
BI (FWIP)
LEAVE IT TO ME, CYNDI!
YEAH-
HYUA (SHOOM)
HIJIRIIDO IS SELF-AWARE.
WHAT HAPPENS NOW...?

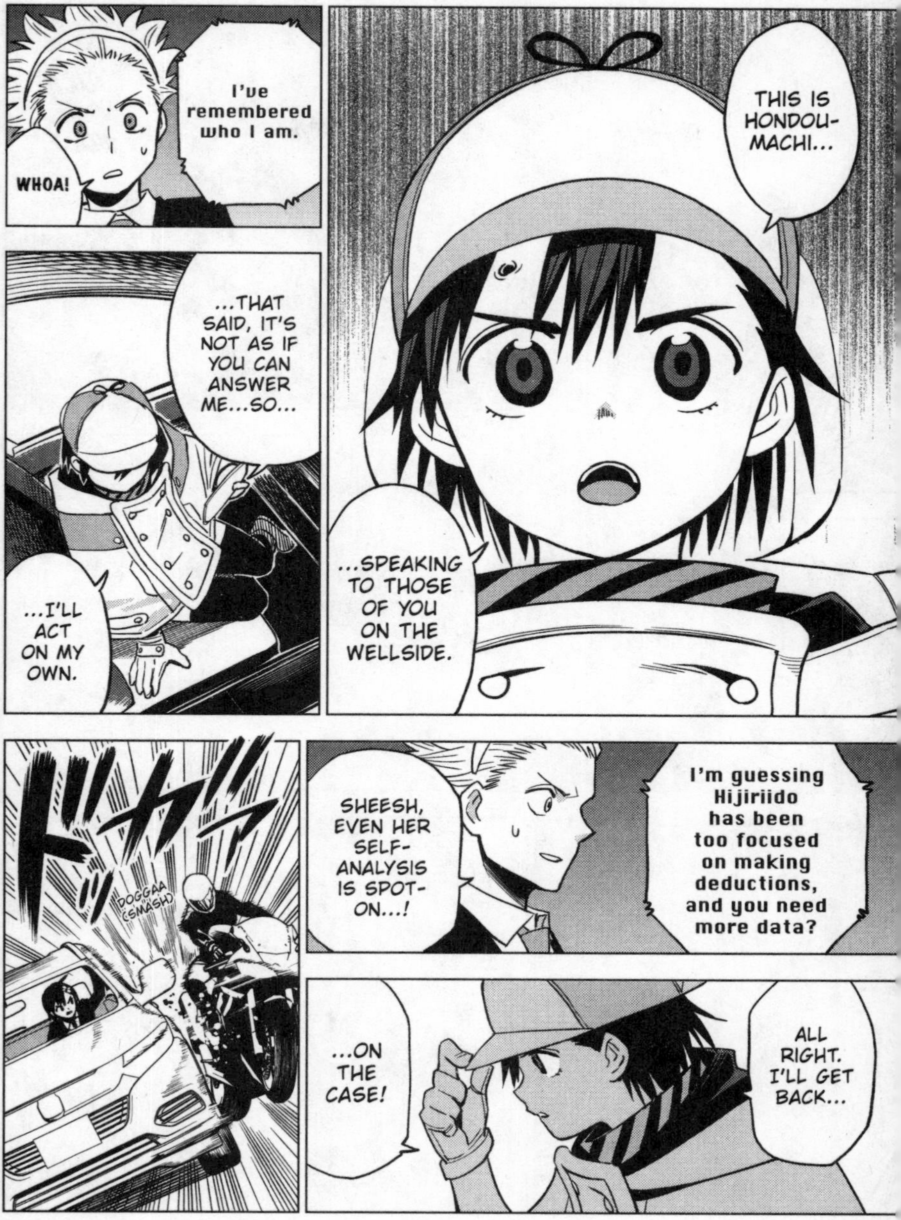
THIS IS HONDOUMACHI...
...SPEAKING TO THOSE OF YOU ON THE WELLSIDE.
I've remembered who I am.
WHOA!
...THAT SAID, IT'S NOT AS IF YOU CAN ANSWER ME...SO...
...I'LL ACT ON MY OWN.
I'm guessing Hijiriido has been too focused on making deductions, and you need more data?
SHEESH, EVEN HER SELF-ANALYSIS IS SPOT-ON...!
ALL RIGHT. I'LL GET BACK...
...ON THE CASE!
DOGGAA (SMASH)

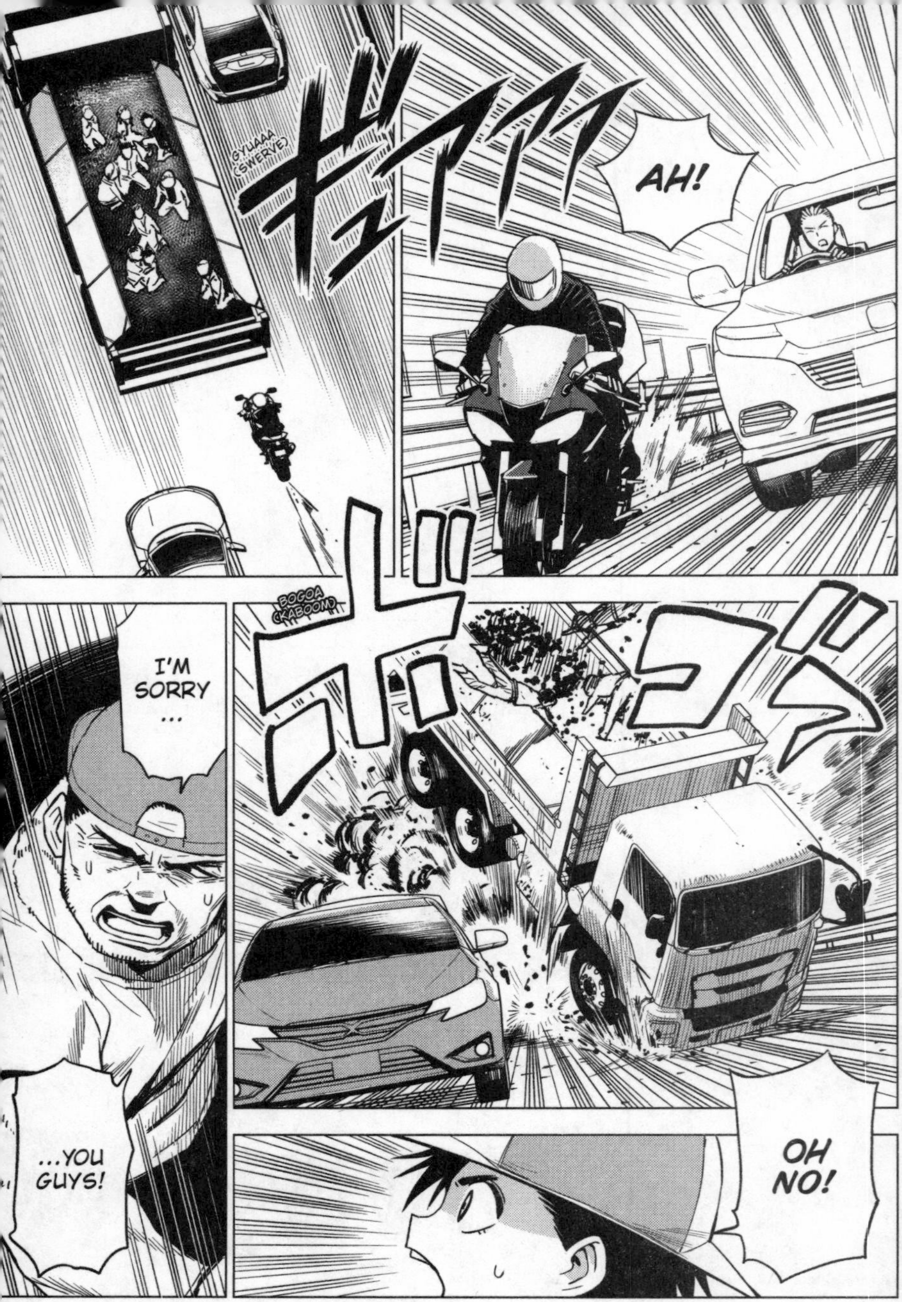
AH!
GYUAAA (SWERVE)
BOGOA (KABOOM)
OH NO!
I'M SORRY ...
...YOU GUYS!

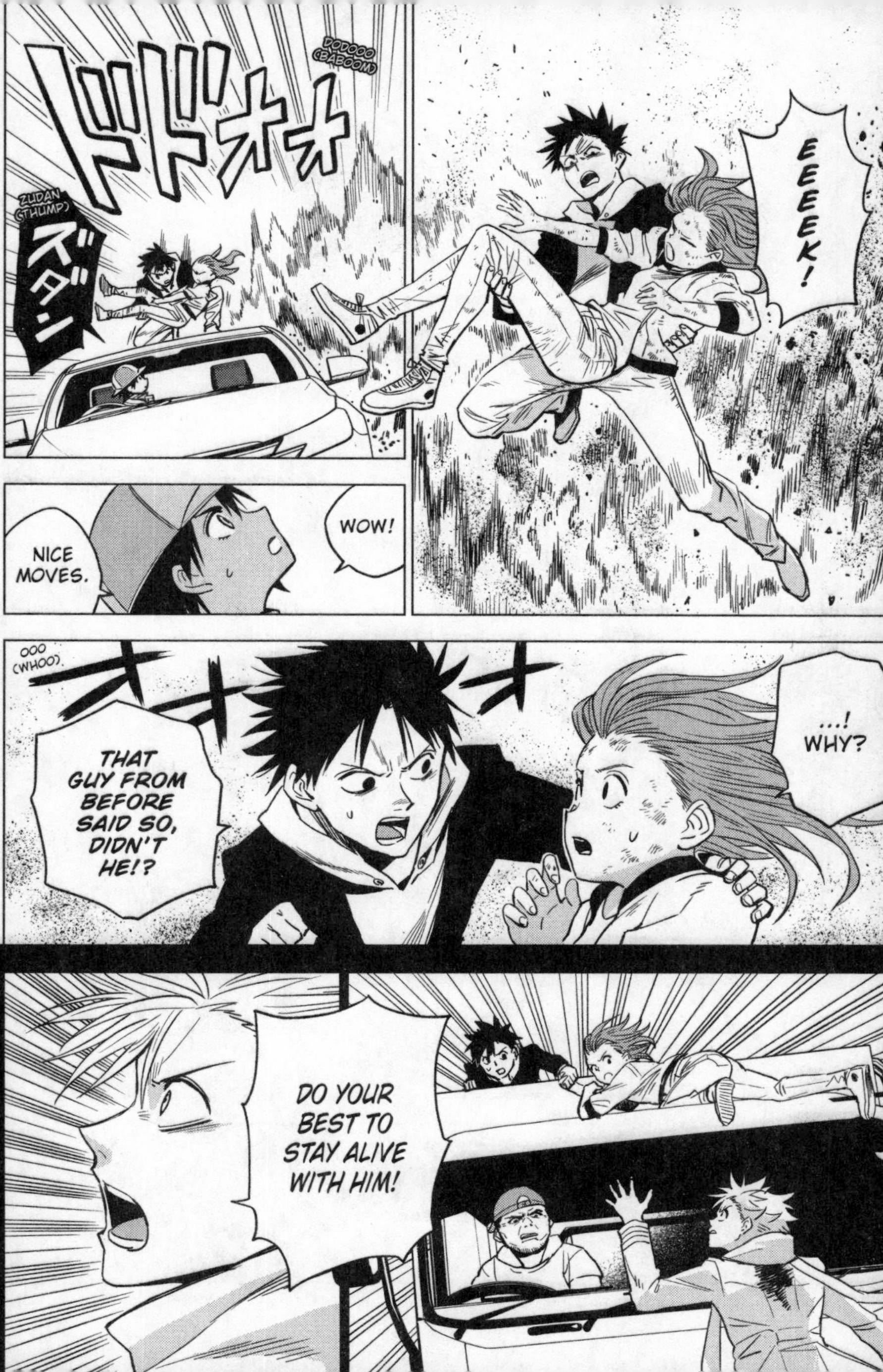
EEEEEK!
DODOOO (BABOOM)
ZUDAN (THUMP)
WOW!
NICE MOVES.
...! WHY?
OOO (WHOO)
THAT GUY FROM BEFORE SAID SO, DIDN'T HE!?
DO YOUR BEST TO STAY ALIVE WITH HIM!

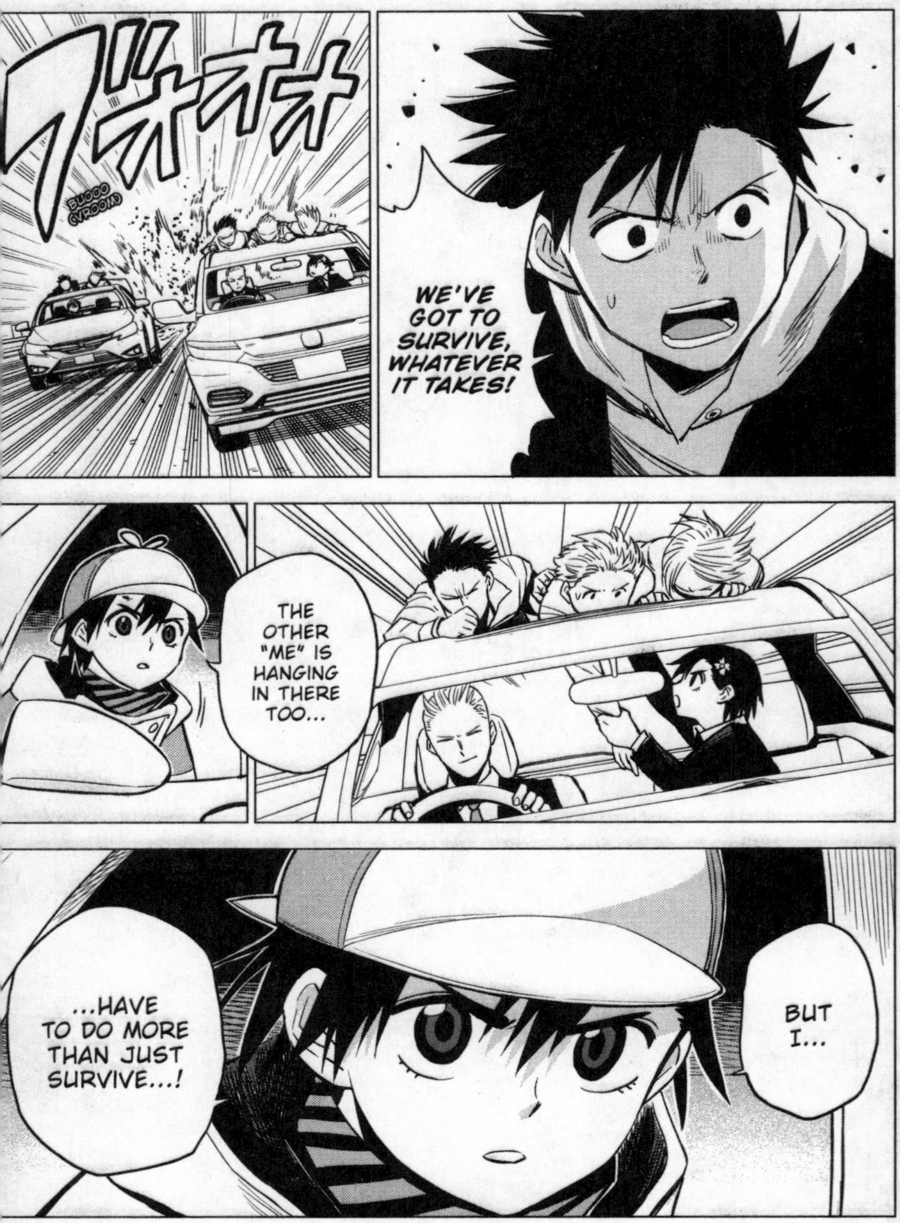
WE'VE GOT TO SURVIVE, WHATEVER IT TAKES!
ブオオオ
BUOOO (VROOM)
THE OTHER "ME" IS HANGING IN THERE TOO...
BUT I...
...HAVE TO DO MORE THAN JUST SURVIVE...!

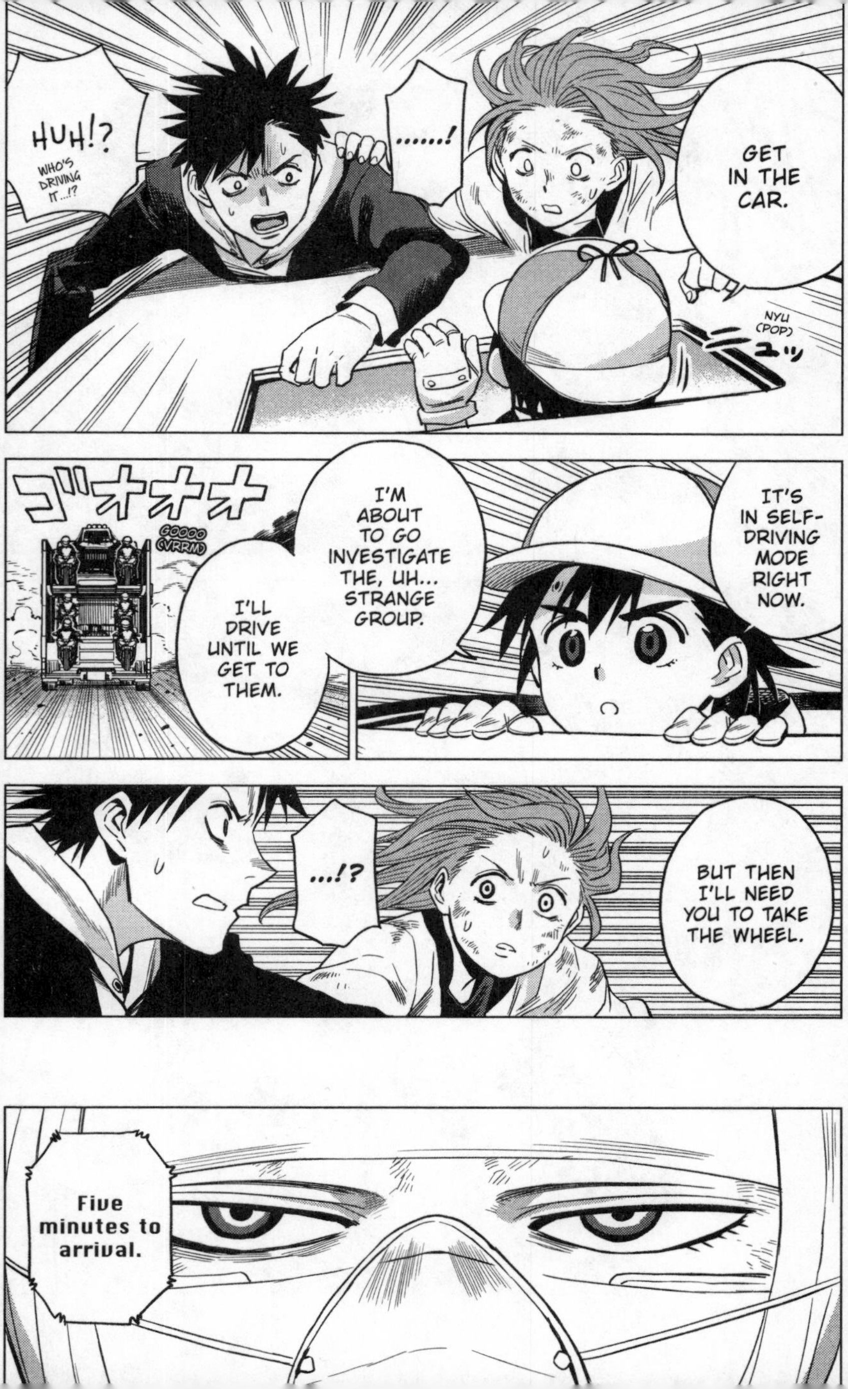
GET IN THE CAR.
NYU (POP)
ユッ
......!
HUH!?
WHO'S DRIVING IT...!?
IT'S IN SELF-DRIVING MODE RIGHT NOW.
I'M ABOUT TO GO INVESTIGATE THE, UH... STRANGE GROUP.
I'LL DRIVE UNTIL WE GET TO THEM.
ゴオオオ
GOOOO (VRRM)
BUT THEN I'LL NEED YOU TO TAKE THE WHEEL.
...!?
Five minutes to arrival.

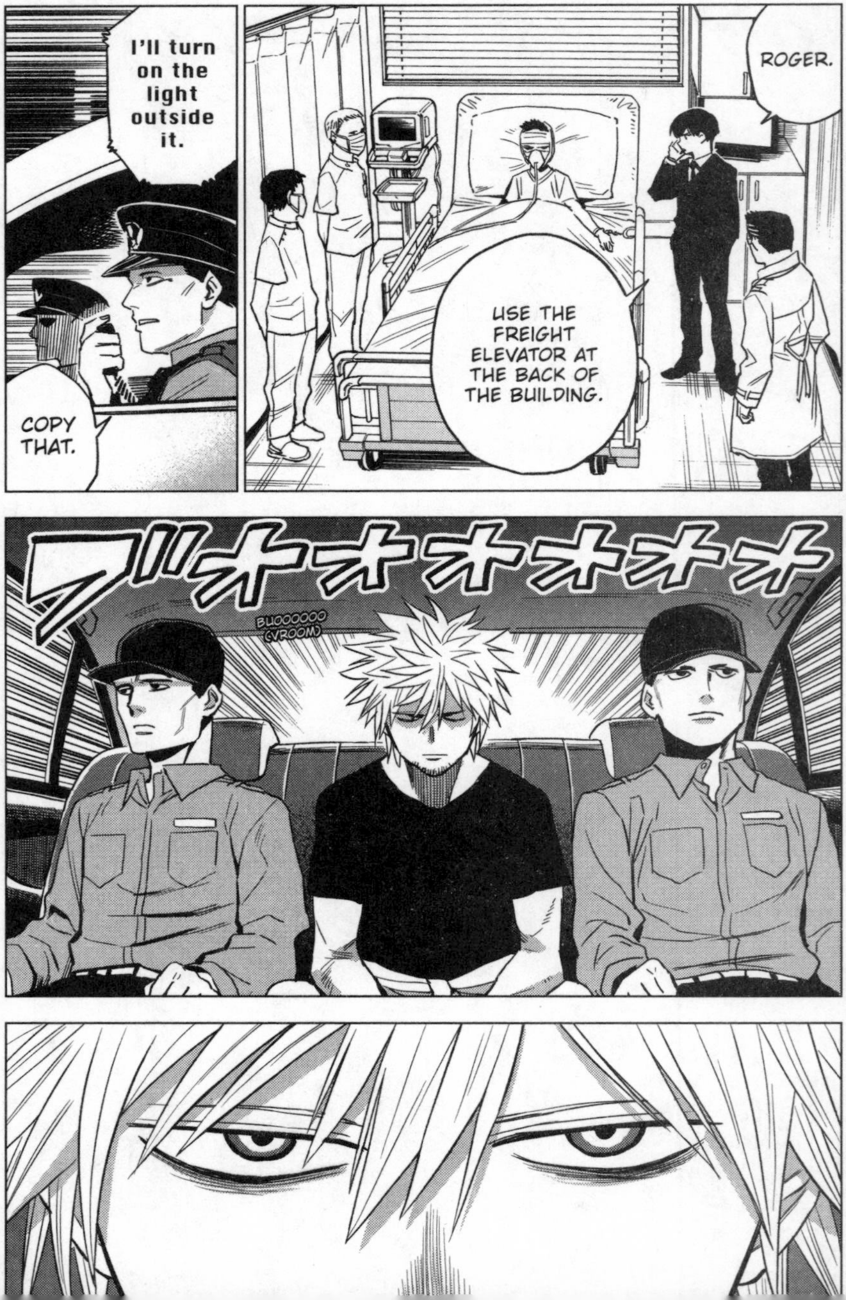
ROGER.
USE THE FREIGHT ELEVATOR AT THE BACK OF THE BUILDING.
I'll turn on the light outside it.
COPY THAT.
ブオオオオオオ
BUOOOOOO (VROOM)

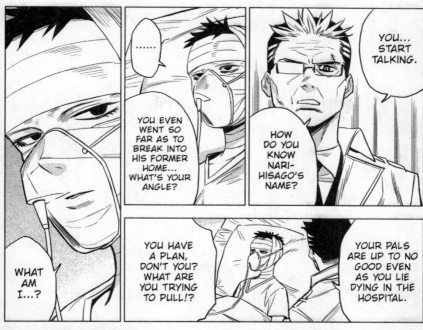

YOU... START TALKING.
HOW DO YOU KNOW NARI-HISAGO'S NAME?
......
YOU EVEN WENT SO FAR AS TO BREAK INTO HIS FORMER HOME... WHAT'S YOUR ANGLE?
YOUR PALS ARE UP TO NO GOOD EVEN AS YOU LIE DYING IN THE HOSPITAL.
YOU HAVE A PLAN, DON'T YOU? WHAT ARE YOU TRYING TO PULL!?
WHAT AM I...?
!
...WHAT!? OUT WITH IT!
WHAT ARE YOU TALKING ABOUT ...?
THE HELL DO YOU MEAN, "WHAT" ...?
AM I MISSING SOME-THING HERE?

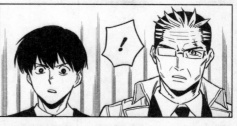

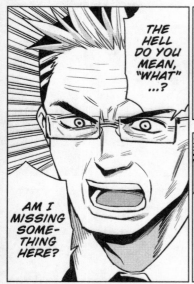

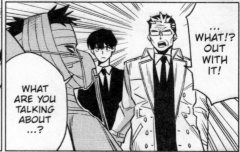

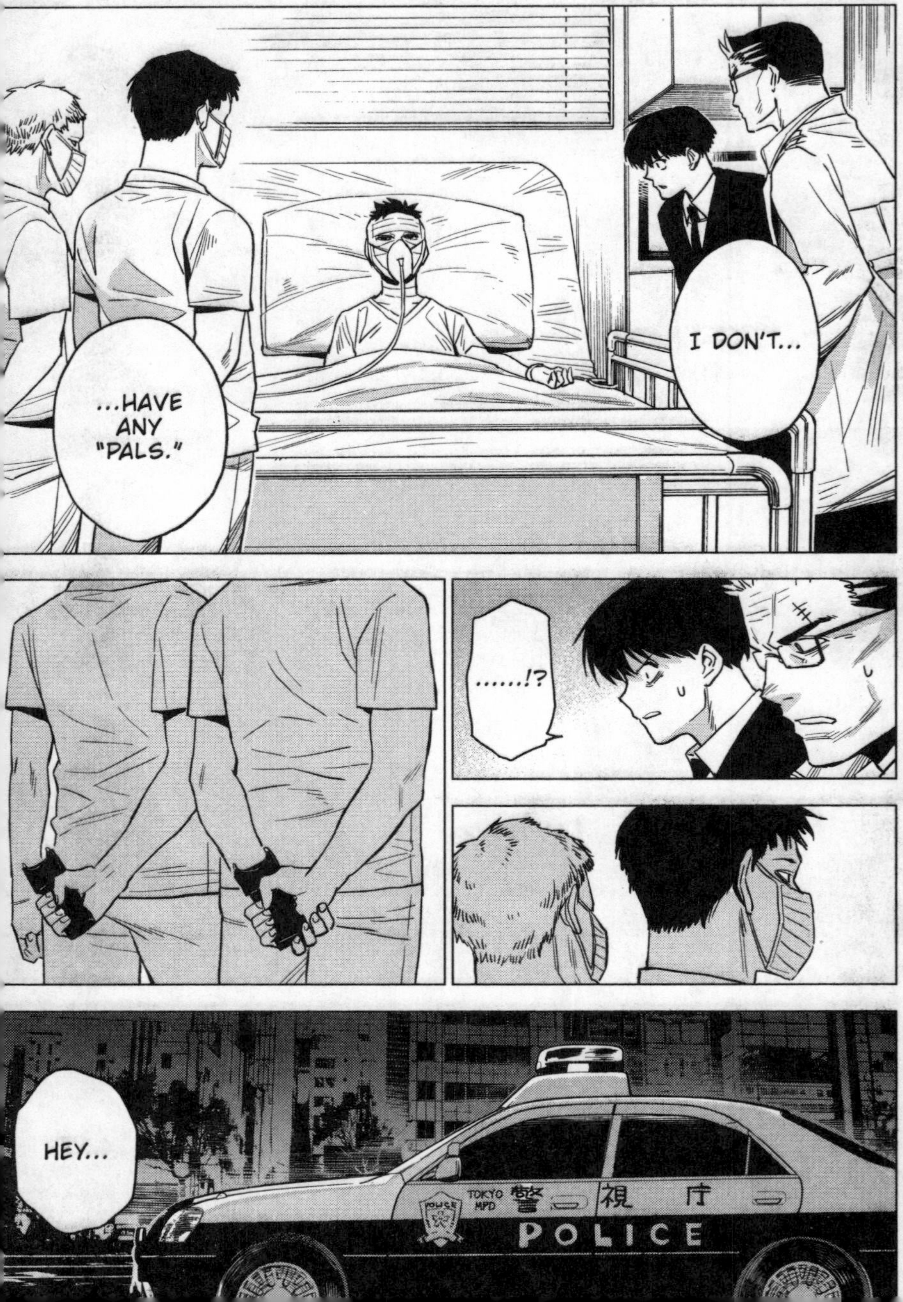
I DON'T...
...HAVE ANY "PALS."
......!?
HEY...
TOKYO MPD 警視庁
POLICE

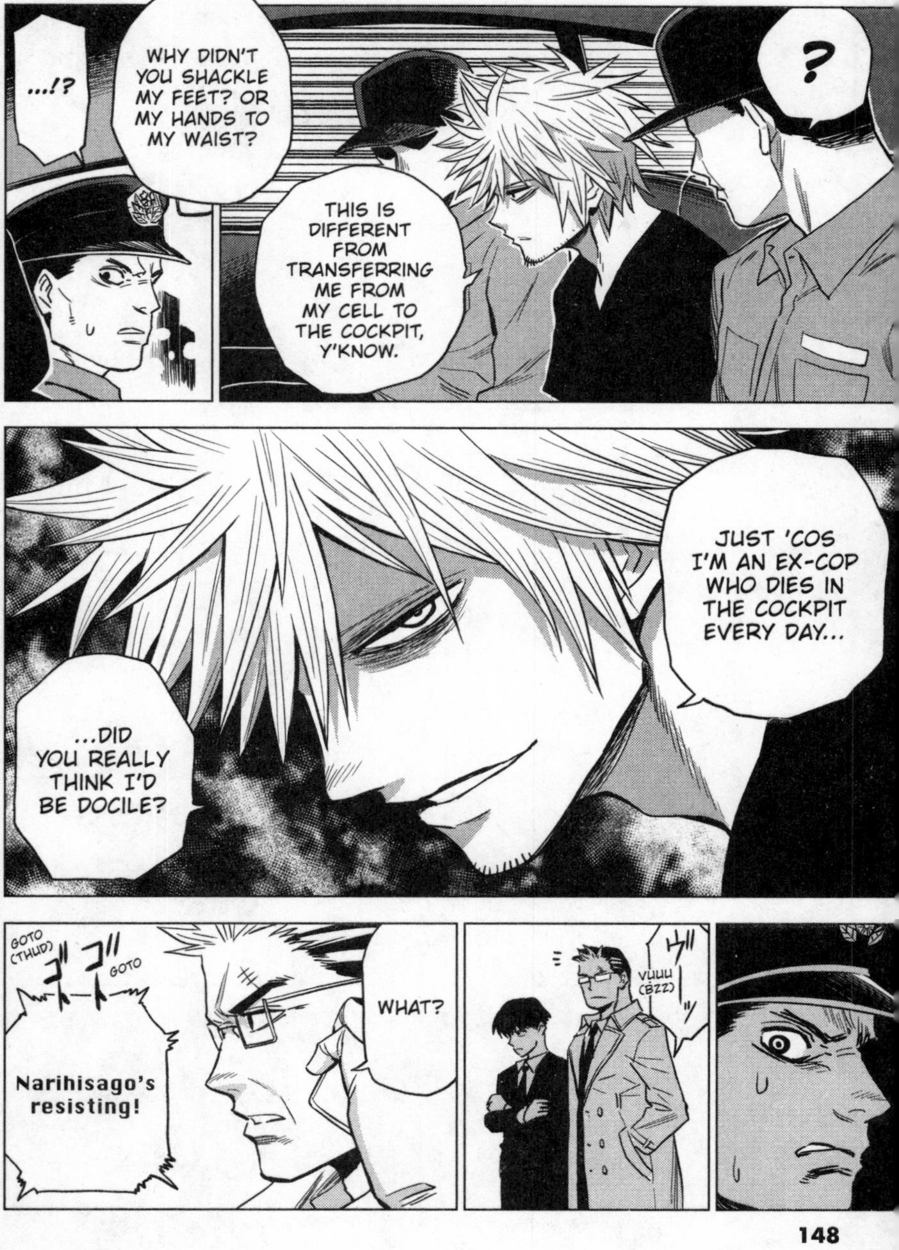
?
WHY DIDN'T YOU SHACKLE MY FEET? OR MY HANDS TO MY WAIST?
THIS IS DIFFERENT FROM TRANSFERRING ME FROM MY CELL TO THE COCKPIT, Y'KNOW.
...!?
JUST 'COS I'M AN EX-COP WHO DIES IN THE COCKPIT EVERY DAY...
...DID YOU REALLY THINK I'D BE DOCILE?
VUUU (BZZ)
WHAT?
GOTO (THUD)
GOTO
Narihisago's resisting!

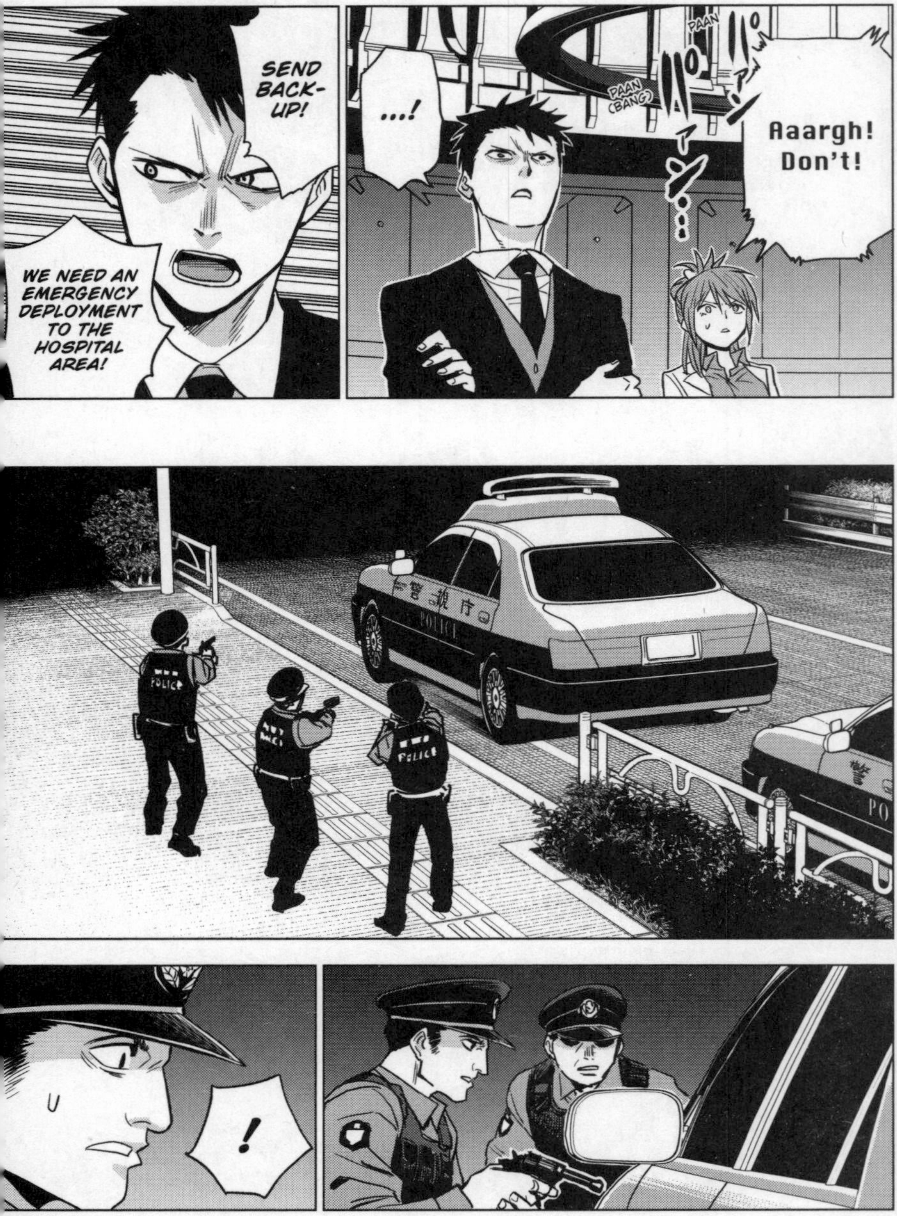
Aaargh! Don't!
PAAN
PAAN (BANG)
...!
SEND BACK-UP!
WE NEED AN EMERGENCY DEPLOYMENT TO THE HOSPITAL AREA!
!

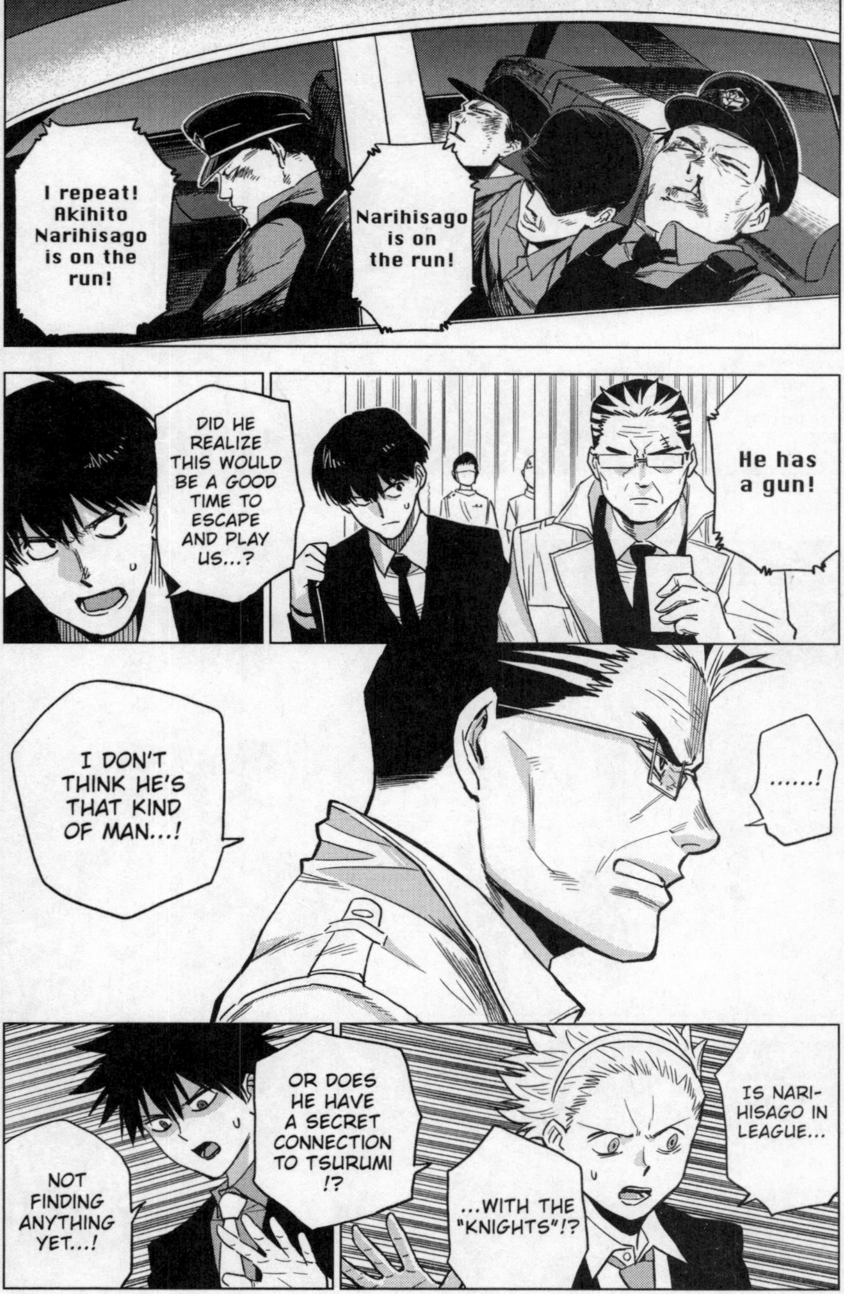
Narihisago is on the run!
I repeat! Akihito Narihisago is on the run!
He has a gun!
DID HE REALIZE THIS WOULD BE A GOOD TIME TO ESCAPE AND PLAY US...?
......!
I DON'T THINK HE'S THAT KIND OF MAN...!
IS NARI-HISAGO IN LEAGUE...
...WITH THE "KNIGHTS"!?
OR DOES HE HAVE A SECRET CONNECTION TO TSURUMI!?
NOT FINDING ANYTHING YET...!

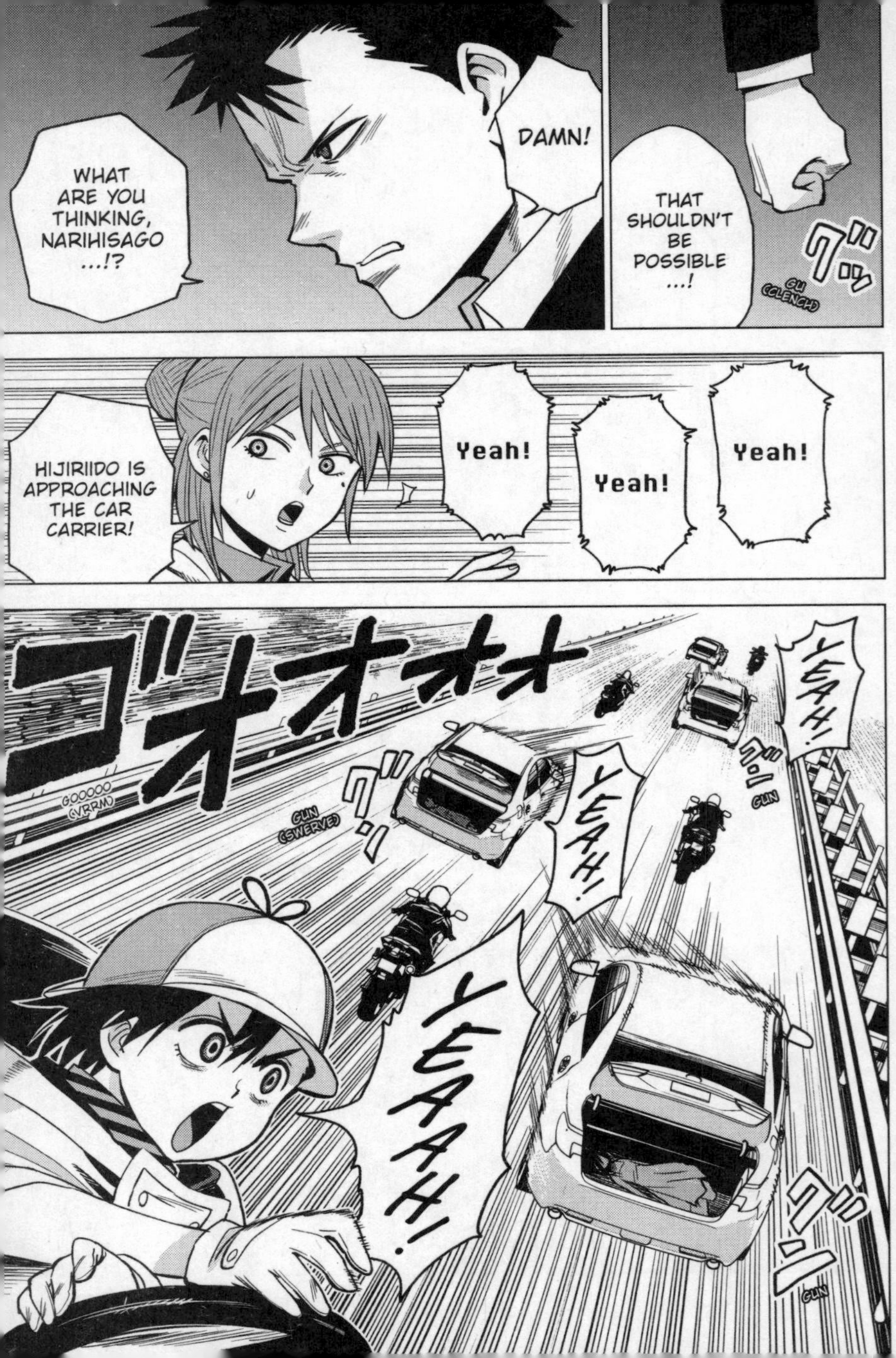
THAT SHOULDN'T BE POSSIBLE ...!
GU (CLENCH)
DAMN!
WHAT ARE YOU THINKING, NARIHISAGO ...!?
Yeah!
Yeah!
Yeah!
HIJIRIIDO IS APPROACHING THE CAR CARRIER!
YEAH!
GUN
YEAH!
GUN (SWERVE)
ゴオオオオ
GOOOOO (VRRM)
YEAAAH!
GUN

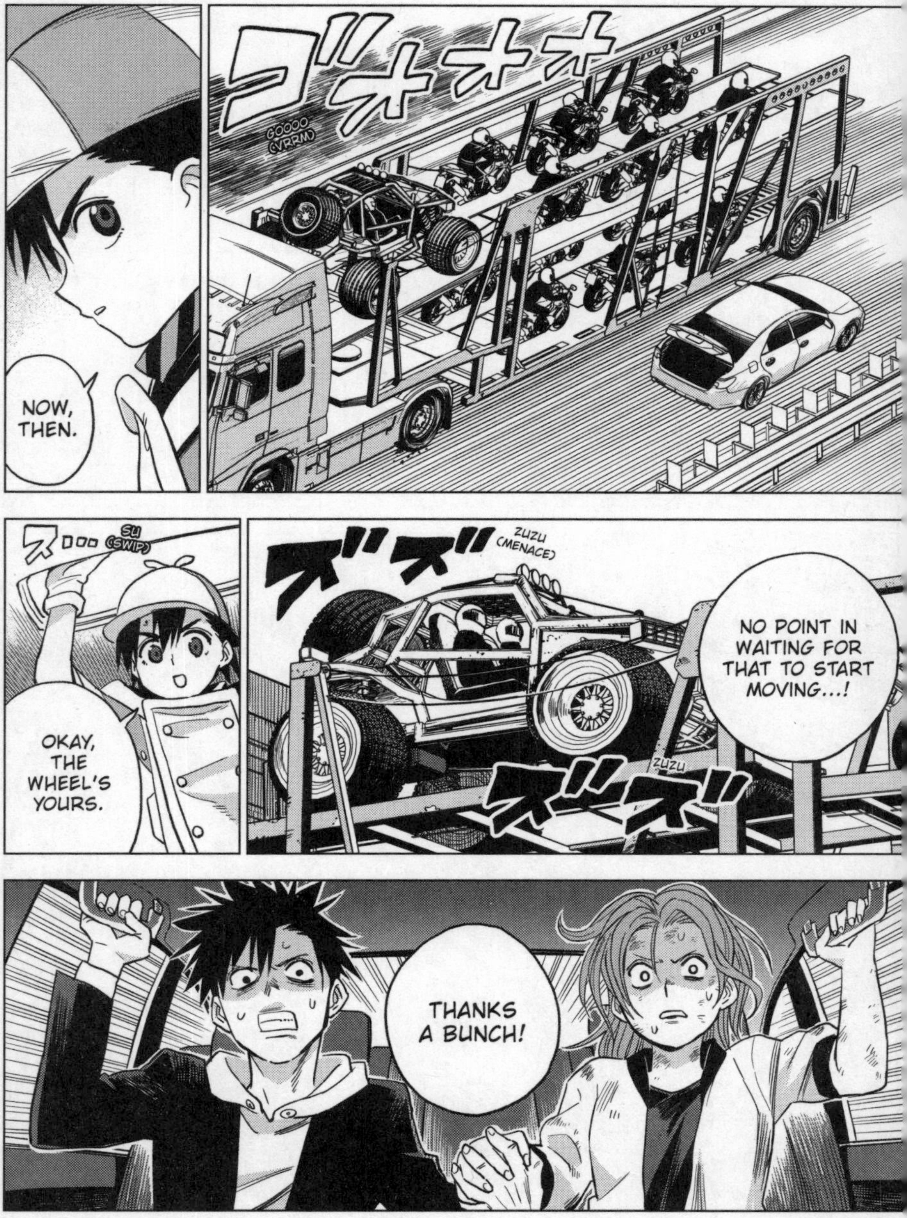
GOOOO (VRRM)
NOW, THEN.
ZUZU (MENACE)
NO POINT IN WAITING FOR THAT TO START MOVING...!
ZUZU
SU (SWIP)
OKAY, THE WHEEL'S YOURS.
THANKS A BUNCH!

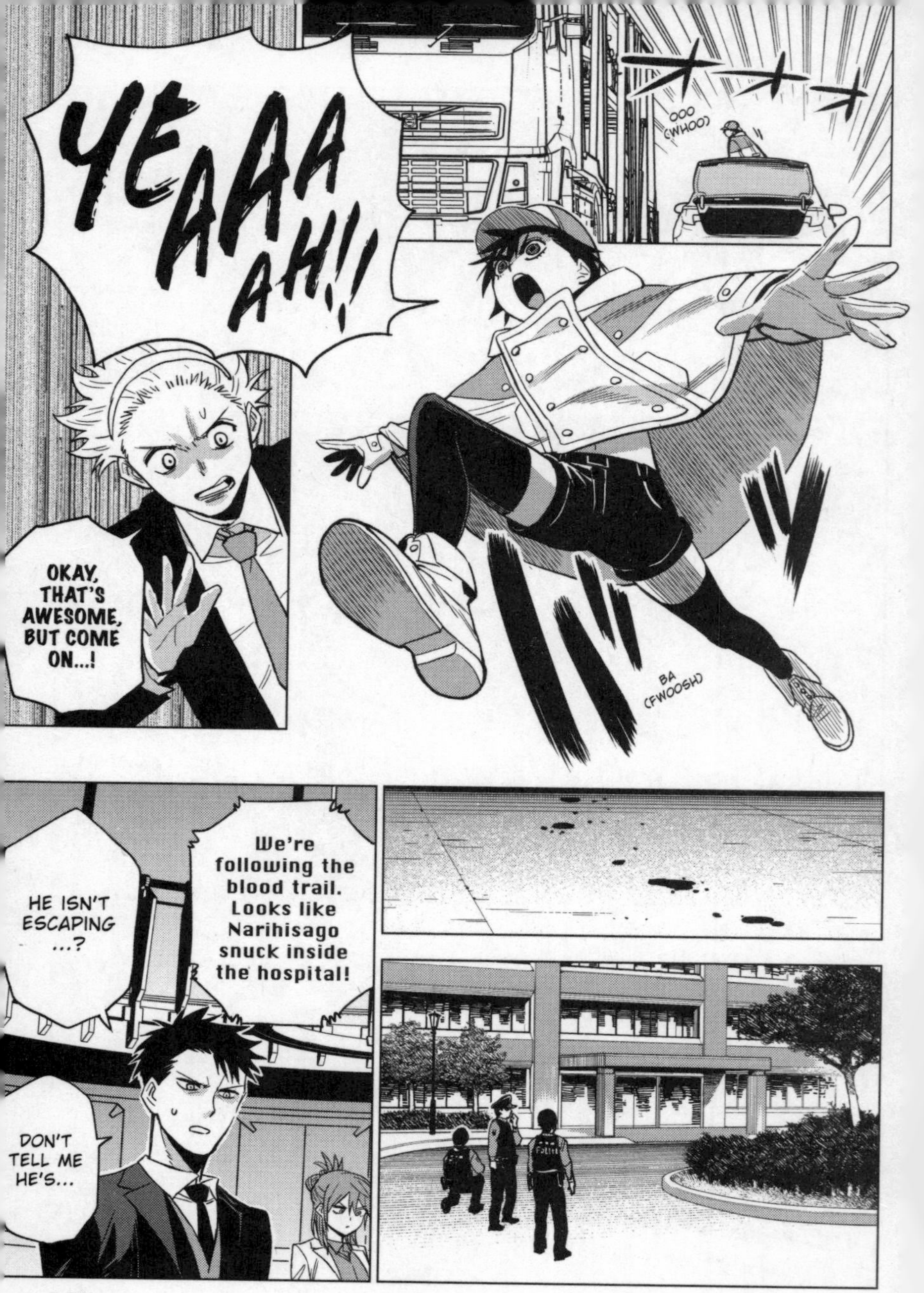
OOO (WHOO)
YEAAAAAH!!
BA (FWOOSH)
OKAY, THAT'S AWESOME, BUT COME ON...!
We're following the blood trail. Looks like Narihisago snuck inside the hospital!
HE ISN'T ESCAPING ...?
DON'T TELL ME HE'S...

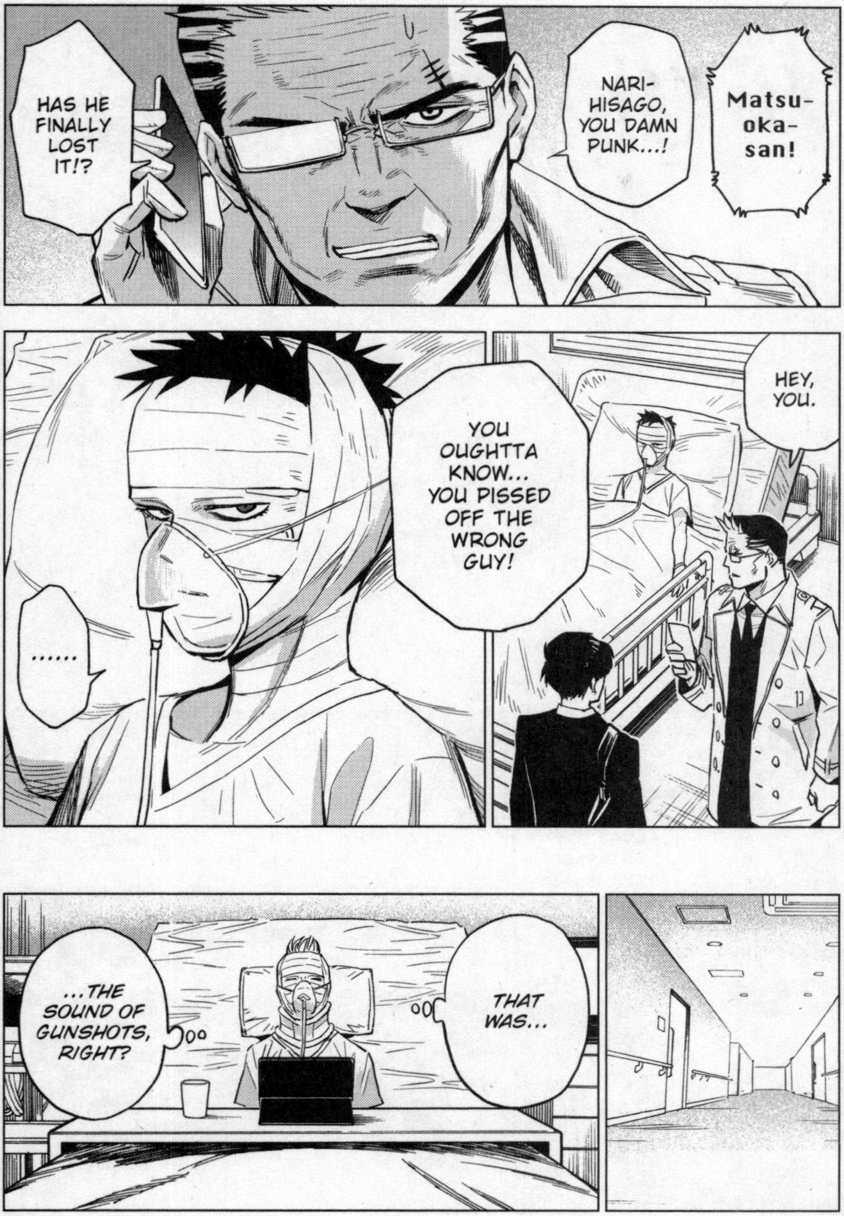
Matsu-oka-san!
NARI-HISAGO, YOU DAMN PUNK...!
HAS HE FINALLY LOST IT!?
HEY, YOU.
YOU OUGHTTA KNOW... YOU PISSED OFF THE WRONG GUY!
......
THAT WAS...
...THE SOUND OF GUNSHOTS, RIGHT?

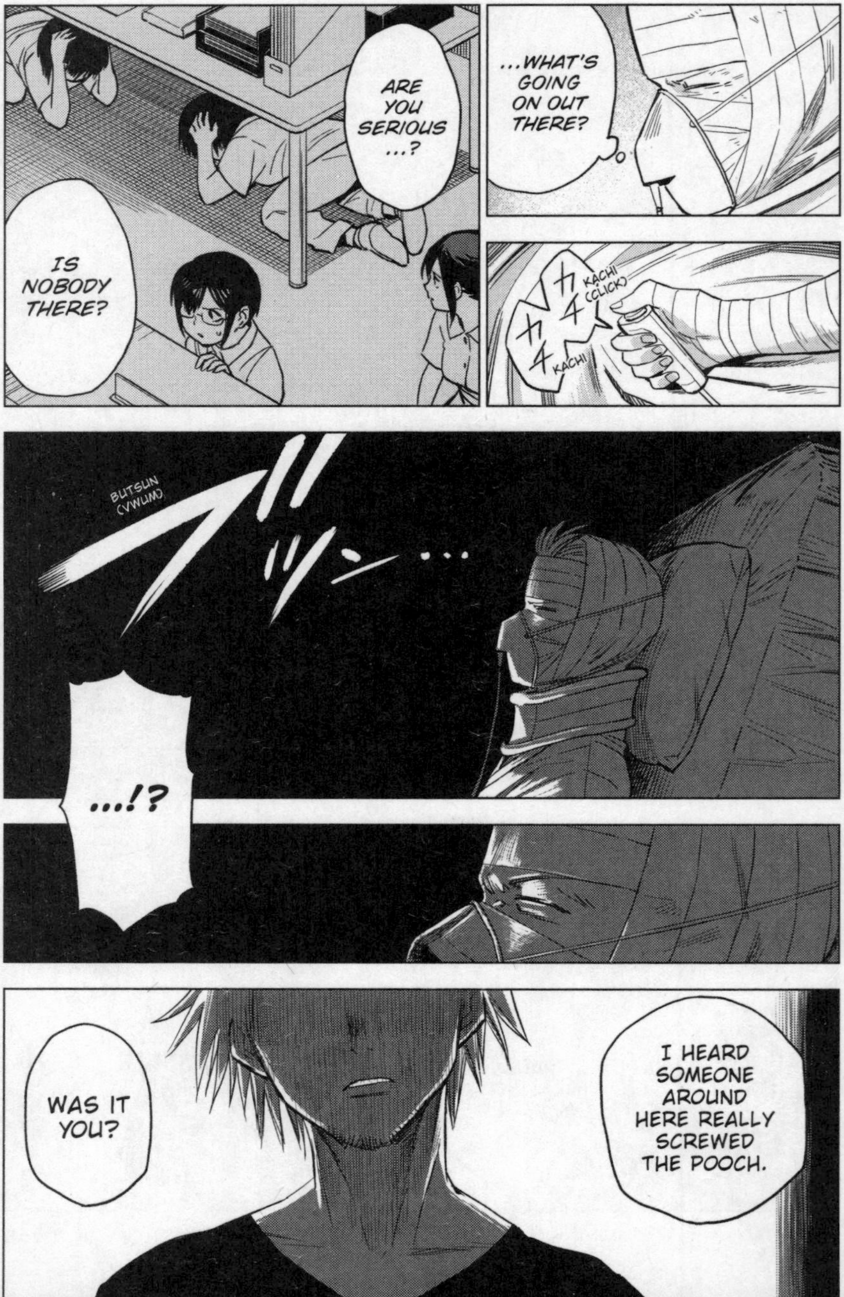
...WHAT'S GOING ON OUT THERE?
カチ
カチ
KACHI (CLICK)
KACHI
ARE YOU SERIOUS ...?
IS NOBODY THERE?
BUTSUN (VWUM)
ブツン
...
...!?
I HEARD SOMEONE AROUND HERE REALLY SCREWED THE POOCH.
WAS IT YOU?

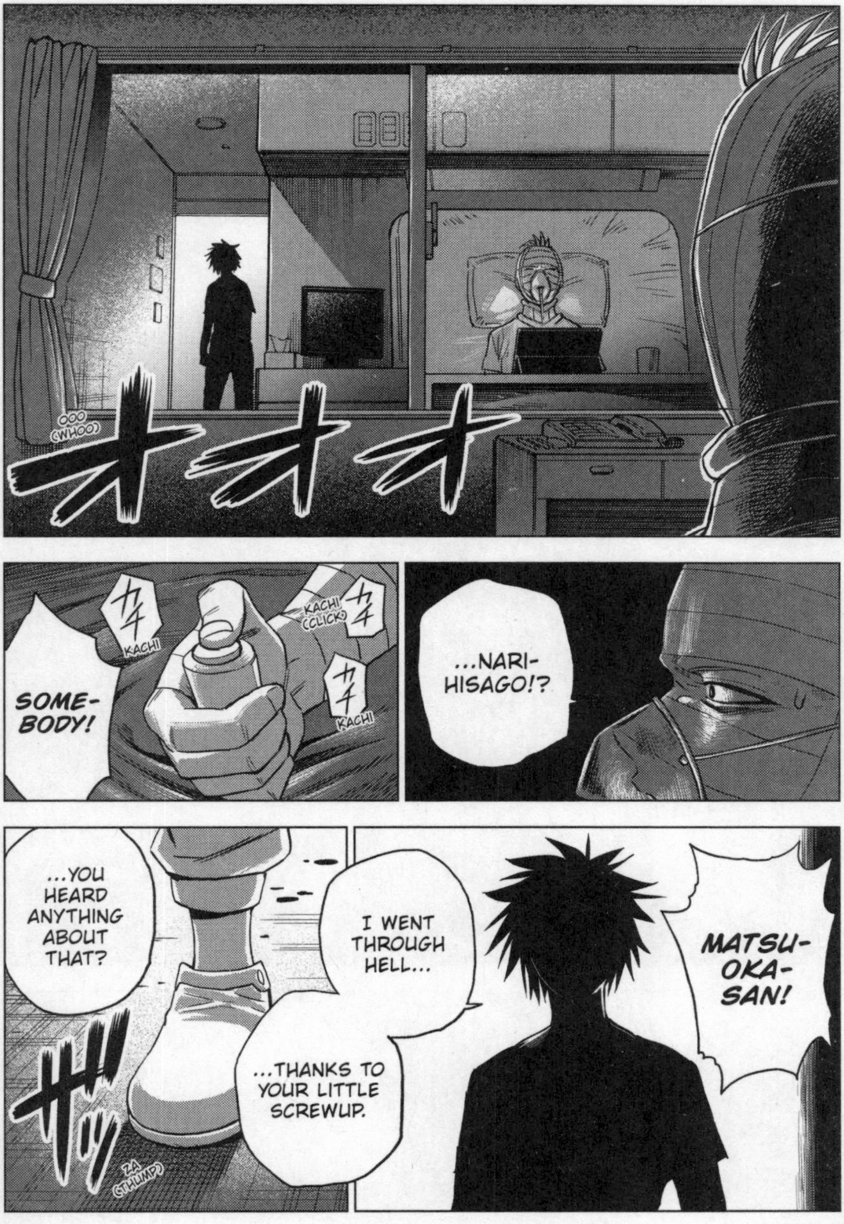
OOO (WHOO)
...NARI-HISAGO!?
KACHI (CLICK)
KACHI
KACHI
SOME-BODY!
MATSU-OKA-SAN!
I WENT THROUGH HELL...
...THANKS TO YOUR LITTLE SCREWUP.
...YOU HEARD ANYTHING ABOUT THAT?
ZA (THUMP)

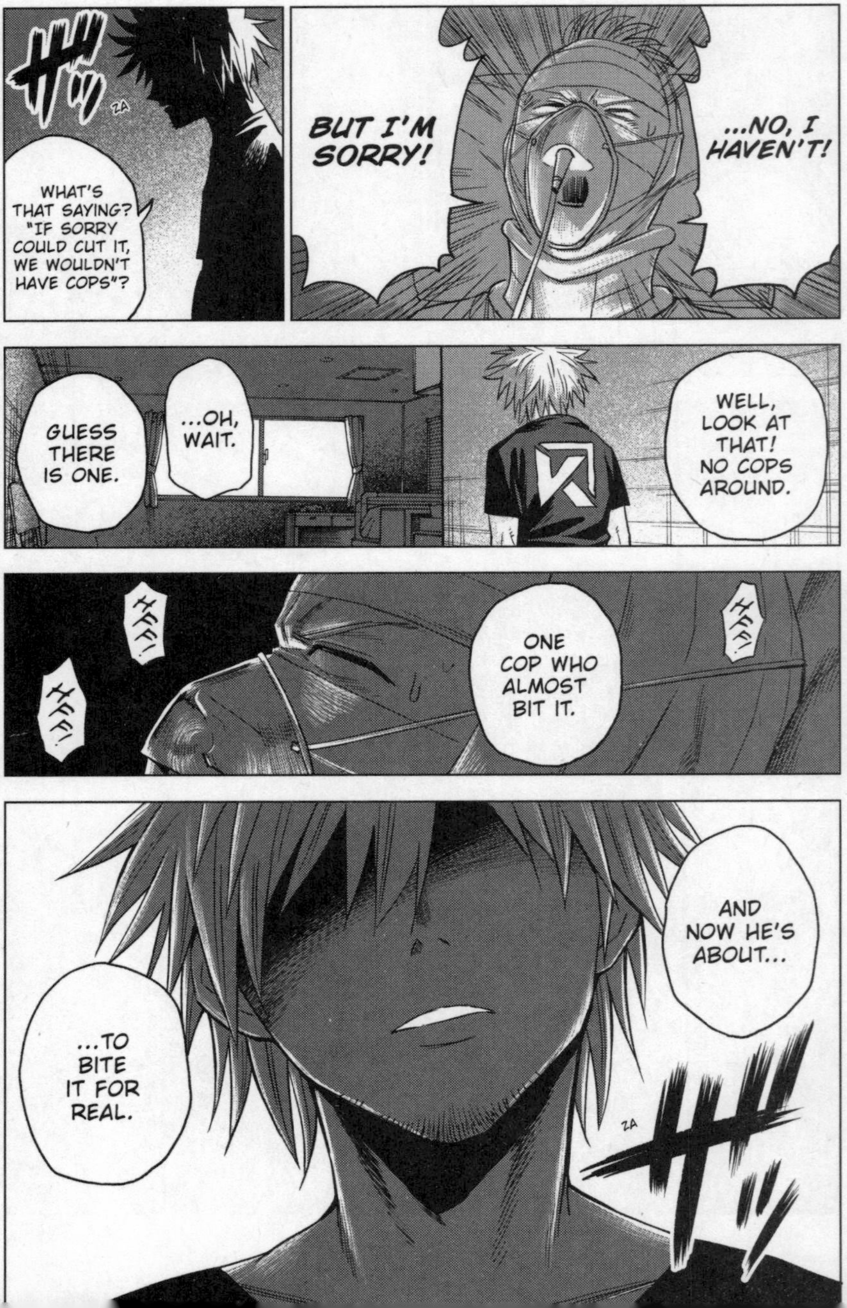
...NO, I HAVEN'T!
BUT I'M SORRY!
ZA
WHAT'S THAT SAYING? "IF SORRY COULD CUT IT, WE WOULDN'T HAVE COPS"?
WELL, LOOK AT THAT! NO COPS AROUND.
...OH, WAIT.
GUESS THERE IS ONE.
HFF!
ONE COP WHO ALMOST BIT IT.
HFF!
HFF!
AND NOW HE'S ABOUT...
...TO BITE IT FOR REAL.
ZA

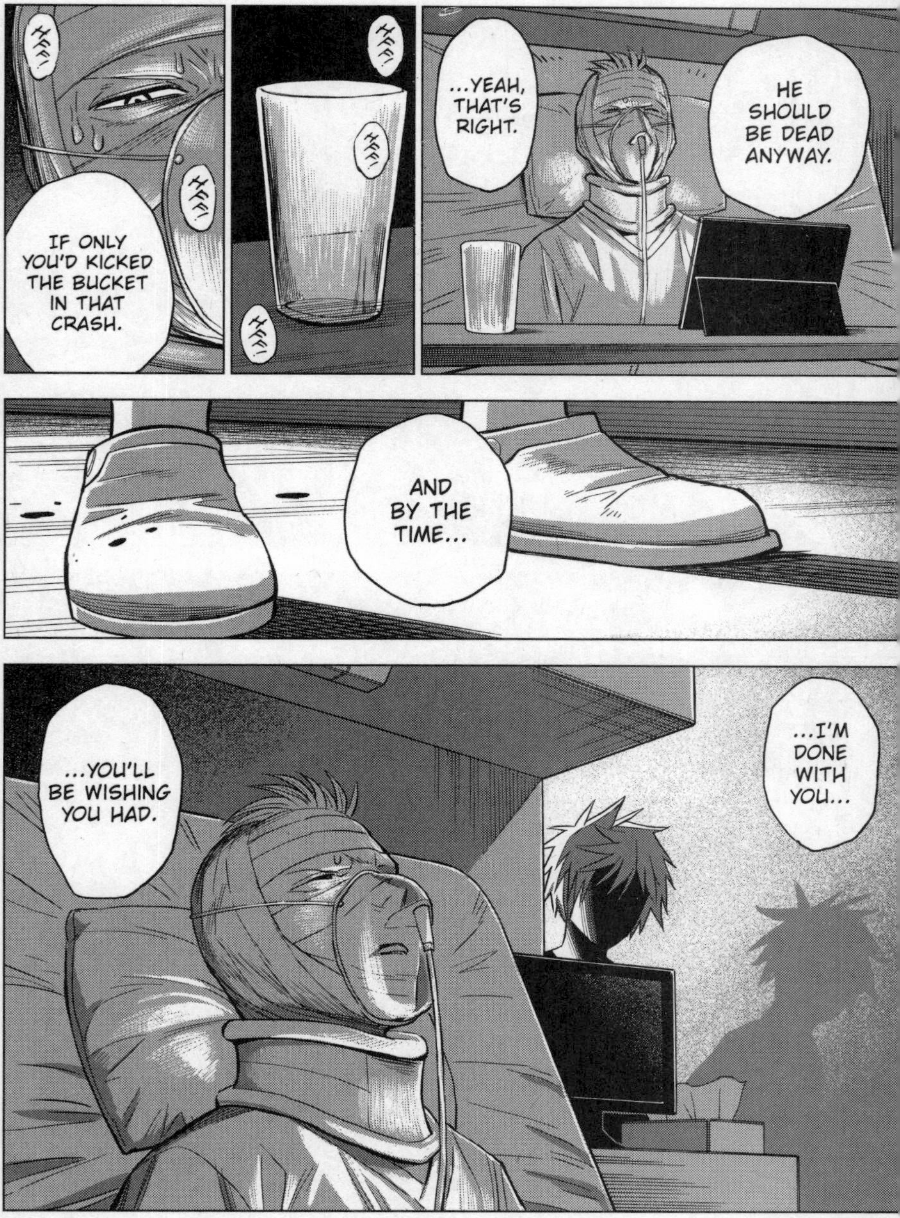
HE SHOULD BE DEAD ANYWAY.
...YEAH, THAT'S RIGHT.
IF ONLY YOU'D KICKED THE BUCKET IN THAT CRASH.
AND BY THE TIME...
...I'M DONE WITH YOU...
...YOU'LL BE WISHING YOU HAD.

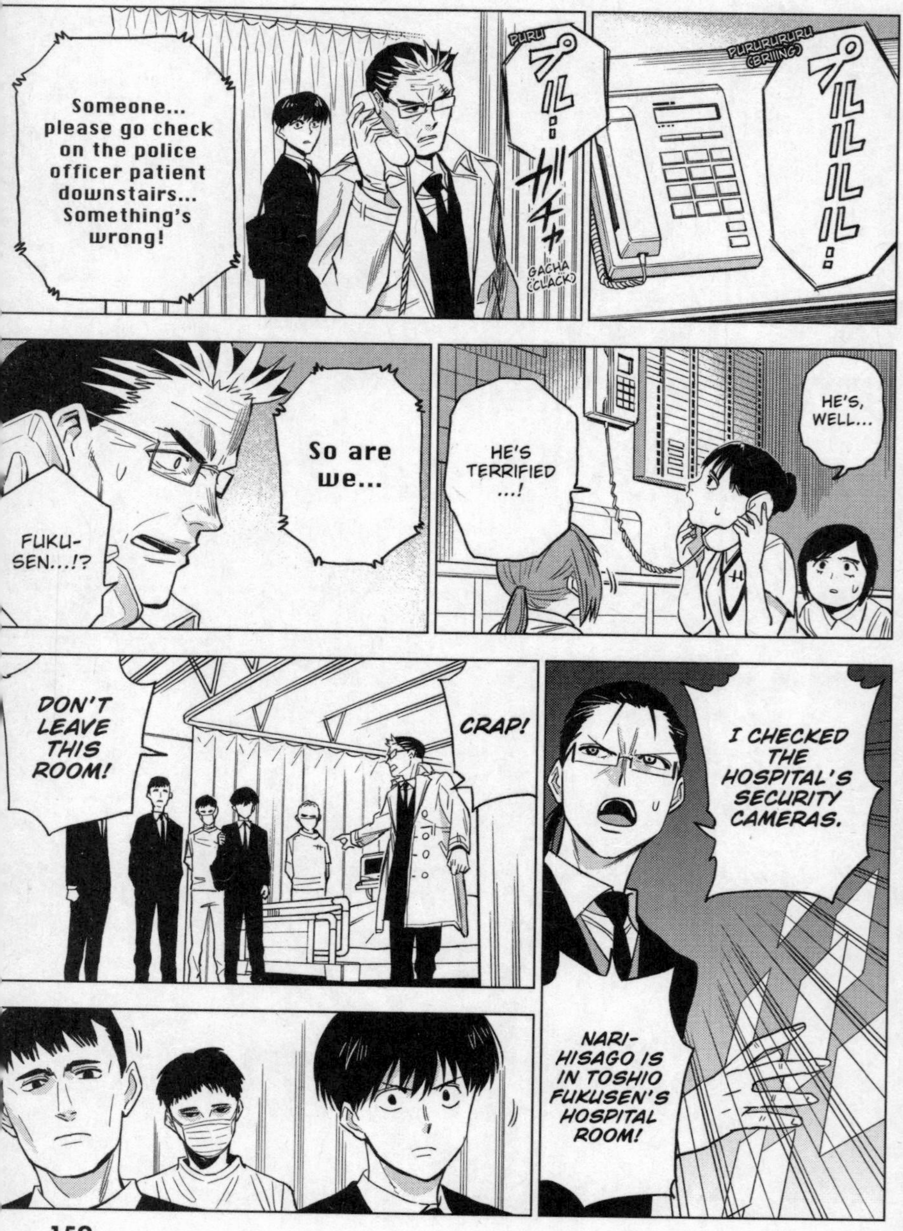
PURURURURU (BRIIING)
パルルルル!!
PURU
パル!!
ガチャ
GACHA (CLACK)
Someone... please go check on the police officer patient downstairs... Something's wrong!
HE'S, WELL...
HE'S TERRIFIED ...!
So are we...
FUKU-SEN...!?
I CHECKED THE HOSPITAL'S SECURITY CAMERAS.
NARI-HISAGO IS IN TOSHIO FUKUSEN'S HOSPITAL ROOM!
CRAP!
DON'T LEAVE THIS ROOM!

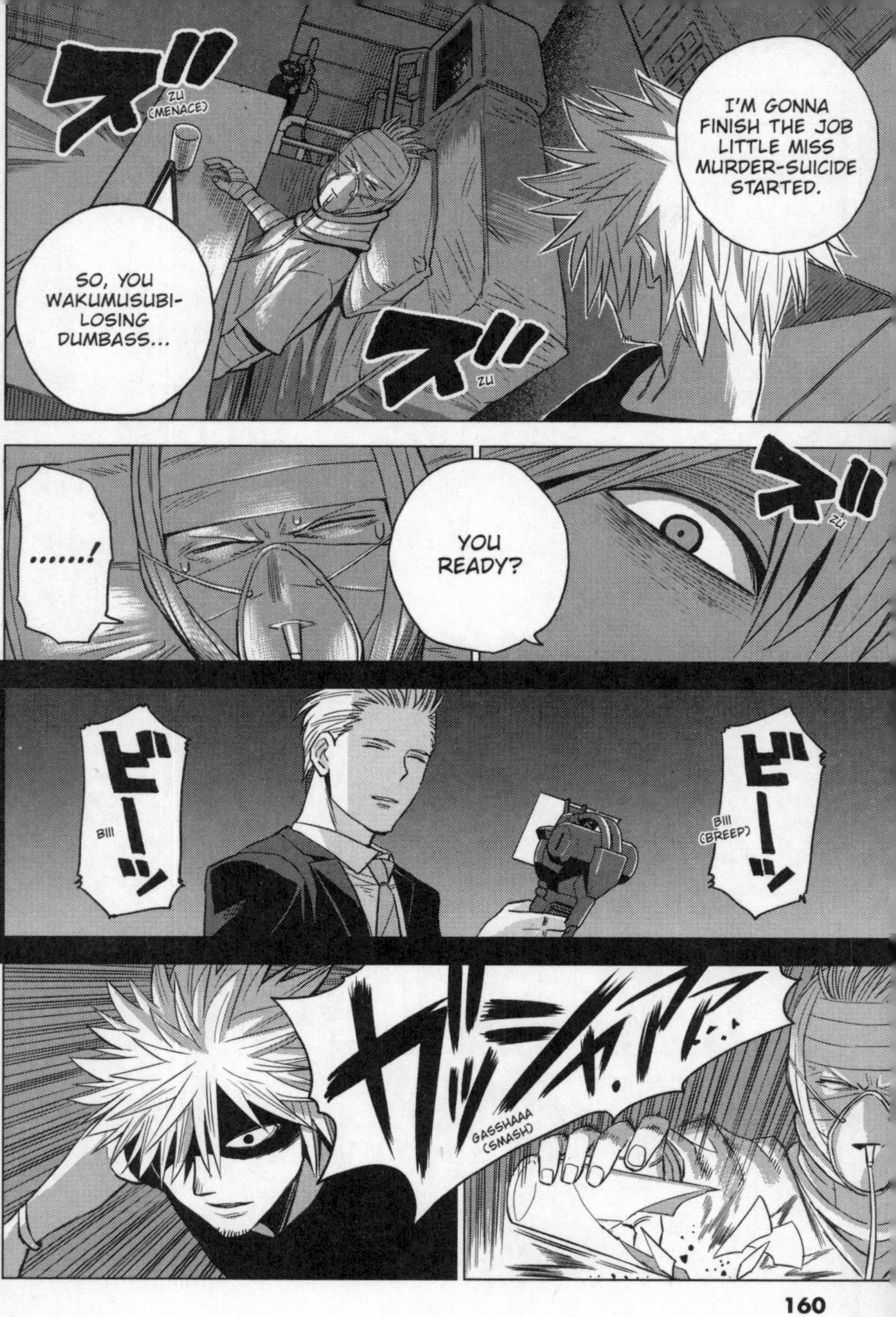
I'M GONNA FINISH THE JOB LITTLE MISS MURDER-SUICIDE STARTED.
ズ
ZU (MENACE)
SO, YOU WAKUMUSUBI-LOSING DUMBASS...
ズ
ZU
ズ
ZU
YOU READY?
......!
ビーッ
BIII (BREEP)
ビーッ
BIII
ガッシャアア
GASSHAAA (SMASH)

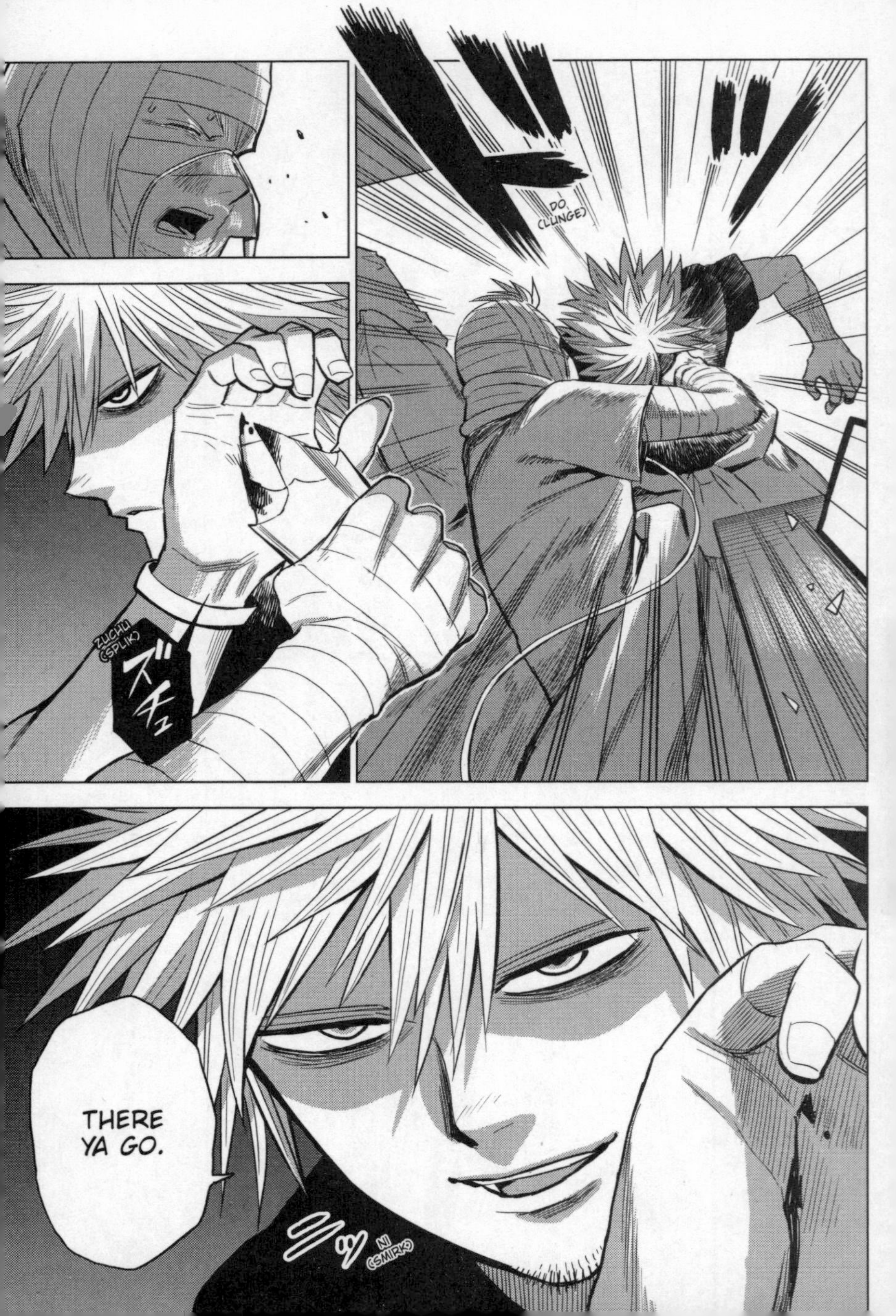
DO (LUNGE)
ZUCHU (SPLIK)
THERE YA GO.
NI (SMIRK)

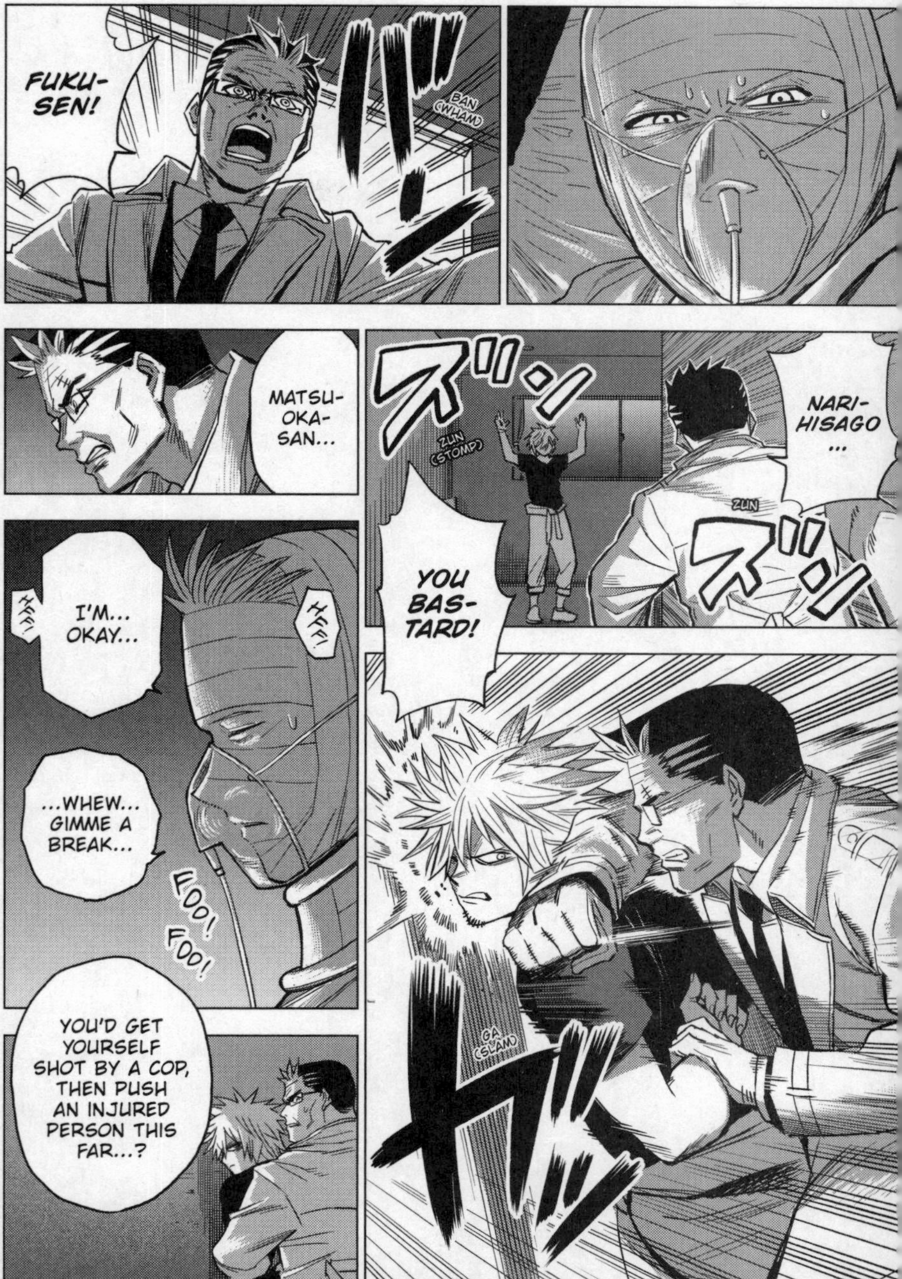
FUKU-SEN!
BAN (WHAM)
NARI-HISAGO...
ZUN
ZUN (STOMP)
YOU BAS-TARD!
MATSU-OKA-SAN...
GA (SLAM)
HFF!
I'M... OKAY...
HFF!
...WHEW... GIMME A BREAK...
FOO! FOO!
YOU'D GET YOURSELF SHOT BY A COP, THEN PUSH AN INJURED PERSON THIS FAR...?

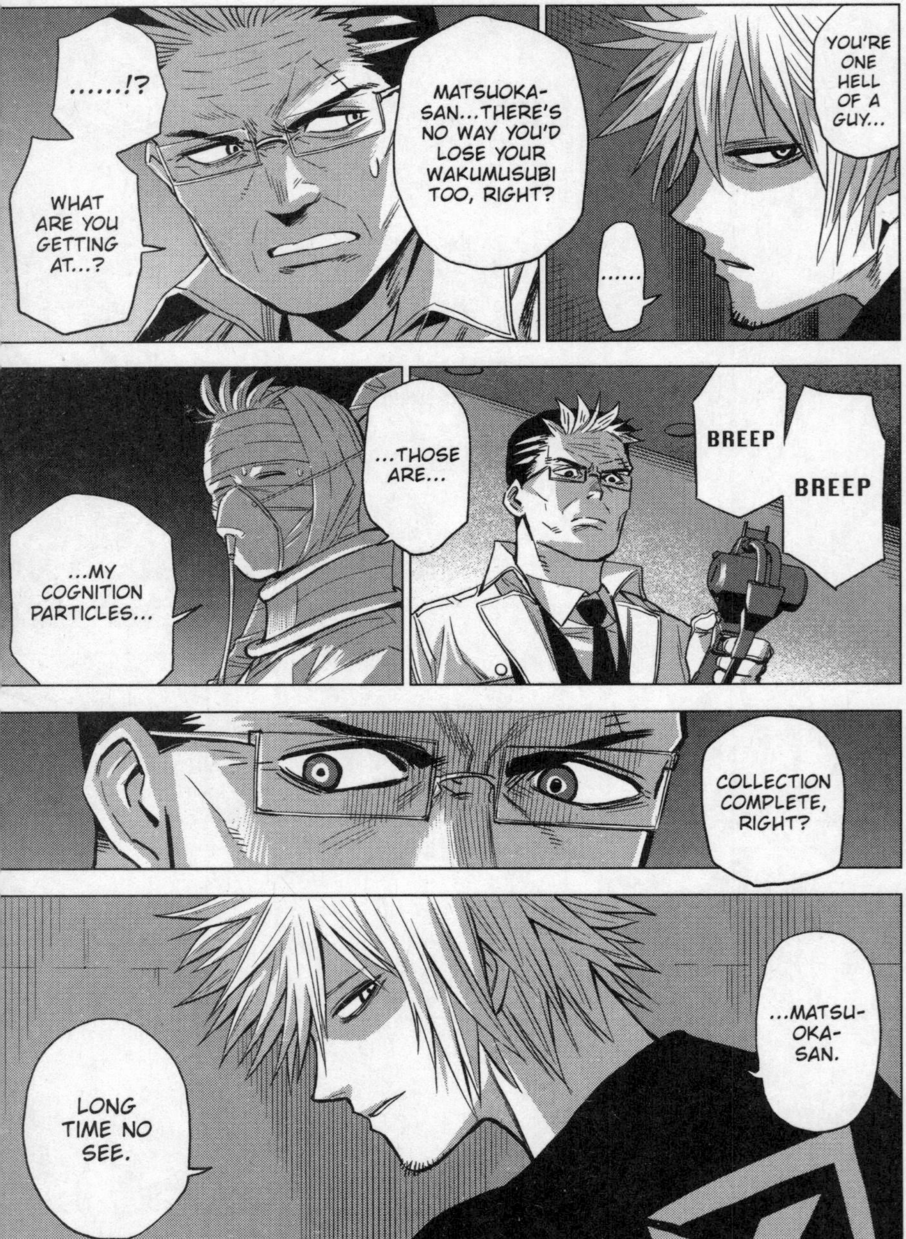
YOU'RE ONE HELL OF A GUY...
......
MATSUOKA-SAN...THERE'S NO WAY YOU'D LOSE YOUR WAKUMUSUBI TOO, RIGHT?
......!?
WHAT ARE YOU GETTING AT...?
BREEP
BREEP
...THOSE ARE...
...MY COGNITION PARTICLES...
COLLECTION COMPLETE, RIGHT?
...MATSU-OKA-SAN.
LONG TIME NO SEE.

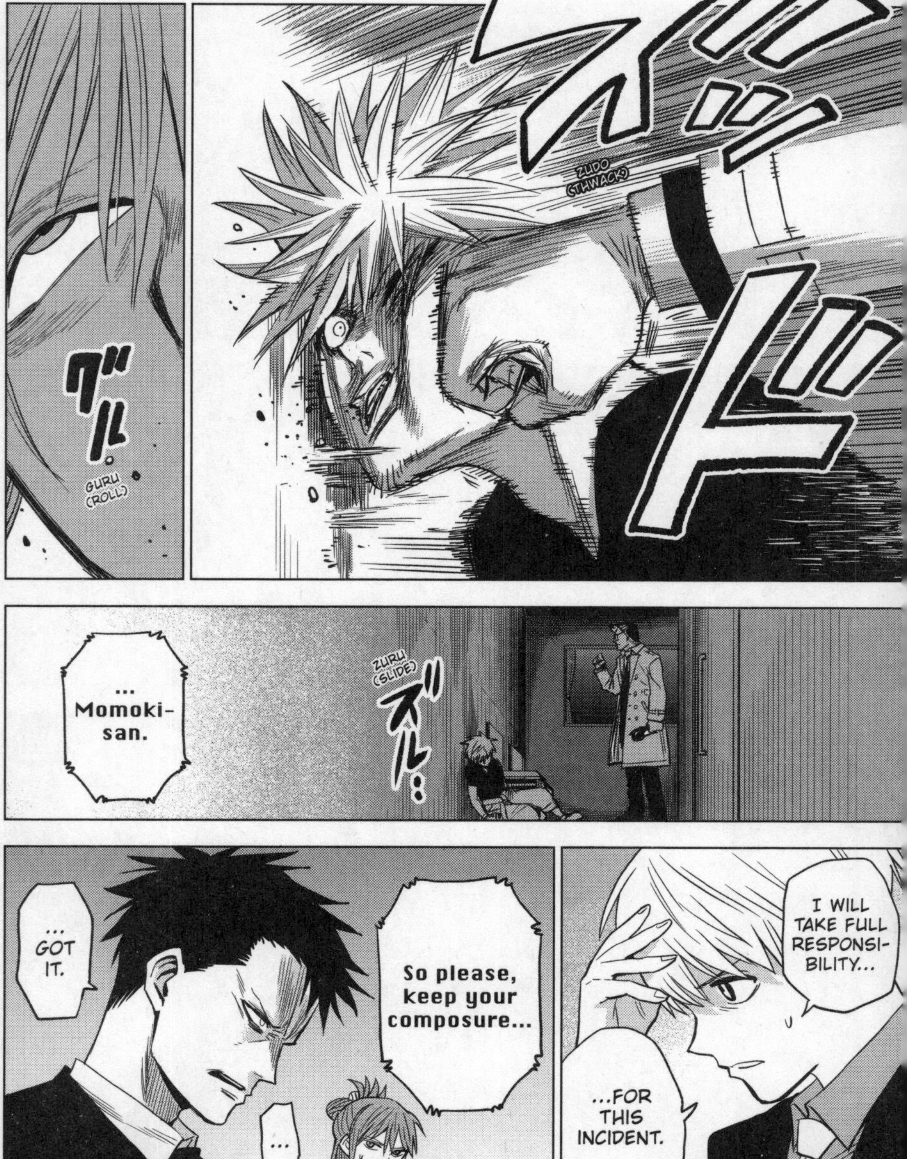
ZUDO (THWACK)
GURU (ROLL)
ZURU (SLIDE)
... Momoki-san.
I WILL TAKE FULL RESPONSI-BILITY...
...FOR THIS INCIDENT.
So please, keep your composure...
...
... GOT IT.

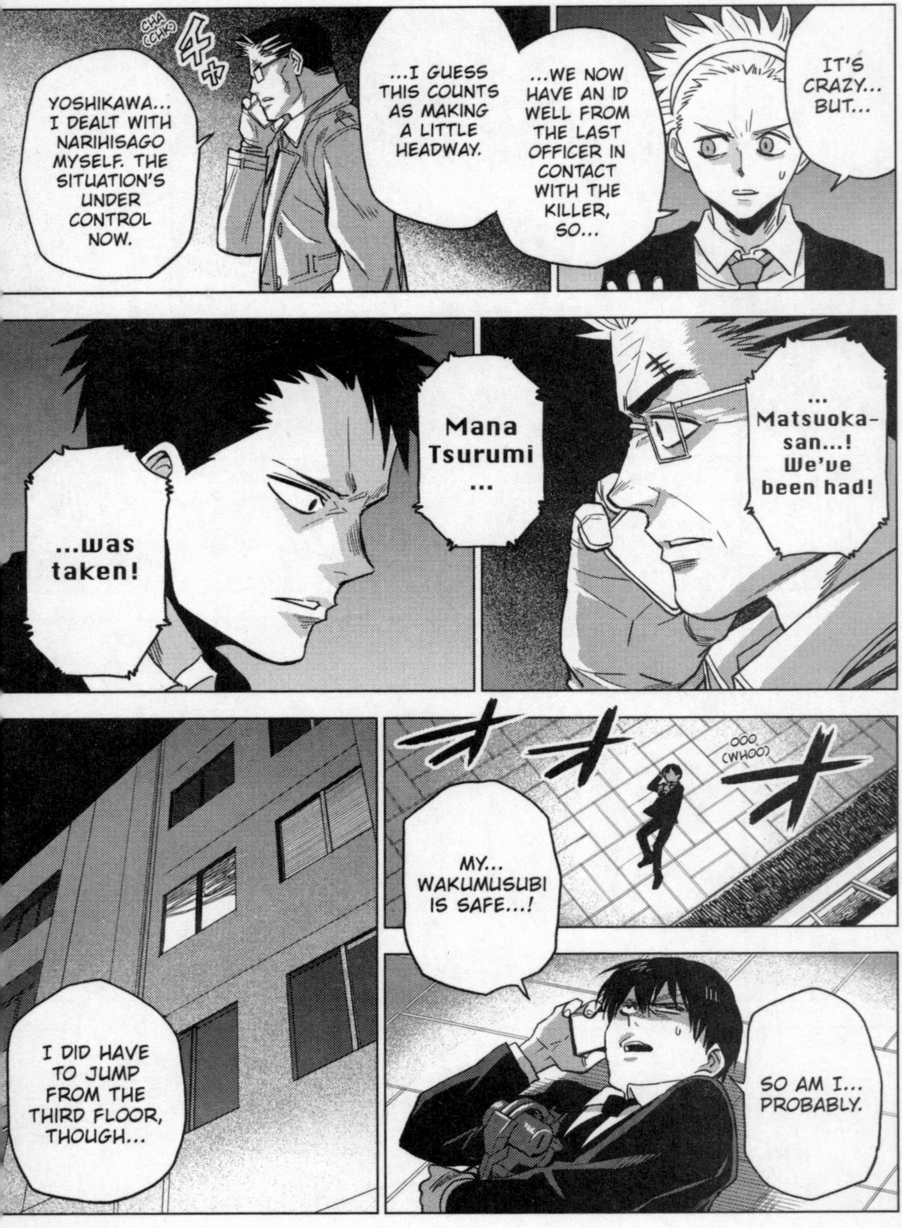
IT'S CRAZY... BUT...
...WE NOW HAVE AN ID WELL FROM THE LAST OFFICER IN CONTACT WITH THE KILLER, SO...
...I GUESS THIS COUNTS AS MAKING A LITTLE HEADWAY.
CHA (CHK)
YOSHIKAWA... I DEALT WITH NARIHISAGO MYSELF. THE SITUATION'S UNDER CONTROL NOW.
...Matsuoka-san...! We've been had!
Mana Tsurumi...
...was taken!
OOO (WHOO)
MY... WAKUMUSUBI IS SAFE...!
SO AM I... PROBABLY.
I DID HAVE TO JUMP FROM THE THIRD FLOOR, THOUGH...

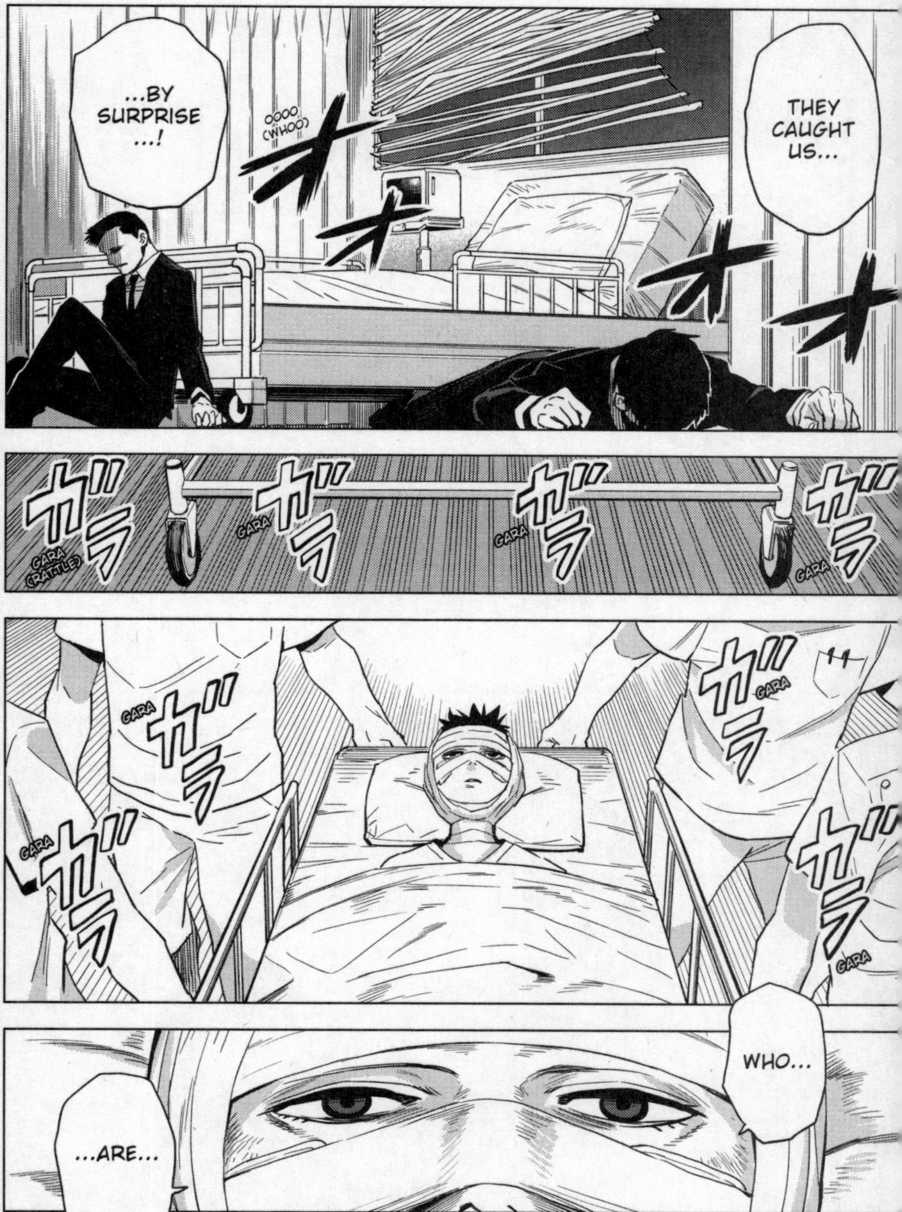
THEY CAUGHT US...
OOOO (WHOO)
...BY SURPRISE ...!
GARA
GARA
GARA
GARA (RATTLE)
GARA
GARA
GARA
GARA
WHO...
...ARE...

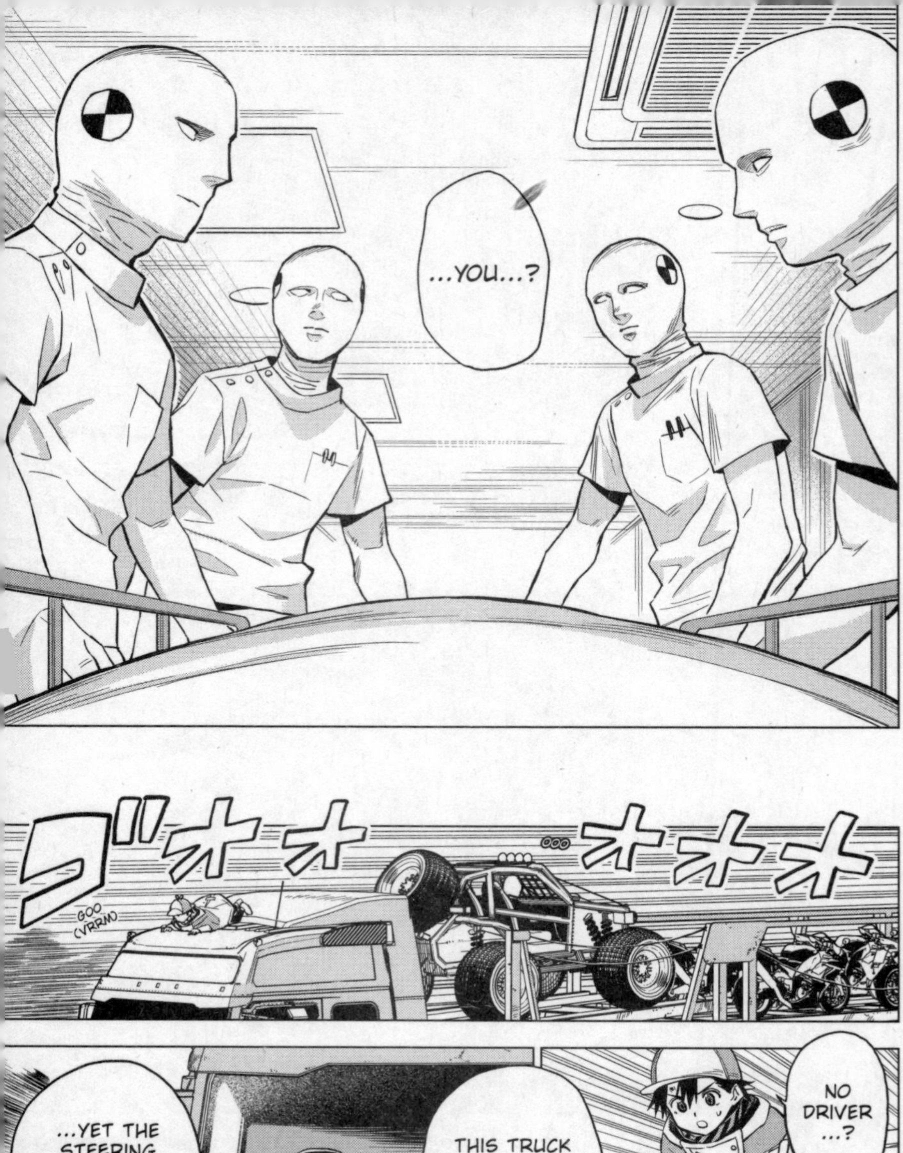
...YOU...?
ゴオオオ…オオオオ
GOO (VRRM)
NO DRIVER ...?
THIS TRUCK HAS NO SELF-DRIVING SYSTEM...
...YET THE STEERING WHEEL IS MOVING ON ITS OWN...

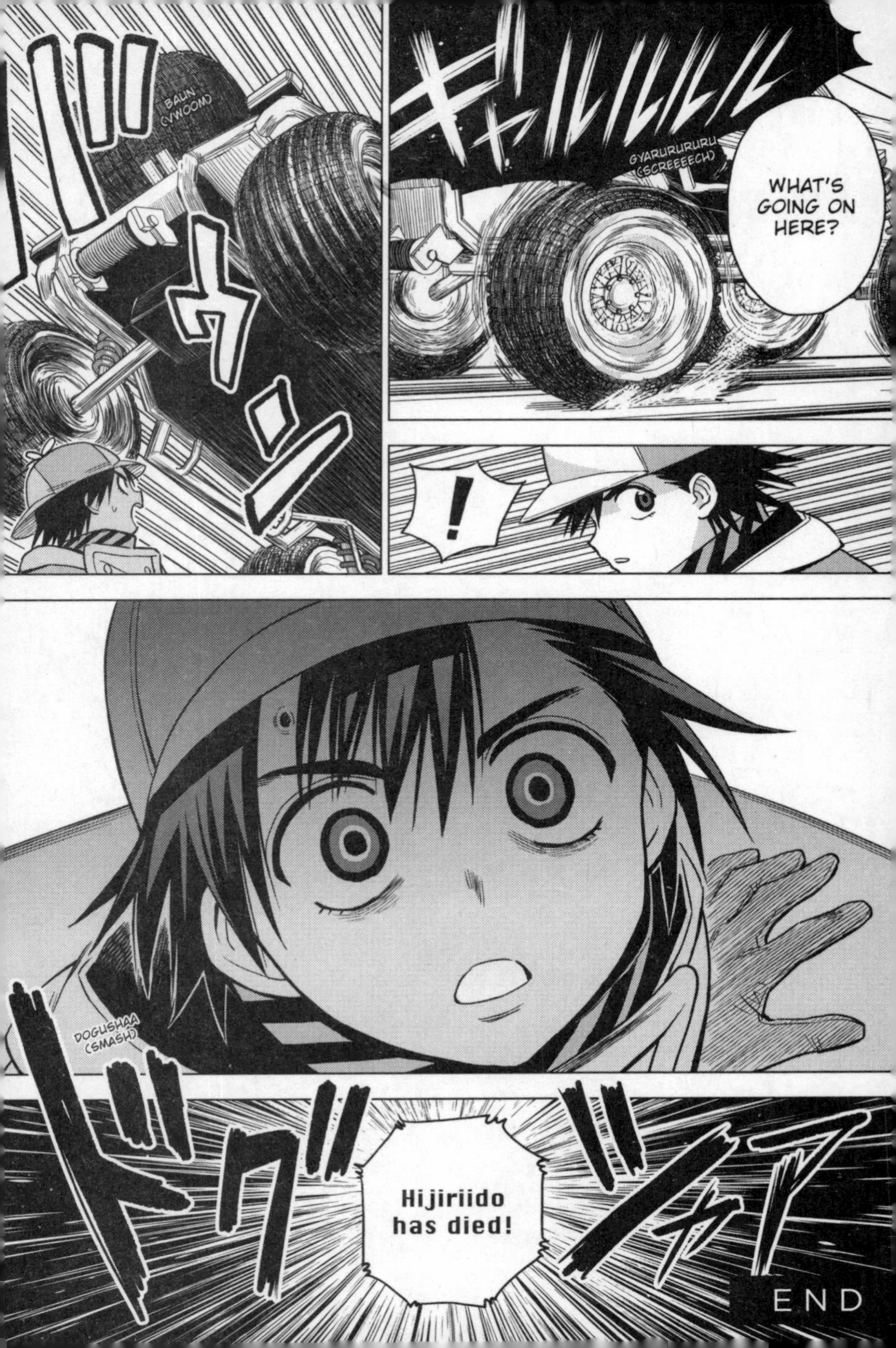
GYARURURURU (SCREEEECH)
WHAT'S GOING ON HERE?
!
BAUN (VWOOM)
DOGUSHAA (SMASH)
Hijiriido has died!
END

TRANSLATION NOTES

COMMON HONORIFICS

no honorific: Indicates familiarity or closeness; if used without permission, addressing someone in this manner would constitute an insult.

-san: The Japanese equivalent of Mr./Mrs./Miss. If a situation calls for politeness, this is the fail-safe honorific.

-sama: Conveys great respect; may also indicate that the social status of the speaker is lower than that of the addressee.

-kun: In a professional setting, this can be used to address a junior coworker, particularly one whom the speaker works closely with; conveys more familiarity or affection than *-san*. Used most often when referring to boys.

-chan: An affectionate honorific indicating familiarity used mostly in reference to girls; also used in reference to cute persons or animals of either gender.

-senpai: A suffix used to address upperclassmen or more experienced coworkers.

PAGE 17

The term **murder-suicide** is actually *shinjuu* (a "lovers' suicide") in the original Japanese. Tragic lovers choosing to die together rather than be forced apart are a common trope in classic Japanese theater and literature (and in fact have a fair amount of real historical precedent, as suicide is more socially acceptable in Japanese culture). *Shinjuu* are, strictly speaking, supposed to be consensual, but the term often gets applied to cases where someone kills themselves and takes others down with them. Since this concept is not as familiar to Western audiences, the more common "murder-suicide" has been used throughout this translation instead.

PAGE 35

"**Frog**" is one of the possible meanings of *kaeru* in Japanese.

PAGE 39

The kanji for "**Mana**" literally read as "true name," which is part of why the Kura operatives think she might have given them an alias to mess with them.

PAGE 42

Tomei Expressway: short for the Tokyo-Nagoya Expressway.

PAGE 75

The name of the instant ramen brand is a pun—**UMA** is both an acronym meaning Unidentified Mysterious Animal (i.e. a cryptid, like Bigfoot or the Loch Ness Monster) and a homophone for "tasty" in Japanese.

PAGE 87

As in Sakaido's name, the *ido* in **Hijiriido** is written with the kanji for "well."

PAGE 88

Paisen is modern, playful slang for "senpai"; using it suggests that the speaker is fairly young and on good terms with the person they are addressing (or just rather immature).

PAGE 97

In the world of Japanese show business, *ohayou gozaimasu* ("**good morning**") is the standard greeting no matter what time of day it is, which is why Narihisago accuses Hondoumachi of being a diva here.

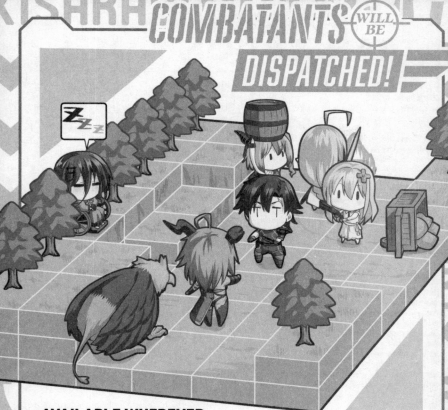

AVAILABLE WHEREVER BOOKS ARE SOLD!

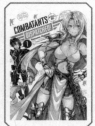

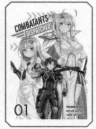

LIGHT NOVEL
VOLUMES 1-6

MANGA
VOLUMES 1-4

©Natsume Akatsuki, Kakao • Lanthanum 2017
KADOKAWA CORPORATION

©Masaaki Kiasa 2018 ©Natsume Akatsuki, Kakao • Lanthanum 2018
KADOKAWA CORPORATION

Always bring a gun to a sword fight!

With world domination nearly in their grasp, the Supreme Leaders of the Kisaragi Corporation—an underground criminal group turned evil megacorp—have decided to try their hands at interstellar conquest. A quick dice roll nominates their chief operative, Combat Agent Six, to be the one to explore an alien planet...and the first thing he does when he gets there is change the sacred incantation for a holy ritual to the most embarrassing thing he can think of. But evil deeds are business as usual for Kisaragi operatives, so if Six wants a promotion and a raise, he'll have to work much harder than that! For starters, he'll have to do something about the other group of villains on the planet, who are calling themselves the "Demon Lord's Army" or whatever. After all, this world doesn't need two evil organizations!

For more information
visit www.yenpress.com

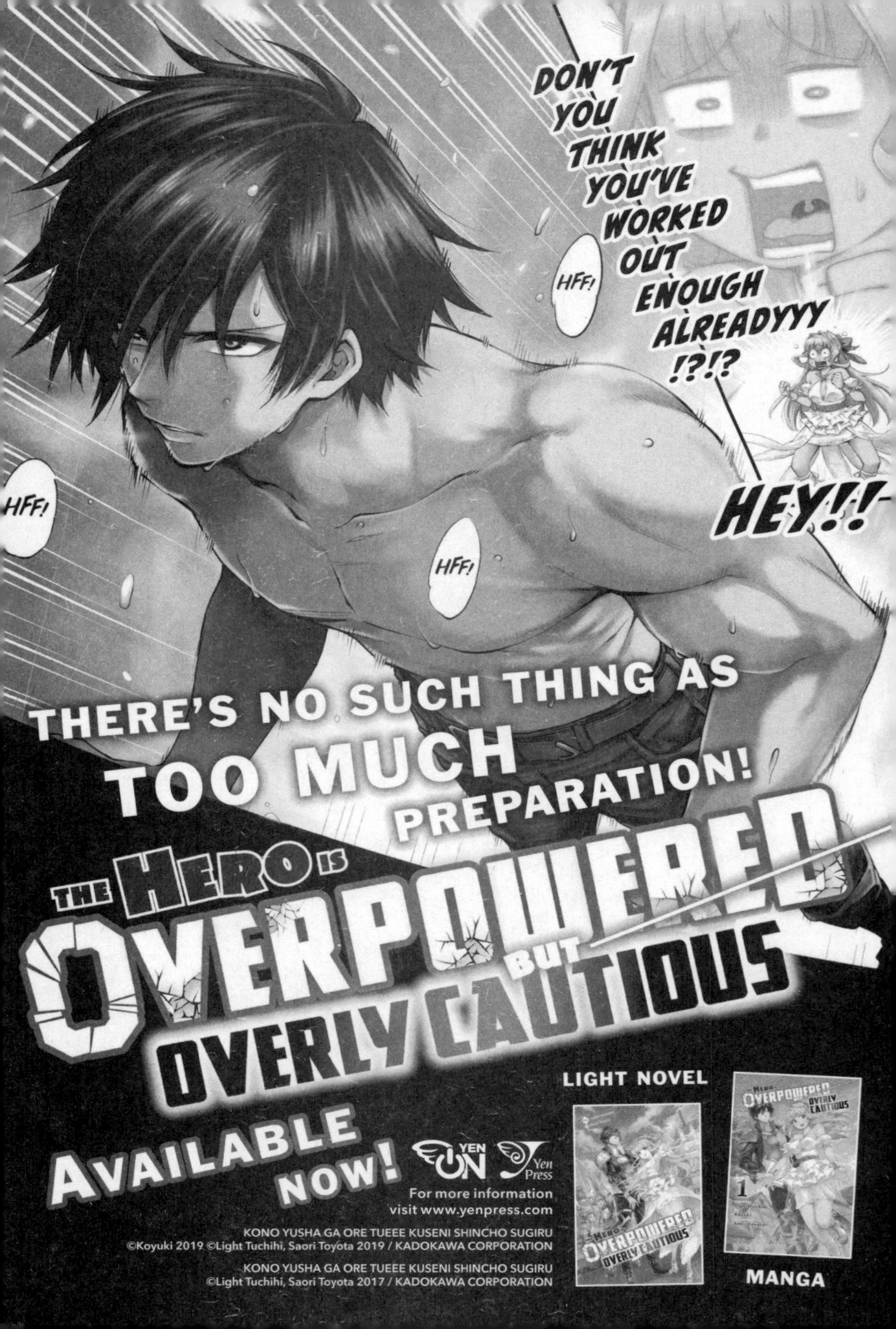
DON'T YOU THINK YOU'VE WORKED OUT ENOUGH ALREADYYY !?!?
HEY!!
HFF!
HFF!
HFF!
THERE'S NO SUCH THING AS TOO MUCH PREPARATION!
THE HERO IS OVERPOWERED BUT OVERLY CAUTIOUS
AVAILABLE NOW!
YEN ON
Yen Press
For more information visit www.yenpress.com
KONO YUSHA GA ORE TUEEE KUSENI SHINCHO SUGIRU
©Koyuki 2019 ©Light Tuchihi, Saori Toyota 2019 / KADOKAWA CORPORATION
KONO YUSHA GA ORE TUEEE KUSENI SHINCHO SUGIRU
©Light Tuchihi, Saori Toyota 2017 / KADOKAWA CORPORATION
LIGHT NOVEL
MANGA

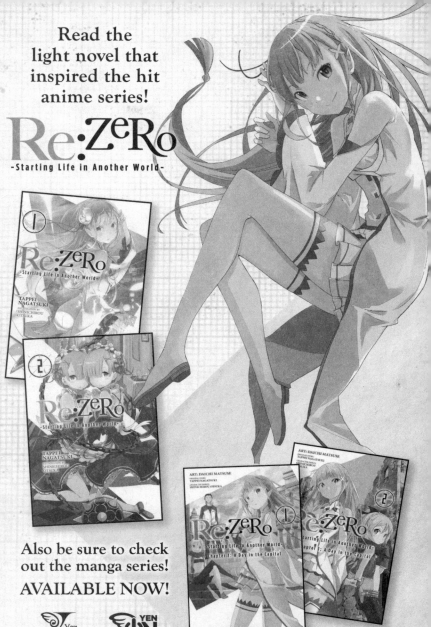

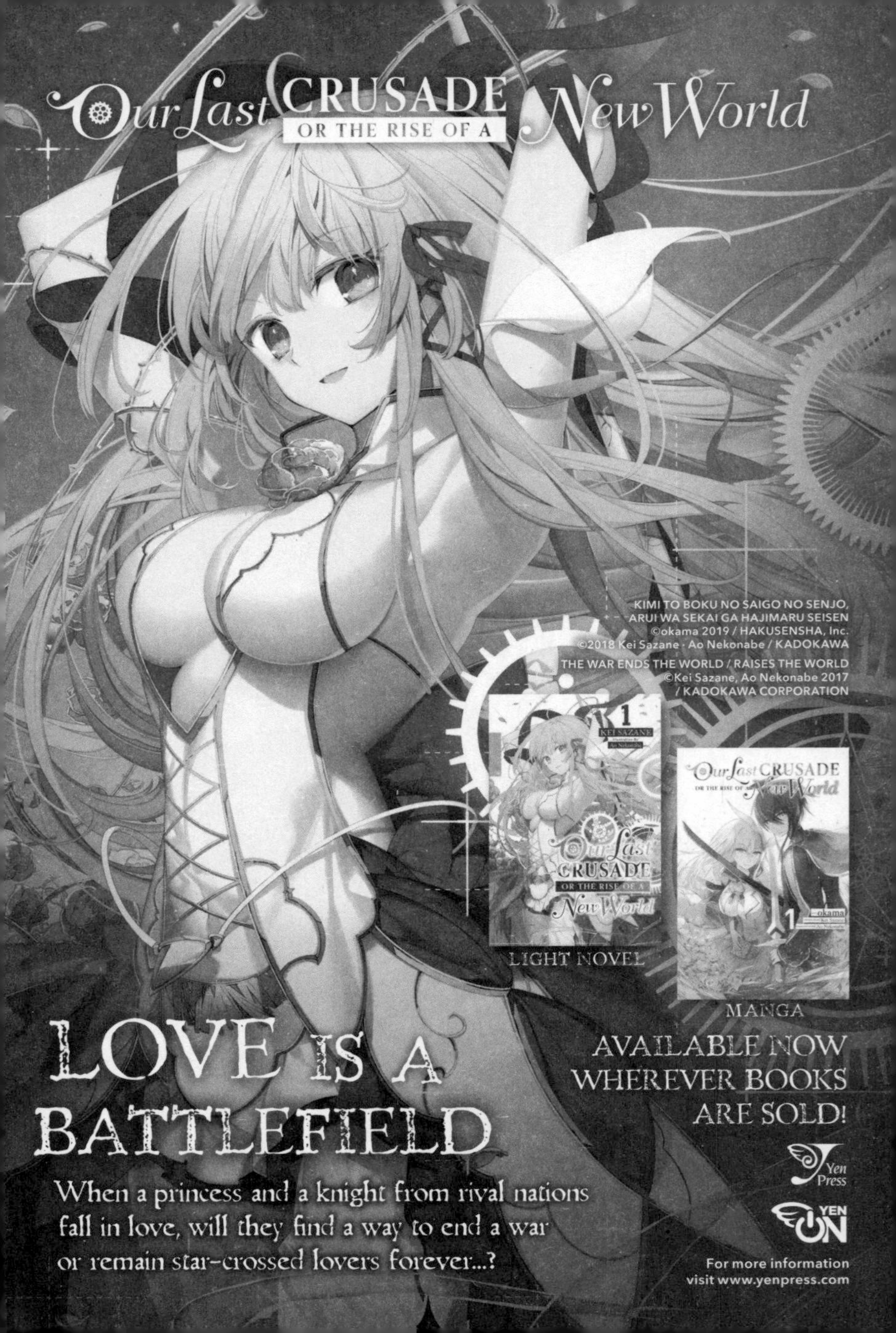
Our Last CRUSADE OR THE RISE OF A New World
KIMI TO BOKU NO SAIGO NO SENJO,
ARUI WA SEKAI GA HAJIMARU SEISEN
©okama 2019 / HAKUSENSHA, Inc.
©2018 Kei Sazane · Ao Nekonabe / KADOKAWA
THE WAR ENDS THE WORLD / RAISES THE WORLD
©Kei Sazane, Ao Nekonabe 2017
/ KADOKAWA CORPORATION
LIGHT NOVEL
MANGA
LOVE IS A BATTLEFIELD
When a princess and a knight from rival nations fall in love, will they find a way to end a war or remain star-crossed lovers forever...?
AVAILABLE NOW WHEREVER BOOKS ARE SOLD!
Yen Press
YEN ON
For more information
visit www.yenpress.com

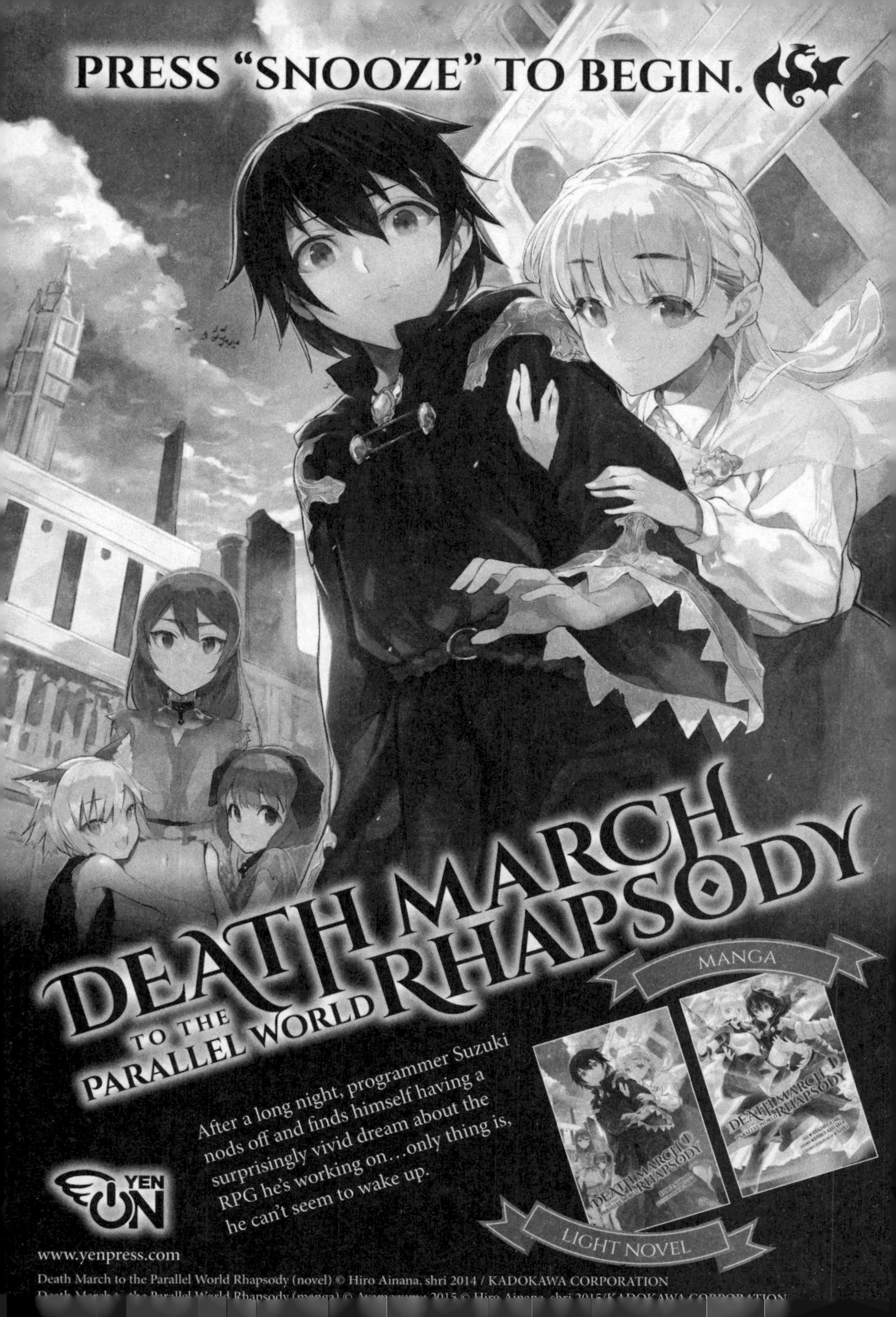
PRESS "SNOOZE" TO BEGIN.
DEATH MARCH TO THE PARALLEL WORLD RHAPSODY
After a long night, programmer Suzuki nods off and finds himself having a surprisingly vivid dream about the RPG he's working on...only thing is, he can't seem to wake up.
MANGA
LIGHT NOVEL
YEN ON
www.yenpress.com
Death March to the Parallel World Rhapsody (novel) © Hiro Ainana, shri 2014 / KADOKAWA CORPORATION

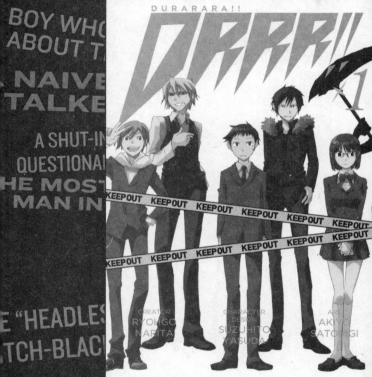

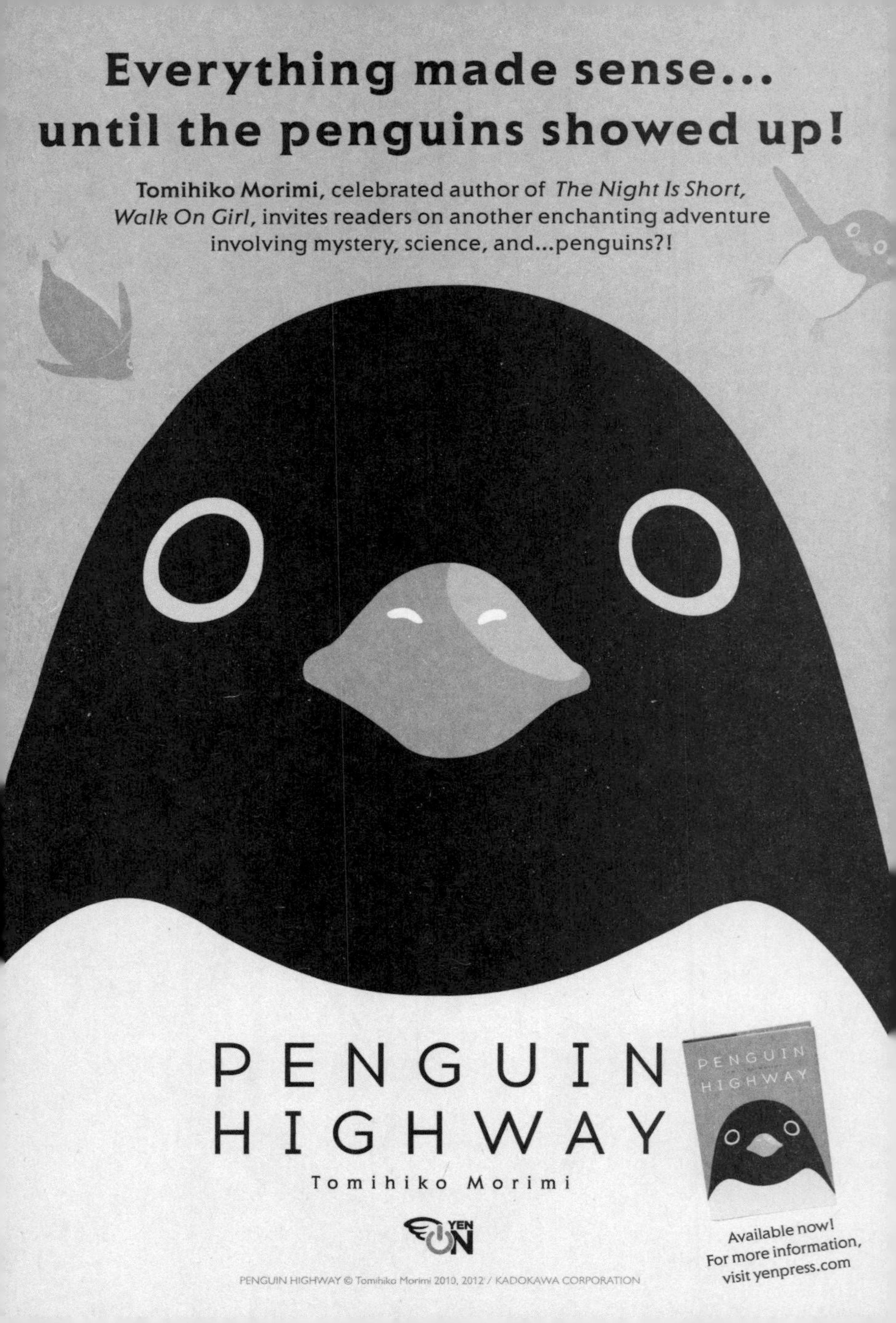
Everything made sense...
until the penguins showed up!
Tomihiko Morimi, celebrated author of The Night Is Short, Walk On Girl, invites readers on another enchanting adventure involving mystery, science, and...penguins?!
PENGUIN
HIGHWAY
Tomihiko Morimi
PENGUIN
HIGHWAY
YEN ON
Available now!
For more information,
visit yenpress.com
PENGUIN HIGHWAY © Tomihiko Morimi 2010, 2012 / KADOKAWA CORPORATION

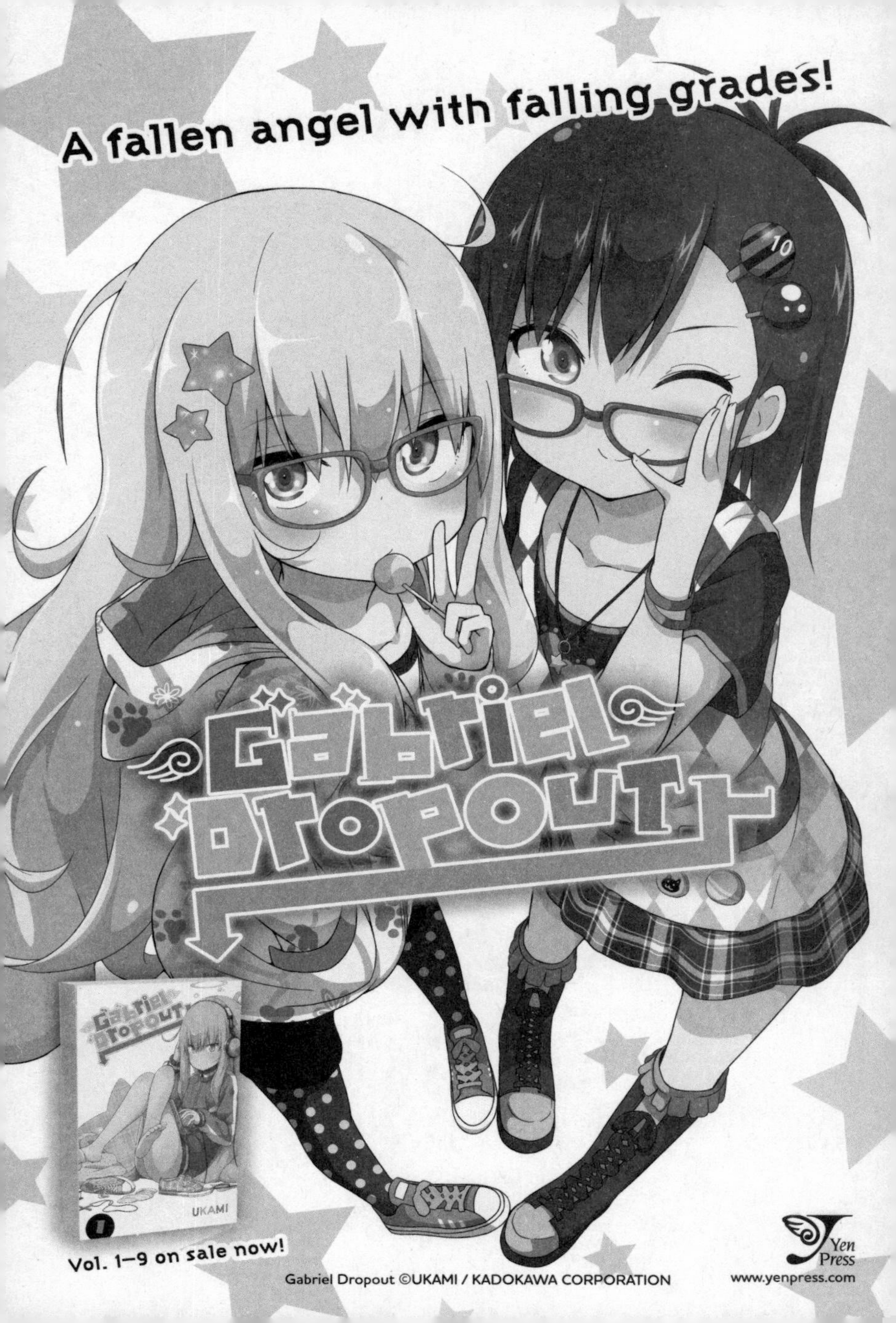
A fallen angel with falling grades!
Gabriel Dropout
Gabriel Dropout
UKAMI
1
Vol. 1–9 on sale now!
Gabriel Dropout ©UKAMI / KADOKAWA CORPORATION
Yen Press
www.yenpress.com

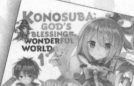

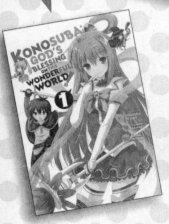

ID:INVADED 2

#BRAKE-BROKEN

Art: Yuuki Kodama   **Original Story:** Otaro Maijo, The Detectives United

Translation: AMANDA HALEY   **Lettering:** BIANCA PISTILLO

ID: INVADED #BRAKE-BROKEN Vol. 2
©IDDU/ID:INVADED Society
©Yuuki Kodama 2020
First published in Japan in 2020 by KADOKAWA CORPORATION, Tokyo. English translation rights arranged with KADOKAWA CORPORATION, Tokyo through TUTTLE-MORI AGENCY, INC., Tokyo.

Yen Press
150 West 30th Street, 19th Floor
New York, NY 10001

Visit us at yenpress.com
facebook.com/yenpress
twitter.com/yenpress
yenpress.tumblr.com
instagram.com/yenpress

First Yen Press Edition: July 2021

Yen Press is an imprint of Yen Press, LLC.
The Yen Press name and logo are trademarks of Yen Press, LLC.

The publisher is not responsible for websites (or their content) that are not owned by the publisher.

Library of Congress Control Number: 2020950211

ISBNs: 978-1-9753-2406-3 (paperback)
        978-1-9753-2407-0 (ebook)

10 9 8 7 6 5 4 3 2 1

WOR

Printed in the United States of America